Changing Human Beliefs and Values, 1981-2007

A Cross-Cultural Sourcebook based on the World Values Surveys and European Values Studies

Edited by

RONALD INGLEHART, MIGUEL BASÁÑEZ,
GABRIELA CATTERBERG, JAIME DÍEZ-MEDRANO,
ALEJANDRO MORENO, PIPPA NORRIS,
RENATA SIEMIENSKA *and* IGNACIO ZUASNABAR

siglo
veintiuno
editores

siglo xxi editores, s.a. de c.v.
CERRO DEL AGUA 248, ROMERO DE TERREROS, 04310, MÉXICO, D.F.

siglo xxi editores, s.a.
GUATEMALA 4824, C1425BUP, BUENOS AIRES, ARGENTINA

Cover design: María Luisa Martínez Passarge
1st edition: 2010

© Siglo XXI Editores, S. A. de C. V.

ISBN 978-607-03-0222-0

All rights reserved
Printed and made in Mexico

Authors' information

Miguel Basáñez
Cultural Change Institute,
Fletcher School
Tufts University
mbasanez@gmail.com

Gabriela Catterberg
Department of Political Science
Universidad de Buenos Aires
gabriela.catterberg@undp.org

Jaime Díez-Medrano
World Values Survey
Archive-ASEP/JDS
Madrid
jdiezmed@jdsurvey.net

Ronald Inglehart
Institute for Social Research
University of Michigan
Ann Arbor, Michigan
RInglehart@gmail.com

Alejandro Moreno
Department of Political Science
Instituto Tecnológico Autónomo
de México, ITAM
amoreno@itam.mx

Pippa Norris
John F. Kennedy School of Government
Harvard University
Cambridge MA 02138
Pippa_Norris@Harvard.edu

Renata Siemienska
Institute of Sociology
Director, Institute for Social Studies
Warsaw University
siemiens@post.pl

Ignacio Zuasnabar
Department of Political Science
Universidad Católica del Uruguay
ignaciozuasnabar@gmail.com

Contents

List of tables	ix
Acknowledgements	xiii
Introduction to the Values Surveys, *Ronald Inglehart*	1
Globalization and Major Trends in Value Change, 1981–2007, *Pippa Norris and Ronald Inglehart*	19
Generational Differences in Support for Democracy and Free Market Economics: Evidence from New and Established Market Democracies, *Renata Siemienska, Miguel Basáñez and Alejandro Moreno*	33
Youth, Values and Democracy: Exploring Tolerance toward Diversity among Third Wave Generations, *Gabriela Catterberg and Ignacio Zuasnabar*	55
Working with the Values Surveys files, *Jaime Diez-Medrano*	73
Questionnaire used in the 2005-2007 World Values Survey	89
Tables	117

List of tables

SECTION A:
PERCEPTIONS OF LIFE

(A001)   Family Important in Life
(A002)   Friends important in life
(A003)   Leisure time important in life
(A004)   Politics important in life
(A005)   Work important in life
(A006)   Religion important in life
(A007)   Feeling of happiness
(A008)   State of health (subjective)
(A009)   Child qualities: independence
(A010)   Child qualities: hard work
(A011)   Child qualities: feeling of responsibility
(A012)   Child qualities: imagination
(A013)   Child qualities: tolerance and respect for other people
(A014)   Child qualities: thrift, saving money and things
(A015)   Child qualities: determination, perseverance
(A016)   Child qualities: religious faith
(A017)   Child qualities: unselfishness
(A018)   Child qualities: obedience
(A019)   Life satisfaction
(A020)   Most people can be trusted
(A021)   Membership in church or religious organization
(A022)   Membership in cultural activities
(A023)   Membership in labor unions
(A024)   Membership in political party
(A025)   Membership in environmental organization
(A026)   Membership in professional organization
(A027)   Membership in charitable/ humanitarian organization
(A028)   Freedom feeling

SECTION B: ENVIRONMENT

(B001)   Environmental protection vs. economic growth
(B002)   Environment: Income
(B003)   Environment: Taxes
(B004)   Environment: No cost

SECTION C: WORK

(C001)   Men more right to a job
(C002)   Employers should give priority to people of own nationality
(C003)   Important aspects in a job first choice
(C004)   Important aspects in a job second choice
(C005)   Satisfaction with the financial situation of household
(C006)   Work: Efficiency is paid more

SECTION D: FAMILY

(D001)   Child needs a home with father and mother
(D002)   Marriage is an out-dated institution
(D003)   Woman as a single parent

x   List of tables

(D004)	Being a housewife just as fulfilling	(E023)	Respect for human rights
(D005)	Men make better political leaders than women do	(E024)	Aims of country: first choice
		(E025)	Aims of country: second choice
(D006)	University is more important for a boy than for a girl	(E026)	Priority: first choice
		(E027)	Priority: second choice
(D007)	Make my parents proud	(E028)	Most important goal: first choice
(D008)	Live up to what my friends expect	(E029)	Most important goal: second choice

SECTION E:
POLITICS AND SOCIETY

		(E031)	Confidence: Churches
		(E016)	Hard work
		(E033)	Confidence: The Press
(E001)	Be willing to fight in war for your country	(E034)	Confidence: Television
		(E035)	Confidence: Labour Unions
(E002)	Less importance placed on work	(E036)	Confidence: The Police
		(E037)	Confidence: Justice System
(E003)	More emphasis on technology	(E038)	Confidence: The Government
(E004)	Greater respect for authority	(E039)	Confidence: The Political Parties
(E005)	More emphasis on family life		
(E006)	Opinion about scientific advance	(E040)	Confidence: Parliament
		(E041)	Confidence: The Civil Services
(E007)	Interest in politics		
(E008)	Political action: signing a petition	(E042)	Confidence: Major Companies
(E009)	Political action: joining in boycotts	(E043)	Confidence: The Environmental Protection Movement
(E010)	Political action: attending lawful demonstrations	(E044)	Confidence: The Women's Movement
(E011)	Self positioning in political scale	(E045)	Confidence: Charitable or humanitarian organizations
(E012)	Income: Larger income differences	(E046)	Confidence: The European Union
(E013)	Government ownership of business	(E047)	Confidence: NATO
		(E048)	Confidence: Education System
(E014)	Government more responsibility		
		(E049)	Confidence: The United Nations
(E015)	Competition is good		
(E016)	Hard work	(E030)	Postmaterialism
(E017)	Wealth accumulation		
(E018)	Immigrant policy	**SECTION F: RELIGION AND MORAL ISSUES**	
(E019)	Having a strong leader		
(E020)	Having experts make decisions		
		(F001)	Thinking about meaning and purpose of life
(E021)	Having the army rule		
(E022)	Having a democratic political system	(F002)	How often do you attend religious services

(F003)	Religious person	(F012)	Justifiable: cheating on taxes
(F004)	Churches give answers: moral problems	(F013)	Justifiable: someone accepting a bribe
(F005)	Churches give answers: the problems of family life	(F014)	Justifiable: homosexuality
		(F015)	Justifiable: prostitution
(F006)	Churches give answers: people's spiritual needs	(F016)	Justifiable: abortion
		(F017)	Justifiable: divorce
(F007)	Churches give answers: the social problems	(F018)	Justifiable: euthanasia
		(F019)	Justifiable: suicide
(F008)	How important is God in your life		
(F009)	Moments of prayer, meditation		
(F010)	Justifiable: claiming government benefits		
(F011)	Justifiable: avoiding a fare on public transport		

SECTION G:
NATIONAL IDENTITY

(G001)   How proud of nationality

Acknowledgements

This book owes large debts to many friends and colleagues. It draws on a unique database, the World Values Survey (WVS) and the European Values Surveys (EVS), conducted from 1981 to 2007. These representative mass surveys provide data from countries comprising almost 90 percent of the world's population and covering the full range of variation, from societies with per capita incomes as low as $200 per year to societies with per capita incomes more than one hundred times that high, and from long-established democracies with market economies to authoritarian states and former socialist states.

We extend our gratitude to the following WVS and EVS participants for creating and sharing this unique dataset: Anthony M. Abela, Q. K. Ahmad, Rasa Alishauskene, Helmut Anheier, José Arocena, W. A. Arts, Dziedzorm Reuben Asafo, Soo Young Auh, Taghi Azadarmaki, Ljiljana Bacevic, Olga Balakireva, Josip Balobn, Miguel Basanez, Elena Bashkirova, Abdallah Bedaida, Jorge Benitez, Jaak Billiet, Alan Black, Eduard Bomhoff, Ammar Boukhedir, Rahma Bourquia, Fares al Braizat, Thawilwade Bureejul, Harold Caballeros, Augustin Canzani, Marita Carballo, Pavel Campeanu, Henrique Carlos de O. de Castro, Pradeep Chhibber, Hei-yuan Chiu, Munqith Daghir, Jaime Diez-Medrano, Juan Diez-Nicolas, Karel Dobbelaere, Peter J. D. Drenth, Javier Elzo, Yilmaz Esmer, Ann Evans, T. Fahey, Nadjematul Faizah, Georgy Fotev, James Georgas, Mark Gill, Renzo Gubert, Linda Luz Guerrero, Peter Gundelach, Christian Haerpfer, Jacques Hagenaars, Loek Halman, Sang-Jin Han, Stephen Harding, Mari Harris, Bernadette C. Hayes, Camilo Herrera, Virginia Hodgkinson, Nadra Muhammed Hosen, Desmond Hui, Kenji Iijima, Ljubov Ishimova, Wolfgang Jagodzinski, Aleksandra Jasinska-Kania, Fridrik Jonsson, Stanislovas Juknevicius, Jan Kerkhofs, S.J., Johann Kinghorn, Hans-Dieter Klingemann, Hennie Kotze, Hans-Peter Kreisi, Zuzana Kusá, Marta Lagos, Bernard Lategan, Abdel-Hamid Abdel-Latif, Carlos Lemoine, Noah Lewin-Epstein, Pei-shan Liao, Ola Listhaug, Jin-yun Liu, Augustin Loada, Brina Malnar, Mahar Mangahas, Mario Marinov, Joan Mico, Jon Miller, Felipe Miranda, Carlos Matheus, Robert Mattes, Rafael Mendizabal, Mansoor Moaddel, José Molina, Jotham Momba, Alejandro Moreno, Gaspar Munishi, Naasson Munyandamutsa, Neil Nevitte, Elone Nwabuzor, F. A. Orizo, Magued Osman, Merab Pachulia, Alula Pankhurst, Dragomir Pantic, Juhani Pehkonen, Paul Perry, Thorleif Pettersson, Pham Minh Hac, Pham Thanh Nghi, Gevork Pogosian, Bi Puranen, Ladislav Rabusic, Andrei Raichev, Angel Rivera-Ortiz, Catalina Romero, David Rotman, Rajab Sattarov, Sandeep Shastri, Shen Mingming, Renata Siemienska, John Sudarsky, Toru Takahashi, Tan Ern Ser, Farooq Tanwir, Jean-François Tchernia, Kareem Tejumola, Larissa Titarenko, Miklos Tomka, Alfredo Torres, Niko

Tos, Jorge Vala, Andrei Vardomatskii, Malina Voicu, Alan Webster, Friedrich Welsch, Christian Welzel, Robert Worcester, Seiko Yamazaki, Birol Yesilada, Ephraim Yuchtman-Yaar, Brigita Zepa, Josefina Zaiter, Ignacio Zuasnabar, and Paul Zulehner.

Most of these surveys were supported financially by sources within a given country, but assistance for surveys where such funding was not available, as well as for central coordination, was provided by the National Science Foundation, the Bank of Sweden Tercentenary Foundation, the Swedish Agency for International Development, the Volkswagen Foundation, the Netherlands Foreign Ministry, and the BBVA Foundation. For more information about the World Values Survey, see the WVS Web site, http://www.worldvaluessurvey.org. The European surveys were conducted by the European Values Study group. For more information, see the EVS Web site, http://www.europeanvalues.nl/.

Introduction: the Values Surveys

Ronald Inglehart

This book gives insight into how people's basic values and attitudes differ across almost 100 countries containing most of the world's population —and how these orientations have been changing from 1981 to 2007. Using data from the World Values Survey and European Values Study Surveys, it examines human values and goals concerning politics, economics, religion, sexual behavior, gender roles, family values, communal identities, civic engagement and ethical concerns, and such issues as environmental protection, scientific progress and technological development and human happiness. This volume provides an initial overview, reporting each country's overall scores on these variables, and how they have changed over time. A great deal of additional information, including many recent publications and the raw data themselves, can be downloaded from the World Values Survey web site, http://www.worldvaluessurvey.org and the European Values Study website, http://www.europeanvalues.nl.

These surveys cover a broader range of variation than has ever before been available for analyzing the changing belief systems of mass publics. They provide data from representative national samples of the publics of societies containing almost 90 percent of the world's population and covering the full range of variation, from societies with per capita incomes below $200 per year, to societies with per capita incomes of more than $45,000 per year; from long-established democracies to authoritarian states; and from societies with market economies to societies that are in the process of emerging from state-run economies. They cover societies that were historically shaped by a wide variety of religious and cultural traditions, from Christian to Islamic to Confucian to Hindu; and from societies whose culture emphasizes social conformity and group-obligations, to societies where the main emphasis is on human emancipation and self-expression.

This sourcebook enables the reader to compare the responses to hundreds of questions across societies throughout the world covering the full spectrum of economic, political, and cultural variation. It also enables the reader to examine the changes that took place from 1981 to 2007 in countries that were surveyed at multiple times. In order to present this material concisely, the responses to each question are dichotomized, with only the percentage ranking "high" being shown (missing data is excluded from the percentage base). For example, one of the tables presented in our data section shows the responses to the question, "How important is religion in your life?" This table A001 is reproduced here to illustrate the overall pattern. As the reader will note, only the percentage saying that religion is "very important" is shown. The first column in this table shows the name of a given country. The next columns compare the results from the various years for which data are available. Thus the first row in this table shows that in the 1990 survey in Albania, 25 percent of the public rated religion as "very important" (the remaining 72 percent rated it as either "fairly important," "not very important," or "not at all important."). In the 2000 survey in Albania, this figure had risen slightly, and 28 percent of the public rated religion as "very important." Albania was not included in the 1981 and 1990 surveys, so the spaces for these years are blank. Data on the responses to some question are available for as many as five time points, but this question was not asked in 1981. Thus, data are available from Argentina from 1990, 1995, 2000 and 2006.

The table doesn't show the breakdown among the other three categories. If the reader wishes to examine these details (or to run any number of additional cross-tabulations) is invited to download the raw data for all of the variables presented here from the World Values Survey web site at http://www.worldvaluessurvey.org. This book shows only one response category for each variable. This sacrifice of detail brings a huge gain in conciseness: if we were to report every response category for every variable, it would be necessary to expand the hundreds of pages of tables and figures presented here into several thousand pages.

This mode of presentation facilitates cross-cultural comparisons. One can simply scan down the columns in each table in order to compare the proportions in each country that consider religion "very important." The countries are listed alphabetically in each table. When we scan table A006, we find that in some countries, such as Indonesia and Egypt, as much as 97 or 98 percent of the public said that religion was very important in their lives— while, at the other extreme, in China as little as 1 percent of the public considered religion to be very important in their lives (though this has risen in recent surveys). This illustrates one of the most striking findings from the Values Surveys: there is enormous cross-cultural variation in people's beliefs and values. This finding appears repeatedly throughout this book: what people believe and what they want out of life varies immensely from one society to another. To assume that everyone sees the world as you, yourself, see it, would be extremely misleading.

Another pervasive finding is the fact that the people of low-income countries tend to emphasize different values and beliefs from those found in high-income countries. Thus, in our sample table the publics of the poorest societies, such as Burkina Faso and El Salvador, tend to place the greatest emphasis on religion. But it is also clear that societies with an Islamic cultural heritage are particularly likely to attach great importance to religion. Thus, Indonesia, Egypt, Jordan, Morocco, Nigeria, Algeria and Bangladesh rank highest in the importance they place on religion. All of these countries except Nigeria (which is about half Islamic) have overwhelmingly Islamic populations.

Time series data are available for many countries, making it possible to examine trends. The sample table shows that the percentage saying that religion was very important in their lives, increased in about as many countries as it declined—but the pattern varies strikingly according to level of economic development. Emphasis on religion declined in most of the advanced industrial societies, such as Austria, Canada, France, Germany, South Korea, Poland, Spain and the United Kingdom. But it increased in most of the developing countries such as Bangladesh, Brazil, India, Mexico, Nigeria and South Africa (there was also a slight increase in the U.S.). But the developing countries have much higher population growth rates than the advanced industrial societies. Conse-

Religion important in life

(A006) For each of the following, indicate how important it is in your life: Religion

Very important (%)

Country	1981	1990	1995	2000	2006	Change
Albania			25	28		3
Algeria				91		
Andorra					8	
Argentina		40	37	46	32	−8
Armenia			27			
Australia			23		20	−3
Austria		25		21		−4
Azerbaijan			30			
Bangladesh			82	88		6
Belarus		12	22	12		0
Belgium		17		21		4
Bosnia and Herz.			40	40		0
Brazil		57	65		52	−5
Britain	18		13	20		2
Bulgaria		12	16	16	19	7
Burkina Faso				84		
Canada		30		33	34	4
Chile		51	43	47	37	−14
China		1	4	3	7	6
Colombia			49			
Croatia			26	24		−2
Cyprus				51		
Czech		9	9	8		−1
Denmark		9		8		−1
Dominican Rep.			51			
Egypt				97	96	−1
El Salvador			87			
Estonia		4	8	5		1
Ethiopia				81		
Finland		14	13	12	18	4
France		14		11	13	−1
Georgia			49		80	31
Germany (East)		16	6	4	9	−7
Germany (West)		13	15	9	13	0
Ghana				90		
Greece				33		
Guatemala				83		
Hong Kong				5		
Hungary		23	22	19		−4
Iceland		24		19		−5
India		49	49	57	51	2
Indonesia				98	95	−3
Iran				80	78	−2
Iraq				94	96	2
Ireland		48		38		−10
Israel						
Italy		31		33	34	3
Japan			6	7	7	6	0
Jordan				96	95	−1

Country	1981	1990	1995	2000	2006	Change
Kyrgyzstan				32		
Latvia		7	13	11		4
Lithuania		16	13	12		−4
Luxembourg				15		
Macedonia			35	48		13
Malaysia					81	
Mali					90	
Malta	72			67		−5
Mexico		34	44	66	59	25
Moldova			31	35	32	1
Montenegro			24	19		−5
Morocco				94	91	−3
Netherlands	21			16	13	−8
New Zealand			20		17	−3
Nigeria		85	91	93		8
Northern Ireland		34		27		−7
Norway		15	12		11	−4
Pakistan			79	82		3
Peru			55	53	50	−5
Philippines			78	87		9
Poland		52	47	45	48	−4
Portugal		19		28		9
Puerto Rico			71	76		5
Romania		42	38	51	58	16
Russia		12	14	13	13	1
Rwanda					39	
Saudi Arabia				89		
Serbia			26	29	26	0
Singapore				59		
Slovakia		25	24	27		2
Slovenia		17	16	12	15	−2
South Africa		64	71	73	71	7
South Korea		26	20	23	21	−5
Spain		21	25	19	15	−6
Sweden		10	10	11	9	−1
Switzerland		24	16		17	−7
Taiwan			13		12	−1
Tanzania				85		
Thailand					56	
Trinidad					78	
Turkey		61	77	78	75	14
Uganda				72		
Ukraine			21	23	17	−4
Uruguay			24		23	−1
USA		53	58	59	56	3
Venezuela			61	64		3
Vietnam				10	7	−3
Zambia					78	
Zimbabwe				78		

4   Introduction: the Values Surveys

quently, although secularization does seem to be taking place in most rich countries, the number of religious people has been increasing in the world as a whole. The once widely-held belief that religion is disappearing, was clearly mistaken.

Most of the findings will seem intuitively plausible to the reader. For example, these tables show that religion tends to be considered much more important by the publics of low-income societies than by those of economically highly developed societies. These findings are consistent with the secularization thesis—and though this thesis has been hotly debated, it is widely known so the finding may not seem surprising. Nevertheless, there are some striking deviant cases, with the peoples of both the United States and Ireland showing a much more religious outlook than their economic levels would predict.

We will not pursue our interpretation of this table any farther (for a more detailed discussion of religious attitudes around the world, see Norris and Inglehart, 2004). This discussion is simply intended to illustrate some of the many possible types of cross-cultural comparisons that this sourcebook facilitates. The reader will find a good deal of fascinating material in the tables presented in the data section below.

As the reader will note, we consistently observe large and systematic differences between the values and attitudes prevailing in rich and poor societies. These differences are consistent with the predictions of modernization theory, a body of social thought that has been influential throughout the past two centuries. Modernization theory has been controversial since its inception, and the Values Surveys provide a massive body of new evidence with which to test its claims. Economic development seems to make a great deal of difference in what people value and believe. As Figure 1-1 below indicates, the people of low-income societies emphasize religion and work as more important than other aspects of life—while the people of high-income societies emphasize friends and leisure as being considerably more important than religion, with friends even slightly more important than work. But, although we find strong and statistically significant rela-

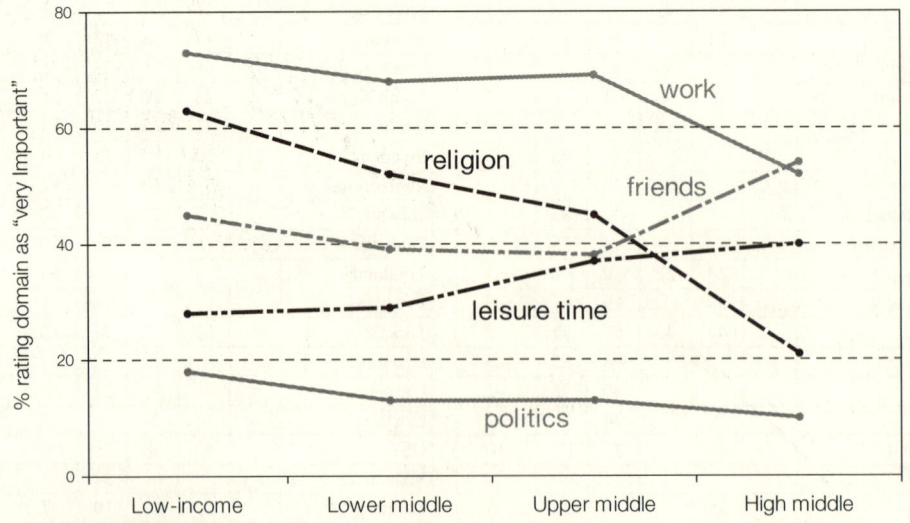

Figure 1-1. Importance of five aspects of life in low-income, middle-income and high-income countries.

tions between levels of economic development and beliefs and values, these relationships are rarely monotonic and we almost always find deviant cases, sometimes dramatic ones.

Though economic development tends to push socio-cultural change in a predictable direction, each society remains unique. This reflects the fact that cultural variation reflects the entire historical experience of given peoples, including political, social, technological, geographic, and other factors and not just economic influences (Inglehart and Baker, 2000; Arts and Halman, 2004; Inglehart and Welzel, 2005).

Implications of Modernization Theory and Human Development

The central claim of modernization theory is that economic, cultural, and political change tend to go together in a coherent pattern, with modern societies showing fundamentally different characteristics from those of pre-modern societies. The two most influential proponents of modernization theory, Karl Marx and Max Weber, agreed on this point. They disagreed profoundly on why economic, cultural, and political changes go together. For Marx and his disciples, they are linked because economic and technological change determines political and cultural changes. For Weber and his disciples, they are linked because culture helps shape economic and political life.

Modernization theory gave rise to heated debate that stimulated influential subsequent work by Deutsch, Lerner, Inkeles and Smith, Bell, Toffler, Nolan and Lenski and many others. Still more recent work analyzing evidence from the Values Surveys, suggests that the central claim of modernization theory is largely correct: economic change, cultural change, and political change are closely linked (Inglehart, 1997, Inglehart and Baker, 2000). More specifically, Inglehart and Welzel (2005) demonstrate that the common theme underlying all these economic, cultural and political changes is "human choice," which tends to grow as people gain more material and intellectual resources, place more emphasis on self-expression and obtain democratic rights. Economic prosperity, rising emphasis on self-expression values and the strengthening of democracy, form a coherent syndrome of Human Development. Though we cannot predict exactly what will happen in a given society at a given time, major trends in Human Development are predictable in broad outline. When given processes of change reshape one aspect of this syndrome, other aspects are likely to emerge in the long run. Growing human choice in economic, cultural, and political aspects of life tend to go together.

While conceding an important role to cultural factors, modernization theorists such as Bell (1973) viewed changes in the structure of the work force as the leading cause of cultural change. For Bell, the crucial milestone in the coming of "Postindustrial society" is reached when a majority of the work force is employed in the tertiary sector of the economy, producing neither raw materials, nor manufactured goods, but offering services. This is paralleled by a massive expansion of formal education, driven by the need for an increasingly skilled and specialized work force. Other writers such as Lerner (1958) and Inkeles and Smith (1974) and Inkeles (1983) emphasized the importance of mass communications and formal education as key factors shaping a "modern" worldview. Still others, such as Ember and Ember (1996) and Nolan and Lenski (1999) see the key factor as the individualizing trend in postmodern service economies, based on the fact that service professions require individual judgment, self-reliance, initiative and intellectual creativity—factors linked with human autonomy and choice.

And Inglehart (1990, 1997), Welzel (2003), and Inglehart and Welzel (2005) emphasize the role of economic security in reducing existential constraints on human choice, giving rise to emancipative values that emphasize human self-expression.

Though any simplistic linear version of modernization theory has long since been refuted, we do find strong empirical evidence that some scenarios of social change are far more probable than others. The Values Surveys show coherent and far-reaching cultural patterns that are closely linked with economic development. In the long term, across many societies, once given processes are set in motion, certain important changes seem likely to happen. Industrialization, for example, tends to bring increasing urbanization, growing occupational specialization and higher levels of formal education in any society that undertakes it. These are core elements of a trajectory called "Modernization."

This trajectory also tends to bring less obvious but equally important long term consequences, such as a shift from traditional religious values toward rational-bureaucratic norms; an increasing emphasis on economic achievement; rising levels of mass political participation and major changes in the types of issues that are most salient in the politics of the respective types of societies.

The modernization trajectory is linked with many other cultural changes. As this sourcebook shows, a wide range of cultural values are closely linked with a given society's level of economic development. For example, the sharply contrasting gender roles that characterize all preindustrial societies tend to give way to increasingly similar gender roles in advanced industrial societies.

The Postmodern Shift

Economic development is linked with social change—but the process is not linear. Though a specific modernization syndrome becomes increasingly probable when societies move from an agrarian mode to an industrial mode, no trend goes on in the same direction forever. It eventually reaches a point of diminishing returns. Modernization is no exception. In the past few decades, advanced industrial societies have reached an inflection point where they begin moving on a new trajectory that Inglehart (1997) describes as "Postmodernization." Inglehart and Welzel (2005) find that this stage brings a pervasive shift in value orientations linked with increasing emphasis on human choice in all aspects of people's lives—including mate selection, gender roles, child rearing goals, working habits, religious orientations, consumer patterns, civic action and voting behavior.

The process of economic development leads to two successive trajectories, Modernization and Postmodernization. Both of them are linked with economic development but Postmodernization represents a later stage of development that emphasizes very different beliefs from those that characterize Modernization. These belief systems are not mere consequences of economic change, but shape socioeconomic conditions as well as being shaped by them, in reciprocal fashion. At the heart of the postmodern shift lies a change of value orientations linked with increasing emphasis on human choice and self-expression. This reflects a change in which authority shifts from religious to secular institutions and ideologies, but authority remains external to the individual. At the peak of modernity, rational science has almost the same absolute authority as religion in pre-modernity. Postmodernity erodes the absoluteness of all kinds of external authority, whether religious or secular: authority becomes internalized.

Why Is the Postmodern Shift Occurring?

This is not the first major cultural shift in human history. The transition from agrarian society to industrial society was facilitated by a Modernization shift, from a worldview shaped by a steady-state economy, which discourages social mobility and emphasized tradition, inherited status, communal obligations, and absolute religious norms-- to a worldview that encourages economic achievement, individualism and innovation, with increasingly secular and flexible social norms. Today, some of these trends have reached their limits in advanced industrial society, where change is taking a new direction.

This change of direction reflects the principle of diminishing marginal utility. Industrialization and modernization required breaking the cultural constraints on accumulation that are found in any steady-state economy. In West European history, this was achieved by what Weber described as the rise of the Protestant Ethic. If it had occurred two centuries earlier, it might have died out. In the environment of its time, it found a niche: technological developments were making rapid economic growth possible and the Calvinist worldview complemented these developments beautifully. These elements created a cultural-economic syndrome that accelerated the rise of capitalism and eventually, the industrial revolution. Once this had occurred, economic accumulation (for individuals) and economic growth (for societies) became top priorities for an increasing part of the world's population, and are still the central goals for much of humanity. Economic growth came to be equated with progress and was seen as the hallmark of a successful society. But eventually, diminishing returns from economic growth lead to a Postmodern shift.

Advanced industrial societies are now changing their basic value systems in a number of related ways. Growing material wealth reduces the basic existential constraints on human choice. The rise of a knowledge-based economy makes people intellectually independent, widening the areas in which people have to rely on their own choices. In that sense, the broadening of human choice is the most pervasive underlying theme of postmodern society.

In postmodern society, the emphasis on economic achievement as the top priority is now giving way to an increasing emphasis on the quality of life. In a major part of the world, the disciplined, self-denying and achievement-oriented norms of industrial society are yielding, leaving an increasingly broad latitude for individual choice of life styles and individual self-expression. The shift from "Materialist" values, emphasizing economic and physical security, to "Postmaterialist" values, emphasizing individual self-expression and quality life concerns, is the most amply documented aspect of this change, but it is only one component of a much broader syndrome of cultural change. Moreover, the relationship between socioeconomic environment and value priorities is not one of immediate adjustment: a substantial time lag is involved because, to a large extent, one's basic values reflect the conditions that prevailed during one's preadult years. This gives rise to substantial differences between the values of older and younger generations—so that cultural change largely takes place as one generation replaces another in the adult population.

The recent economic history of advanced industrial societies has significant implications in the light of the scarcity hypothesis. For these societies are a striking exception to the prevailing historical pattern: they still contain poor people, but most of their population does not live under conditions of hunger and economic insecurity. This has led to a gradual shift in which needs for belonging, esteem, and intellectual and esthetic satisfaction became more prominent. Other things being equal, we would expect prolonged periods of high prosperity to encourage the spread of Postmaterialist values; economic problems, such as the current recession and welfare state retrenchment would have the opposite effect, re-strengthening Materialist values.

Materialist/Postmaterialist values have been measured in every wave of the Values Surveys. Materialist priorities are tapped by emphasis on such goals as economic growth, fighting rising prices, maintaining order and fighting crime; while Postmaterialist values are reflected when top priority is given to such goals as giving people more say on the job or in government decisions, or protecting freedom of speech or moving toward a less impersonal, more humane society. The shift toward Postmaterialist values is only one aspect of a much broader Postmodern trend toward values that emphasize human choice and emancipation. This shift from survival values towards self-expression values involves changing political, religious, sexual, and other norms.

Changing Moral Orientations, Gender Roles, and Sexual Norms

Postmaterialist values are part of a broader Postmodern shift that is reshaping the political outlook, religious orientations, gender roles, and sexual norms of advanced industrial society. This shift involves an intergenerational change in a wide variety of basic social norms, from cultural norms linked with ensuring survival of the species, to norms linked with the pursuit of individual well being. For example, Postmaterialists and the young are markedly more tolerant of homosexuality than are Materialists and the old. This is part of a pervasive pattern. Postmaterialists have been shaped by security during their formative years, and are far more permissive than Materialists in their attitudes toward abortion, divorce, extramarital affairs, prostitution, and euthanasia. Materialists, conversely, tend to adhere to the traditional societal norms that favor child-bearing, but only within the traditional two-parent family—and that heavily stigmatized sexual activity outside that setting. Accordingly, we find a pervasive shift toward more tolerant attitudes toward homosexuality in virtually all advanced industrial societies from 1981 to 2006—but relatively little change in low-income societies.

Traditional gender role norms from East Asia to the Islamic world to Western society discouraged women from taking jobs outside the home. Virtually all preindustrial societies emphasized child-bearing and child-rearing as the central goal of any woman, her most important function in life, and her greatest source of satisfaction. In recent years, this perspective has been increasingly called into question, as growing numbers of women postpone having children or forego them completely in order to devote themselves to careers outside the home. The sharply differentiated gender roles that characterize virtually all preindustrial societies, give way to increasingly similar gender roles in advanced industrial society.

As the data section demonstrates, we find enormous differences in attitudes toward equal employment opportunity for women. In Egypt, 90 percent of the public agrees that men have more right to a job than women, while in Sweden only 2 percent agree. The publics of rich countries are much more supportive of gender equality than the publics of low-income societies. Outside of advanced industrial societies, much of the world still takes it for granted that practically everyone lives in a traditional family, with a male as their principal provider. People who see the world from this perspective are willing to accord men preferential employment opportunities. Thus in Africa, Asia, and above all, the Islamic countries, pluralities or even absolute majorities of the public feel that men have more right to a job than women. In Catholic Europe and Latin America, by contrast, solid pluralities of the public feel that men do not have more right to a job than women; in the U.S., Canada, and Northern Europe, support for gender equality is overwhelming: less than one in five agree that men have more right to a job than women.

The differences linked with Materialist/Postmaterialist values are also strong: Materialists are more than twice as likely as Postmaterialists to feel that men have more right to a job than women. The more educated, and the upper income groups are also more supportive of gender equality than the less educated and lower income groups. The overall picture strongly suggests that economic development is conducive to increasing support for gender equality (see Inglehart and Norris, 2003).

Not surprisingly, women are more likely to favor equal employment opportunity than are men—the only surprising finding is the fact that the overall gender gap amounts to only 6 percentage points. Across these societies, 38 percent of the men feel that their sex has more right to a job, while only 32 percent of the women agree. But we find relatively large gender differences in the less developed societies. In the ten richest societies, on the other hand, there is a broad consensus favoring equal rights, and a gender gap of only two points.

A Cultural Map of the World

Figure 1-2 below shows where scores of societies fall on two main dimensions of cross-cultural variation that are linked with the processes of "Modernization" and "Postmodernization" respectively (for a detailed discussion of these dimensions and how they were derived, see Inglehart and Baker, 2000; for a similar type of analysis applied to the European context, see Hagenaars, Halman and Moors, 2003).
These two broad dimensions reflect a large number of the key values examined in the Values Surveys. Since hundreds of questions were asked in these surveys, it would be unworkable to compare the values of each public on each topic separately. Figure 1 compares the orientations of these publics on two important dimensions that sum up the cross-national variation on scores of values. These two dimensions tap:

1. **Traditional vs. Secular-Rational values.** This dimension reflects emphasis on obedience to traditional authority (usually religious authority), and adherence to family and communal obligations, and norms of sharing-- or, on the other hand, a secular worldview in which authority is legitimated by rational-legal norms, linked with an emphasis on economic accumulation and individual achievement.

2. **Survival values vs. Self-Expression values.** This reflects the fact that in postindustrial society, historically unprecedented levels of wealth and the emergence of the welfare states have given rise to a shift from scarcity norms, emphasizing hard work and self-denial, to postmodern values emphasizing the quality of life, emancipation of women and sexual minorities and related Postmaterialist priorities such as emphasis on self-expression.

The two respective phases of modernization—industrialization, and the emergence of the knowledge society— each give rise to a major dimension of cross-cultural variation. This makes it possible to locate any society in the world on a two-dimensional map of cross-cultural variation. Figure 1 show this map. The Traditional/Secular-rational values dimension constitutes the vertical axis: as one moves from south to north, one moves from societies that emphasize Traditional values to those that emphasize Secular-rational values. The Survival/Self-expression values dimension constitutes the horizontal axis: as one moves from left to right, one moves from societies that emphasize Survival values to those that emphasize Self-expression values.

Figure 1-2 sums up an immense amount of information. It reflects the responses to scores of questions, given by over many thousands of respondents in scores of societies. There is a great deal of constraint among cultural systems. The first two dimensions that emerge from the principal components factor analysis depicted in Figure 1-2 account for over half of the cross-national variation among ten key variables. Additional dimensions explain relatively small amounts of variance. And these dimensions are robust, showing little change if we drop some of the items, even high-loading ones. This cross-cultural map is so robust that, using a completely different way of measuring basic values, different types of samples and a different type of dimensional analysis, Schwartz (2006) finds very similar transnational groupings among 76 countries.

The Traditional/Secular-rational values dimension reflects the contrast between societies in which religion is very important and those in which it is not-- but deference

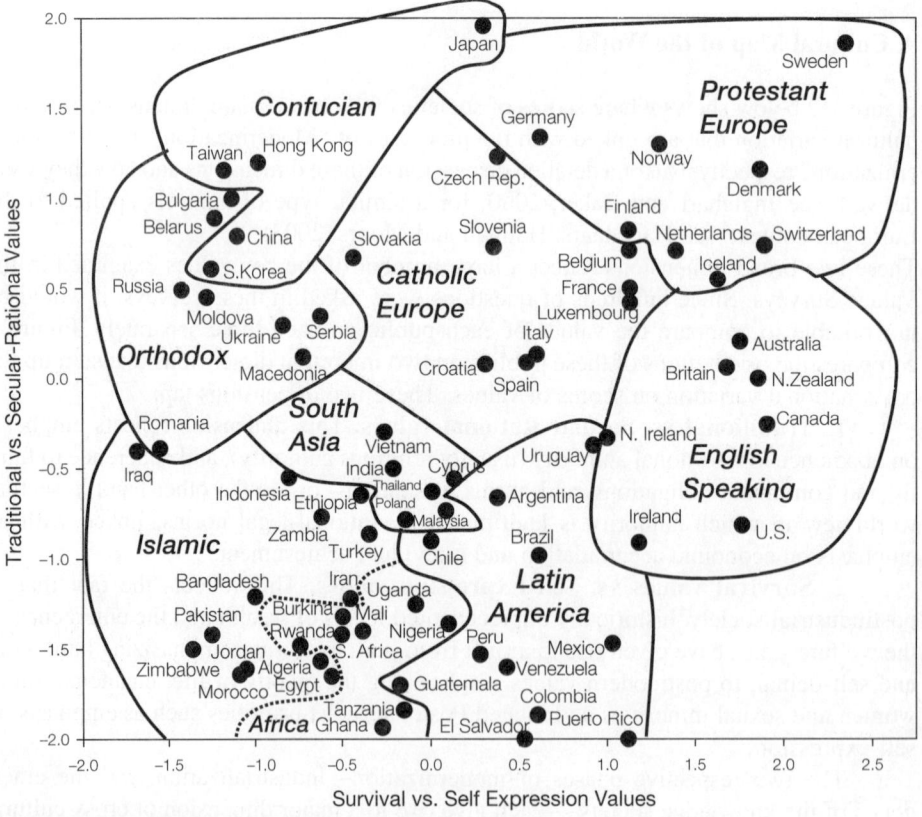

Figure 1-2. Location of 80 societies on a global map of cross-cultural differences.

(Based on most recent available data for the given country, in most cases from 2005-2007 World Values Survey)

to the authority of God, Fatherland and Family are all closely linked. In traditional societies, a main goal in most people's lives is to make their parents proud; they idealize large families, and have large numbers of children. They also have high levels of national pride, favor more respect for authority, and reject divorce, abortion, euthanasia, and suicide. Societies with secular-rational values have the opposite preferences on all of these topics.

The Survival/Self-expression dimension taps a syndrome of tolerance, trust, subjective well-being, political activism and self-expression that emerges in postindustrial societies with high levels of existential security. People in societies shaped by insecurity tend to emphasize economic and physical security above all, and feel threatened by foreigners, by ethnic diversity and by cultural change— which leads to intolerance of gays and other outgroups, insistence on traditional gender roles and an authoritarian political outlook. Societies that emphasize survival values show relatively low levels of subjective well-being, report relatively poor health, are low on interpersonal trust, relatively intolerant of outgroups, and low on support for gender equality. They emphasize economic and physical security more than autonomy and self-expression, have relatively high levels of faith in science and technology, are relatively low on environmental activism, and relatively favorable to authoritarian government. Societies high on Self-expression values tend to have the opposite preferences on all of these topics.

Each individual's score on the Traditional/Secular-rational values dimension and on the Survival/Self-expression dimension is included as a variable on the dataset that can be downloaded from http://www.worldvaluessurvey.org, with the names "Tradrat5" [factor score on Traditional/Secular-rational values] and "SurvSelf" [factor score on Survival/Self-expression values]).[1] Each person's score on Materialist/Postmaterialist values is also available. This cultural map closely resembles earlier ones in Inglehart (1997: 334-337) and Inglehart and Welzel (2005: 63) based on the 1990-1991 and 1995-1997 Values Surveys respectively. Although Figure 1-2 is based on an analysis that uses less than half as many variables and a much larger number of societies than were analyzed by Inglehart (1997), the locations of the respective societies are strikingly similar to those on the cultural maps he generated from earlier surveys. The same cultural zones appear, in similar locations, but some of them now contain many more societies. The similarity between this map and the earlier ones reflects the fact that these two key dimensions of cross-cultural variation are robust.

The maps show consistent cultural clusters based on religion. For example, the historically Protestant societies tend to rank higher on the Survival/Self-expression dimension than the historically Roman Catholic societies. Conversely, all of the former communist societies rank relatively low on the Survival/Self-expression dimension. The historically Orthodox societies form a coherent cluster within the broader ex-communist zone—except for Greece, an Orthodox society that did not experience communist rule, and ranks substantially higher on Self-expression values than the other communist societies. The Islamic societies fall into a relatively compact group in the Southwest

---

[1] If one of the ten questions used to construct them was not asked in a given country, these dimensions can not be constructed for that sample. The individual-level scores are not directly equivalent to the national-level scores shown on Figures 1-2 and 1-3. If one wishes to plot given groups on these maps, the individual-level scores can be converted into a close approximation of the national-level scores by multiplying Tradrat5 by 1.56 and by multiplying Survself by 1.76.

quadrant of the map. And the influence of colonial ties is apparent in the existence of a Latin American cultural zone. Former colonial ties also help account for the existence of an English-speaking zone containing Britain, Ireland, Northern Ireland, the United States, Canada, Australia, and New Zealand.

At first glance, the configuration in Figure 1-2 might seem to reflect geographic clusters, but closer observation makes it clear that this is true only in so far as geographic proximity happens to coincide with cultural similarity. Thus, the English-speaking cluster spans immense geographic distances, with Australia and New Zealand being half-way around the world from Great Britain and Ireland and on the opposite side of the Pacific Ocean from the United States and Canada—but all seven of the English-speaking societies included in this study show relatively similar cultural characteristics, and they occupy neighboring positions on this cultural map. Similarly, the Latin American countries span a vast geographic distance, from Tiajuana to Patagonia, with very different terrain, climates, and racial compositions, but they have similar value systems, reflecting a common cultural heritage imported from Spain and Portugal—which themselves have value systems that place them close to Latin America despite being on opposite sides of the Atlantic Ocean. The Islamic cultural zone also spans a vast geographic distance from Morocco to Indonesia, but the Muslim-majority countries all fall into the same region of the global cultural map.

Economic development and cultural change

The classic version of modernization theory emphasized economic determinism; as we have just seen, it must be modified to take into account the remarkable persistence of cultural factors. Nevertheless, a society's level of economic development plays an extremely important role in shaping its value system.

As modernization theory implies, these two major dimensions of cross-cultural variation are closely linked with a society's level of economic development. As Figure 1-3 demonstrates, the value systems of richer countries differ dramatically from those of poorer countries. All of the high-income societies (as defined by the World Bank), rank relatively high on both dimensions, falling into a zone near the upper right-hand corner of the global cultural map. Conversely, all of the low-income and lower-middle-income societies fall into a cluster at the lower left of Figure 3. All of the upper-middle-income societies fall into an intermediate cultural-economic zone. One rarely finds such a striking and consistent correspondence between an objective independent variable such as GNP per capita, and subjective values and attitudes as is found here. Economic development seems to push societies in a predictable common direction, regardless of their cultural heritage.

We find a remarkable degree of coherence. All of the high-income societies rank relatively high on both of our two major dimensions of cross-cultural variation, and the low-income societies rank relatively low on both dimensions. Furthermore, the societies fall into compact and historically meaningful clusters, such as Protestant Europe, Catholic Europe, Latin America, an English-speaking zone, an Islamic zone, and ex-communist zone, sub-Saharan Africa or the Confucian zone. As the reader examines the following tables, he or she will find that again and again, across scores of variables, the societies that are located near each other show relatively similar values and beliefs; while those that are far apart on this figure show dissimilar values and beliefs.

Introduction: the Values Surveys   13

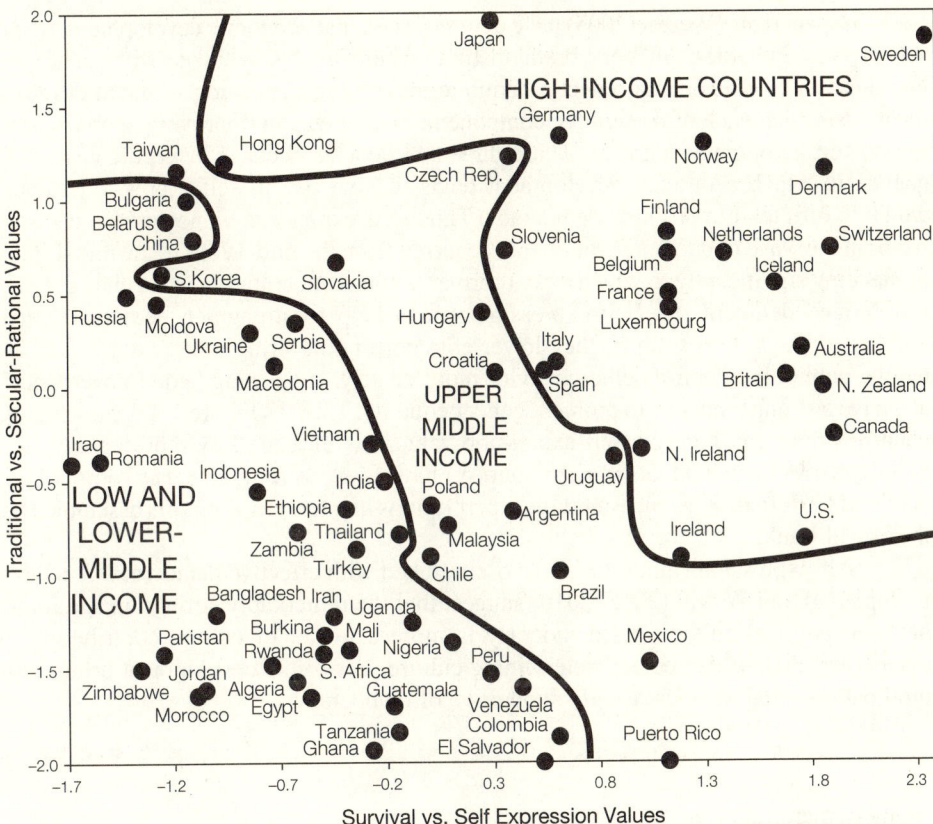

Figure 1-3. Economic development and cultural values: cultural locations of rich and poor countries.

(Based on most recent available data for the given country, in most cases from 2005-2007 World Values Survey)

Individual-level values and societal-level phenomena

Human beliefs and values are not just an epiphenomenon that is shaped by a society's economic infrastructure. The fact that the Values Surveys cover scores of societies, makes it possible to carry out statistically significant cross-level analyses, examining the impact of individual-level values and beliefs on societal-level phenomena such as fertility rates or political institutions. The results indicate that cultural factors play a major role in shaping the societal-level characteristics of given societies.

Moreover, an analysis of the empirical linkages between culture and democracy demonstrates that democracies have strikingly different political cultures from authoritarian societies. Almost without exception, stable democracies rank high on self-expression values, and authoritarian societies rank low on them. These linkages persist when we control for economic level and social structure: a pro-democratic political culture seems to play an important role in sustaining democratic institutions over the long term.

14   Introduction: the Values Surveys

Inglehart and Welzel (2005) have demonstrated that economic development, rising self-expression values, and democratic institutions are so closely linked with each other that these three phenomena reflect a common underlying dimension—human development—to which each of these three components contributes in improving people's ability to exert autonomous choices. These three components occur in a specific causal sequence in which economic development tends to give rise to self-expression values, which in turn tend to promote democracy. Thus, self-expression values were a decisive factor in the wave of democratization that occurred from the mid-1980s to the mid-1990s, influencing significantly to which extent formerly non-democratic societies changed into full-fledged democracies. Self-expression values help to strengthen democracy in a number of ways: for example, they lower elite corruption, bring a more active and attentive public that controls elite behavior more closely, supporting "good governance" and have a strong tendency to promote gender equality. Thus, as Figure 1-4 demonstrates, countries that rank high on Self-expression values (as measured by representative national surveys of individuals in each country) have a very strong tendency to rank high on Good Governance, as measured by expert ratings and travelers' reports assembled by the World Bank.

Self-expression values are also closely linked with effective democracy. Analyses by Inglehart and Welzel (2005, 2010) suggest that the remarkably strong linkage found between political culture and democracy is more a matter of culture contributing to democracy, than of democracy determining culture. Economic development brings cultural patterns that are increasingly supportive of democracy.

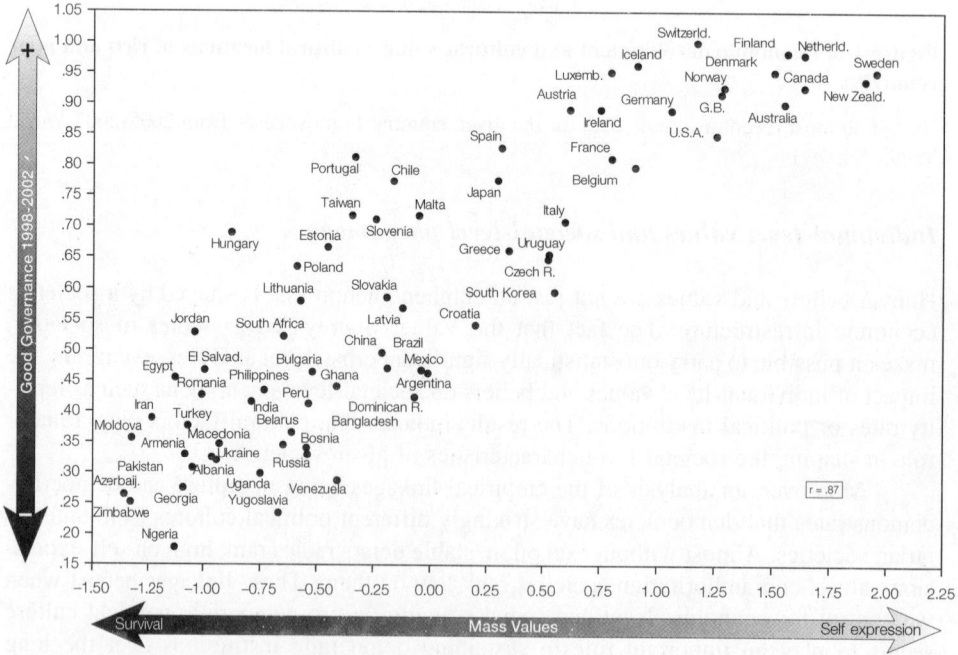

Figure 1-4. Self-expression values and Good Governance.

About the *World Values Survey* and *European Values Study*

These surveys build on the 1981 European Values Study, which evoked so much interest that it was replicated in a number of non-European countries. In 1990 this investigation was carried out on a worldwide basis, using a questionnaire designed with input from social scientists on six continents, and was referred to as the World Values Survey. In subsequent years, the WVS and EVS became separate organizations, with the WVS group carrying out surveys every five years, while the EVS did fieldwork every nine years. Accordingly, the WVS carried out another wave of surveys in 1995. In 1999-2001, the two groups collaborated in a third wave of surveys, while the WVS went on to do another wave in 2005-2007. The World Values Survey is a network of social scientists in that has carried out representative national surveys in almost 100 countries containing almost 90 percent of the world's population. A non-profit association seated in Stockholm with partners in each of the participating countries, the World Values Survey completed five waves of surveys on all six inhabited continents, in 1981, 1990, 1995, 2000 and 2005-2006 and is carrying out a new wave of surveys in 2010-2011.

The WVS is a unique resource for social scientists, policy-makers and journalists. Its findings suggest that mass values and attitudes have a significant impact on important political, social and economic phenomena. And its time series data demonstrate that important changes in basic values are taking place throughout advanced industrial society. These changes are linked with economic development: they are occurring most rapidly in high-income societies, though they are also taking place in developing countries. Thus, as Table C001 below demonstrates, the percentage of the public saying that "men have more right to a job than women" has diminished since 1990 in almost every country in the world. Similarly, as Table F014 demonstrates, the percentage saying that "homosexuality is never justified" has decreased since 1981 in the vast majority of

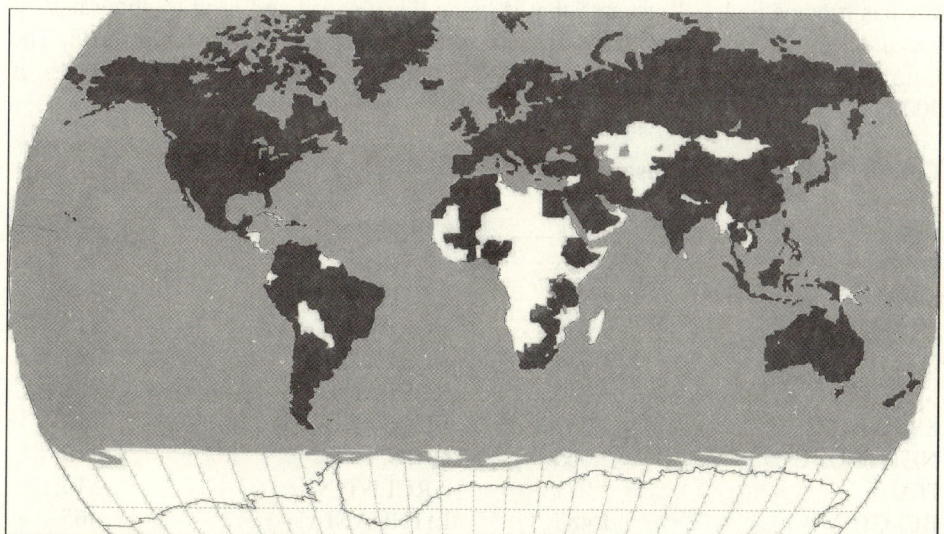

Figure 1-5. Countries included in the World Values Survey.

(The shaded countries have been covered in at least one wave of the WVS as of 2007)

16   Introduction: the Values Surveys

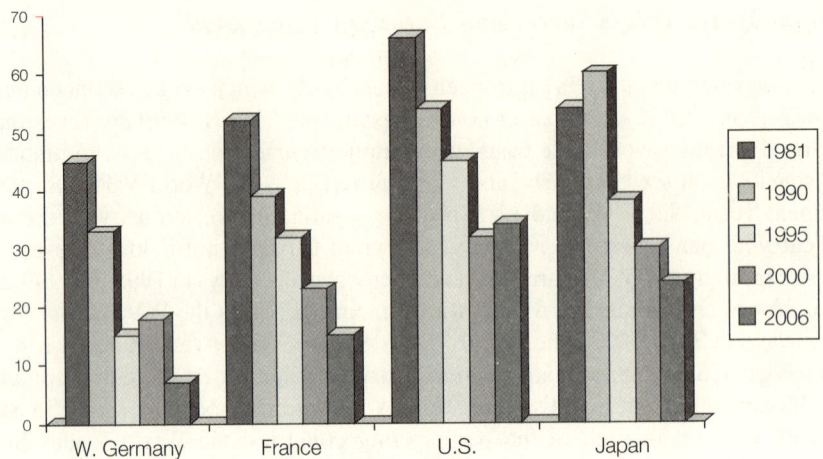

Figure 1-6. Percentage saying that "homosexuality is never justified."

countries—but the changes are most dramatic in high-income countries such as the U.S., Germany, France and Japan. As Figure 1-6 indicates, a majority of the public in most high-income countries absolutely rejected homosexuality in 1981—but by 2006, the percentage taking this position had fallen to about half its earlier level in these countries.

In the World Values Survey network, people on all six continents are working together to gain a better understanding of social change and cultural differences. The members of this network have produced hundreds of publications, and the data have been used by others in thousands of publications. The data from the World Values Survey has become a global resource that is being downloaded and used by thousands of social scientists, journalists, decision-makers and students throughout the world. The following table shows the number of users who had downloaded WVS data as of 2007:

Country and number of users

U.S.A.	30,485	TURKEY	1,077
GERMANY	4,954	FRANCE	1,066
SPAIN	4,897	SWITZERLAND	964
GT. BRITAIN	4,848	NORWAY	814
CANADA	4,686	AUSTRALIA	795
MEXICO	3,241	KOREA (S.)	767
SWEDEN	2,667	BULGARIA	715
NETHERLANDS	2,665	CHINA	515
ITALY	2,071	ARGENTINA	515
BELGIUM	1,487	LITHUANIA	465
DENMARK	1,460	TAIWAN	451
POLAND	1,240	LATVIA	428
JAPAN	1,115	FINLAND	418

SINGAPORE	389	SAUDI ARABIA	42
AUSTRIA	380	EGYPT	40
PORTUGAL	368	BELARUS	39
BRAZIL	367	DOMINICAN REPUBLIC	38
LEBANON	355	BOLIVIA	37
HONG KONG	348	BOSNIA	36
ISRAEL	345	PUERTO RICO	33
RUSSIA	344	VIET NAM	33
CHILE	319	UNITED ARAB EMIRATES	32
ESTONIA	317	JAMAICA	27
ROMANIA	315	SLOVAKIA	27
MOROCCO	306	MALAYSIA	22
IRELAND	276	BANGLADESH	22
HUNGARY	263	MALTA	21
CZECH REP.	258	CYPRUS	21
IRAN	256	AZERBAIJAN	19
NEW ZEALAND	223	RWANDA	17
COLOMBIA	206	MOLDOVA	16
PHILIPPINES	200	GEORGIA	15
SOUTH AFRICA	190	CAMBODIA	15
INDIA	181	OMAN	15
SERBIA	175	ALGERIA	15
GREECE	169	NIGERIA	9
ICELAND	141	GUATEMALA	9
CROATIA	122	KENYA	9
THAILAND	121	COSTA RICA	8
PAKISTAN	114	COTE D'IVOIRE	8
PERU	113	KYRGYZSTAN	8
VENEZUELA	111	SUDAN	7
HONDURAS	107	ARMENIA	7
URUGUAY	102	MACEDONIA	6
UKRAINE	60	ALBANIA	6
INDONESIA	50	KAZAKHSTAN	5
ECUADOR	45	SRI LANKA	5

This introduction is followed by chapters that discuss: (1) trends in changing values from 1981 to 2007; (2) generational differences in support for democracy and free market economics; (3) generational differences in tolerance of ethnic diversity; and (4) technical problems in working with the Values Surveys data. This is followed by the English-language version of the questionnaire used in the 2005 – 2005 World Values Surveys, showing the exact text of the questions asked in this wave of surveys. The text of the questionnaires used in each country, in each wave, can be found at http://www.world-valuessurvey.org. The book concludes with a tables section that presents hundreds of data tables. Those who wish to carry out more detailed analyses can download and analyze the original data from this web site.

The authors hope that this sourcebook will be a useful tool to anyone concerned with the role of human values and beliefs in contemporary society.

REFERENCES

Arts, Wil and Loek Halman (eds.) 2004. *European Values at the End of the Millennium*. Leiden and Boston: Brill.
Baker, Wayne E. 2004. *America's Crisis of Values: Perceptions and Realities*. Princeton: Princeton University Press.
Bell, Daniel. 1973. *The Coming of Postindustrial Society*. New York: Basic Books.
Ember, Carol R. and Melvin Ember. 1996. *Cultural Anthropology*. London: Prentice Hall.
Hagenaars, Jacques, Loek Halman and Guy Moors. 2003. "Exploring Europe's Basic Values Map." In Wil Arts, Jacques Hagenaars and Loek Halman (eds.), *The Cultural Diversity of European Unity: Findings, Explanations and Reflections from the European Values Study*. Leiden and Boston: Brill: 23-58.
Huntington, Samuel P. 1996. *The Clash of Civilizations and the Remaking of World Order*. New York: Simon and Schuster.
Inglehart, Ronald. 1997. *Modernization and Postmodernization: Cultural, Economic and Political Change in 43 Societies*. Princeton: Princeton University Press.
Inglehart, Ronald and Christian Welzel. 2005. *Modernization, Cultural Change and Democracy: The Human Development Sequence*. New York: Cambridge University Press.
Inglehart, Ronald and Pippa Norris. 2003. *Rising Tide: Gender Equality and Cultural Change around the World*. New York and Cambridge: Cambridge University Press.
Inglehart, Ronald and Wayne E. Baker. 2000. "Modernization, Cultural Change, and the Persistence of Traditional Values," *American Sociological Review* 65 (February): 19-51.
Inkeles, Alex. 1983. *Exploring Individual Modernity*. New York: Columbia University Press.
Lerner, Daniel. 1958. *The Passing of Traditional Society: Modernizing the Middle East*. New York: Free Press.
Lipset, Seymour Martin. 1990. "American Exceptionalism Reaffirmed." *Toqueville Review* 10.
Lipset, Seymour Martin. 1996. *American Exceptionalism*. New York: Norton.
Nolan, Patrick and Gerhard Lenski. 1999. *Human Societies: An Introduction to Macrosociology* (8th ed.). New York: McGraw-Hill.
Norris, Pippa and Ronald Inglehart. 2004. *Sacred and Secular: Religion and Politics around the World*. New York: Cambridge University Press.
Schwartz, Shalom H. (2006). A Theory of Cultural Value Orientations: Explication and Applications. *Comparative Sociology* 5: 137-182.
Welzel, Christian, Ronald Inglehart and Hans-Dieter Klingemann. 2003. "The Theory of Human Development: A Cross-Cultural Analysis. *European Journal of Political Research*, 42 (April).
Welzel, Christian. 2002. *Fluchtpunkt Humanentwicklung: Die Grundlagen der Demokratie und die Ursachen ihrer Ausbreitung*. Opladen: Westdeustcher Verlag.

Globalization and Major Trends in Value Change, 1981–2007

Pippa Norris and Ronald Inglehart

Many of the basic values measured in the World Values Survey and European Values Study have changed significantly over the past twenty-five years. These surveys contain hundreds of items, so it would be tedious to examine the changes in every item. Instead, this chapter will focus on changes observed in five key clusters of attitudes that reflect some of the most important changes— examining response to questions that have been replicated in identical form in many successive waves, making it possible to examine trends. Our first step was to identify subsets of items that tap important orientations and that were replicated in a form suitable for time-series analysis from 1981 to 2007. Factor analysis identified five separate dimensions reflecting the following underlying values: (1) religiosity, (2) sexual morality, (3) free market economics, (4) political engagement, and (5) nationalism. The factor analysis results in Table 1 show the items used to tap each dimension and the factor loadings, which indicate how strongly a given item taps the underlying dimension.

The increasing globalization of communication flows in the past few decades has been dramatic. Figure 2-1 demonstrates the extent to which information flows have expanded across national borders for the world as a whole from 1980 to 2004. The increase has been dramatic. Some authorities have claimed that it is homogenizing the value systems of societies around the world, producing a global village. To what extent have accelerated information flows across national borders been linked with value changes? And have these changes been greatest in the societies that are most open to these flows?

The rise in cosmopolitan communications has varied from one society to another, as Figure 2-2 indicates. There is a strong tendency for high-income societies such as Finland, Germany, Japan, Sweden and the United States, Britain, and Japan to be relatively cosmopolitan, with relatively open borders to information flows. These countries show relatively high levels on the cosmopolitan communications index, and these levels have been rising over time. By contrast, middle-income societies, such as Argentina, Mexico and South Africa, are relatively parochial—that is, less open to global communication flows. Although they show some increase in trans-national communications flows over time, they remain at relatively low levels. We believe that global communication flows contribute to value change (along with economic modernization and the changing values it brings). In so far as this is true, we would expect to find larger and more rapid value changes in the relatively cosmopolitan high-income societies than in the more parochial middle-income societies.

Table 1. Dimensions of Cultural Values

	Religiosity	Liberal Sexual Morality	Free Market Economics	Political Engagement	Nationalism
Religious identity	.829				
Importance of God	.827				
Frequency of attendance at religious services	.749				
Approval of divorce		.840			
Approval of abortion		.786			
Approval of homosexuality		.780			
Approval of income differences as incentives			.720		
People should take responsibility to provide for themselves			.694		
Left–right self-placement scale			.504		
Participated in a demonstration				.778	
Participated in a boycott				.774	
Political interest				.606	
Willingness to flight for country					.783
National pride					.682

Note: Individual-level principal-component factor analysis. Rotation method: varimax with Kaiser normalization.
Source: World Values Survey (1981–2005).

Trends in Religiosity

Since the 19th century, influential social thinkers have argued that modernization brings secularization, causing organized religion to decline in importance— leading to its eventual disappearance. In recent years, it has become obvious that religion is not disappearing—in fact, its persisting importance has been so manifest that some analysts have claimed that we are witnessing a Global Resurgence of Religion. Norris and Inglehart (2004) have presented a more nuanced view of what is happening, showing extensive evidence of long-term processes of secularization that have eroded religious values and practices in most affluent nations during the 20th century-- although the historical imprints of religious traditions such as Protestantism, Catholicism and Islam remain evident even in high-income societies. Predominant religious cultures seem to be path dependent, adapting and evolving in response to developments in the contemporary world, and yet

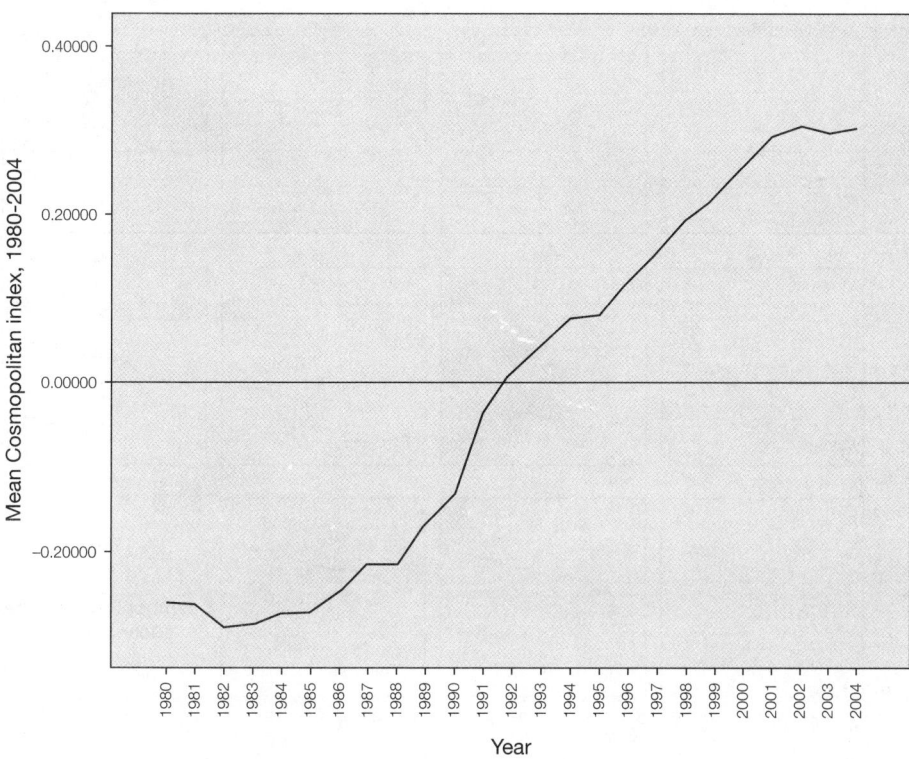

Figure 2-1. The rise in cosmopolitanism worldwide, 1980-2004.

Note: The Cosmopolitanism index is conceptualized as the permeability of societies to information flows and it is constructed according to levels of globalization, media freedom, and economic development, with all indices standardized around the mean (z-scores). See text for details.
For the construction of the 100-point Cosmopolitanism Index scale, see Norris and Inglehart, 2009, Chapter 5 and Technical Appendix A.

also strongly reflecting the legacy of past centuries (Inglehart and Baker, 2000). We have demonstrated elsewhere that religiosity persists most strongly among vulnerable populations, especially those of poor nations, that are facing personal threats to survival. We argue that feelings of vulnerability to physical, societal, and personal risks are a key factor driving religiosity, and we show that the process of secularization – a systematic erosion of religious practices, values, and beliefs – has occurred mainly among the most prosperous social sectors in affluent and secure postindustrial nations. Moreover, secularization in recent decades has been linked with a sharp decline in human fertility rates, which have fallen below the population replacement level in virtually all high-income societies. Relatively religious societies, on the other hand, continue to have fertility rates that are far above the population replacement level. Consequently, Norris and Inglehart (2004) do not foresee any decline in religiosity for the world as a whole—on the contrary, their calculations indicate that in the world as a whole, a higher percentage of the population has traditional religious values today than it did twenty years ago.

22 Globalization and Major Trends in Value Change, 1981–2007

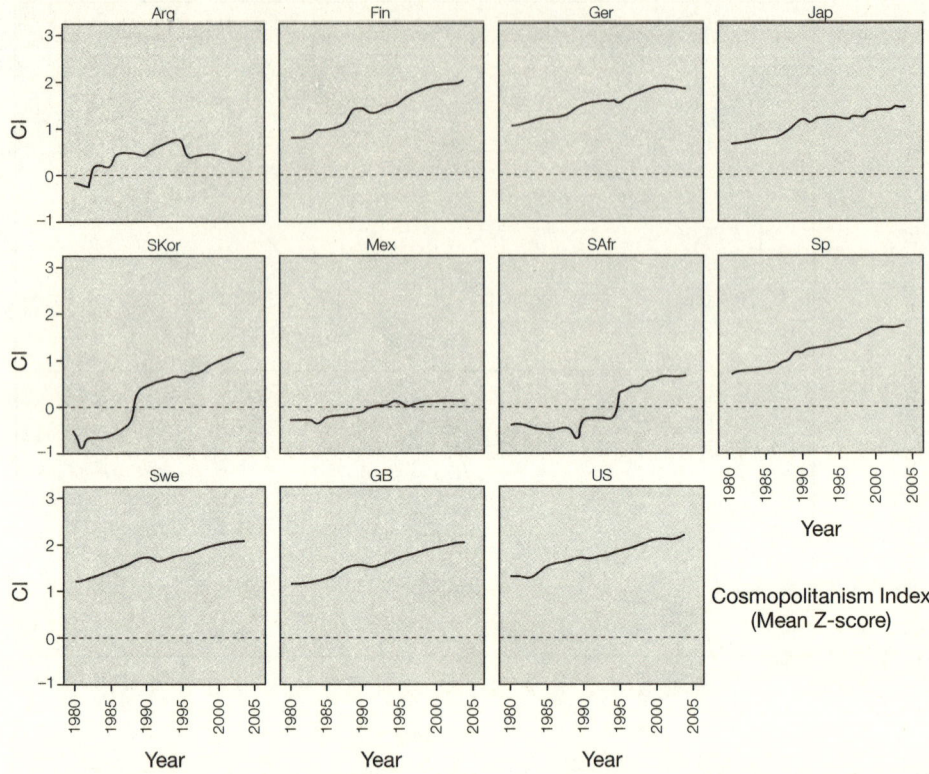

Figure 2-2. The rise in cosmopolitanism, selected nations.

Note: For the construction of the 100-point Cosmopolitanism Index scale, see Norris and Inglehart, 2009, Chapter 5 and Technical Appendix A. The graph illustrates the standardized (z-score) national means for each year, from 1980 to 2005.

The analysis in Norris and Inglehart (2004) was based on the first four waves of the WVS, from 1981 to 2001. Figure 2-3 updates this analysis to include the fifth wave, in 2005–2007. The eleven nations for which we have consistent time-series data throughout this period include predominately Protestant and Catholic societies, as well as countries with a Confucian cultural tradition (South Korea and Japan). And it includes several cosmopolitan high-income countries, as well three middle-income countries (Argentina, Mexico and South Africa). Because the first wave of the values survey (in 1981) did not include any low-income countries, we can not analyze changes in low-income countries across the full 25-year period.

The graphs show trends in the standardized religiosity scale, reflecting: (1) whether people expressed a religious identity; (2) the degree to which they value religion, as measured by their belief in the importance of God, and (3) the frequency of their attendance at religious services. The religiosity scale was standardized around the mean. In predominantly Protestant European countries, the level of religiosity across the five waves of the WVS is relatively steady and persistently lower than in most other countries. In secular Sweden, for example, only one-third of the public expressed a religious iden-

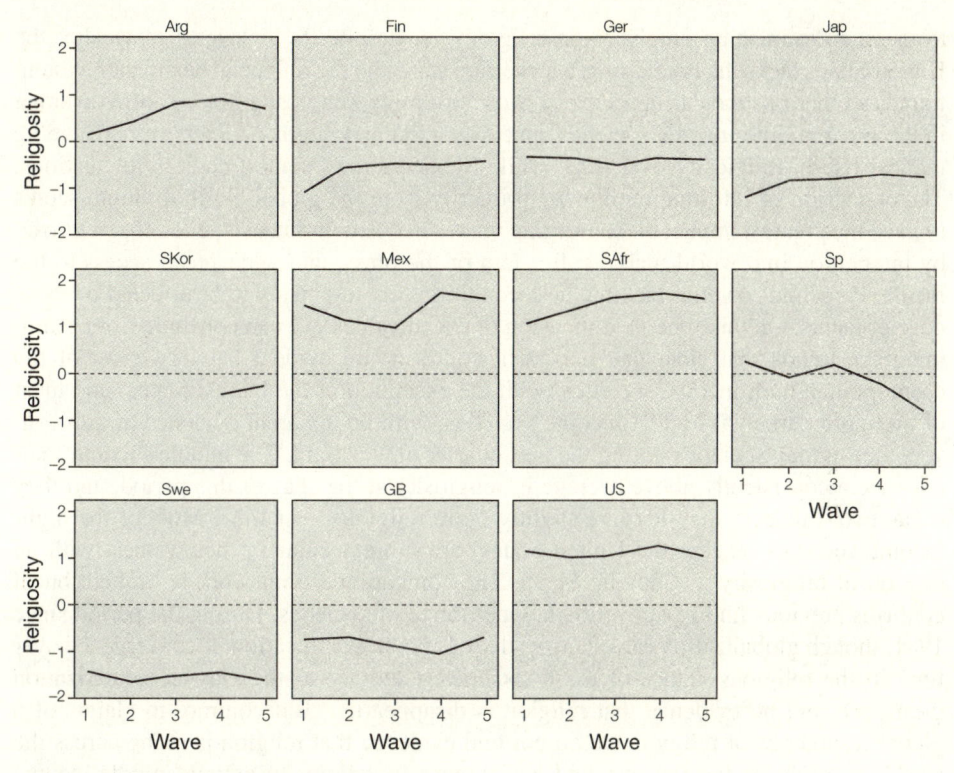

Figure 2-3. Trends in religiosity, 1981-2007.

Note: For the construction of the 100-point religiosity scale, see Table 1. The graph illustrates the standardized (z-score) national means for each wave of the Values Surveys from Wave 1 (1981-3) to Wave 5 (2005-7).
Source: Values Surveys, 1981-2007.

tity and church attendance was consistently low. Similar patterns were found in Britain and Germany. By contrast, from 1995 to 2005 Catholic Spain registered a sharp decline in religiosity, across all of the indicators were included in the composite scale; thus, the proportion of Spaniards expressing a religious identity fell from two-thirds to less than one-half. The distinction observed here reflects trends in attendance at religious services documented in the series of Eurobarometer surveys since the early 1970s, where active religious practices appear to have fallen farther and earlier in Protestant than in Catholic European societies (Norris and Inglehart, 2004). The time-series evidence for South Korea is limited, but the available data indicate that the two Asian nations in the comparison are also relatively secular; for example, only one-quarter of the Japanese public expressed a religious identity.

Yet there are also some persistent contrasts, particularly the high level of religiosity found in the United States, which remains a special case among affluent societies and cosmopolitan nations, as many others have observed, and where all the indicators remain relatively high (Gerard and Wilcox, 2002). Many factors contribute to American exceptionalism. As we have argued elsewhere, rising levels of existential security tend to bring a diminishing emphasis on religion; but despite its high level of wealth, the United States lacks the cradle-to-grave welfare state and the universal health care system found in other postindustrial societies. Most strikingly, religiosity is well above average in the three middle-income societies, and Argentina and South Africa have registered a modest rise in religiosity over time, while Mexico shows some trendless fluctuations. The expansion of information flowing primarily from the global North to South seems to have the greatest impact on converging values in cosmopolitan societies characterized by integration into world markets, freedom of the press, and widespread access to the media. Parochial societies lacking these conditions are less likely to be affected by these developments. On this specific dimension of social values, we can conclude from examining the trends that clear and persistent contrasts are evident between most of the cosmopolitan high-income societies (with the exception of the United States) and most of the more parochial middle-income societies, with no apparent evidence of any convergence among societies during the past quarter of a century. The middle-income societies were consistently above average in religiosity at the start of this period, and they remain so – indeed, they became slightly more religious over time. Most of the high-income societies (except the United States) are more secular in their values, with an erosion of religiosity in Catholic Spain. The comparative framework is limited, but it confirms previous findings covering a wider range of societies. During the period since 1981, though globalization rose sharply, there is no clear indication of convergence over time in the religious values of these societies. Contrary to the classic secularization thesis, we find no evidence that religion is disappearing. But contrary to claims of a global resurgence of religion, we do not find evidence that religion is rising across the world as a whole. Instead, we find an increase in religiosity among middle-income countries, but stagnation or decline among high-income countries.

Trends in Sexual Morality, 1981–2005

In previous work (Inglehart and Norris, 2003), we have documented how perceptions of sexual morality, issues such as tolerance of homosexuality and support for gay rights, attitudes toward marriage and divorce, and ideas about the appropriate division of sex roles in the home and family, paid employment, and the political sphere, are shaped by the interaction of two types of fators: societal modernization, which is bringing pervasive change—but also by the persistent influence of a society's religious and historical traditions. Relatively liberal social values are found in the most affluent postindustrial societies – in particular, high levels of tolerance toward homosexuality and egalitarian roles for women – while more conservative values are characteristic of most developing nations (Inglehart and Welzel, 2005; Scott, 1998) . Social values are monitored in this chapter by the liberal sexual morality scale, which compares attitudes toward divorce, abortion, and homosexuality.

Figure 2-4 illustrates the trends, revealing a complex pattern. If we compare the positions of countries at the start and end of the time series, it is apparent that most of the high-income societies have become more liberal and tolerant in their values during the past quarter of a century. This shift is strongest (despite different religious traditions) in Sweden, Spain, Japan, and the United States. By contrast, South Africa remains the most conservative society in its moral values in the modern era. Argentina and Mexico are also relatively conservative, but they register a more liberal trend. South Korea is an

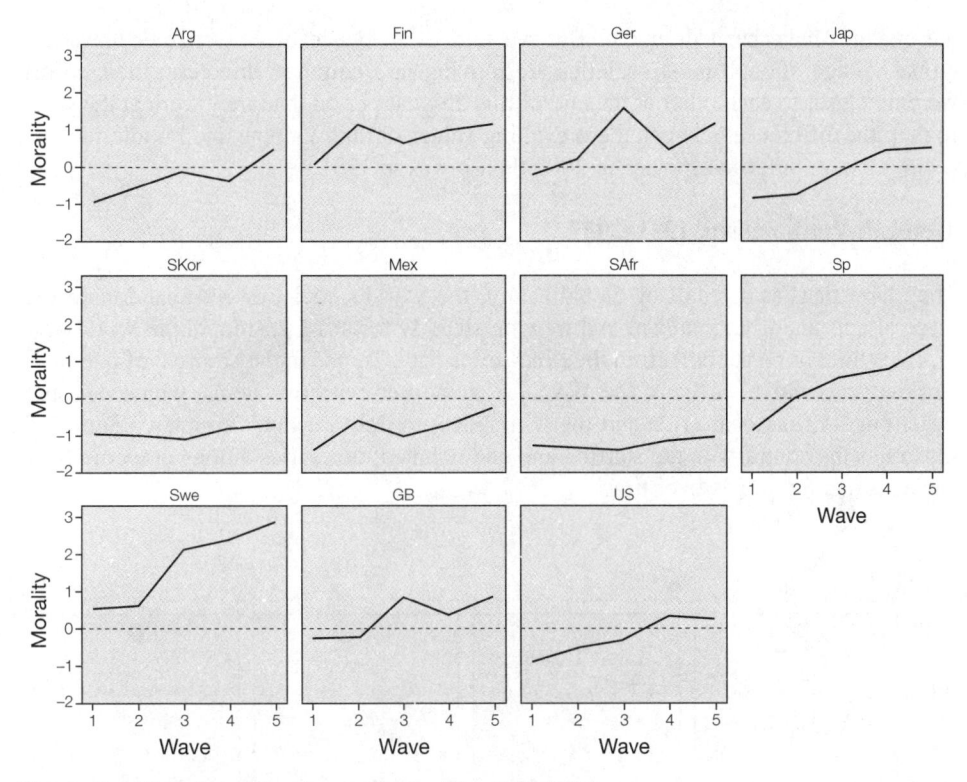

Globalization and Major Trends in Value Change, 1981–2007   25

Figure 2-4: Trends in liberal sexual morality, 1981-2007.

Note: For the construction of the 100-point liberal sexual morality scale, see Table 1. The graph illustrates the standardized (z-score) national means for each wave of the Values Surveys from Wave 1 (1981-3) to Wave 5 (2005-7).
Source: Values Surveys, 1981-2007.

interesting case, remaining fairly conservative in moral values according to the composite scale, but Korean attitudes have become more liberal toward homosexuality and divorce, while becoming less permissive toward abortion rights. Fluctuations in public opinion are also notable in certain waves of the survey in Germany (1995), Finland (1990), and the United Kingdom (1995), which may reflect contemporary policy debates and legislation about these issues, elite opinion and rhetoric, and the strength of conservative and liberal social movements in each of these countries (Jelen and Wilcox, 2003). Overall the trends suggest that societies continue to differ sharply in their attitudes toward sexual morality issues, as evidenced by the contrasts between contemporary Sweden and South Africa, or between contemporary Spain and Mexico. South Africa is the clearest example of a middle-income society with conservative social values that have not changed during the past quarter of a century, in contrast to the dramatic transformation that has occurred during this period in Spain. The pattern is complex, but it does not support the claim that these societies are converging in their social and moral values. In fact, we find divergent trends. The people of most countries have become substantially more liberal in their social norms— and in some cases, such as Spain and Sweden,

26 Globalization and Major Trends in Value Change, 1981–2007

the changes have been dramatic. But we find no evidence of convergence toward a global village: though most societies are moving in a common direction, their norms were no closer to each other at the end of this 25-year period than they were at the start. In fact, the difference between the prevailing values of high-income and middle-income societies was somewhat greater in 2006 than it was in 1981.

Trends in Nationalism, 1981–2007

The claim that, as a result of globalization, the world's societies are abandoning the visceral appeals of nationalism and moving steadily toward a cosmopolitan worldview receives little or no support from the time-series data. Trends in the strength of nationalism over successive waves of the WVS are monitored with two items, which measure the strength of national pride and the willingness to fight for one's country. Figure 2-5 illustrates the contrasts in the starting and end points of this series among contemporary societies and the trends over time.

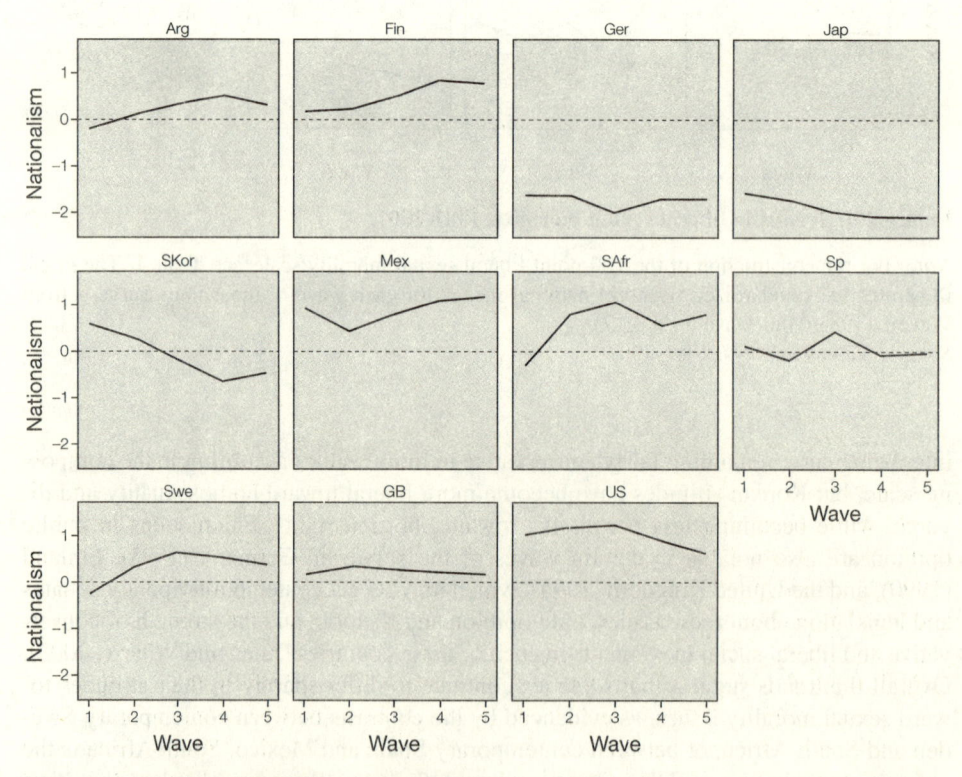

Figure 2-5. Trends in nationalism, 1981-2007.

Note: For the construction of the 100-point liberal nationalism scale, see Table 1. The graph illustrates the standardized (z-score) national means for each wave of the Values Surveys from Wave 1 (1981-3) to Wave 5 (2005-7).

Source: Values Surveys, 1981-2007.

The citizens of Germany and Japan express the lowest support for nationalism – a persistent pattern that seems attributable to the enduring legacy of their defeat in World War II and the backlash that this experience generated against the use of military force by these countries. This outlook is also reflected in current debates in each country about the deployment of their armed forces overseas in a peacekeeping role. There has also been a sharp erosion of nationalism in South Korea during this era, especially in willingness to fight for the country. On the other hand, the United States displays relatively high levels of nationalism, although there has been a decline on both indicators during the past decade (thus predating contemporary controversies over the Bush administration's use of force after 9/11 in Afghanistan and Iraq). Public opinion is also relatively nationalistic in two middle-income societies, Mexico and South Africa, while rising over time in Argentina. The trends in nationalist feelings vary considerably across the eleven nations under comparison, with the United States again something of an outlier among postindustrial societies. Overall at least two of the three middle-income societies are more nationalistic than average, and there is no evidence that the appeal of nationalism has been eroded; there is no indication that these attitudes have been converging toward the low levels of nationalism found in Spain, Britain or Germany.

Trends in Political Engagement, 1981–2007

Trends in civic activism are monitored by political interest and by the propensity to demonstrate and engage in demonstrations and boycotts (see Figure 2-6). Sweden consistently ranks highest on civic activism, among the countries examined here. This confirms previous findings that the publics of the Scandinavian countries rank high on democratic engagement, including voting turnout and campaign activism, membership in voluntary associations, and generalized social trust, as well as involvement in protest politics (Norris, 2002). After Sweden, the United States and Germany show relatively high levels of political engagement, although with greater volatility. Certain fluctuations can probably be attributed to specific events, such as the reunification of Germany during the early 1990s, or to particular elections that mobilized and activated the public, such as the 2000 U.S. presidential election, the exceptionally close outcome of which generated so much controversy. Similarly, the end of apartheid and the rise of majority rule in South Africa gave rise to an outpouring of political activism and interest during the early 1990s. Despite the fluctuations over time, we again find no indications that all of these countries (or even the most cosmopolitan high-income societies) have been converging toward the mean or toward the level of the dominant media sources. On the contrary, persistent cross-national differences remain evident, even among relatively similar nations, such as those found between active Sweden and relatively apathetic Britain, or between Argentina and Mexico.

Trends in Economic Values, 1990–2007

We lack sufficient time-series data to monitor support for capitalist economic values over the full time series, but we do have time-series data from 1990 to 2006 that enable us to compare ideological left–right orientations, support for greater income equality, and attitudes toward the role of the state and markets. If the spread of cosmopolitan communications, especially the consumer values reflected in commercial advertising and popu-

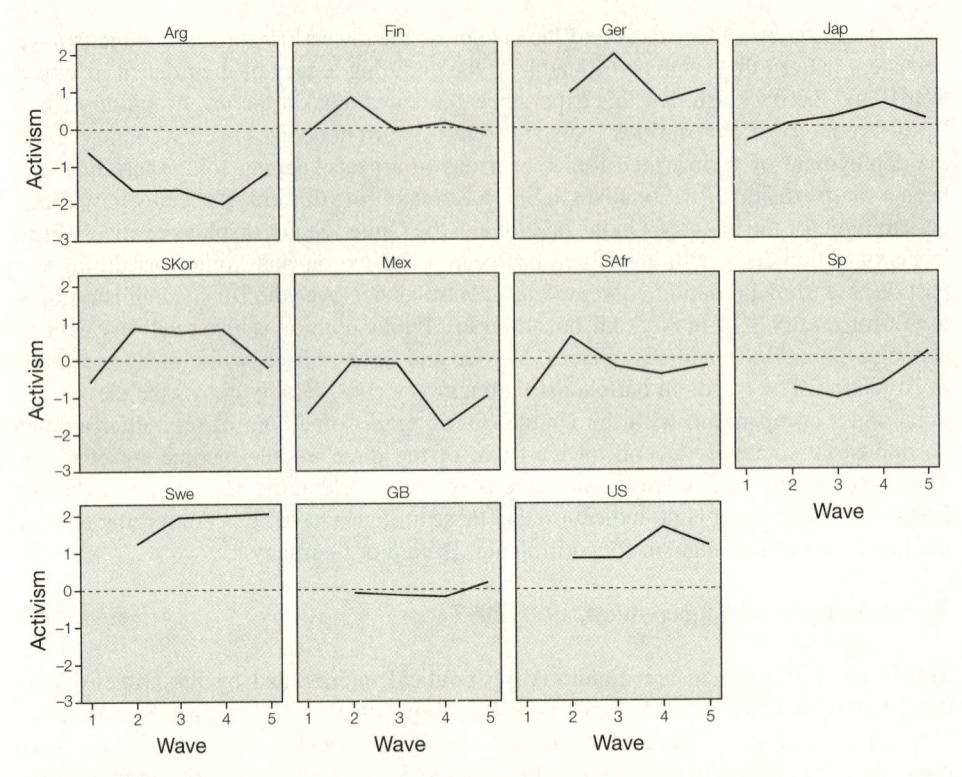

28   Globalization and Major Trends in Value Change, 1981–2007

Figure 2-6. Trends in political engagement, 1981-2007.

Note: For the construction of the 100-point political engagement scale, see Table 1. The graph illustrates the standardized (z-score) national means for each wave of the Values Surveys from Wave 1 (1981-3) to Wave 5 (2005-7).
Source: Values Surveys, 1981-2007.

lar entertainment, has encouraged the diffusion of support for global capitalism in recent decades, as McChesney claims, then this should be evident from trends in public opinion (McChesney, 1999). Figure 2-7 shows the relevant evidence. On economic values, public opinion across the eleven countries compared here indeed displays a greater cross-national consensus than is found with the other dimensions of public opinion examined so far. Despite the diverse roles played by the state in these countries and despite the diverse political ideologies of the regimes in power, we find broadly similar and relatively steady levels of support for liberal economic values. Indeed, the overall trends in the relatively small welfare state of Sweden and in the pro–free market and neoliberal United States are surprisingly similar. Although free trade agreements and the reduction of protectionism have gradually opened economic borders throughout this period, especially within the European Union, we actually find a gradual trend in economic values toward more *collectivist* or leftist values, as shown most clearly in Germany, Argentina, and even the United States. The shift is modest, but it is in exactly the *opposite* direction from that predicted by the thesis that globalization is converting people to capitalist values. Since the dramatic move away from state-run economies that occurred from the

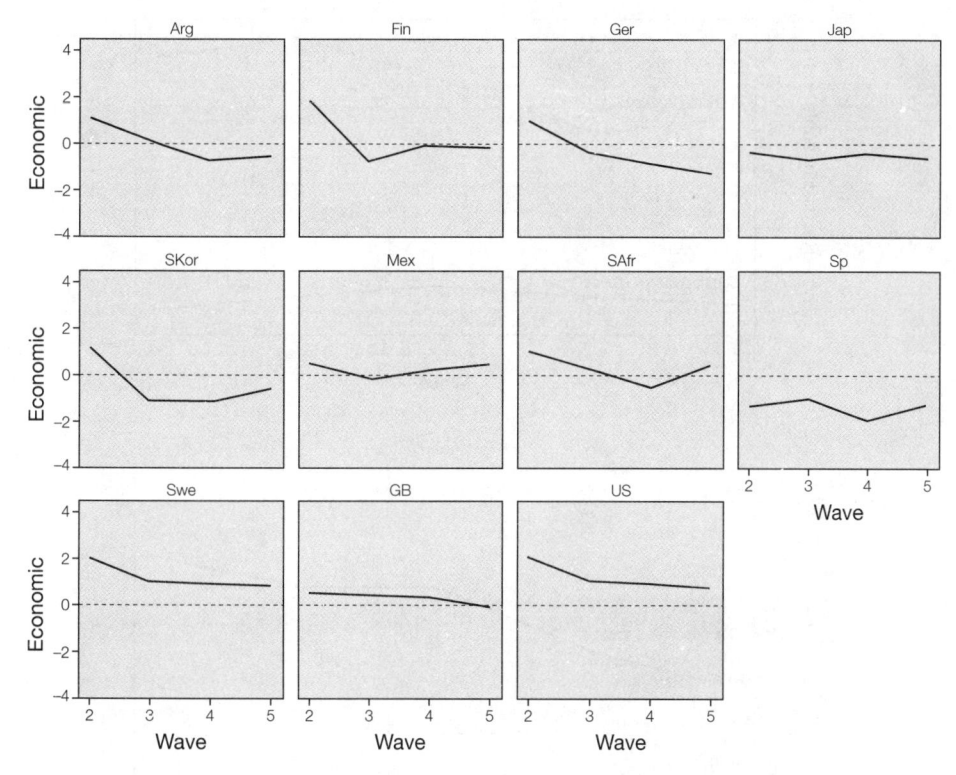

Figure 2-7: Trends in support for free market economic values, 1990-2007

Note: For the construction of the 100-point economic values scale, see Table 1. The graph illustrates the standardized (z-score) national means for each wave of the Values Surveys from Wave 2 (1990-1) to Wave 5 (2005-7).
Source: Values Surveys, 1981-2007.

mid-1980s to the mid-1990s, there has been a general shift in the opposite direction: though it was clear by the 1980s that the state can be too big, more recent years have seen a growing feeling that the role of the state can be too small.

Now let us sum up the overall findings concerning the changes observed from 1981 to 2007. We find contrasting patterns of change across these scales between relatively parochial and cosmopolitan societies. The countries included in all five waves of the Values Surveys were classified on the basis of each country's the mean annual ratings on the Cosmopolitan index during this 25 year period. The results indicate that three countries-- Mexico, Argentina and South Africa-- could be classified as clearly and consistently more parochial than average. Seven other nations-- Sweden, Finland, Germany, Britain, the United States, Japan and Spain-- could be classified as consistently more cosmopolitan than average in every year. The case of South Korea didn't fit into either category, because it moved from being a relatively parochial society to being a relatively cosmopolitan society during this era. Figure 2-8 examine trends in three of the value scales for each wave of the survey and for each type of society. This summary demonstrates that, during the past 25 years, the gap in values between middle-income

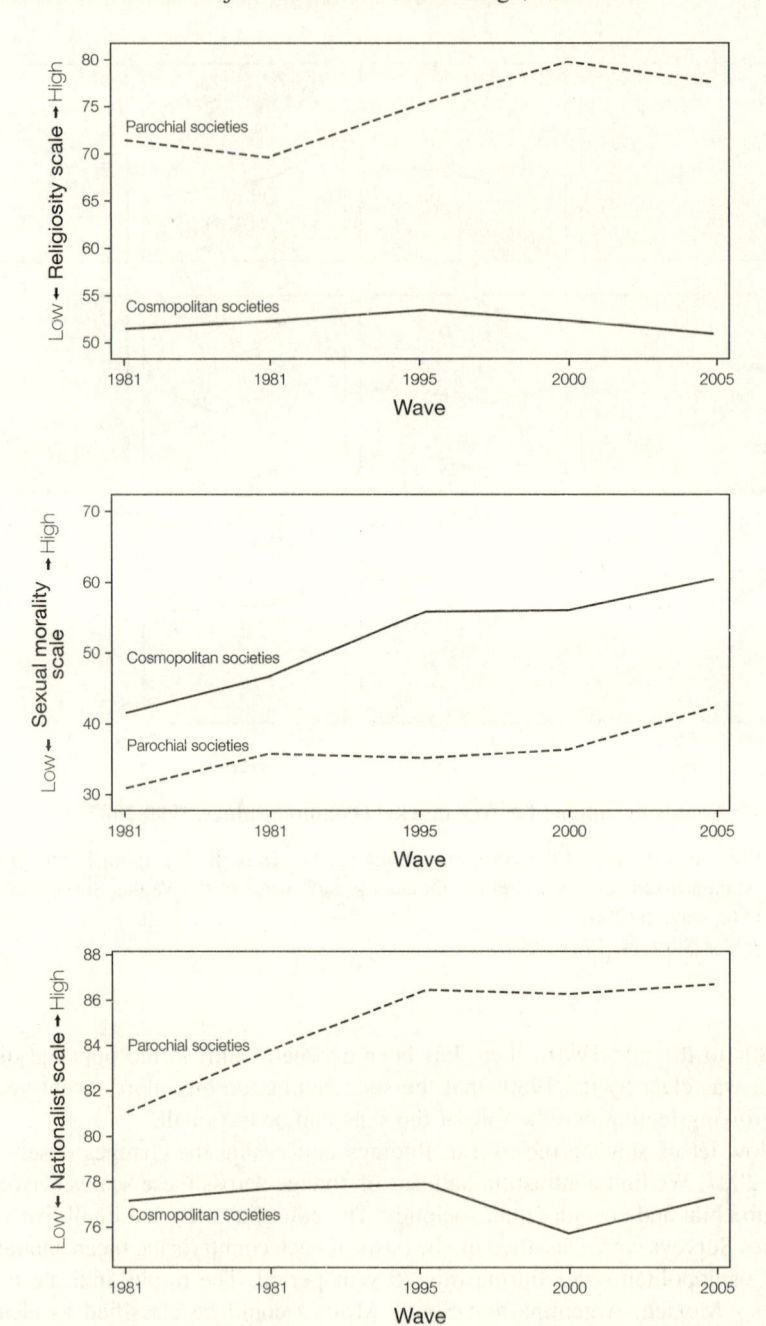

Globalization and Major Trends in Value Change, 1981–2007

Figure 2-8. Divergence between parochial and cosmopolitan societies, 1981-2007.

Note: Trends from 1981-2007 in mean value scales in successive waves of the Values Surveys in 10 nations, including three persistently parochial societies (Mexico, Argentina and South Africa) and seven persistently cosmopolitan societies (Sweden, Finland, Germany, Britain, the United States, Japan and Spain). For the construction of the 100-pt value scales, see Table 1.
Source: Values Surveys 1981-2007.

and high-income societies either persisted (on the liberal sexual morality scale), or even widened (concerning feelings of nationalism and the strength of religiosity). There is no evidence here (or with the other value scales) of convergence between the two types of societies. Cultural change *is* occurring, but it is path dependent. Enduring cultural differences persist between nations—even between societies that are most interconnected and tied together by deep cultural bonds and communication networks, such as Britain and the United States in the Anglophone world, or Sweden and Finland in Europe, Argentina and Mexico in Latin America, or Japan and South Korea in Asia. The slopes may be similar (the degree of change over time, such as the shift towards more liberal and tolerant views on sexual morality in high-income and middle-income societies), but the intercept (the starting point for the series for each nation and type of society) continues to be distinct. It has been claimed that the globalization of communication flows is producing convergence and homogenization over time. The empirical evidence does not support this claim. It reveals the enduring imprint of distinctive historical traditions that are as apparent today as they were 25 years ago.

Change over Time

Is there any evidence that national cultures have become increasingly similar during the past quarter of a century – especially the open high-income societies that were most subject to the potential forces of globalization? Trends over time in the successive waves of the WVS enable us to test this proposition in eleven nations, from which a full time-series of survey data is available from 1981 to 2007. The descriptive figures and the cross-national time-series regression analysis establish two important findings. First, far from there being convergence over time, the values gap between middle-income and high-income societies was maintained (in the case of liberal social values) or even widened (with feelings of nationalism and the strength of religiosity). This happened because culture in affluent postindustrial nations is not static, as the convergence thesis implicitly assumes; on the contrary, values and attitudes continue to evolve in these nations. Thus, the relative gap between types of societies has not been closing (Inglehart and Norris, 2003). Moreover, even among postindustrial societies such as the United States and Britain, Sweden and Germany, and Japan and South Korea, which are tightly interconnected through communication networks, trade flows, and economic interdependence, with a particularly high share of cultural trade in audiovisual programs, there remain distinctive and persistent cultural differences that show no signs of disappearing. These societies do not share a monolithic Western culture toward which developing societies are converging. Instead, both developing societies and Western societies are changing in ways shaped by broad forces of modernization, while retaining distinctive national cultures. These cultures are not the same today as they were a generation ago, but it is by no means evident that all of the changes that have taken place are negative, as globalization's critics generally claim: they include a growing tolerance for gender equality and social diversity, and a growing emphasis on democracy and self-expression.

REFERENCES

Inglehart, Ronald and Christian Welzel. 2005. *Modernization, Cultural Change and Democracy.* Cambridge: Cambridge University Press.

Inglehart, Ronald and Pippa Norris. 2003. *Rising Tide: Gender Equality and Cultural Change Around the World* Cambridge: Cambridge University Press

Inglehart, Ronald and Wayne E. Baker. 2000. 'Modernization, globalization and the persistence of tradition: Empirical evidence from 65 Societies.' *American Sociological Review.* 65: 19–55.

Jelen, Ted Gerard and Clyde Wilcox. 2003. 'Causes and consequences of public attitudes toward abortion: A review and research agenda.' *Political Research Quarterly* 56 (4): 489–500.

Jelen, Ted Gerard and Clyde Wilcox. Eds. 2002. *Religion and Politics in Comparative Perspective: The One, the Few and the Many.* Cambridge: Cambridge University Press.

McChesney, Robert W. 1999. *Rich Media, Poor Democracy: Communication Politics in Dubious Times.* Urbana: University of Illinois Press.

Norris, Pippa and Ronald Inglehart. 2004. *Sacred and Secular: Politics and Religion Worldwide.* Cambridge: Cambridge University Press.

Norris, Pippa. 2002. *Democratic Phoenix: Political Activism Worldwide.* Cambridge: Cambridge University Press.

Scott, John. 1998. 'Changing attitudes to sexual morality: A cross-national comparison.' *Sociology: Journal of the British Sociological Association* 32 (4): 815–845.

Generational Differences in Support for Democracy and Free Market Economics: Evidence from New and Established Market Democracies

Alejandro Moreno, Renata Siemienska and Miguel Basáñez

More than three decades have passed since the third wave of democratization began in Southern Europe, and twenty years have elapsed since the fall of the Berlin wall. During this time, a great number of countries have democratized and many of them have transformed previously centralized economies into free market systems. The emergence of (1) free and fair elections and (2) market economies have been the central elements of change. These are profound changes. They raise the question, "How quickly do such basic changes take root in a society?" Does the entire public accept them at the same time? Or do they take root through a process of intergenerational change, with the younger generation accepting them more fully than the older generation— who remain attached to the older norms to a somewhat greater extent?

This paper analyzes generational differences in support for democracy and capitalism, comparing the patterns found in established market-based democracies and in and societies in which market economies and democracy have emerged more recently. If assimilation of new basic economic and political norms takes place through generational change, we would expect the new democracies to show differences between the extent to which older and younger generations have adopted the values of democratic politics and free market economies— while in long-established market democracies, intergenerational differences would be smaller, since both old and young have grown up under these institutions.

In previous research, Siemienska (2003) asked: "To what extent do young people differ from older generations and are their attitudes and conceptions of life conducive to building a democratic system and a free market economy?" We hypothesized that older cohorts of society were more likely to resist the values of democracy and free market economics or to adopt them slowly, while younger cohorts were more likely to develop democratic attitudes and capitalist views more rapidly. Perhaps the former's nostalgia for the old regime would be an obstacle to the values of political and economic competition, whereas the former's increasing exposure to globalization encouraged them to pursue more open and more competitive politics and economics. The findings pointed to "growing similarities in attitudes and behaviors among young generations… as a consequence of cultural and economic globalization that encourages processes of change and adaptation in the new democracies" (Siemienska, 2003:145). We must also take into account the fact that education also seems to play a role in this process, and that younger generations are, overall, more educated than their elders.

We use data from the World Values Survey to examine generational differences cross-nationally and cross-regionally. We treat the 2000 and 2005 waves of surveys as one point in time, in order to have more countries and larger samples sizes to analyze differences by subgroups of age—comparing these 21st century findings with those from earlier decades. Our analyses include over 180,000 interviews conducted in more than 80 countries. The generational differences allow us to track societal change by focusing on the values and priorities of the younger generations. This means that differences between the young and the old are not just a life-cycle effect, but indeed a source of values change through generational replacement (Inglehart 1997). In that sense, the ways in which values and beliefs are changing in society can be illuminated by examining the differences between older and younger citizens.

Our previous research considered two contrasting possibilities: (1) that the political values of younger and older publics in post-Communist new democracies would not be very different from each other simply because value systems change slowly; and (2) that the rapid processes of political and economic transformation in new democracies tend to make the values and preferences of younger publics become rapidly differentiated from those of their elders, creating a visible generational gap with potentially important political implications. This paper hypothesizes that: (1) There should be observable differences between younger and older generations in their political and economic values; (2) younger generations in new democracies will gradually tend to converge in those views; and (3) such convergence is generally favorable to democratic politics and market economics.

Generational differences in values

Before we analyze generational differences in political and economic views, the central task of our paper, we should note that the World Values Survey has already provided a great deal of evidence that the values of developed nations differ greatly from the values of developing ones (Inglehart 1997; Inglehart and Welzel 2005). In addition, in many countries, the values of younger generations are also clearly differentiated from those of their elders. These are at least two sources of distinction in value orientations: the level of development and differences in age.

Results from the World Values Survey rely have delineated two major dimensions of value orientations in the world: The first is a dimension of traditional versus secular-rational values, which emphasizes religion, family and the persistence of tradition, on one hand, and secular-rational values, which reflect the processes of secularization and modernization, on the other. The second dimension is a contrast between survival values, which reflects a culture of scarcity and emphasize physical and economic security, and self-expression values, which reflect a sense of subjective well-being, and tend to be supportive of freedom of choice, tolerance, and the quality of life, among other things.

As mentioned, these two value dimensions enable us to observe a significant cross-national variation: the more developed and richer societies are more likely to hold self-expression values, and less developed and poorer societies emphasize more traditional values, reflecting the greater impact of scarcity in shaping their views. In addition to this, generational differences have also been documented: "For we find that in developed societies, the younger generations emphasize secular-rational values and self-expression values much more highly than do the older generations" (Inglehart and Welzel 2005:94).

We have replicated the two value dimensions using the World Values Survey data to determine the extent to which generational differences are observed (similarly to Inglehart and Welzel 2005:112). Figure 3-1 shows the average placement of four age groups in ten different types of societies arranged regionally. In this analysis we grouped the societies for which the 2000 and 2005 WVS has data available into ten regions: Scandinavian societies; Western Europe; Southern Europe; East Central and South East Europe; North America; Latin America; the Soviet successor states including Russia; the Middle East and North Africa; Africa; and Asia.[1] Some of these regions, such as Africa, contain both democracies and non-democratic regimes, but the rest of the regional categories have, along with a regional logic, a political one as well. For example, the categories for Southern Europe, Latin America and EC&SE Europe consist almost entirely of third wave democracies, whereas the Middle East and North Africa consist almost entirely of non-democratic regimes. In contrast, all the countries of Scandinavia, Western Europe and North America are established, developed democracies.

The grouping of countries into these regional categories follows a previous classification developed by the Bertelsmann Transformation Index (Bertelsmann Stiftung 2008), which has tracked significant changes in political management and market economies throughout the world. Since we focus precisely on those two variables, we considered it appropriate to use these categories. (The countries included in each of these ten regions is shown in this paper's Appendix).

The age groups used in the analysis correspond to different years of birth reported by the interviewers: those born before 1940, between 1940 and 1958, between 1959 and 1976, and between 1977 and 1991. This last cohort is almost perfectly parallel to the third wave of democratization and, consequently, it includes respondents that have naturally been much more exposed to democracy than their elders in all new democracies. In many countries, the youngest cohort can almost take democracy for granted.

The data in Figure 3-1 show that there are, indeed, noticeable generational differences on the two value dimensions, and that these differences are considerably greater in richer countries than in poorer ones. Moreover, generational differences in values seem also linked to the length of democratic experience: the longer it has been, the higher the differences, although Southern Europe, which democratized in the 1970s, shows the greatest difference between the youngest and oldest age groups than any other region. But all of the high-income countries (which also consist of the long-established democracies) show significantly larger generational differences than those of the new democracies from Latin America and East Central Europe. Generational differences are small or almost nonexistent in the Asian countries included in this analysis, as well as in the Middle East and North Africa, and, especially, in Africa. This reflects that fact that the high-income societies have experienced significant economic growth throughout most

---

[1] Israel, Japan, Australia and New Zealand were omitted from these general regional groups.

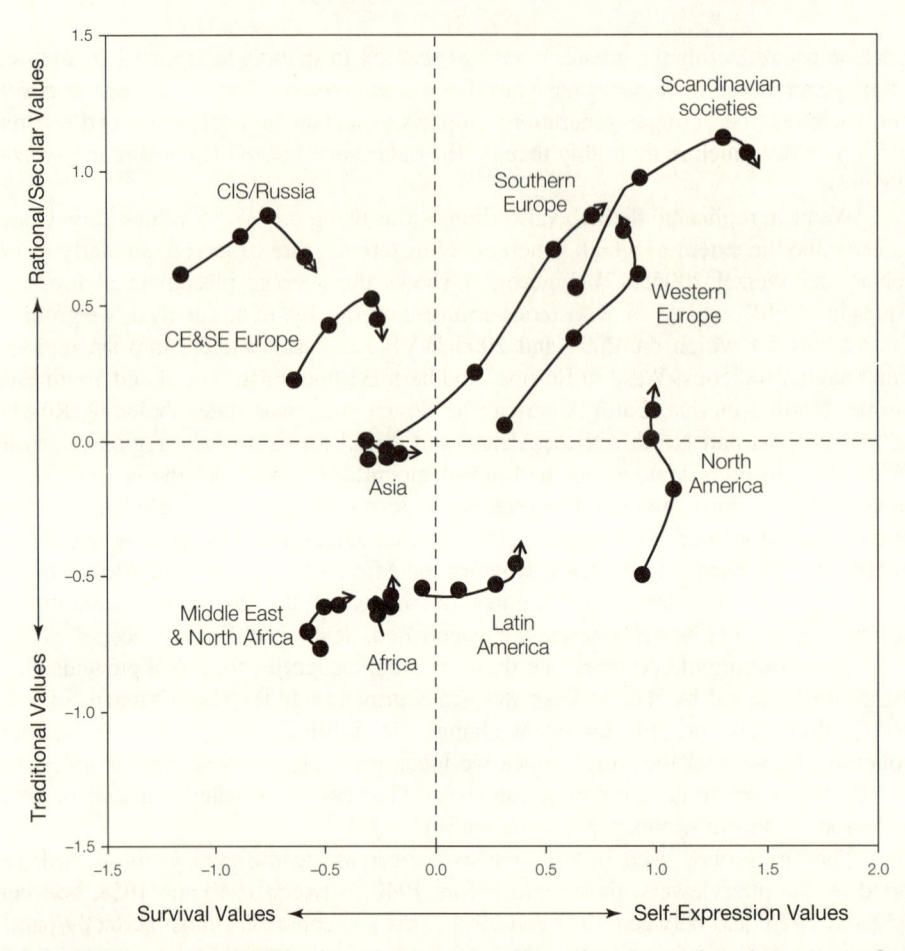

Figure 3-1. Generational differences in two value dimensions by region. Arrows run from oldest to youngest age group.

of the past five decades (which has made them high-income societies); the oldest birth cohorts grew up under conditions of relative scarcity, but the youngest birth cohorts have grown up under unprecedentedly high levels of existential security, leading them to take survival for granted. The large differences between the formative experiences of older and younger generations in today's high-income societies have produced large intergenerational differences in basic values. The younger and older generations of the Soviet successor states and of Central and Eastern Europe also were shaped by different levels of existential security, experiencing substantial economic growth during the 1950s and 1960s—but the 1980s were an era of economic stagnation, and the collapse of communism around 190 was followed by sharp economic decline; only since about 2000 has the been a resumption of rising prosperity. On the whole, the younger birth cohorts among the publics of these ex-communist countries have experienced higher levels of existential security than the older ones, but they have not reached levels comparable to those of the high-income countries, and the differences between younger and older cohorts are not as great as in the high-income countries with established democracies.

Latin America has experienced a somewhat similar pattern of intermittent economic growth, producing an intergenerational shift toward secular-rational value and self-expression values, but the intergenerational differences are smaller than those in the high-income countries. The publics of Africa and the Middle East, on the other hand, have not experienced dramatic increases in prosperity during the past several decades. The younger generations have not grown up with markedly higher levels of existential security than the older generations, and we find little or no difference between the basic values of young and old.

The data in Figure 3-1 demonstrate that there are impressive differences between the prevailing values found in different regional settings. The people of Russia and the other Soviet successor states emphasize survival values far more than do the people of North America, Western Europe or the Scandinavian societies. And the publics of the Middle Eastern countries, Africa and Latin America tend to emphasize traditional values far more heavily than the publics of other regions. These differences reflect the interaction of different levels of economic development, and the historic cultural heritage of given societies.

Another finding is even more important for our purposes. It concerns the value orientations of the different age groups in each region. For example, the youngest group of Latin Americans is closer to the self-expression side than the oldest group, and it is also slightly less traditional. In East Central Europe, Russia and the other Soviet successor countries, the youngest groups is similarly more prone to self-expression values (or less driven by survival values), but the younger generations show a marked movement away from secular-rational values. The young publics of formerly Communist countries seem to be shifting away from the values of modernity. This may reflect the fact that the collapse of communism has left an ideological vacuum; there has been a resurgence of emphasis on religious and traditional cultural values, particularly among the younger birth cohorts. This shifts, although moderate in size, may signal a changing set of values among the new generations. In Latin America as a whole there is no shift away from rational secular values, though the Mexican surveys demonstrate a change in that direction (see Moreno 2005). And there has been a significant shift toward self-expression values.

Let us stop for a moment at this point and discuss some of the observed patterns in given countries. Figures A, B and C in the Appendix show the generational differences in selected countries from Europe, the former Communist block, and Latin America, respectively. As shown in Figure 3-A in the Appendix, younger publics in Europe generally express more secular-rational values and self-expressive values. The two Southern European countries, Portugal and Spain, show certain linearity in the positions of their different groups, younger and older. However, the trends in Italy, Sweden, Germany and Britain suggest that the youngest generations are becoming less driven by self-expression values. We do not know if this is a temporary shift, linked with the unprecedentedly high levels of unemployment that have emerged among the younger cohorts in recent decades, or the beginning of a deeper trend. However, the global economic crisis of 2008 and 2009 would be expected to push societies in that direction, away from self-expression values. This is a point to which we will return later, when we discuss public views about free market economics.

Figure 3-B in the Appendix shows countries from the former Communist bloc that show similar patterns to those observed in Portugal and Spain, where younger cohorts are more rational-secular and more self-expressive. This is the case more noticeably in Belarus and Romania. However, in this set of countries we also observe some shifts in trends. In Russia, Bulgaria, Slovakia, the Czech Republic, and, more significantly, in Hungary, the youngest group is generally more self-expressive than their elders, but that group has marked a clear "return" towards traditional values (or a shift away from rational-secular ones). In the Czech case the youngest generation has shows a double shift: away from rational-secularity and away from self-expression. In Poland, the youngest group has not engaged in that trend yet, but it has certainly stopped its shift towards self-expression, given the lack of difference from the immediately older group.

The Latin American findings are shown in Figure 3-C in the Appendix. In these cases, we find a linear trend, with each younger cohort emphasizing both rational secular values and self-expression values more heavily than their elders. This is particularly the case in Uruguay, Chile, Argentina, Mexico and Colombia. The only noticeable exception is Peru, where the youngest group is slightly (though not significantly) less self-expressive and slightly more traditional than its immediately older group. This figure also includes the generational differences in the United States, where the pattern resembles the ones observed in some European countries, where the youngest generations are more likely to emphasize secular-rational values than their elders, but seem to be turning away from self-expression values. In this sense, the younger American and Latin Americans are converging in their values, mainly because the youngest Americans are turning away from the self-expression pole, perhaps reflecting the economic stagnation of recent years.

This section has shown significant generational differences in several regions and countries and signaled the possible patterns of value change based on the value-orientations of the younger publics. Perhaps the most striking one is the shift toward traditional religious values in formerly Communist countries and the shift away from self-expression in several developed nations of Europe and North America.

Now let us examine these publics' views concerning democracy and market economies. Do we find any significant generational differences—and if we do, what are their implications for the future of democratic politics and free trade economics?

Generational differences in views towards democracy

Are younger people in new democracies more supportive of democracy and capitalism than their elders? In this section we analyze intergenerational differences in responses to the World Values Survey, focusing on indicators of support for democracy and evaluations of the democratic political system, and an assessment of freedom of choice. In the following section, we will examine ideological preferences for state and market mechanisms of economic redistribution and construct a single variable that allows us to differentiate between views that we label a "Redistributive Left" from views that we call "Capitalist Right". We then analyze generational differences both in a descriptive and in a statistical way. We also incorporate education and values to determine whether generational differences are statistically significant when we control for the effects of education and values.

Figure 3-2 shows the regional variation in attitudes toward democracy. The horizontal axis reflects the percent of respondents who value democracy highly, based on their responses to a question about how important democracy is to them. The vertical

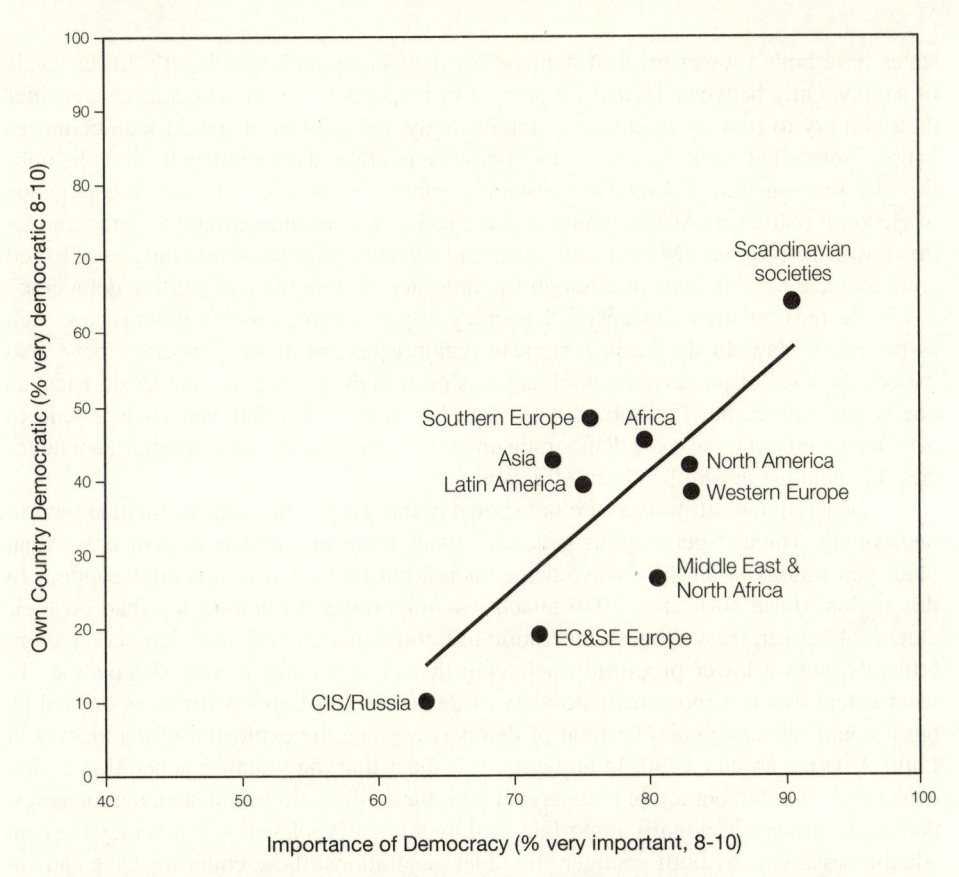

Figure 3-2. Assessments of Democracy: Percent of respondents who consider democracy very important and who believe their country is very democratic, by region.

axis reflects how democratic people think their own country is—based on the percent of respondents who believe their country to be very democratic. As this figure indicates, there is a rather strong positive correlation between these two measures: those who believe that democracy is very important, tend to rate their own country as relatively democratic. Scandinavian societies show the highest emphasis on the importance of democracy *and* the highest assessment of how democratic their society is. At the other end of the spectrum, the publics of the Soviet successor states (including Russia) attach the least importance to democracy and give the lowest ratings to how democratic their own society is.

These two variables could be viewed as measures of demand for, and supply of, democracy. Demand is based on how important it is to have a democratic political system, while supply reflects the extent to which citizens consider their country to be democratic. In this fashion, the publics of the Scandinavian societies show both a high demand and a relatively high supply. Although the two tend to go together, it varies from one society to another. Thus, the publics of the Middle Eastern and Northern Africa societies express a high demand for democracy but feel they have a substantially lower supply. East central and Southeast European countries, as well as the Soviet successor states have both a lower level of demand for democracy and significantly lower levels of supply. Only between 10 and 20 percent of respondents in those countries consider their country to be very democratic. Interestingly, the publics of the African countries express somewhat higher assessments of how democratic their country is, than the publics of Latin America or Asia. One possible explanation for this is the recent emergence of electoral politics in Africa, which is perceived as a clear indication that democratization has made progress. Most, Latin American societies have relatively long-established competitive electoral systems (though the presence of genuine competitive democracy has fluctuated) and their concept of democracy may be turning towards other issues, such as the rule of law. In the Latin American region assessments of democracy have also varied: the level of perceived democracy has been high in Uruguay and Costa Rica, as one would expect, but Latinobarómetro data has also shown that Venezuelans tend to evaluate their country as very democratic under Chávez: despite his authoritarian tendencies, his populist appeal has been effective.

Generational differences are not shown in this graph, but some of them are worth mentioning. Younger generations generally attach more importance to democracy than older generations do in third wave democracies, but Latin America is an exception. In this region, those born after 1976 attach less importance to democracy than do their elders. Moreover, the youngest generation in Latin America evaluates democracy more critically, with a lower proportion believing that their country is very democratic. To what extent this is a more realistic view of democracy in Latin America is debatable, but it could reflect a general retreat of democracy since the explosion of democracy in Latin America around 1990. In any case, it is clear that the younger generation is disenchanted with democracy in comparison with their elders. In established democracies, democracy is seen as equally important, and their country's level of democracy is given equal assessments by both younger and older generations: these countries have had secure democratic institutions for so long that generational differences have disappeared

The largest generational differences are observed in Latin America and the Soviet successor states, reflecting its relatively recent emergence in both regions— but the generational differences have opposite polarity. As mentioned, younger Latin Americans value democracy slightly less and are the more critical of their country's perceived level of democracy than their elders. But in the Soviet successor countries, the younger generations value democracy more than their elders and evaluate democracy more favorably (or, one might say, less unfavorably) than their elders. It seems clear that younger citizens are *not* necessarily more supportive of democracy than older ones. This pattern holds true in former Communist countries, less so in advanced democracies, and the finding is reversed in Latin America, where the young seem clearly less favorable towards democracy than the old. One interpretation of this finding is that democratic institutions are gaining acceptance among the younger generation in the ex-communist societies, but not in Latin America, where successive Latinobarometer surveys show declining public assessments of democracy during the past two decades. But this interpretation seems at odds with the fact that young Latin Americans are moving towards increasing emphasis on self-expression values, which are supportive of democratic government and practices. This topic merits additional research and exploration of its possible implications for the consolidation of democracy in the region. Additional data from Venezuela, Bolivia and Honduras may help clarify how attitudes towards democracy and authoritarianism are evolving among younger Latin Americans.

Generational Differences in Support for Democracy and Free Market Economics   41

Figure 3-3 shows generational differences in the degree to which given publics support democracy, on one hand; and the extent to which they feel that they have freedom. Our measure of support for democracy is an index of democratic attitudes based on two questions: how good or bad it is to have a democratic political system, and how good or bad it is to have the military rule. The measure shown on the vertical axis of Figure 3-3 reflects the percentage who think that having a democratic system is good, *and* that having the army rule is bad. This provides a measure of support for democracy and rejection of authoritarian rule (none of the other categories are supportive of democracy). This is a different measure from the one shown in the previous graph, where the vertical axis reflects an evaluation of how democratic the country is.

The horizontal axis on Figure 3-3 shows the percentage of respondents who believe that they have a high level of individual freedom of choice (categories 8 to 10 on a 10-point scale). This measure may be taken as an indirect indicator not only of civil and political liberties, but of a more extended sense of freedom in various areas of life.

As this figure shows, Scandinavian societies express the highest level of support for democracy (along with Southern Europe) and they also express the highest level of perceived freedom of choice— along with the Latin American societies, which are sig-

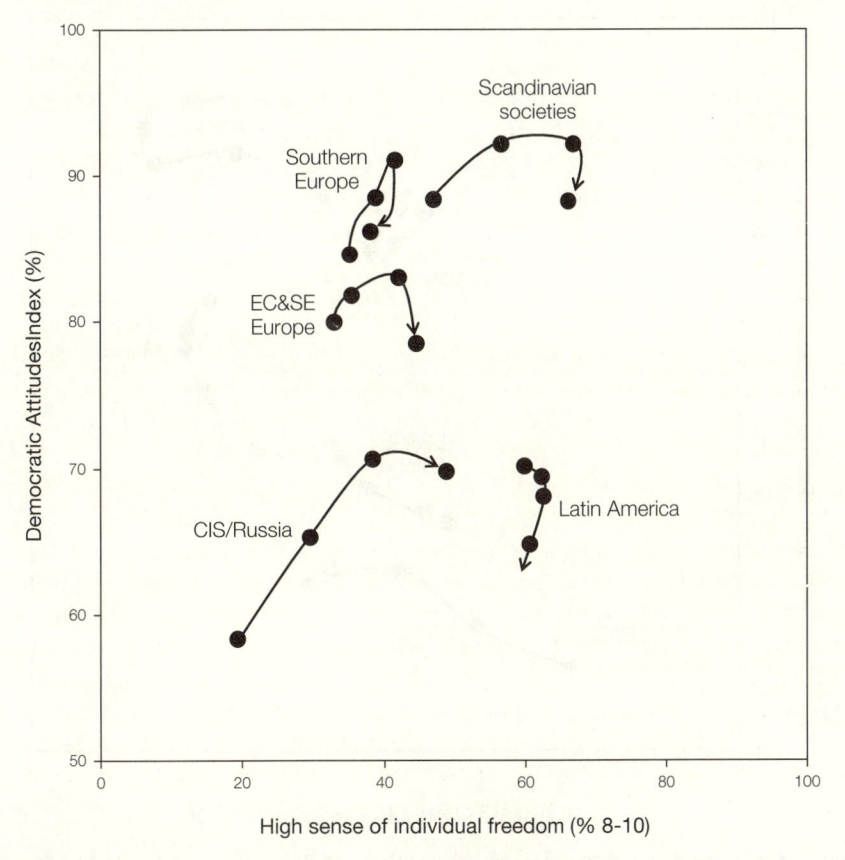

Figure 3-3. Generational differences in support for democracy and individual sense of freedom. Arrows run from oldest to youngest age group.

nificantly less supportive of democracy. In the Soviet successor states including Russia, younger generations are markedly more supportive of democracy and feel that they have markedly greater personal freedom than do older respondents. Older respondents manifest much a much more negative outlook, which may reflect their decades of experience under Communism. This pattern suggests that democracy is gradually winning support in the ex-Soviet societies. But this does not seem to be the case in Latin America, where younger generations are less supportive of democracy and feel slightly less free than their elders. Here again, we find indications of a trend toward disenchantment with democracy in Latin America.

This pattern is not unique to Latin America. In the Scandinavian societies, Southern Europe and Central and Eastern Europe, we find a somewhat similar pattern, in which the youngest birth cohort seems to be turning away from democracy. The publics of these countries show much more positive orientations toward democracy than is the case in Latin America or the Soviet successor states, and the decline is limited to the youngest cohort, but this disillusionment" with democracy among the younger groups gives cause for concern.

With the exception of Latin America, this shift away from support for democracy among the youth does not reflect perceptions of living in a less democratic environment.

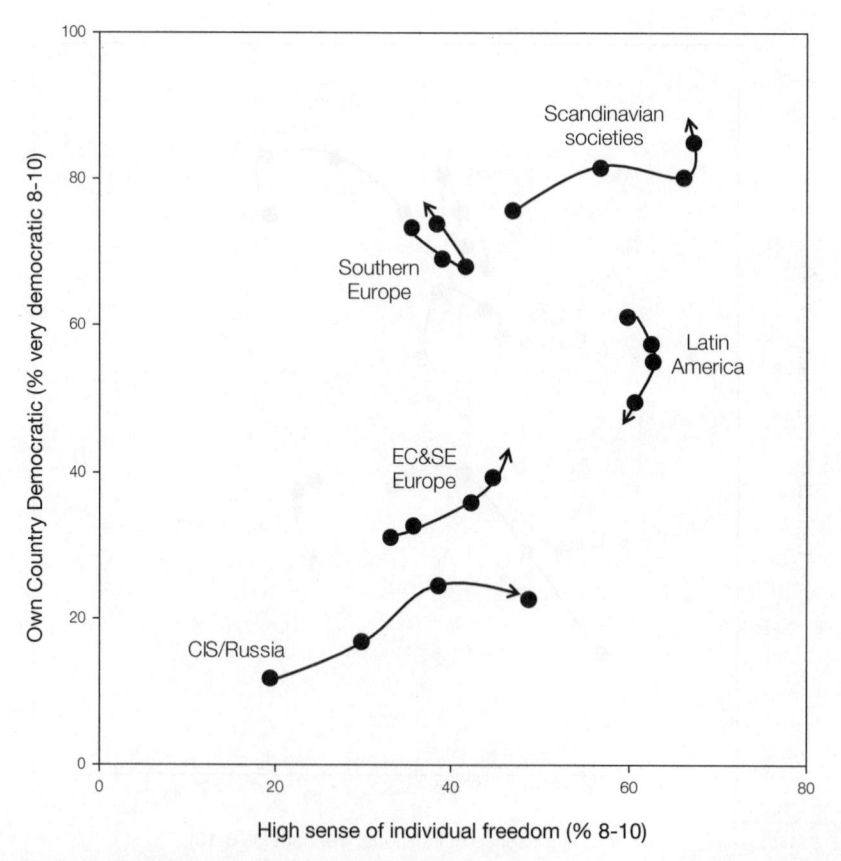

Figure 3-4. Generational differences in perceptions of democracy and individual sense of freedom. Arrows run from oldest to youngest age group.

As Figure 3-4 indicates, the youngest Latin Americans not only feel less free than do their older compatriots- they also think that their country is not as democratic as do older Latin Americans. In contrast, the younger members of most other societies tent to have more positive orientations toward democracy than do their elders. We find multiple indications of a trend toward disenchantment with democracy in Latin America.

Generational differences in views towards free market economics

Do we find generational differences in preferences for state interventionism and capitalism? Are younger generations more supportive of free market economies than older generations? The current global economic crisis has redefined much of the pro-market discourse and the new wave of surveys scheduled for 2010 and 2011 may provide evidence of significant changes in public views of the market. But it seems that ongoing trends do not simply reflect rising unemployment, negative economic growth and the recent recession, but the rise of an anti-market discourse. As Ian Bremmer (2009:40 and 41) recently noticed,

"Across the United States, Europe, and much of the rest of the developed world, the recent wave of state interventionism is meant to lessen the pain of the current global recession and restore ailing economies to health. For the most part, the governments of developed countries do not intend to manage these economies indefinitely. However, an opposing intention lies behind similar interventions in the developing world: there the state's heavy hand in the economy is signaling a strategic rejection of free market doctrine. [...] the challenged posed by this potent brand of state-managed capitalism has been sharpened by the international financial crisis and the global recession. Now, the champions of free trade and open markets have to prove these systems' value to an increasingly skeptical international audience."

The survey measures examined here were obtained before the current economic crisis, and they do not reflect either the economic distress or changes in economic discourse and policies. They reflect trends toward gradually growing criticism of a free market ideology that were established well before the current recession—which may further strengthen them. Let us analyze inter-generational differences in support for capitalism and state interventionism.

Figure 3-5 shows the percent of respondents in each region that shares redistributive leftist views, capitalist rightist preferences or a combination of both (mixed). This variable was constructed using two variables originally measured with ten-point scales: support for increasing income equality vs. individual incentives; and support for state responsibility vs. individual responsibility. The two variables were used to construct an index of support for a Redistributive Left, versus a Capitalist Right (the two load highly on the same factor and show high Cronbach alphas —see Norris and Inglehart, 2010 in this volume).

As one might expect, the North American publics show the highest level of support for capitalist policies, with twice as many respondents supporting individual incentives and individual responsibility as state intervention. Despite their large welfare states, the Scandinavian societies rank second in support for capitalism, followed by Asia, Western Europe, and Africa. In Russia and the other ex-Soviet countries the balance is still favorable to capitalism over state interventionism, but only narrowly. In Latin America, support for the two views is evenly balanced, and in the remaining three regions, East

44   Generational Differences in Support for Democracy and Free Market Economics

■ Redistributive Left   □ Mixed   □ Capitalist Right

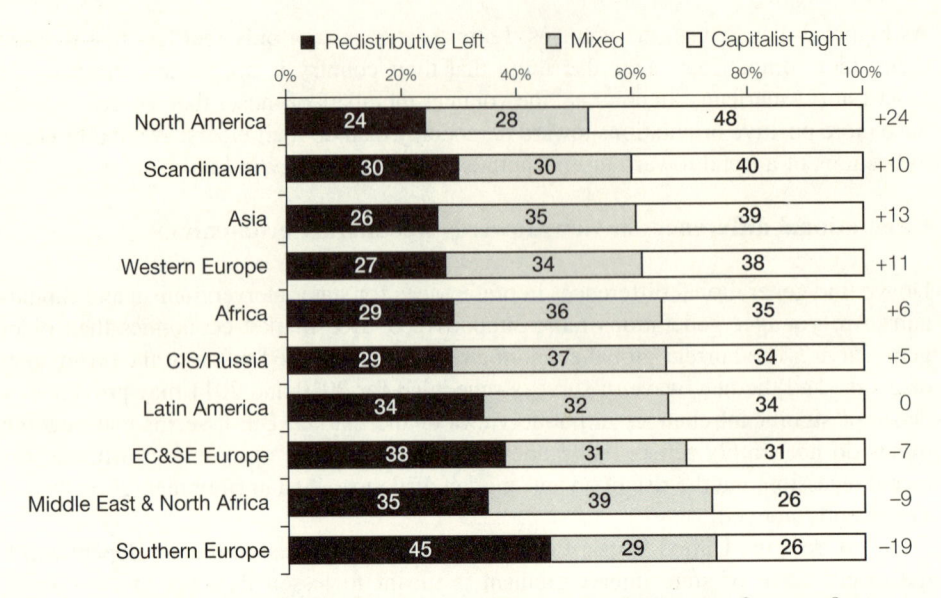

Region	Redistributive Left	Mixed	Capitalist Right	Net
North America	24	28	48	+24
Scandinavian	30	30	40	+10
Asia	26	35	39	+13
Western Europe	27	34	38	+11
Africa	29	36	35	+6
CIS/Russia	29	37	34	+5
Latin America	34	32	34	0
EC&SE Europe	38	31	31	−7
Middle East & North Africa	35	39	26	−9
Southern Europe	45	29	26	−19

Figure 3-5. State and Market Preferences: Average regional percent of respondents on a Distributive-Left vs. Capitalist Right attitudinal index. (The number on the right is the net difference between the capitalist proportion minus the redistributive proportion of respondents in each region).

Central Europe, Southern Europe and the Middle East and Northern Africa, support for redistributive leftist policies outweighs support for individual incentives and individual responsibility. This is particularly true in Southern Europe (Portugal, Spain, and Greece).

These data show that there are significant cross-regional variations in support for free market economics, but what about generational differences? Figures 6a and 6b show the percentage of respondents who support redistributive leftist and capitalist views respectively by birth cohort and by region: the horizontal axis shows the birth years of given cohorts, moving from older respondents to younger ones. In North America, for example, as we move from older to younger groups, we find sharply decreasing support for free market economics and growing support for state interventionism—although the former still outweighs the latter. Generational differences are pronounced. In Western Europe the differences are not as great, but the trend from old to young is in the same direction, and the youngest generation is balanced between the two economic worldviews. Generational differences are slight in Southern Europe—but support for state intervention is relatively high and remains so among every age group. The balance between the two views was already skewed rather strongly in favor of the redistributive left, and there is no indication of change.

Generational differences are dramatic in the new Latin American and the post-communist countries of Central and Eastern Europe as well as the Soviet successor states—and they move in the opposite direction from the trend found in North America and Western Europe. In these new democracies, the younger generations are more favorable to free market economies, while the older generations tend to prefer state intervention. The generational differences are most dramatic in the ex-communist societies, where the political and economic transformations during the last two decades seem to

Generational Differences in Support for Democracy and Free Market Economics 45

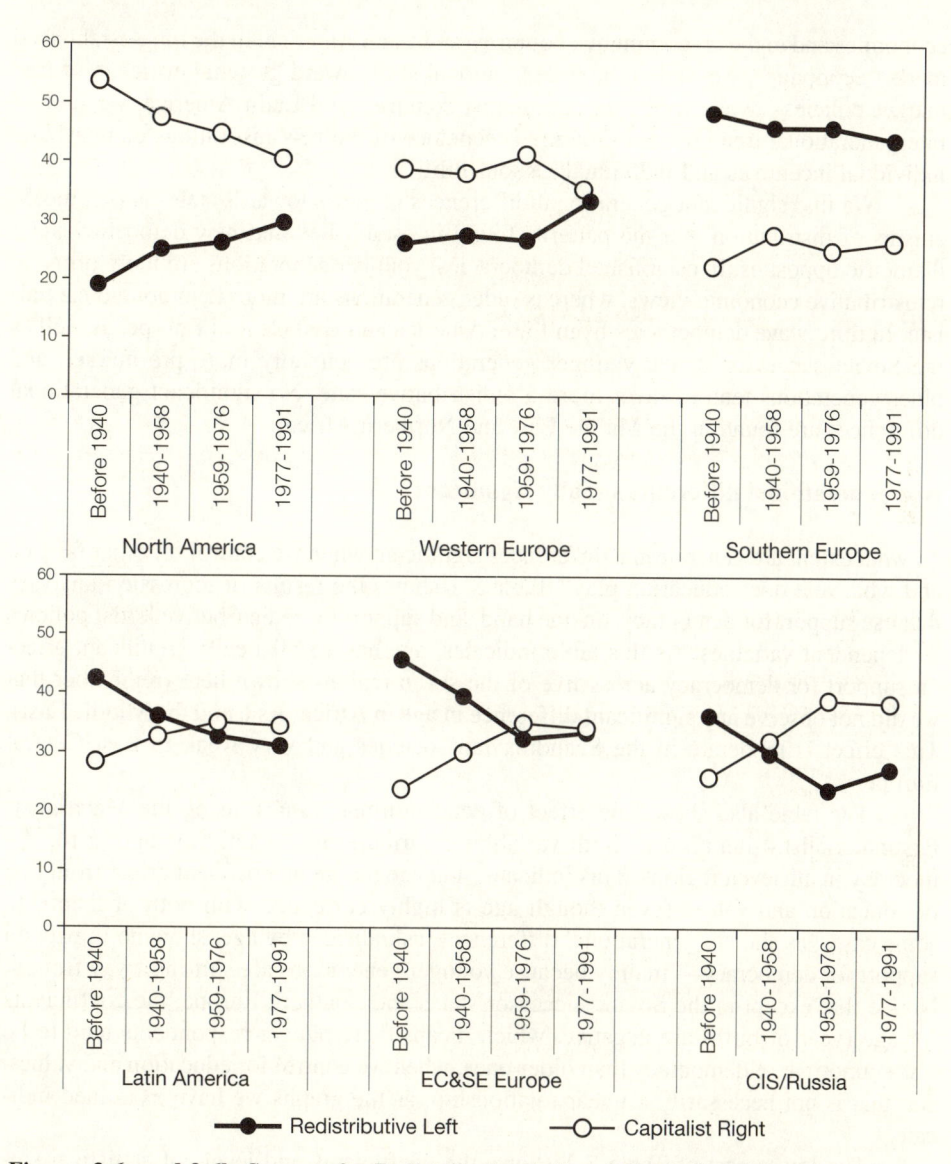

Figures 3-6a and 3-6b. Support for Redistributive Left and Capitalist Right Views by age.

have divided younger and older generations. Both in Latin America and in the ex-communist countries, the younger cohorts are move supportive of market economies than are their elders—and in both Latin America and Eastern Europe, the younger generations are evenly divided between the two alternatives. The two ideologies are equally competitive, which may have important implications for party competition. In the 2006 Mexican election, for example, the polarized campaign discourse divided voters in an open left-right confrontation, and the presidential candidates representing the two ideological poles drew roughly equal support among the different age groups. Thus, we find two contrasting patterns of intergenerational differences among established market economies and in the ex-communist countries and Latin America. In the long-established market economies, we find an inter-generational shift toward growing criticism of free market policies—while in the ex-communist countries and Latin America, we find an intergenerational trend toward growing acceptance of the new institutions emphasizing individual incentives and individual responsibility.

We find significant generational differences in views towards state-market mechanisms of distribution, but the patterns found in established and new democracies are diametric opposites. In established democracies, younger generations are more prone to redistributive economic views, whereas older generations are more favorable to capitalism. In third wave democracies from Latin America and East Central Europe, as well as the Soviet successor states, younger generations are generally more pro-market, and older generations tend to favor more a redistributive state. No significant generational differences are found in the Middle East and Northern Africa.

Are generational differences really significant?

To what extent are generational differences significant when we control for other factors, and what role does education play? Table 3-1 shows the results of regression analyses that use support for democracy, on one hand, and support for redistributive leftist policies as dependent variables. As this table indicates, age has a statistically significant effect on support for democracy across five of the seven regions shown here (remember that we did not observe any significant difference in age in Africa, Asia and the Middle East). This effect is moderate in the Scandinavian societies and very weak in East Central Europe.

The table also shows the effect of education and values, using the Materialist-Postmaterialist 4-item index. Both variables contribute significantly to support for democracy in all seven regions. This indicates that age has an independent effect from that of education and values (even though age is highly correlated with both of them). In some cases, as shown, generational differences, as indicated by age, show no impact on support for democracy— mainly because younger generations are shifting away from it. Notice that except in the Soviet successor states and Southern Europe, the coefficients for age (year of birth) are negative, which means that younger respondents tend to be *less* supportive of democracy than older ones, when we control for education and values. But this is not necessarily a linear relationship, as the graphs we have examined indicate.

The lower part of Table 3-1 shows the coefficients and levels of statistical significance in support for the redistributive Left versus the capitalist Right, using multinomial logit analysis. In this case, negative coefficients mean that younger respondents are more favorable to state intervention, while positive coefficients mean that younger groups are more favorable to free market economics. As it was observed in previous graphs, younger cohorts are less pro-capitalist in the Scandinavian societies, Western Europe, and North America. However, the effect of age is mildly significant in the former two regions. It is not significant at all in Southern Europe, and it is very significant— but with positive effects— in the new democracies of Latin American and the post-Communist world.

In these analyses, the independent effects of age and education are more noticeable. In North America, for example, age has a significant effect but education does not.

Table 3-1. The effects of age, education and values on support for democracy and free market orientations.

	Scandinavian Societies		Western Europe		Southern Europe		EC&ES Europe		North America		Latin America		Ex-Soviet/ Russia	
	B	Sig.	B	Sig.	B	Sig.	B	Sig.	B	Sig.	B	Sig.	B	Sig.
Support for Democracy														
Logit analysis														
Year of birth	-.103	.015	-.320	.000	.121	.002	-.031	.071	-.330	.000	-.172	.000	.162	.000
Education	.681	.000	.694	.000	.341	.000	.586	.000	.943	.000	.648	.000	.505	.000
M/PM values	.533	.000	.545	.000	.187	.002	.382	.000	.367	.000	.220	.000	.271	.000
Constant	-.110	.556	-.040	.711	.055	.677	-.840	.000	-.767	.000	-.666	.000	-1.938	.000
Redistributive Left vs. Capitalist Right														
Multinomial logit analysis														
Year of birth	-.109	.005	-.129	.000	.001	.990	.122	.000	-.217	.000	.061	.005	.159	.000
Education	.282	.000	.399	.000	.231	.008	.662	.000	.063	.314	.419	.000	.368	.000
M/PM values	-.329	.000	-.081	.041	.003	.976	.307	.000	-.274	.000	.074	.029	.397	.000
Constant	.565	.002	-.042	.688	-.961	.000	-2.354	.000	1.610	.000	-1.116	.000	-1.669	.000

Dependent variables:
Support for democracy (dichotomous variable where 1 means having a democratic political system is very good or good and having a military regime is very bad or bad, 0 means all other outcomes in the combination of variables).
Redistributive Left vs. Capitalist Right is the preference for income equality and state responsibility vs. individual incentives and responsibility. The multinomial analysis also included an intermediate position but the table only shows the left-right comparison. "Redistributive Left" is the reference category.

In contrast, results for Latin America show that the effects of age and values are moderate but education has a strong influence on economic views. Respondents with more formal education are more favorable to free market economics. All three variables have a statistically significant effect in the post-Communist new democracies.

Conclusions

As we have seen, intergenerational differences in support for democracy are modest in the long-established democracies. In the Soviet successor states including Russia, the younger generations are markedly more supportive of democracy and feel that they have markedly greater personal freedom than do older respondents. This pattern suggests that democracy is gradually winning support in the ex-Soviet societies. But this does not seem to be the case in Latin America, where younger generations are less supportive of democracy and feel slightly less free than their elders— indications of a disquieting trend toward disenchantment with democracy in Latin America. In Scandinavia, Southern Europe and Central and Eastern Europe, we find a faintly similar pattern, which suggests that the very youngest birth cohort may be turning away from democracy.

In support for state intervention versus free market policies, we find a dramatic contrast between the generational differences in long-established market economies, and the ex-communist countries and Latin America. In the established market economies of North America and Western Europe, we find decreasing support for free market economics and growing support for state interventionism as we move from older to younger groups. Generational differences are dramatic in the post-communist countries and Latin American— but they move in the opposite direction from the trend found in North America and Western Europe. In these countries, the younger generations are more favorable to free market economies, while the older generations tend to prefer state intervention.

Basic social norms generally change slowly, giving rise to intergenerational differences that reflect the fact that younger generations absorb new emerging norms more readily than older generations. But the direction in which change occurs reflects the environment in which it takes place. When communism collapsed in Central and Eastern Europe and the Soviet Union around 1990, one of the reasons why it collapsed was because the state had taken on a vastly oversized role. Although in Western countries, for generations it had seemed self-evident that the political Left stood for increasing state intervention, by 1990 the meaning of Left and Right had reversed itself in the Soviet Union: in that setting, the "Left" referred to the young reformers who were attempting to roll back the state and make way for a market economy and democratic political competition; the "Right" denoted the hard liners who were trying to hold on to a state-run economy and a one-party dominated political system. Subsequently, ex-communist countries have been experiencing an intergenerational shift in which as younger birth cohorts enter the adult population, they have brought growing acceptance of free markets and democratic politics. By contrast, in North America and much of Western Europe, the deregulation and privatization that dominated the 1980s and 1990s, shifted the balance to a point where subsequent years brought an intergenerational shift away from laissez-faire capitalism, toward a better balance between state and society. We find extensive evidence of intergenerational differences, but the direction it takes is not predetermined: it reflects the conditions in which it emerges.

APPENDIX

Countries included in the ten regional categories used here.

Scandinavian Societies	Western Europe	Southern Europe	North America	East Central and Southeast Europe	Latin America	Ex-Soviet/Russia	Asia	Africa	Middle East and North Africa
Denmark	France	Spain	USA	Hungary	Mexico	Tambov (Russia)	S Korea	S Africa	Pakistan
Norway	Britain	Portugal	Canada	Poland	Argentina	Belarus	India	Nigeria	Turkey
Sweden	West Germany	Greece		Czech Republic	Brazil	Ukraine	China	Ghana	Saudi Arabia
Iceland	Italy			Slovenia	Chile	Russia	Taiwan	Zimbabwe	Egypt
Finland	Netherlands			Bulgaria	Peru	Moldova	Philippines	Tanzania	Morocco
	Belgium			Romania	Venezuela	Georgia	Thailand	Uganda	Iran
	Ireland			Slovakia	Uruguay	Armenia	Bangladesh	Burkina Faso	Jordan
	Switzerland			Lithuania	El Salvador	Azerbaijan	Indonesia	Ethiopia	Algeria
	Austria			Latvia	Dominican R.		Vietnam	Mali	Iraq
				Estonia	Colombia		Singapore	Rwanda	
				Albania	Guatemala		Hong Kong	Zambia	
				Serbia			Malaysia		
				Macedonia					
				Croatia					
				Bosnia					
				Serbia and Montenegro					

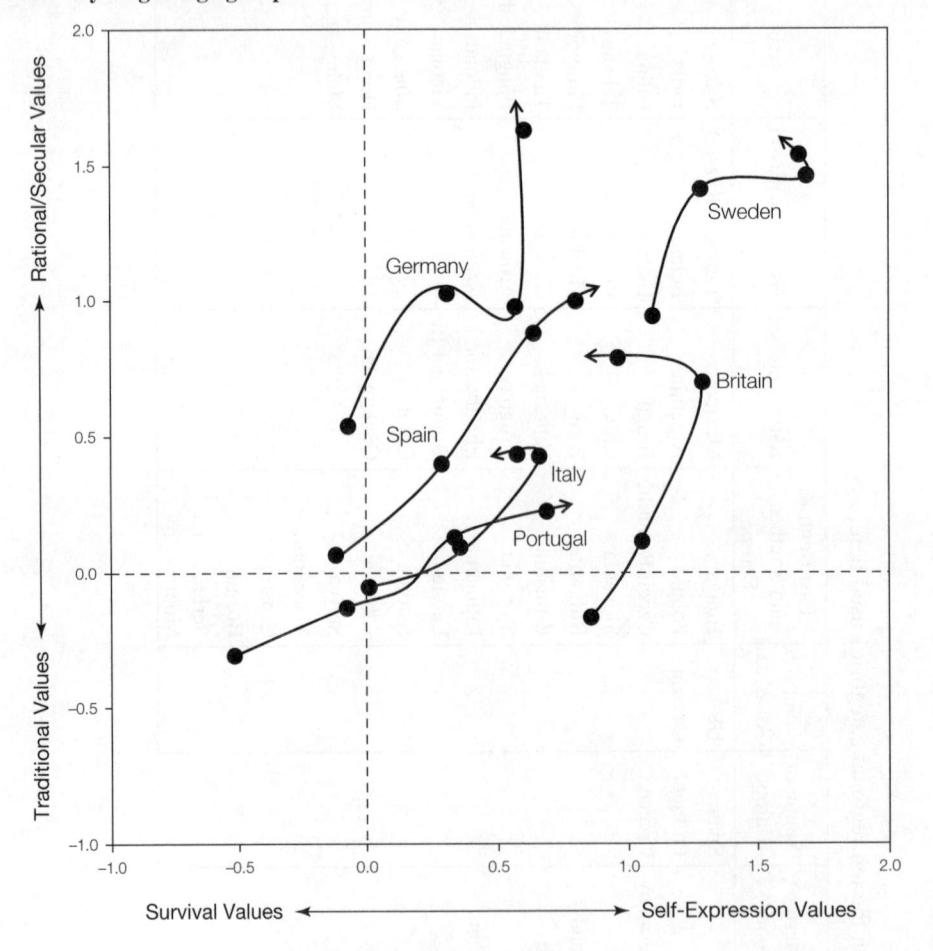

Figure 3-A. Generational differences in two value dimensions in Eruope. Arrows run from oldest to youngest age group.

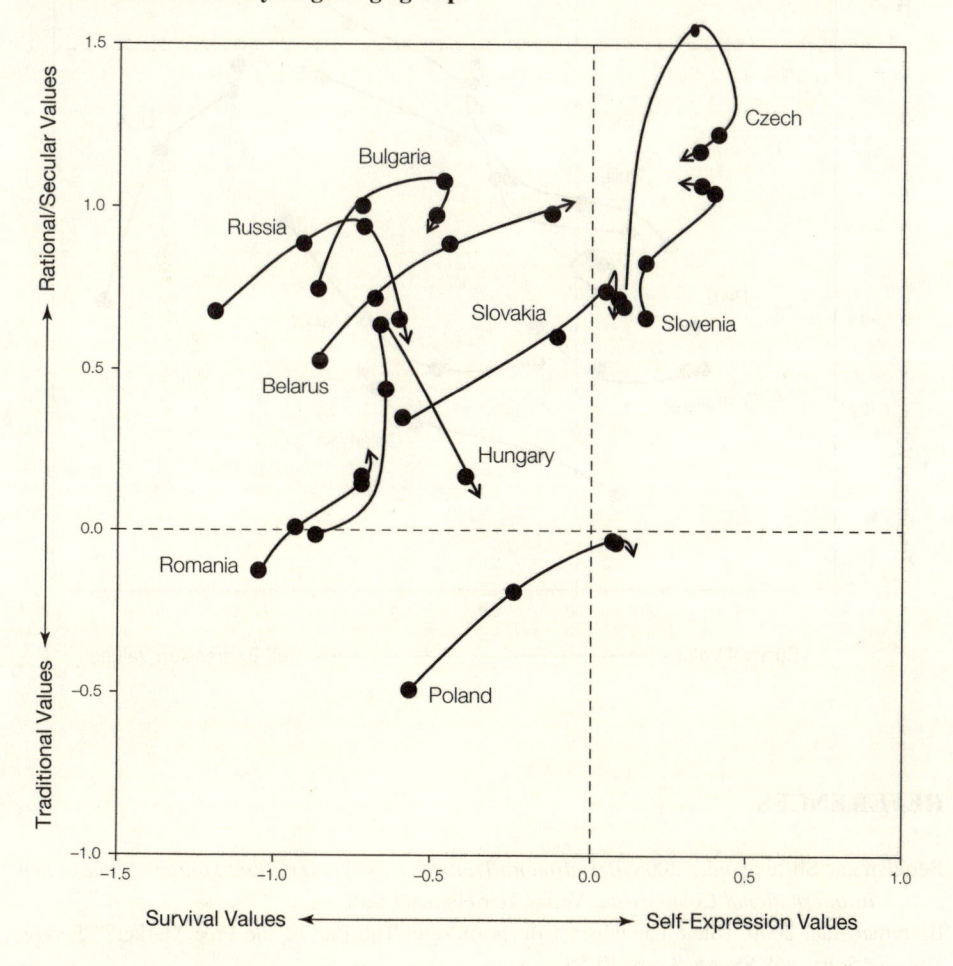

Generational Differences in Support for Democracy and Free Market Economics

Figure 3-B. Generational differences in two value dimensions in East Central Europe. Arrows run from oldest to youngest age group.

Figure 3-C. Generational differences in two value dimensions in Latin America and the United States. Arrows run from oldest to youngest age group.

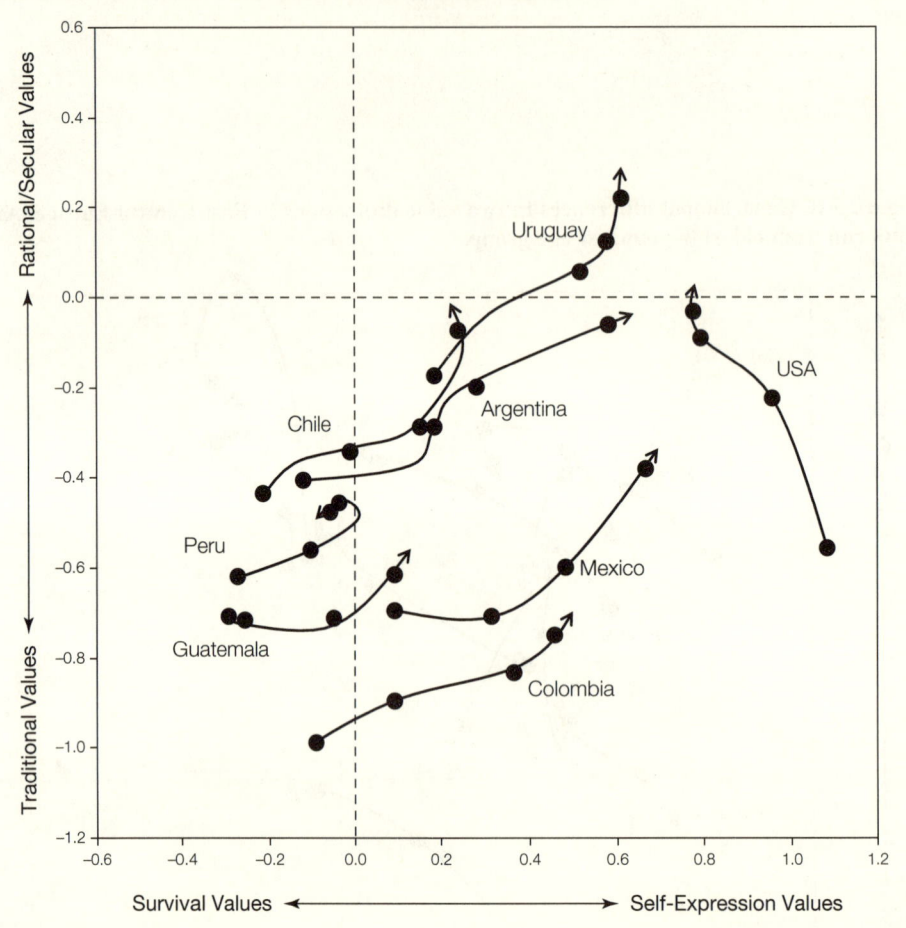

REFERENCES

Bertelsmann Stiftung (ed.). 2008. *Bertelsmann Transformation index 2008: Political Management in International Comparison*. Verlag Bertelsmann Stiftung.

Bremmer, Ian. 2009. "State capitalism Comes of Age: The End of the Free Market?" *Foreign Affairs*, vol. 88, no. 3, pp. 40-55.

Inglehart, Ronald. 1997. *Modernization and Postmodernization*. Princeton: Princeton University Press.

Inglehart, Ronald, and Christian Welzel. 2005. *Modernization, Cultural Change, and Democracy*. Cambridge: Cambridge University Press.

Moreno, Alejandro. 2005. *Nuestros Valores: Los Mexicanos en México y Estados Unidos al inicio del Siglo 21* [Our Values: Mexicans in Mexico and the U.S. at the Turn of the Century]. Mexico City. Banamex.

Norris, Pippa and Ronald Inglehart. 2010 (in this volume). "Globalization and Major Trends in Value Change, 1981-2007." Mexico City: Siglo XXI.

Siemienska, Renata. 2003. "Intergenerational Differences in Political Values and Attitudes in Stable and New Democracies". In Ronald Inglehart (ed.), *Islam, Gender, Culture, and Democracy: Findings from the World Values Survey and the European Values Survey*. Willowdale, Canada: de Sitter Publications.

Youth, Values and Democracy: Exploring Tolerance toward Diversity among Third Wave Generations[1]

Gabriela Catterberg and Ignacio Zuasnabar

How democratic is the Third Wave Generation? This chapter examines the factors that have shaped the generation that has grown up since the Third Wave of democratization that occurred around 1990. Is a new generation of democratic supporters emerging?

More than two decades after the Third Wave expanded democracy into new countries throughout Latin America, Central and Eastern Europe, and South Asia, it is still unclear to what extent inter-generational value change has taken place, and how democratic the orientations of the younger generations are, in comparison to those of their elders. A new generation of citizens has been raised under democratic regimes, but recent findings indicate that they show detachment and distrust toward the political system. This is disquieting (though it might be interpreted as a healthy distrust of authority on the part of "Critical Citizens," as is argued by Norris, et al., [1999]). Tolerance of other groups has been shown to be a crucial element of a pro-democratic political culture (Inglehart, 2003). This chapter examines whether younger citizens in the new democracies are more or less tolerant of outgroups than their elders.

In established democracies, high levels of existential security during one's formative years, were conducive to the emergence the pro-democratic values that characterize the post war cohorts even more than their elders (Inglehart 1997; Inglehart and Welzel, 2005). Throughout advanced industrial society, rising levels of economic and physical security led to increasingly higher levels of tolerance, trust, and mass participation among younger generations. But research on democratization has given little attention to the effects of early socialization on the Third Wave Generation's political orientations (for an exception, see Niemi, Catterberg et al., 1991). We believe this is crucial component in understanding the survival and consolidation of democracy.

Is the youngest generation in the new democracies growing with supportive orientations toward democracy? In contrast to the 'natural' socialization hypothesis usually assumed in established democracies, inter-generational transmission of democratic values in Third Wave nations is uncertain. As Niemi (1996) put it, "In newer democra-

---

[1] We thank Antonella Bonacina for her statistical support.

cies, 'automatic' transmission of democratic values from one generation to the next cannot be taken for granted ...Older generations are themselves untutored about democratic processes, and they may fail to embrace democratic values or waiver in their own commitment to them" (p. 465).

Whether given generations continue to hold antidemocratic values after democratization has been a continuing theme in studies of the former Soviet Union (Gibson 1998). In the Southern Cone of Latin America, an absence of democratic values among the adult population has been identified since the early stages of democratization. As E. Catterberg (1991) noted, on the basis of surveys conducted during the military regime and after the transition to constitutional government, "during the first five years of the constitutional government [responses on] many libertarian dimensions moved backward" (107-108).

There is also the question whether education fosters democratic values in new democracies. Recent research suggests that those who are relatively well educated may *not* necessarily emphasize democratic ideals. In Soviet studies, a concern has been if education encouraged support for democratic values or if, in earlier years, it increased support for the prevailing authoritarian system. Szabo (1991) pointed out, for instance, that schools promoted the development of a conformist, anti-political authoritarian personality. It has also been argued that since young people in less affluent countries often leave school at an earlier age than in the U.S. and Western Europe, repeated exposure to democratic values over many classes (or even the experience of a single high school civics course) is often not a factor.

Despite these concerns about the absence of natural socialization to democratic attitudes or the learning of such values in the classroom, an almost universal fact about democratization is that it brought more openness in formal and informal institutional settings, more freedom of expression and association, and more exposure to independent media. As Huntington points out in a 1997 article about the future of the Third Wave, "A quarter-century ago, authoritarian governments —communist politburos, military juntas, personal dictatorships— were the rule. Today, hundreds of millions of people who previously suffered under tyrants live in freedom" (p3).

Yet, as Niemi anticipated, research on the trajectories of political orientations in new democracies over time after regime change uncovers a worrisome trend that calls into question the impact of the Third Wave political socialization on people's democratic orientations. On average, political participation and trust in new democracies *declined* in the years following regime change, while tolerance toward elite corruption and detachment with the law increased (Catterberg, Moreno, & Zuasnabar 2008; Uslaner 2004; Norris 2002).

Nevertheless, we contend that socialization processes after the Third Wave did positively affect at least one crucial aspect of democracy. As this chapter shows, tolerance toward diversity increased among the publics of most new democracies between regime change and 2005. People are becoming more willing to accept and coexist with groups traditionally subjected to stereotypes and negative evaluations, such as minorities of a different race and foreign workers. Moreover, as a Tolerance Index constructed by the present authors shows, the publics of twelve out of fourteen new democracies have become increasingly tolerant during the last fifteen years. On average, the percentage of those defined as "tolerant" increased by nine percentage points, rising from 37 percent to 46 percent of the population.

Tolerance is a critical value for democratic functioning and survival. As Sartori argues (2001), pluralism, the "genetic code of an open society," presupposes and requires high doses of tolerance. Pluralism holds that diversity and dissent enhance both the individual and his political community, and tolerant people concede that others have the right to hold 'wrong beliefs.' As Inglehart (2003) puts it, in democracies an underlying culture of tolerance, is crucial: the very essence of democracy is that one concedes to other groups—even groups one dislikes—the right to advocate their views and to contend for political power. At this point in history, tolerance of homosexuals is a particularly good litmus test of how tolerant a society is. "Tolerance or intolerance of homosexuals, although it does not overtly refer to support for democracy, provides a substantially stronger predictor of the degree to which democratic institutions exist, than does any question that explicitly asks how one feels about democracy."

This paper analyzes (1) if a positive shift in tolerance toward diversity during the last fifteen years took place in new democracies, comparing their experience with that of established democracies, (2) if the Third Wave generation—those who have grown up since the transition to democracy— is more tolerant than its older elders, and (3) if tolerance's rate of change was higher among younger cohorts in newer regimes. To explore these questions, we use World Values Surveys data from 1990-1991 (the approximate time when most Third Wave democracies experienced regime change) and 2005-2007 (the most recent wave of surveys). The fact that the World Values Survey (WVS) was launched a decade before the Third Wave of democratization enables us to study the impact of political socialization in recently democratized countries over time. The fact that the WVS became a global project during an era of widespread democratization was not pure coincidence; the new openness experienced by more than 30 nations across the globe made it possible for cross-national survey research to expand into societies that had previously excluded it.

A Note on the Data

The WVS has been conducted in more than 90 societies in successive waves of interviews from 1981 to 2007, including new and established democracies, as well as non-democratic countries. The first wave took place in 1981-83, followed by a second one in 1990-91, a third one in 1995-96, and then a forth one in 2000-2001. The fifth wave was conducted in 2005-08, and the next wave will be carried out in 2010-2011. In 1990, the WVS critically expanded to cover 45 nations, including almost 20 countries that were undergoing transitions to democracy.

A more detailed description of this unique dataset can be found elsewhere in this sourcebook and the raw data and documentation can be obtained from the Inter-University Consortium for Political and Social Research (ICPSR), at the University of Michigan. More information about the World Values Survey can also be found at http://www.worldvaluessurvey.org and the raw data can be downloaded from this source. Comparable data is available for fifteen new democracies and ten established democracies that were surveyed in both 1990 and 2005. Each national representative sample includes about 1,000 face to face interviews, though sample sizes vary from country to country. Most surveys are conducted among populations over eighteen, although in some surveys the age range starts at fifteen.

Methodological Considerations

We define the Third Wave Generation as including all respondents born after 1965. This means that in 1990, the year of regime change, they ranged from 15 to 25 years of age. For analytic purposes, we distinguish between those born from 1965 to 1974, and those born from 1975 to 1990. Since the latter group was less than 15 years old in 1990, it was too young to be included in the 1990 surveys, this distinction prevents us from comparing non-equivalent populations over time and enables us to determine whether there are important differences between those who were young adults at the time of the transition and those who were still adolescents.

Our focus, therefore, is on youth and young adults. Traditional studies of political development and socialization generally focus on young children. But, young adulthood, as recent studies shows, also represents a period of rapid change to adult-like learning capacities and adult attitudes (Sapiro 2004). Two crucial factors in these studies are young adults' cognitive competence— shaped by their biological maturation, abilities and experiences— and the relevance of politics to young adults' lives—shaped by their interest and exposure to political information and discussion. As Niemi argues, "The period from about 14 through the mid 20s should receive much more attention from political scientists interested in the process of political socialization. The reason is two-fold. First, there is little dispute that youth is a time of extraordinary psychological and social change. Second, those are the years during which our society traditionally attempts to educate youth for citizen participation" (Niemi & Hepburn, 1995: 9).

In order to identify intergenerational differences, the orientations of three older cohorts are compared with those of the two Third Wave cohorts. The birth years of the five respective cohorts are:

		Established Democracies*		News Democracies**	
		n	%	n	%
	1901-1924	2,565	9.42	1,417	3.81
	1925-1944	7,169	26.32	7,885	21.22
	1945-1964	10,507	38.57	14,035	37.77
3WG	1965-1974	4,667	17.13	7,417	19.96
	1975-1990	2,333	8.56	6,401	17.23
	Total	27,241	100	37,155	100

*Britain, Finland, France, Italy, Netherlands, Spain, Sweden, Switzerland, U.S, and West Germany.
**Argentina, Brazil, Bulgaria, Chile, East Germany, mexico, Peru, Poland, Romania, Russia, South Korea, Slovenia, Taiwan, Turkey, and Uruguay.
Source: World Values Surveys.

To measure tolerance toward diversity, we use a WVS battery that inquires about attitudes toward various minorities. It asks: "On this list are various groups of people. Could you please sort out any that you would not like to have as neighbors?" The extent to which a wide range of groups are accepted or rejected, provides a broad, general indication of the extent to which tolerant orientations are present within each cohort. To provide an overall measure of tolerance, we constructed, a Tolerance Index that the sums the number of groups that are rejected among five groups that are widely stigmatized: people of a different race, immigrants or foreign workers, homosexuals, drug addicts and people with AIDS. We then reversed polarity, so that high scores indicate high levels of tolerance. The resulting Tolerance Index is an ordinal measure that runs from 0 to 5, where 0 indicates high intolerance (all five groups are rejected), and 5 indicates high tolerance toward diversity (none of the five groups is rejected). Intermediate values show intermediate orientations toward the acceptance of minorities as neighbors.

To test for significant differences over time within age groups (by country and between old versus new democracies), we conducted two-sample mean tests of proportions. Differences significant at the .05 level are identified in the following tables.

Trends in Tolerance

Our first major finding is the fact that tolerance toward diversity has risen in most new democracies since regime change. Although the publics of the established democracies showed much higher levels of tolerance in 1990 then did the publics of the new democracies—and still did so in 2005-2007—the publics of the new democracies showed much larger *increases* in their levels of tolerance than did the publics of the established democracies. As Table 4-1 indicates, our overall measure of tolerance, the Tolerance Index, increased in all of the new democracies but two (Taiwan and Turkey). On average, the percentage of "Tolerants" (those who rejected none or at most one of the five groups) rose from 37 percent to 47 percent. The largest change took place in Russia, where the proportion rejecting immigrants fell from 12 percent to 32 percent. All of the other shifts were smaller than 5 percentage points.

The publics of almost all Third Wave democracies showed rising levels of tolerance toward people of a different race, and toward immigrants or foreign workers and homosexuals from 1990 to 2005. Positive shifts took place in twelve out of fourteen nations in the percentage of respondents not excluding people of different race as potential neighbors, in ten out of fifteen countries in the percentage not rejecting immigrants or foreign workers and in thirteen out of fourteen countries in the percentage willing to accept homosexuals in their communities (see Table 4-A1 in Appendix).

But rejection of some minority groups is still widespread, with attitudes toward homosexuals being by far the most negative. Although the percentage saying they would not want to have homosexuals as neighbors fell by 12 percentage points, in 2005-2007, almost half of the respondents still indicated that they would not like to have homosexuals as neighbors—a rejection rate that is more than twice as high as the proportion rejecting people of a different race, or immigrants. An extreme case is Turkey, where 94 percent would not accept homosexuals as potential neighbors. In the Southern Cone of South America (Argentina, Brazil and Uruguay) and East Germany, on the contrary, only two out of ten say that they would not like to have homosexuals as neighbors. The Southern Cone nations are also positioned at the top of the Tolerance Index ranking, while Turkey is in its last place.

The Tolerance Index remained relatively constant from 1990 to 2005 in the established democracies, rising slightly from 62 percent to 65 percent— although different trajectories characterized its three individual components analyzed in our study. While

Table 4-1. Tolerance toward diversity over time.
Tolerance Index. % tolerants, totals by country.

	1990	2005	Change
Established Democracies			
Britain	62	61	−1*
Finland	53	56	3*
France	69	43	−26*
Italy	54	59	5*
Netherlands	72	73	1
Spain	56	75	19*
Sweden	83	89	6*
Switzerland			
US	53	55	2*
W. Germany	58	70	12*
mean	**62**	**65**	**3***
New Democracies			
Argentina	58	77	19*
Brazil	72	73	1
Bulgaria	23	34	11*
Chile	41	60	19*
E. Germany	58	68	10*
Mexico	27	51	24*
Peru	39	48	9*
Poland	30	36	6*
Romania	21	38	17*
Russia	18	21	3*
S. Korea			
Slovenia	38	48	10*
Taiwan	22	13	−9*
Turkey	8	4	−4*
Uruguay	65	73	8*
mean	**37**	**47**	**10***

* $p < .05$
[1] 1995 wave used for Sweden, Brazil, Peru, Poland, Taiwan and Uruguay.
Source: World Values Surveys.

rejection of people of a different race stayed at 10 percent and intolerance toward immigrants increased by six percentage points (largely because of a very large increase in xenophobic in France), prejudice toward homosexuals decreased by seven points. Despite this decrease, as in the case of new democracies, homosexuals remain particularly stigmatized. The percentage expressing negative orientations toward them is twice as large as the percentages rejecting people of a different race, or immigrants. Overall, the Tolerance Index ranking indicates that Sweden is the most tolerant society among the ten established democracies, with 89 percent of the public being classified as "Tolerants," while the U.S. is the least tolerant established democracies, with 55 percent "Tolerants."[2]

The tolerance gap between the new democracies and the established democracies has been gradually narrowing. The Tolerance Index gap between established and new democracies has fallen from a ratio of 62:37 in the percentage of "Tolerants" in 1990, to a ratio of 65:47 in 2005-2007. This tendency toward convergence characterized all age groups, but it was especially strong among the Third Wave birth cohorts.

Let's now examine the dynamics of specific types of tolerance, within each of the five birth cohort from 1990 to 2005-2007.

Tolerance toward people of a different race

In new democracies, growing tolerance toward people of a different race took place among all age groups. Within the older half of the Third Wave generation (those born from 1965 to 1974), tolerance experienced a positive shift of seven percentage points. We have no time series data for the younger half of the Third Wave generation, but it shows a similar level of tolerance. Roughly similar changes took place among the 1945-1964 cohort and the 1901-1924 cohort, both of which showed a six point increase in tolerance. The 1925-1945 group levels of tolerance did not show significant changes over time.

Among the new democracies, the publics of the Southern Cone countries are particularly open toward people of a different race, showing acceptance levels of 90 percent or higher among all age groups. In this respect, the tolerance's levels of these Latin American countries are similar to, or even higher, than those found in most established democracies. Only Sweden and Switzerland show higher levels of racial tolerance than those found in the Southern Cone countries. In contrast with these countries, in South Korea, Russia and Turkey the rejection of people of a different race is often 30 percent or higher.

In almost all countries, the younger cohorts are more tolerant than the older ones. On average, in 2005-2007, only 12 percent of the older segment of the Third Wave generation in new democracies rejected having people of a different race as neighbors. The younger segment of the Third Wave generation (born after 1975), is even more tolerant, with only 10 percent rejecting people of another race. Among the older cohorts

---

[2] In established democracies, tolerance toward people with AIDS stayed practically constant, while acceptance of drug addicts experienced a visible decrease (with the exceptions of Italy and Germany). In new democracies, in contrast, tolerance toward people with AIDS sharply increased in all nations (including Turkey), while prejudice toward drug addicts experienced a small increase.

Table 4-2. Tolerance of diversity over time.
Proportion rejecting *people of a different race* by age cohort in 1990 & 2005.
% saying they would *not* want to have as neighbors.

	1901-1924		1925-1944		1945-1964		3rd Wave Generation		
							1965-1974		1975-1990
	1990[1]	2005	1990[1]	2005	1990[1]	2005	1990[1]	2005	2005
Established Democracies									
Britain	11	10	9	6	7	5	4	4	3
Finland	24	19	31	15*	22	11*	29	11*	12
France	15	41*	11	34*	8	24*	6	16*	15
Italy			15	18	8	11*	9	9	6
Netherlands	20	23	11	12	4	7*	2	6*	8
Spain	18	6	12	7*	8	6	6	6	6
Sweden	3	0	6	2*	2	2	1	1	0
Switzerland	5	13*	2	8*	2	6*	1	4*	2
US	12	6	9	4*	7	3*	12	5*	4
W. Germany	18	12	12	10	6	8	7	7	6
mean	14	14	12	12	7	8*	8	7	6
New Democracies									
Argentina	3	8	4	4	3	2	1	1	2
Brazil			3	4	4	3	1	4*	6
Bulgaria			43	25*	36	20*	34	20*	17
Chile	12	8	16	15	8	6	10	8	6
E. Germany	19	14	14	7*	8	5*	10	8	10
Mexico	30	27	14	12	16	8*	18	7*	8
Peru			12	6*	12	7*	10	6*	5
Poland	36	27	28	19*	17	13*	9	11	7
Romania	34	17*	29	24*	30	18*	20	18	11
Russia			12	36*	10	30*	10	29*	32
S. Korea			46	49	59	43*	70	30*	16
Slovenia	52	34*	35	28*	42	13*	40	11*	6
Taiwan	31	27	17	30*	7	10			2
Turkey			43	49	34	26*	26	28	27
Uruguay	7	11	9	4	8	5*	4	3	3
mean	25	19	22	21*	20	14*	19	13*	10

* mean difference, $p < .05$
100% = not mention + mention within each cohort.
[1] 1995 wave used for Sweden, Brazil, Peru, Poland, Taiwan and Uruguay.
Source: World Values Surveys.

in new democracies, from 14 to 21 percent rejected having people of another race as neighbors in 2005-2007. Intolerance toward people of a different race seems to be undergoing an intergenerational decline.

The younger generations in established democracies also show higher tolerance levels toward people of different race than do the old. But in contrast to the newer democracies, racial tolerance remained relatively constant over time. Although this pattern tends to produce convergence between the racial tolerance levels of the two groups of nations (especially within the younger Third Wave group, where there was only a four-point gap in 2005), racial tolerance is still significantly higher among the established democracies than in the new democracies.

Tolerance toward foreign workers

Tolerance toward immigrants or foreign workers is qualitatively different from tolerance toward people of a different race. Here, the respondent's attitudes are not only related to the 'neighborhood' dimension but also to the job market. This distinction may help explain some differences between new and established democracies in their trajectories over time with this variable. In the last two decades, most established democracies have experienced massive in-migration, which has interacted with high levels of unemployment to produce rising xenophobia in many countries. But in-migration has been negligible in virtually all of the new democracies. Consequently, while the presence of foreign workers has become a sensitive issue in most established democracies, in new democracies this phenomenon has very low salience.

As with tolerance toward people of a different race, tolerance toward foreign workers in the new democracies increased in all cohorts, apart from those born from 1925 to 1944. The percentage of people saying would not like to have foreign workers as neighbors fell from 20 percent to 15 percent among the Third Wave generation. Similar changes impacted the 1901-1924 and 1945-1964 generations. The evidence suggests that democratization has been conducive to growing tolerance of outgroups, and that it has had roughly equal impact on all birth cohorts. Nevertheless, the young continue to be more tolerant than the old—apparently for other reasons than democratization.

Argentina, Uruguay, Brazil and Peru are characterized by relatively high levels of tolerance, similar to those in Switzerland, Sweden and Spain. And the least tolerant societies among the new democracies are, again, Turkey, Russia and South Korea. Although the Third Wave generation is more tolerant than their elders, in these countries, about 30 percent of this generation's respondents are not willing to accept foreign workers as neighbors.

In the established democracies we find a very different pattern. A negative shift took place across all generations, with intolerance of foreign workers increasing by five to six points. In some countries this effect was particularly strong. This phenomenon was strongest in France, where xenophobia rose dramatically across all generations, reaching levels by 2005 that were three times as high as they were in 1990.

Rising intolerance toward foreign workers in established democracies reflects the effects of globalization and technological changes that have produced much higher levels of unemployment than those that existed a few decades ago—and unemployment is dramatically higher among the young than among older respondents, largely neutralizing

Table 4-3. Tolerance of diversity over time.
Immigrants or foreign workers by age cohort in 1990 & 2005.
% saying they would *not* want to have as neighbors.

| | 1901-1924 | | 1925-1944 | | 1945-1964 | | 3rd Wave Generation |||
| | | | | | | | 1965-1974 || 1975-1990 |
	1990[1]	2005	1990[1]	2005	1990[1]	2005	1990[1]	2005	2005
Established Democracies									
Britain	18	31*	10	21*	9	13*	5	13*	11
Finland	10	29*	4	24*	3	16*	10	14*	12
France	18	50*	17	44*	10	37*	8	33*	30
Italy			18	21*	10	15*	10	12	7
Netherlands	24	23	12	11	5	9*	4	8*	10
Spain	16	6	10	5*	7	8	6	7	5
Sweden	6	0	7	3*	4	2*	2	4	1
Switzerland	3	9*	2	7*	1	7*	2	7*	6
US	12	21*	11	17*	8	11*	10	14*	14
W. Germany	24	15	16	13	13	11	15	14	11
mean	15	20*	11	17*	7	13*	7	13*	11
New Democracies									
Argentina	1	0	2	3	3	2	1	3*	4
Brazil			2	7*	5	6	2	7*	7
Bulgaria	39	14*	40	23*	32	17*	27	15*	16
Chile	12	8	15	13	11	9	12	8*	7
E. Germany	23	36*	21	14*	15	13	19	17	15
Mexico	22	33	19	16	15	9*	20	8*	9
Peru			15	9*	9	7*	9	5*	5
Poland	31	18	27	16*	18	15	14	11	11
Romania	34	15*	32	22*	30	16*	28	13*	13
Russia			13	36*	11	30*	11	29*	32
S. Korea			46	38*	53	44*	63	36*	29
Slovenia	55	24*	34	27*	42	17*	43	14*	11
Taiwan			30	45*	21	21	20	17*	23
Turkey	35	0	33	35	27	30	25	29*	28
Uruguay	7	6	8	4*	6	6	7	6	5
mean	26	15	22	21	20	16*	20	15*	14

* mean difference, *p* < .05
100% = not mention + mention within each cohort.
[1] 1995 wave used for Sweden, Brazil, Peru, Poland, Taiwan and Uruguay.
Source: World Values Surveys.

the effects of cultural changes that otherwise tend to make younger generations relatively tolerant of diversity. Although the presence of foreign workers is not the root cause of unemployment, it symbolizes a genuine economic threat to the local population. This decline of tolerance occurred during a period of economic growth in the established democracies. It seems likely that the current international economic recession will give rise to even more adverse conditions for this aspect of social tolerance in consolidated democracies.

Tolerance toward homosexuality

As we have seen, tolerance toward homosexuality is much lower than tolerance toward foreign workers or people of a different race. This is the case both in established democracies and, even more so, in newer regimes. But intolerance of homosexuality declined across all age groups, including the Third Wave generations. Here again, we find evidence that democratization affects not only the younger generations but society as a whole. Tolerance increased by 14 points among the Third Wave generation, by 12 points among those born in 1945-1964, by eight points in the next older cohort (1925-1944) and by 12 points among the oldest group. Nevertheless, the Third Wave generation is markedly more tolerant than the older ones. In 2005-2007, rejection of homosexuals was expressed by 35 percent of the youngest age group in the new democracies, and by 53 percent of the oldest cohort .

Tolerance of homosexuality rose in all new democracies, but in some far more than others. In South American countries (Argentina, Brazil, Uruguay, and also Chile and Peru) tolerance rose at a higher rate than in Eastern and Central European nations. Indeed, in some European countries negative attitudes remain very strong, even among the Third Wave generation. This is true of Turkey, where 90 percent reject homosexuals as potential neighbors, in Russia where 62 percent do so, in Romania (with 56 percent) and in Bulgaria (with 51 percent).

Although the publics of established democracies showed growing rejection of foreign workers, they have become increasingly tolerant toward homosexuals, with the old changing almost as much as the young. Among the youngest age groups there was a 9 points reduction in rejection of homosexuality from 1990 and 2005, all of the other generations experienced a 7 points decrease. But because the younger birth cohorts already were much more tolerant of homosexuality in 1990 than were the old (and have remained much more tolerant), the change was proportionally greater among the young than among the old: among the youngest cohort, rejection of homosexuality fell from 21 percent to only 12 percent (a 43% decline); while among the oldest group, it fell from 41 percent to 34 percent (a 16% decline).

The Overall Tolerance Index

The Tolerance Index shows the overall pattern of change in tolerance of diversity from 1990 to 2005-2007. The changes take very distinct trajectories in the new democracies, as compared with the established democracies. While a significant increase in tolerance took place in the new democracies following the transition to democracy, there was little overall change in the established democracies, largely because rising tolerance of homosexuality was offset by rising rejection of foreign workers.

Table 4-4. Tolerance of diversity over time.
Rejection of *Homosexuals* by age cohort in 1990 & 2005.
% saying they would *not* want to have as neighbors.

	1901-1924		1925-1944		1945-1964		3rd Wave Generation		
							1965-1974		1975-1990
	1990[1]	2005	1990[1]	2005	1990[1]	2005	1990[1]	2005	2005
Established Democracies									
Britain	51	49	37	28*	26	12*	18	15	8
Finland	33	57*	33	32	21	22	30	18*	15
France	42	47	28	49*	21	29*	14	19	17
Italy			46	32*	30	25	26	16*	11
Netherlands	29	8*	13	10	5	3*	10	4*	4
Spain	46	29*	37	10*	22	7*	21	6*	3
Sweden	26	5*	15	10*	9	2*	4	3	2
Switzerland									
US	50	56	36	36	34	24*	40	21*	21
W. Germany	51	24*	38	21*	27	11*	21	10*	10
mean	**41**	**34***	**32**	**25***	**22**	**15***	**21**	**12***	**10**
New Democracies									
Argentina	53	38	45	30*	35	11*	30	9*	12
Brazil			32	31	27	22*	23	18*	20
Bulgaria	66	43	65	53*	71	50*	65	51*	43
Chile	69	31*	58	41*	55	37*	58	31*	25
E. Germany	50	32	38	22*	26	13*	31	14*	12
Mexico	70	80	72	39*	57	35*	57	27*	24
Peru			57	53	56	48*	53	42*	37
Poland	75	59*	74	63*	67	53*	57	47*	43
Romania	80	57	82	65*	75	61*	67	56*	51
Russia			81	70*	81	67*	79	62*	63
S. Korea									
Slovenia	45	55	42	53*	42	36*	45	25*	24
Taiwan	70	60	71	88*	63	66			29
Turkey	87	100	93	94	93	93	89	90	83
Uruguay	52	33*	35	20*	27	17*	22	18*	20
mean	**65**	**53***	**60**	**52***	**55**	**43***	**52**	**38***	**35**

* mean difference, $p < .05$
100% = not mention + mention within each cohort.
[1] 1995 wave used for Sweden, Brazil, Peru, Poland, Taiwan and Uruguay.
Source: World Values Surveys.

Table 4-5. Tolerance of diversity over time.
Tolerance Index by age cohort in 1990 & 2005.
% *"Tolerants"*

	1901-1924		1925-1944		1945-1964		3rd Wave Generation		
							1965-1974		1975-1990
	1990[1]	2005	1990[1]	2005	1990[1]	2005	1990[1]	2005	2005
Established Democracies									
Britain	44	38	57	58	68	76*	79	73*	78
Finland	43	29	55	54	63	68*	49	73*	75
France	55	29*	65	32*	75	51*	82	59*	61
Italy			43	47*	58	61*	61	69*	71
Netherlands	46	54	71	73	87	80*	84	84	82
Spain	39	65*	49	75*	67	80*	70	79*	86
Sweden	68	84*	82	84	88	96*	94	93	97
Switzerland	95	57*	97	78*	98	84*	98	89*	85
US	42	32	55	51*	60	68*	53	69*	71
W. Germany	40	65*	53	64*	67	78*	74	73	78
mean	**52**	**50**	**63**	**62**	**73**	**74**	**75**	**76**	**78**
New Democracies									
Argentina	41	62*	52	71*	64	89*	74	88*	88
Brazil			69	66	71	74	77	79*	74
Bulgaria	22	29	24	32*	22	37*	25	38*	38
Chile	31	69*	42	50*	45	59*	45	62*	73
E. Germany	45	50	56	68*	68	79*	65	74*	76
Mexico	22	27	21	55*	34	57*	31	67*	71
Peru			38	44*	38	47*	42	53*	59
Poland	21	32	22	26*	32	41*	43	46*	54
Romania	14	43*	17	32*	23	34*	33	42*	45
Russia			14	19*	18	22*	21	23	22
S. Korea									
Slovenia	39	31	41	35*	38	56*	35	71*	67
Taiwan	18	20	19	5*	27	15*			
Turkey			5	5	5	4	9	5*	11
Uruguay	43	56	65	75*	71	80*	80	81	87
mean	**30**	**42**	**35**	**42***	**40**	**50***	**45**	**56***	**59**

* mean difference, $p < .05$
100% = tolerants + ambivalents + intolerants within each cohort.
[1] 1995 wave used for Sweden, Brazil, Peru, Poland, Taiwan and Uruguay.
Source: World Values Surveys.

These findings suggest that democratization brings a more open society is conducive to rising tolerance of diversity. Moreover, it also indicates that increasing tolerance is not due to intergenerational population replacement. Although the younger generations are more tolerant than older ones, rising tolerance occurred among all age groups in the new democracies—but not in the established democracies (which nevertheless show large intergenerational differences that can not be attributed to the experiences of the past 15 years).

In both groups of nations, the younger generations are more tolerant than the older ones. This suggests that process of intergenerational change will tend to bring rising tolerance in the long run—other things being equal. Other things have not been equal in the established democracies in recent years, which have experienced rising unemployment juxtaposed with massive immigration that has been widely seen as the cause of rising unemployment. In some new democracies the younger generations still show very low levels of tolerance. The paradigmatic case is Turkey, where the percentage of "Tolerants" is only 11 percent and 5 percent among two segments of the Third Wave generation. Other relatively intolerant nations are Russia and Taiwan.

The years since 1990 have seen a clear tendency toward convergence between new and old democracies in the levels of tolerance found among each birth cohort, especially the Third Wave generation.

Discussion

Our analysis points to three main findings. (1) Tolerance toward diversity rose in most countries from 1990 to 2005. But the change mainly took place in the new democracies, which have been converging toward the still-higher levels found in the established democracies; (2) The Third Wave generation is substantially more tolerant than its older compatriots; and (3) Change occurred across all age groups, with the rate of change being only slightly greater among the younger cohorts in new democracies, than among the older cohorts.

Let's discuss each point. First, we found a rather coherent pattern of increasing in tolerance in new democracies, but not in established democracies. Almost all of the new democracies experienced positive shifts on all three forms of tolerance examined here; in the established democracies, tolerance toward homosexuality increased, tolerance toward people of a different race remained stable, and tolerance toward foreign workers diminished. Accordingly, our overall measure of tolerance, the Tolerance Index, shows two distinct trajectories for old and new democracies since 1990.

Second, although tolerance in both old and new democracies is higher among the younger cohorts, the recent shifts can not be attributed solely to intergenerational change: rising tolerance occurred across all birth cohorts in the new democracies; while tolerance levels remained relatively constant across all cohorts in the established democracies. Neither life-cycle effects nor intergenerational population replacement could fully explain this pattern. There are clear indications of significant period effects.

Third, the publics of the established democracies are substantially more tolerant than those of the new democracies despite the recent changes examined here. But the publics of the new democracies have been rising toward the tolerance levels found in the established democracies, at a rate the suggests that long-term convergence is likely.

These findings suggest, but do not prove, that democratization is conducive to rising tolerance of social diversity. It is clear that, during the years since 1990, tolerance rose substantially in the new democracies but only very slightly in the established democracies. This suggests that democratization caused the change. But an alternative interpretation is possible—that a rising sense of security is conducive to an intergenerational shift toward greater tolerance. This would explain (1) why the younger cohorts are more tolerant than the older ones, in both new and old democracies; and (2) why the established democracies, despite recent trends, are substantially more tolerant than the new democracies. But recent economic conditions have superimposed different period effects on these generational differences: while the established democracies experienced rising unemployment and massive immigration (much of it from the new democracies), most of the new democracies experienced significant economic improvement and little or no immigration. As a result, although the publics of the established democracies became more tolerant of gays and lesbians, they became less tolerant of foreign workers, with the two effects largely neutralizing each other on the overall Tolerance Index. Rising hostility to foreign workers was generally absent in the new democracies, which show a significant recent increase in overall tolerance.

The two interpretations are not inconsistent, and both may contribute to the observed findings. In any event, the evidence examined here indicates that changes in tolerance of diversity (in contrast to the post-honeymoon decline of political trust and political participation discussed in Inglehart and Catterberg, 2003) are not necessarily related to economic performance. In fact, Mexico and Argentina, two countries affected by recurrent economic turmoil, experienced the largest increases on the Tolerance Index among the new democracies. Moreover, recent studies indicate that this upward shift in tolerance after regime change has not been an isolated phenomenon but rather part of a broader trend of support for self-expression values and individual freedom among younger generations in newer regimes (Siemienska, Basanez, and Moreno, 2010).

Our findings suggest transitions to democracy may be conducive to increasing tolerance of racial and other forms of diversity. It is clear that the publics of the new democracies have been becoming more tolerant, converging with the publics of the established democracies in this respect. This is definitely good news for the Third Wave democracies.

APPENDIX

Table 4-A1. Tolerance toward diversity over time. Totals by country.

	Different race[1]			Immigrants[1]			Homosexuals[1]		
	% said would not have as neighbors								
	1990[2]	2005	Change	1990[2]	2005	Change	1990[2]	2005	Change
Established Democracies								
Britain	8	7	−1*	11	20	9*	33	26	−7*
Finland	27	14	−13*	7	21	14*	29	32	3
France	10	29	19*	13	41	28*	26	36	10*
Italy	11	13	2*	13	16	3*	34	24	−10*
Netherlands	9	12	3	11	13	2	14	6	−8*
Spain	11	6	−5*	10	7	−3*	32	13	−19*
Sweden	3	1	−2*	5	2	−3*	14	5	−9*
Switzerland	2	8	6*	2	7	5*			
US	10	4	−6*	10	16	6*	40	34	−6*
W. Germany	11	9	−2	17	13	−4*	34	16	−18*
mean	**10**	**10**	**0**	**10**	**16**	**6***	**29**	**22**	**−7***
New Democracies								
Argentina	3	4	1	2	2	0	41	22	−19*
Brazil	3	4	1	3	6	3*	27	23	−4*
Bulgaria	38	22	−16*	34	17	−17*	67	49	−18*
Chile	12	9	−3	12	10	−2	60	35	−25*
E. Germany	13	8	−5*	19	20	1*	36	20	−16*
Mexico	19	14	−6*	19	17	−2*	64	45	−19*
Peru	11	7	−4*	11	7	−4*	55	48	−7*
Poland	23	17	−6*	23	15	−8*	68	56	−12*
Romania	28	19	−9*	31	16	−15*	76	60	−16*
Russia	11	32	21*	12	32	20*	81	66	−15*
S. Korea	58	41	−17*	54	39	−16*			
Slovenia	42	21	−21*	43	21	−22*	43	42	−1*
Taiwan	19	17	−2	24	26	2*	68	65	−3*
Turkey	34	34	0	30	23	−7*	90	94	4
Uruguay	7	6	−1*	7	5	−2	34	22	−12*
mean	**21**	**17**	**−4***	**22**	**17**	**−5***	**58**	**47**	**−11***

* $p < .05$
[1] 100% = mention+not mention
[2] 1995 wave used for Sweden, Brazil, Peru, Poland, Taiwan and Uruguay.
Source: World Values Surveys.

REFERENCES

Catterberg, Edgardo. 1991. *Argentina Confronts Politics: Political Culture and Public Opinion in the Argentine Transition to Democracy*. Boulder: Lynne Rienner.

Catterberg, Gabriela, Alejandro Moreno, and Ignacio Zuasnabar. 2008. "What do we measure when we ask attitudes towards corruption in Latin America? Survey evidence from Argentina, Mexico, and Uruguay." Paper prepared for 61st WAPOR conference, New Orleans, May 14-15.

Gibson, James. 1998. "A Sober Second Thought: An Experiment in Persuading Russians to Tolerate," *American Journal of Political Science*, 42, July, 819-850.

Huntington, Samuel. 1997. "After Twenty Years: the Fuuure of the Third Wave," *Journal of Democracy*, 8:4, 3-12.

Inglehart, Ronald. 1997. *Modernization and Post-Modernization*. Princeton: Princeton University Press.

Inglehart, Ronald. 2003. "How Solid is Mass Support for Democracy— And How Do We Measure It ?" *PS: Political Science and Politics,* January, 2003:51-57.

Inglehart, Ronald and Christian Welzel. 2005. Modernization, Cultural Change and Democracy. New York: Cambridge University Press.

Inglehart, Ronald and Gabriela Catterberg. 2003. "Cultural Change and the Rise of Participatory Publics." *International Journal of Comparative Sociology.* 44:1: pp. 300-316. March, 2003.

Niemi, Richard and Mary Hepburn. 1995. "The Rebirth of Political Socialization," *Perspectives on Political Science,* 24:1.

Niemi, Richard, Edgardo Catterberg, Frank Bell, and Roxana Morduchowicz. 1996. "Teaching Political Information and Democratic Values in a New Democracy: An Argentine Experiment", *Comparative Politics,* July, 465-476.

Norris, Pippa. 2002. *Democratic Phoenix: Reinventing Political Activism*. Cambridge: Cambridge University Press.

Norris, Pippa, ed. 1999. *Critical Citizens: Global Support for Democratic Governance*. Cambridge: Cambridge University Press.

Sapiro, Virginia. 2004. "Not your parents' political socialization: introduction for a new generation," *Annual Review of Political Science,* 7, 1-23.

Sartori, Giovanni. 2001. *La Sociedad Multietnica. Pluralismo, Multiculturalismo, y Extranjeros*. Madrid: Taurus.

Siemienska, Renata, Miguel Basanez and Alejandro Moreno. 2010. "Generational Differences in Support for Democracy and Free Market Economics: Evidence from New and Established Democracies," in Miguel Basanez et al., *Changing Human Values and Beliefs*. Mexico City: Siglo XXI..

Szabo, Mate. 1991. "Political Socialization in Hungary," in Dekker and Meyenberg (eds.) *Politics and the European Younger Generations*. Oldenburg: Bibliotheks.

Uslaner, Eric. 2004. "Coping and Social Capital: The Informal Sector and the Democratic Transition." Paper prepared for the "Unlocking Human Potential: Linking the Formal and Informal Sectors Conference" Helsinki, Finland, September 17-18.

Working with the Values Surveys files

Jaime Diez-Medrano *WVS Archive – ASEP/JDS*

Introduction

The World Values Survey / European Value Study dataset has grown over time as new waves are added with new or repeating countries. As it expands over time and space, its value to researchers interested in social change and comparative analysis increases geometrically— but it has become a complex tool that requires some mastering.

Every day, the WVS archive responds to many questions from researchers around the world. Most of these questions deal with weighting, special indexes and wave merging issues: Which variable should be used? Why are there so many? How are they calculated within countries? How are the post-materialist and autonomy indexes built? How can I merge the 2005-2007 wave with the previous combined four-wave data base?

This chapter seeks to answer these questions, and to introduce users to some new concepts such as the *population balanced weight*. We will use syntax examples to illustrate the procedures or else refer the reader to documents that can be downloaded from the internet site at www.worldvaluessurveys.org.

Working with weighted samples in the Values Studies

The World Values Surveys consist of representative national samples, apart from Chile and Argentina, where standard sampling excludes the southern part of each country, which is large but sparsely populated. Similarly, normal sampling practice for representative national samples in the U.S. (including the National Election Studies) omits Alaska, which is larger than Germany, Great Britain and France combined, but so sparsely populated that inclusion would not be cost-effective and its omission does not substantially change the results. The WVS has also carried out regional surveys, covering Valencia, Galicia, Andalusia and the Basque Country in Spain; and Moscow and Tambov oblast in Russia. These were distributed with the 1995 dataset but to avoid confusion, they are no longer included with the official WVS releases.

The official four-Wave Values Survey, that can be downloaded from the WVS site www.worldvaluessurveys.org includes six different weighting variables. One immediately wonders which one to use. The existing variables are:

S017 – S017A	Original country weight
S018 – S018A	1000-equilibrated weight
S019 – S019A	1500-equilibrated weight

Original country weight

S017 is the original weight provided by each participating country. The purpose of S017 is to compensate for **small** deviations in the resulting sample with respect to one or more important dimensions. These dimensions can be the sex-age distribution, the rural-urban distribution, or the respondent education's distribution. The weighting method is decided by each participant country. In general, it is not good practice to use weighting to compensate for large deviations from the target figures.

Whatever the criteria chosen, the procedure to compute weighting factors is similar. Usually, a matrix is defined with the estimated proportion of each combination of categories that the sample contains. This estimate may come from the census or other sources. This is the **target** distribution matrix. Then, the **actual** distribution of each combination of categories is calculated for the given sample. The weight is, by definition, the matrix of factors that should be multiplied by the actual sample matrix to obtain the target matrix's distribution.

An example illustrates this for a simple Sex-Age weighting.

- First, we write down the sex-age distribution according to the census (for example):

Target sample	Male	Female
18-29	11,8%	11,3%
30-49	18,5%	18,3%
50-64	9,5%	9,9%
65 and more	8,8%	12,0%

- Second, we write down the sex-age distribution of the actual sample, resulting from field-work:

Actual sample	Male	Female
18-29	10,1%	9,8%
30-49	20,7%	19,3%
50-64	9,9%	10,4%
65 and more	8,8%	11,0%

- And, third, we calculate the weighting matrix to be applied in order to correct the sample:

Weight factors	Male	Female
18-29	1.1710	1.1491
30-49	0.8902	0.9482
50-64	0.9559	0.9570
65 and more	0.9940	1.0927

In this example, the value 1.1710 obtained for (18-29,Male) results from dividing 11.8% (the target percentage of Males of 18-29 years) by 10.1%, the actual percentage, as calculated on the data file. So each respondent record corresponding to males aged 18 to 29 should count as 1.1710 instead of 1 case.

This method *preserves the sample size*. This means that if the file had an N of 1200 cases, then using the weighting factors calculated above will still give an N of 1200 cases.

The WVS site (www.worldvaluessurveys.org) includes the *Technical Information* and *Documentation of Data* special sections with methodology information at the country sample level. You will find there the specific criteria followed for calculating the weight, if any.

Original country weight 1000-balanced and 1500-balanced

S018 and **S019** are both weighting factors derived from S017 whose goal is to transform the sample's N to 1000 or 1500. Making all sample's N equal may serve several purposes.

The first one is to make all samples have equal impact in a combined analysis. In WVS2005 India's sample is 2001 while US's sample is 1249. Using S017 as a weight in a combined analysis India would count more than the US because their total N is bigger. Using S018, which is proportional to S017, both samples would show 1000 cases (and 1500 if using S019).

The second reason for creating S018 is that it helps building a population scaled weight. A population scaled weight is a one that gives an N for each country equal to the population size of the region covered by the sample. With such a weight, India's N would now be 1,165,720,000 and US's N would be 306,790,000 (using 2009 estimates of their respective populations). In this way, US and India would count differently in a combined analysis, but at least there would be a criteria for this difference in weight.

In general, S018 can be used to compute any special weight that ranks countries in any quantified dimension (economic, cultural, and so on).

The formula for such a weight is simple:

$$W_{country} = S018/1000 \times Population_{country}$$

Note that for most statistical analysis the influence of the country Ns will not matter much. Also, when comparing relative figures by country there is no impact at all of the country N, since relative figures will not change at the country level.

Building a population based weight for the four-wave dataset

The four-wave aggregate that can be downloaded from the World Values Survey site doesn't include any population oriented weight. It's up to the researcher to build it.

In order to help users, here is the syntax, in SPSS style for building such a variable.

COMPUTE POPWEIGHT=0.
FORMAT POPWEIGHT (F15.5).

IF (S003=8) POPWEIGHT=S018/1000*3639459. /*Albania*/
IF (S003=12) POPWEIGHT=S018/1000*33769669. /*Algeria*/
IF (S003=20) POPWEIGHT=S018/1000*887000. /*Andorra*/
IF (S003=31) POPWEIGHT=S018/1000*8238672. /*Azerbaijan*/
IF (S003=32) POPWEIGHT=S018/1000*40135000. /*Argentina*/
IF (S003=36) POPWEIGHT=S018/1000*21831000. /*Australia*/
IF (S003=40) POPWEIGHT=S018/1000*8356707. /*Austria*/
IF (S003=50) POPWEIGHT=S018/1000*150448340. /*Bangladesh*/
IF (S003=51) POPWEIGHT=S018/1000*3230100. /*Armenia*/
IF (S003=56) POPWEIGHT=S018/1000*10741000. /*Belgium*/
IF (S003=70) POPWEIGHT=S018/1000*3981239. /*Bosnia and Herzegovina*/
IF (S003=76) POPWEIGHT=S018/1000*191403000. /* Brazil*/
IF (S003=100) POPWEIGHT=S018/1000*7602100. /* Bulgaria*/
IF (S003=112) POPWEIGHT=S018/1000*9671900. /*Belarus*/
IF (S003=124) POPWEIGHT=S018/1000*33698000. /*Canada*/
IF (S003=152) POPWEIGHT=S018/1000*16929000. /*Chile*/
IF (S003=156) POPWEIGHT=S018/1000*1331540000. /*China*/
IF (S003=158) POPWEIGHT=S018/1000*23027672. /*Taiwan*/
IF (S003=170) POPWEIGHT=S018/1000*44981000. /*Colombia*/
IF (S003=191) POPWEIGHT=S018/1000*4432000. /*Croatia*/
IF (S003=196) POPWEIGHT=S018/1000*8016. /*Cyprus*/
IF (S003=203) POPWEIGHT=S018/1000*10474600. /*Czech Republic*/
IF (S003=208) POPWEIGHT=S018/1000*5515287. /*Denmark*/
IF (S003=214) POPWEIGHT=S018/1000*9365818. /*Dominican Republic*/
IF (S003=222) POPWEIGHT=S018/1000*7185218. /*El Salvador*/
IF (S003=231) POPWEIGHT=S018/1000*79221000. /*Ethiopia*/
IF (S003=233) POPWEIGHT=S018/1000*1340341. /*Estonia*/
IF (S003=246) POPWEIGHT=S018/1000*5337719. /*Finland*/
IF (S003=250) POPWEIGHT=S018/1000*65073482. /*France*/
IF (S003=268) POPWEIGHT=S018/1000*4382100. /*Georgia*/
IF (S003=276) POPWEIGHT=S018/1000*82062200. /*Germany*/
IF (S003=288) POPWEIGHT=S018/1000*23416500. /*Ghana*/
IF (S003=300) POPWEIGHT=S018/1000*11262500. /*Greece*/
IF (S003=320) POPWEIGHT=S018/1000*13000000. /*Guatemala*/
IF (S003=344) POPWEIGHT=S018/1000*7008900. /*Hong Kong*/
IF (S003=348) POPWEIGHT=S018/1000*10029900. /*Hungary*/
IF (S003=352) POPWEIGHT=S018/1000*319326. /*Iceland*/
IF (S003=356) POPWEIGHT=S018/1000*1165720000. /*India*/
IF (S003=360) POPWEIGHT=S018/1000*230512000. /*Indonesia*/
IF (S003=364) POPWEIGHT=S018/1000*70495782. /*Iran*/
IF (S003=368) POPWEIGHT=S018/1000*31234000. /*Iraq*/
IF (S003=372) POPWEIGHT=S018/1000*4517800. /*Ireland*/
IF (S003=376) POPWEIGHT=S018/1000*7411500. /*Israel*/
IF (S003=380) POPWEIGHT=S018/1000*60090400. /*Italy*/
IF (S003=392) POPWEIGHT=S018/1000*127580000. /*Japan*/
IF (S003=400) POPWEIGHT=S018/1000*6198677. /*Jordan*/
IF (S003=410) POPWEIGHT=S018/1000*48379392. /*South Korea*/

IF (S003=417) POPWEIGHT=S018/1000*5356869. /*Kyrgyzstan*/
IF (S003=428) POPWEIGHT=S018/1000*2256400. /*Latvia*/
IF (S003=440) POPWEIGHT=S018/1000*3350400. /*Lithuania*/
IF (S003=442) POPWEIGHT=S018/1000*4917000. /*Luxembourg*/
IF (S003=458) POPWEIGHT=S018/1000*27730000. /*Malaysia*/
IF (S003=466) POPWEIGHT=S018/1000*12000000. /*Mali*/
IF (S003=470) POPWEIGHT=S018/1000*4126000. /*Malta*/
IF (S003=484) POPWEIGHT=S018/1000*109955400. /*Mexico*/
IF (S003=498) POPWEIGHT=S018/1000*3572700. /*Moldova*/
IF (S003=504) POPWEIGHT=S018/1000*31491578. /*Morocco*/
IF (S003=528) POPWEIGHT=S018/1000*16517532. /*Netherlands*/
IF (S003=554) POPWEIGHT=S018/1000*4314100. /*New Zealand*/
IF (S003=566) POPWEIGHT=S018/1000*140003542. /*Nigeria*/
IF (S003=578) POPWEIGHT=S018/1000*4825300. /*Norway*/
IF (S003=586) POPWEIGHT=S018/1000*166783500. /*Pakistan*/
IF (S003=604) POPWEIGHT=S018/1000*29180900. /*Peru*/
IF (S003=608) POPWEIGHT=S018/1000*90500000. /*Philippines*/
IF (S003=616) POPWEIGHT=S018/1000*38130300. /*Poland*/
IF (S003=620) POPWEIGHT=S018/1000*10631800. /*Portugal*/
IF (S003=630) POPWEIGHT=S018/1000*3916632. /*Puerto Rico*/
IF (S003=642) POPWEIGHT=S018/1000*21496700. /*Romania*/
IF (S003=643) POPWEIGHT=S018/1000*141837000. /*Russian Federation*/
IF (S003=646) POPWEIGHT=S018/1000*8648248. /*Rwanda*/
IF (S003=682) POPWEIGHT=S018/1000*27601038. /*Saudi Arabia*/
IF (S003=702) POPWEIGHT=S018/1000*4839400. /*Singapore*/
IF (S003=703) POPWEIGHT=S018/1000*5413548. /*Slovakia*/
IF (S003=704) POPWEIGHT=S018/1000*86116559. /*Vietnam*/
IF (S003=705) POPWEIGHT=S018/1000*2053355. /*Slovenia*/
IF (S003=710) POPWEIGHT=S018/1000*48697000. /*South Africa*/
IF (S003=716) POPWEIGHT=S018/1000*13349000. /*Zimbabwe*/
IF (S003=724) POPWEIGHT=S018/1000*45828172. /*Spain*/
IF (S003=752) POPWEIGHT=S018/1000*9276509. /*Sweden*/
IF (S003=756) POPWEIGHT=S018/1000*7725200. /*Switzerland*/
IF (S003=764) POPWEIGHT=S018/1000*63389730. /*Thailand*/
IF (S003=780) POPWEIGHT=S018/1000*1047366. /*Trinidad and Tobago*/
IF (S003=792) POPWEIGHT=S018/1000*71517100. /*Turkey*/
IF (S003=800) POPWEIGHT=S018/1000*29592700. /*Uganda*/
IF (S003=804) POPWEIGHT=S018/1000*46143700. /*Ukraine*/
IF (S003=807) POPWEIGHT=S018/1000*2048900. /*Macedonia*/
IF (S003=818) POPWEIGHT=S018/1000*76797512. /*Egypt*/
IF (S003=826) POPWEIGHT=S018/1000*59175000. /*Great Britain*/
IF (S003=834) POPWEIGHT=S018/1000*40213160. /*Tanzania*/
IF (S003=840) POPWEIGHT=S018/1000*306790000. /*United States*/
IF (S003=854) POPWEIGHT=S018/1000*13228000. /*Burkina Faso*/
IF (S003=858) POPWEIGHT=S018/1000*3477778. /*Uruguay*/
IF (S003=862) POPWEIGHT=S018/1000*28359313. /*Venezuela*/
IF (S003=891) POPWEIGHT=S018/1000*10832545. /*Serbia and Montenegro*/

IF (S003=894) POPWEIGHT=S018/1000*11862740. /*Zambia*/
IF (S003=900) POPWEIGHT=S018/1000*61131000. /*Germany West*/
IF (S003=909) POPWEIGHT=S018/1000*1800000. /*Northern Ireland*/
EXECUTE.

To check the results, you should run frequencies for variable **S021**, which is the (Country - wave - study - set - year) variable. This is a variable that has a different value for each different sample.

Not surprisingly, the above frequencies show that several samples exist for each country. This reflects the fact that most countries have fielded surveys in several different waves. In a few cases, more than one survey was carried out in a given country in the same wave. This applies to Spain and Turkey, from which data are available from both the WVS and the EVS surveys, and for Morocco, where two surveys were fielded in 2001 to measure the impact of the September 11, 2001 terrorist strike.

When doing combined analysis using more than one sample per country, it is important to consider the impact of using such a weight. Corrections may be introduced to the mentioned syntax by dividing the weight by the number of times the country appears in the combined set to be analyzed. In general, this is left to the researcher's judgment.

S017A, S018A, S019A and other As

We have seen that S018 and S019 are variants of the main weight variable, which is S017. You may wonder what is the meaning of variables S017A, S018A, S019A, that also appear in the aggregate files.

The existence of these variables reflects an historical fact. Until 1990 West Germany and East Germany were two separate countries. The 1981 survey was carried out in West Germany only, so if one wishes to do analyses that cover the full time series from 1981 on, one needs to compare the results from the successive West German samples. This complicates the construction of the combined multi-wave dataset..

S003 could include codes for West and East Germany, as well as for the new unified Germany. But this would prevent researchers from doing time-series analysis for Germany, since waves 1 and 2 were carried out in different countries. The solution adopted was to merge East and West Germany (with weight correction to correct for oversampling of East Germany) and to code the country as Germany in S003 (code 276). This could only be made of course when both countries were available in the same wave. For 1981, however, only West Germany was fielded and S003 reflects it with a different code (900).

In order to allow analysis of East and West Germany separately (for example, if one is interested in measuring to what extent their publics continue to have distinct values) S003A was constructed with these samples coded as 900 (West Germany) and 901 (East Germany), that is with Germany split.

Since weights were corrected when merging 1990 East and West Germany, or when splitting Germany in 1995 and later surveys, the alternate weight had to be coded in S017A. As for S018A and S019A, they are the 1000 and 1500 balanced versions of S017A. Similarly, S021A, S024A and S025A are special versions of S021, S024, S025 for the split Germany. In future releases of the dataset, these variables may disappear, allowing East/West Germany to be differentiated by the region codes.

Creating a merged "five-wave" aggregate of the Values Surveys

The WVS2005 data file is based on a new wave of the World Values Survey carried out in 2005-2007. It includes data from 57 countries around the world.

The files distributed for this dataset use a naming convention that corresponds to the official WVS2005 questionnaire, and so it is not compatible with the combined four-wave dataset produced jointly by WVS and EVS. In order to merge the WVS2005 dataset with the four-wave aggregate to carry out time series analysis across all five waves, a conversion of the file is necessary. This conversion can be done by using an SPSS syntax that is available from the *Additional documents* section of the WVS site (www.worldvaluessurveys.org).

Of the 395 variables of the WVS2005, 155 are new, and 240 are replicated from earlier surveys, making it possible to perform time series with previous four-wave variables. The table below summarizes how the WVS2005 variables correspond to variables in the combined four-wave dataset:

4-wave aggregate variables	Label	WVS2005 variables	Comments
S002	Wave	V1	Set to 5
S003 / S003A	Country/region	V2 / V2A	Recode using the correspondence of WVS country codes and four-wave country codes
S006	Original respondent number	V3	
A001	Important in life: Family	V4	
A002	Important in life: Friends	V5	
A003	Important in life: Leisure time	V6	
A004	Important in life: Politics	V7	
A005	Important in life: Work	V8	
A006	Important in life: Religion	V9	
A008	Feeling of happiness	V10	
A009	State of health (subjective)	V11	
A029	Important child qualities: independence	V12	
A030	Important child qualities: hard work	V13	
A032	Important child qualities: feeling of responsibility	V14	
A034	Important child qualities: imagination	V15	Recode 2 as 0
A035	Important child qualities: tolerance and respect for other people	V16	
A038	Important child qualities: thrift saving money and things	V17	

Working with the Values Surveys files

4-wave aggregate variables	Label	WVS2005 variables	Comments
A039	Important child qualities: determination perseverance	V18	
A040	Important child qualities: religious faith	V19	Recode 2 as 0
A041	Important child qualities: unselfishness	V20	
A042	Important child qualities: obedience	V21	
A170	Satisfaction with your life	V22	
A165	Most people can be trusted	V23	
A098	Active/Inactive membership of church or religious organization	V24	
A099	Active/Inactive membership of sport or recreation	V25	
A100	Active/Inactive membership of art, music, educational	V26	
A101	Active/Inactive membership of labour unions	V27	
A102	Active/Inactive membership of political party	V28	
A103	Active/Inactive membership of environmental organization	V29	
A104	Active/Inactive membership of professional organization	V30	
A105	Active/Inactive membership of charitable/ humanitarian organization	V31	
A106	Active/Inactive membership of any other organization	V33	
A124_08	Neighbours: Drug addicts	V34	
A124_02	Neighbours: People of a different race	V35	
A124_07	Neighbours: People who have AIDS	V36	
A124_06	Neighbours: Immigrants/foreign workers	V37	Recode 2 as 0
A124_09	Neighbours: Homosexuals	V38	
A124_12	Neighbours: People of a different religion	V39	
A124_03	Neighbours: Heavy drinkers	V40	
A124_14	Neighbours: Militant minority	V43	
C001	Jobs scarce: Men should have more right to a job than women	V44	Recode 2 as 3, 3 as 2
C002	Jobs scarce: Employers should give priority to (nation) people than immigrants	V45	Recode 2 as 3, 3 as 2
A173	How much freedom of choice and control	V46	

4-wave aggregate variables	Label	WVS2005 variables	Comments
C009	First choice, if looking for a job	V48	
C010	Second choice if looking for a job	V49	
C036	To develop talents you need to have a job	V50	
C037	Humiliating to receive money without having to work for it	V51	
C038	People who don´t work turn lazy	V52	
C039	Work is a duty towards society	V53	
C041	Work should come first even if it means less spare time	V54	
X007	Marital status	V55	
X011	How many children do you have	V56	
D018	Child needs a home with father and mother	V57	Recode 2 as 0
D022	Marriage is an out-dated institution	V58	Recode 2 as 0
D023	Woman as a single parent	V59	Recode 2 as 0, 3 as 2
D057	Being a housewife just as fulfilling	V60	
D059	Men make better political leaders than women do	V61	
D060	University is more important for a boy than for a girl	V62	
D054	One of main goals in life has been to make my parents proud	V64	
D055	Make effort to live up to what my friends expect	V66	
C006	Satisfaction with financial situation of household	V68	
E001	Aims of country: first choice	V69	
E002	Aims of country: second choice	V70	
E003	Aims of respondent: first choice	V71	
E004	Aims of respondent: second choice	V72	
E005	Most important: first choice	V73	
E006	Most important: second choice	V74	
E012	Willingness to fight for country	V75	Recode 2 as 0
E015	Future changes: Less importance placed on work	V76	
E016	Future changes: More emphasis on technology	V77	

82 Working with the Values Surveys files

4-wave aggregate variables	Label	WVS2005 variables	Comments
E018	Future changes: Greater respect for authority	V78	
E019	Future changes: More emphasis on family life	V79	
E022	Opinion about scientific advances	V90	
E023	Interest in politics	V95	
E025	Political action: signing a petition	V96	
E026	Political action: joining in boycotts	V97	
E027	Political action: attending lawful/peaceful demonstrations	V98	
B008	Protecting environment vs. Economic growth	V104	
B001	Would give part of my income for the environment	V105	
B002	Increase in taxes if used to prevent environmental pollution	V106	
B003	Government should reduce environmental pollution	V107	
E033	Self positioning in political scale	V114	
C059	Fairness: One secretary is paid more	V115	Recode 2 as 0
E035	Income equality	V116	
E036	Private vs state ownership of business	V117	
E037	Government responsibility	V118	Invert 1 to 10 scale
E039	Competition good or harmful	V119	
E040	Hard work brings success	V120	
E041	Wealth accumulation	V121	
E143	Immigrant policy	V124	
D001	How much do you trust your family	V125	Recode 3 as 4, 4 as 5
G007_18	Trust: Your neighborhood	V126	Recode 3 as 4, 4 as 5
E069_01	Confidence: Churches	V131	
E069_02	Confidence: Armed Forces	V132	
E069_04	Confidence: The Press	V133	
E069_10	Confidence: Television	V134	
E069_05	Confidence: Labour Unions	V135	
E069_06	Confidence: The Police	V136	
E069_17	Confidence: Justice System	V137	
E069_11	Confidence: The Government	V138	

4-wave aggregate variables	Label	WVS2005 variables	Comments
E069_12	Confidence: The Political Parties	V139	
E069_07	Confidence: Parliament	V140	
E069_08	Confidence: The Civil Services	V141	
E069_13	Confidence: Major Companies	V142	
E069_14	Confidence: The Environmental Protection Movement	V143	
E069_15	Confidence: The Women´s Movement	V144	
E069_18	Confidence: The European Union	V146	
E069_20	Confidence: The United Nations	V147	
E114	Political system: Having a strong leader	V148	
E115	Political system: Having experts make decisions	V149	
E116	Political system: Having the army rule	V150	
E117	Political system: Having a democratic political system	V151	
E124	Respect for individual human rights nowadays	V164	
E135	Who should decide: international peacekeeping	V179	
E136	Who should decide: protection of the environment	V180	
E137	Who should decide: aid to developing countries	V181	Recode 3 as 2, 2 as 4, 4 as 3
E138	Who should decide: refugees	V182	
E139	Who should decide: human rights	V183	
F001	Thinking about meaning and purpose of life	V184	
F025	Religious denomination	V185	
F028	How often do you attend religious services	V186	Recode 5 as 6, 6 as 7, 7 as 8
F034	Religious person	V187	
F035	Churches give answers: moral problems	V188	
F036	Churches give answers: the problems of family life	V189	
F037	Churches give answers: people´s spiritual needs	V190	Recode 2 as 0
F038	Churches give answers: the social problems	V191	
F063	How important is God in your life	V192	

4-wave aggregate variables	Label	WVS2005 variables	Comments
F065	Moments of prayer, meditation...	V193	Recode 2 as 0
F102	Politicians who don´t believe in God are unfit for public office	V194	
F103	Religious leaders should not influence how people vote	V195	
F104	Better if more people with strong religious beliefs in public office	V196	
F105	Religious leaders should not influence government	V197	
F114	Justifiable: claiming government benefits	V198	
F115	Justifiable: avoiding a fare on public transport	V199	
F116	Justifiable: cheating on taxes	V200	
F117	Justifiable: someone accepting a bribe	V201	
F118	Justifiable: homosexuality	V202	
F119	Justifiable: prostitution	V203	
F120	Justifiable: abortion	V204	
F121	Justifiable: divorce	V205	
F122	Justifiable: euthanasia	V206	
F123	Justifiable: suicide	V207	
G006	How proud of nationality	V209	
G016	Language at home	V222	
E179	Which party would you vote for: first choice	V231	
E180	Which party would you vote for: second choice	V232	
E182	Party that would never vote	V233	
X001	Sex	V235	
X002	Year of birth	V236	
X003	Age	V237	
X025	Highest educational level attained	V238	Recode 2 as 1; 3 as 2; 4 as 3; 5 as 4; 6 as 5; 7 as 6; 8 as 7; 9 as 8
X025CS	Education (country specific)	V238CS	
X023	What age did you complete your education	V239	Recode 0 as -3
X026	Do you live with your parents	V240	Recode 2 as 0
X028	Employment status	V241	

Working with the Values Surveys files   85

4-wave aggregate variables	Label	WVS2005 variables	Comments
X036	Profession/job	V242	1 as 13; 2 as 16; 3 as 21; 4 as 23; 5 as 25; 6 as 31; 7 as 32; 8 as 33; 9 as 34; 10 as 41; 11 as 42; 12 as 51; 13 as 61
X031	Are you supervising someone	V247	Recode 2 as 0
X040	Are you the chief wage earner in your house	V248	Recode 2 as 0
X041	Is the chief wage earner employed now	V249	Recode 2 as 0
X043	Chief wage earner profession/job	V250	1 as 13; 2 as 16; 3 as 21; 4 as 23; 5 as 25; 6 as 31; 7 as 32; 8 as 33; 9 as 34; 10 as 41; 11 as 42; 12 as 51; 13 as 61
X044	Family savings during past year	V251	
X045	Social class (subjective)	V252	
X047	Scale of incomes	V253	
X047CS	Income (country specific)	V253CS	
S013	Respondent interested during the interview	V254	
X049	Size of town	V255	
X049CS	Size of town (country specific)	V255CS	
X051	Ethnic group	V256	
X048	Region where the interview was conducted	V257	
S016	Language in which interview was conducted	V258	
S017	Weight	V259	
S017A	Weight [with split ups]	V259A	
S020	Year survey	V260	

Calculating the post-materialist values indexes and the Autonomy index

The four-wave aggregate includes three important constructed variables named Y001, Y002 and Y003. These are Inglehart's post-materialist variables and the autonomy index.

An explanation of how each of them is computed follows:

- **Y001 (Post-materialist index 12-items):** This variable is computed from V69 to V74 (using WVS2005 names) or E001 to E006 (using 4-wave aggregate names)

E001	Aims of country: first choice	V69
E002	Aims of country: second choice	V70
E003	Aims of respondent: first choice	V71
E004	Aims of respondent: second choice	V72
E005	Most important: first choice	V73
E006	Most important: second choice	V74

Y001 is calculated by setting it to 0 and adding 1 for each condition that is satisfied among the following:

- A code 3 in E001/V69 or E002/V70 ("*People have more say about how things are done*").
- A code 2 ("*Give people more say*") or 4 ("*Protecting freedom of speech*") in E003/V71.
- A code 2 ("*Give people more say*") or 4 ("*Protecting freedom of speech*") in E004/V72.
- A code 2 ("*Progress toward a less impersonal and more humane society*") or 3 ("*Ideas count more than money*") in E005/V73
- A code 2 ("*Progress toward a less impersonal and more humane society*") or 3 ("*Ideas count more than money*") in E006/V74

Thus, a total of 5 points can be added and Y001 can range from 0 to 5. Note that any "no answer" or "missing" code for any of these variables results in a missing value for Y001.

Y001 is named the 12-item index because it is based on a battery of questions containing 12 different items from which the respondent chooses, generating six component variables.

The syntax in SPSS to compute Y001 in the WVS2005 is as follows:

COMPUTE Y001=0.
IF ((V69=3) or (V70=3)) Y001=Y001+1.
IF ((V71=2) or (V71=4)) Y001=Y001+1.
IF ((V72=2) or (V72=4)) Y001=Y001+1.
IF ((V73=2) or (V73=3)) Y001=Y001+1.
IF ((V74=2) or (V74=3)) Y001=Y001+1.
IF ((MISSING(v69) and MISSING(v70)) or MISSING(v71) or MISSING(v72) or MISSING(v73) or MISSING(v74)) Y001=-5.
EXECUTE.

VARIABLE LABELS Y001 'Post-Materialist index 12-item'.
VALUE LABELS Y001
-5 'Missing'
0 'Materialist'
1 '1'
2 '2'
3 '3'

4 '4'
5 'Post-materialist'.
MISSING VALUES Y001 (-5).

- **Y002 (Post-materialist index 4-item)**: This variable is computed from V71 and V72 (using WVS2005 names) or E003 and E004 (using 4-wave aggregate names)

| E003 | Aims of respondent: first choice | V71 |
| E004 | Aims of respondent: second choice | V72 |

Y002 is calculated as follows:

- Missing values in E003/V71 or E004/V72 implies a missing value for Y002.
- A code 2 ("*Give people more say*") in E003/V71 and a 4 ("*Protecting freedom of speech*") in E004/V72 or vice versa implies a value of 3 for Y002.
- A code 1 ("*Maintaining order in the nation*") in E003/V71 and a 3 ("*Fighting rising prices*") in E004/V72 or vice versa implies a value of 1 for Y002.
- Otherwise, a value 2 is coded in Y002.

So Y002 ranges from 1 (materialist) to 3 (post-materialist). It uses only a battery of questions with only 4 items and two possible choices, thus the name.

The syntax in SPSS to compute Y002 in the WVS2005 is as follows:

COMPUTE Y002=-5.
IF (((V71=1) or (V71=2) or (V71=3) or (V71=4)) and ((V72=1) or (V72=2) or (V72=3) or (V72=4))) y002 = 2 .
IF (((V71=1) and (V72=3)) or ((V71=3) and (V72=1))) Y002=1.
IF (((V71=2) and (V72=4)) or ((V71=4) and (V72=2))) Y002=3.
EXECUTE.

VARIABLE LABELS Y002 'Post-Materialist index 4-item'.
VALUE LABELS Y002
-5 'Missing'
1 'Materialist'
2 '2'
3 'Post-materialist'.
MISSING VALUES Y001 (-5).

The datasets are distributed with the **individual-level** scores for two major dimensions of cross-cultural variation: Traditional versus Secular-rational values; and Survival versus Self-expression values. For a discussion of the theoretical basis of these variables, and how these scores are calculated, see Inglehart and Welzel (2005), Chapter 2.

- **Y003 (Autonomy index)**: This variable is computed from v19, v21, v12 and v18 (using WVS2005 names) or A040, A042, A029, A039 and E004 (using 4-wave aggregate names).

A029	Important child qualities: independence	V12
A039	Important child qualities: determination perseverance	V18
A040	Important child qualities: religious faith	V19
A042	Important child qualities: obedience	V21

Note that in the WVS2005 dataset, the answers are coded 1=Mentioned and 2=Not mentioned, while in the 4-wave combined dataset, the codes are 1=Mentioned and 0=Not mentioned. Consequently, the 4-wave variable can be computed as:

$$\text{Variable}_{4\text{wave}} = 2 - \text{Variable}_{\text{WVS2005}}$$

Y003 is defined with the formula:

$$Y003 = (V19 + V21) - (V12 + V18) = (A029 + A039) - (A040 + A042)$$

(Because A029=2-V12 and A039=2-V18, A040=2-V19 and A042=2-V21)

Y003 ranges from –2 (when only religious faith and obedience are mentioned) to +2 (when only independence and determination are mentioned).

The syntax in SPSS to compute Y003 in the WVS2005 dataset is as follows:

```
COMPUTE Y003=-5.
if (V19>0 and V21>0 and V12>0 and V18>0) y003=(V19 + V21)-(V12 +V18).
RECODE y003 (-4=SYSMIS).
VALUE LABELS Y003
-2 'Obedience/Religious Faith'
-1 '-1'
0 '0'
1 '1'
2 'Determination, perseverance/Independence'.
```

Questionnaire used in the 2005-2007 World Values Survey

V1. Survey wave number: **5**

V1a. Split Ballot (*only for OECD-countries*): 1 Split A
2 Split B (*code one number!*)

V2. Country code:

8 Albania	152 Chile	332 Haiti
12 Algeria	156 China	340 Honduras
16 American Samoa	158 Taiwan	344 Hong Kong
20 Andorra	170 Colombia	348 Hungary
24 Angola	180 Dem. Repub. of Congo	352 Iceland
28 Antigua and Barbuda	184 Cook Islands	356 India
31 Azerbaijan	188 Costa Rica	360 Indonesia
32 Argentina	191 Croatia	364 Iran
36 Australia	192 Cuba	368 Iraq
40 Austria	196 Cyprus	372 Ireland
50 Bangladesh	203 Czech Republic	376 Israel
51 Armenia	208 Denmark	380 Italy
52 Barbados	214 Dominican Republic	384 Côte d'Ivoire
56 Belgium	218 Ecuador	388 Jamaica
60 Bermuda	222 El Salvador	392 Japan
64 Bhutan	226 Equatorial Guinea	398 Kazakhstan
68 Bolivia	231 Ethiopia	400 Jordan
70 Bosnia	232 Eritrea	404 Kenya
72 Botswana	233 Estonia	408 North Korea
76 Brazil	246 Finland	410 South Korea
84 Belize	250 France	414 Kuwait
100 Bulgaria	268 Georgia	417 Kyrgyzstan
854 Burkina Faso	270 Gambia	418 Laos
104 Myanmar	275 Palestine	422 Lebanon
108 Burundi	276 Germany	426 Lesotho
112 Belarus	288 Ghana	428 Latvia
116 Cambodia	292 Gibraltar	430 Liberia
120 Cameroon	300 Greece	434 Libya
124 Canada	320 Guatemala	438 Liechtenstein
144 Sri Lanka	324 Guinea	440 Lithuania
148 Chad	328 Guyana	442 Luxembourg

450 Madagascar	624 Guinea-Bissau	792 Turkey
454 Malawi	626 Timor-Leste	795 Turkmenistan
458 Malaysia	630 Puerto Rico	800 Uganda
466 Mali	634 Qatar	804 Ukraine
470 Malta	642 Romania	807 Macedonia
474 Martinique	643 Russia	818 Egypt
478 Mauritania	646 Rwanda	826 Great Britain
480 Mauritius	682 Saudi Arabia	834 Tanzania
484 Mexico	686 Senegal	840 United States
492 Monaco	690 Seychelles	850 U.S. Virgin Islands
496 Mongolia	694 Sierra Leone	854 Burkina Faso
498 Moldova	702 Singapore	858 Uruguay
504 Morocco	703 Slovakia	860 Uzbekistan
508 Mozambique	704 Viet Nam	862 Venezuela
512 Oman	705 Slovenia	887 Yemen
516 Namibia	706 Somalia	891 Serbia and
524 Nepal	710 South Africa	Montenegro
528 Netherlands	716 Zimbabwe	894 Zambia
554 New Zealand	724 Spain	900 West Germany
558 Nicaragua	736 Sudan	901 East Germany
562 Niger	740 Suriname	902 Tambov
566 Nigeria	752 Sweden	903 Moscow
578 Norway	756 Switzerland	904 Basque Country
586 Pakistan	760 Syria	906 Andalusia
591 Panama	762 Tajikistan	907 Galicia
598 Papua New Guinea	764 Thailand	909 North Ireland
600 Paraguay	768 Togo	910 Valencia
604 Peru	780 Trinidad	911 Serbia
608 Philippines	784 United Arab	912 Montenegro
616 Poland	Emirates	913 SrpSka Republic
620 Portugal	788 Tunisia	

(*Introduction by interviewer*):
Hello. I am from the _____ (*mention name of the interview organization*). We are carrying out a global study of what people value in life. This study will interview samples representing most of the world's people. Your name has been selected at random as part of a representative sample of the people in _____ (*mention country in which interview is conducted*). I'd like to ask your views on a number of different subjects. Your input will be treated strictly confidential but it will contribute to a better understanding of what people all over the world believe and want out of life.

(*Show Card A*)
For each of the following, indicate how important it is in your life. Would you say it is (*read out and code one answer for each*):

		Very important	Rather important	Not very important	Not at all important
V4.	Family	1	2	3	4
V5.	Friends	1	2	3	4

		Very important	Rather important	Not very important	Not at all important
V6.	Leisure time	1	2	3	4
V7.	Politics	1	2	3	4
V8.	Work	1	2	3	4
V9.	Religion	1	2	3	4

(*NOTE: Code but do not read out — here and throughout the interview*):
- −1 **Don't know**
- −2 **No answer**
- −3 **Not applicable**

V10. Taking all things together, would you say you are (*read out and code one answer*):

1 Very happy
2 Rather happy
3 Not very happy
4 Not at all happy

V11. All in all, how would you describe your state of health these days? Would you say it is (*read out*):

1 Very good
2 Good
3 Fair
4 Poor

(Show Card B)
Here is a list of qualities that children can be encouraged to learn at home. Which, if any, do you consider to be especially important? Please choose up to five! (*Code five mentions at the maximum*):

		Mentioned	Not mentioned
V12.	Independence	1	2
V13.	Hard work	1	2
V14.	Feeling of responsibility	1	2
V15.	Imagination	1	2
V16.	Tolerance and respect for other people	1	2
V17.	Thrift, saving money and things	1	2
V18.	Determination, perseverance	1	2
V19.	Religious faith	1	2
V20.	Unselfishness	1	2
V21.	Obedience	1	2

(Show Card C)
V22. All things considered, how satisfied are you with your life as a whole these days? Using this card on which 1 means you are "completely dissatisfied" and 10 means you are "completely satisfied" where would you put your satisfaction with your life as a whole? (*Code one number*):

Completely dissatisfied   Completely satisfied
1   2   3   4   5   6   7   8   9   10

V23. Generally speaking, would you say that most people can be trusted or that you need to be very careful in dealing with people? (*Code one answer*):

    1   Most people can be trusted.
    2   Need to be very careful.

Now I am going to read off a list of voluntary organizations. For each one, could you tell me whether you are an active member, an inactive member or not a member of that type of organization? (*Read out and code one answer for each organization*):

		Active member	Inactive member	Don't belong
V24.	Church or religious organization	2	1	0
V25.	Sport or recreational organization	2	1	0
V26.	Art, music or educational organization	2	1	0
V27.	Labor Union	2	1	0
V28.	Political party	2	1	0
V29.	Environmental organization	2	1	0
V30.	Professional association	2	1	0
V31.	Humanitarian or charitable organization	2	1	0
V32.	Consumer organization	2	1	0
V33.	Any other (*write in*): _____	2	1	0

(Show Card D)
On this list are various groups of people. Could you please mention any that you would not like to have as neighbors? (*Code an answer for each group*):

		Mentioned	Not mentioned
V34.	Drug addicts	1	2
V35.	People of a different race	1	2
V36.	People who have AIDS	1	2
V37.	Immigrants/foreign workers	1	2
V38.	Homosexuals	1	2
V39.	People of a different religion	1	2
V40.	Heavy drinkers	1	2

		Mentioned	Not mentioned
V41.	Unmarried couples living together	1	2
V42.	People who speak a different language	1	2
V43.	(*optional: minority relevant to given country, write in*):____	1	2

Do you agree, disagree or neither agree nor disagree with the following statements? (*Read out and code one answer for each statement*):

		Agree	Neither	Disagree
V44.	When jobs are scarce, men should have more right to a job than women.	1	2	3
V45.	When jobs are scarce, employers should give priority to [**British**]* people over immigrants.	1	2	3

*[*Substitute your own nationality for "British"!*]

(Show Card E)
V46. Some people feel they have completely free choice and control over their lives, while other people feel that what they do has no real effect on what happens to them. Please use this scale where 1 means "none at all" and 10 means "a great deal" to indicate how much freedom of choice and control you feel you have over the way your life turns out (*code one number*):

None at all   A great deal
  1   2   3   4   5   6   7   8   9   10

(Show Card F)
V47. Do you think most people would try to take advantage of you if they got a chance, or would they try to be fair? Please show your response on this card, where 1 means that "people would try to take advantage of you," and 10 means that "people would try to be fair" (*code one number*):

People would try to   People would
take advantage of you   try to be fair
  1   2   3   4   5   6   7   8   9   10

V48. Now I would like to ask you something about the things which would seem to you, personally, most important if you were looking for a job. Here are some of the things many people take into account in relation to their work. Regardless of whether you're actually looking for a job, which one would you, personally, place first if you were looking for a job (*read out and code one answer*):
1   A good income so that you do not have any worries about money
2   A safe job with no risk of closing down or unemployment
3   Working with people you like
4   Doing an important job that gives you a feeling of accomplishment

V49. And what would be your second choice (*code one answer*):
1   A good income so that you do not have any worries about money
2   A safe job with no risk of closing down or unemployment
3   Working with people you like
4   Doing an important job that gives you a feeling of accomplishment

Please specify for each of the following statements how strongly you agree or disagree with it! Do you strongly agree, agree, neither agree nor disagree, disagree or strongly disagree? (*Read out and code one answer for each statement*):

		Strongly agree	Agree	Neither	Disagree	Strongly disagree
V50.	To fully develop your talents, you need to have a job.	1	2	3	4	5
V51.	It is humiliating to receive money without working for it.	1	2	3	4	5
V52.	People who don't work become lazy.	1	2	3	4	5
V53.	Work is a duty toward society.	1	2	3	4	5
V54.	Work should always come first, even if it means less free time.	1	2	3	4	5

(*Show Card G*)
V55. Are you currently (*read out and code one answer only*):
1   Married
2   Living together as married
3   Divorced
4   Separated
5   Widowed
6   Single

V56. Have you had any children? (*Code 0 if no, and respective number if yes*):
0   No children
1   One child
2   Two children
3   Three children
4   Four children
5   Five children
6   Six children
7   Seven children
8   Eight or more children

V57. If someone says a child needs a home with both a father and a mother to grow up happily, would you tend to agree or disagree? (*Code one answer*):
1   Tend to agree
2   Tend to disagree

V58. Do you agree or disagree with the following statement (*read out*): "Marriage is an out-dated institution." (*Code one answer*):
   1 Agree
   2 Disagree

V59. If a woman wants to have a child as a single parent but she doesn't want to have a stable relationship with a man, do you approve or disapprove? (*Code one answer*):
   1 Approve
   2 Disapprove
   3 Depends (*do not read out, code only if volunteered*)

For each of the following statements I read out, can you tell me how strongly you agree or disagree with each. Do you strongly agree, agree, disagree, or strongly disagree? (*Read out and code one answer for each statement*):

		Strongly agree	Agree	Disagree	Strongly disagree
V60.	Being a housewife is just as fulfilling as working for pay.	1	2	3	4
V61.	On the whole, men make better political leaders than women do.	1	2	3	4
V62.	A university education is more important for a boy than for a girl.	1	2	3	4
V63.	On the whole, men make better business executives than women do.	1	2	3	4

People pursue different goals in life. For each of the following goals, can you tell me if you strongly agree, agree, disagree or strongly disagree with it? (*Read out and code one answer for each statement*):

		Strongly agree	Agree	Disagree	Strongly disagree
V64.	One of my main goals in life has been to make my parents proud.	1	2	3	4
V65.	I seek to be myself rather than to follow others.	1	2	3	4
V66.	I make a lot of effort to live up to what my friends expect.	1	2	3	4
V67.	I decide my goals in life by myself.	1	2	3	4

(*Show Card H*)
V68. How satisfied are you with the financial situation of your household? Please use this card again to help with your answer (*code one number*):

   Completely dissatisfied   Completely satisfied
   1   2   3   4   5   6   7   8   9   10

(Show Card I)

V69. People sometimes talk about what the aims of this country should be for the next ten years. On this card are listed some of the goals which different people would give top priority. Would you please say which one of these you, yourself, consider the most important? (*Code one answer only under "first choice"*)

V70. And which would be the next most important? (*Code one answer only under "second choice"*)

	First choice	Second choice
A high level of economic growth	1	1
Making sure this country has strong defense forces	2	2
Seeing that people have more say about how things are done at their jobs and in their communities	3	3
Trying to make our cities and countryside more beautiful	4	4

(Show Card J)

V71. If you had to choose, which one of the things on this card would you say is most important? (*Code one answer only under "first choice"*):

V72. And which would be the next most important? (*Code one answer only under "second choice"*):

	First choice	Second choice
Maintaining order in the nation	1	1
Giving people more say in important government decisions	2	2
Fighting rising prices	3	3
Protecting freedom of speech	4	4

(Show Card K)

V73. Here is another list. In your opinion, which one of these is most important? (*Code one answer only under "first choice"*):

V74. And what would be the next most important? (*Code one answer only under "second choice"*):

	First choice	Second choice
A stable economy	1	1
Progress toward a less impersonal and more humane society	2	2
Progress toward a society in which Ideas count more than money	3	3
The fight against crime	4	4

V75. Of course, we all hope that there will not be another war, but if it were to come to that, would you be willing to fight for your country? (*Code one answer*):

    1 Yes
    2 No

Working with the Values Surveys files 97

I'm going to read out a list of various changes in our way of life that might take place in the near future. Please tell me for each one, if it were to happen, whether you think it would be a good thing, a bad thing, or don't you mind? (*Code one answer for each*):

		Good	Don't mind	Bad
V76.	Less importance placed on work in our lives	1	2	3
V77.	More emphasis on the development of technology	1	2	3
V78.	Greater respect for authority	1	2	3
V79.	More emphasis on family life	1	2	3

(Show Card L)
Now I will briefly describe some people. Using this card, would you please indicate for each description whether that person is very much like you, like you, somewhat like you, not like you, or not at all like you? (*Code one answer for each description*):

		Very much like me	Like me	Somewhat like me	A little like me	Not like me	Not at all like me
V80.	It is important to this person to think up new ideas and be creative; to do things one's own way.	1	2	3	4	5	6
V81.	It is important to this person to be rich; to have a lot of money and expensive things.	1	2	3	4	5	6
V82.	Living in secure surroundings is important to this person; to avoid anything that might be dangerous.	1	2	3	4	5	6
V83.	It is important to this person to have a good time; to "spoil" oneself.	1	2	3	4	5	6
V84.	It is important to this person to help the people nearby; to care for their well-being.	1	2	3	4	5	6
V85.	Being very successful is important to this person; to have people recognize one's achievements.	1	2	3	4	5	6
V86.	Adventure and taking risks are important to this person; to have an exciting life.	1	2	3	4	5	6
V87.	It is important to this person to always behave properly; to avoid doing anything people would say is wrong.	1	2	3	4	5	6

Working with the Values Surveys files

		Very much like me	Like me	Some-what like me	A little like me	Not like me	Not at all like me
V88.	Looking after the environment is important to this person; to care for nature.	1	2	3	4	5	6
V89.	Tradition is important to this person; to follow the customs handed down by one's religion or family.	1	2	3	4	5	6

V90. In the long run, do you think the scientific advances we are making will help or harm mankind? (*Code one answer*):
   1   Will help
   2   Will harm
   3   Some of each [DO NOT READ OUT]

(Show Card O)
Now, I would like to read some statements and ask how much you agree or disagree with each of these statements. For these questions, a 1 means that you "completely disagree" and a 10 means that you "completely agree." (*Code one number for each statement*):

		Completely disagree								Completely agree
V91.	Science and technology are making our lives healthier, easier, and more comfortable.	1	2	3	4	5	6	7	8	9	10
V92.	Because of science and technology, there will be more opportunities for the next generation.	1	2	3	4	5	6	7	8	9	10
V93.	Science and technology make our way of life change too fast.	1	2	3	4	5	6	7	8	9	10
V94.	We depend too much on science and not enough on faith.	1	2	3	4	5	6	7	8	9	10

V95. How interested would you say you are in politics? Are you (*read out and code one answer*):
   1   Very interested
   2   Somewhat interested
   3   Not very interested
   4   Not at all interested

(Show Card M)
Now I'd like you to look at this card. I'm going to read out some forms of political action that people can take, and I'd like you to tell me, for each one, whether you have

done any of these things, whether you might do it or would never under any circumstances do it (*read out and code one answer for each action*):

		Have done	Might do	Would never do
V96.	Signing a petition	1	2	3
V97.	Joining in boycotts	1	2	3
V98.	Attending peaceful demonstrations	1	2	3
V99.	Other (*write in*): _____	1	2	3

Have you or have you not done any of these activities in the last five years? (*Read out and code one answer for each action*):

		Have done	Have not done
V100.	Signing a petition	1	2
V101.	Joining in boycotts	1	2
V103.	Attending lawful demonstrations	1	2
V103.	Other (*write in*): _____	1	2

V94, V98: „peaceful" instead of „lawful" used in Split B, OECD-countries

V104. Here are two statements people sometimes make when discussing the environment and economic growth. Which of them comes closer to your own point of view? (*Read out and code one answer*):
  1 Protecting the environment should be given priority, even if it causes slower economic growth and some loss of jobs.
  2 Economic growth and creating jobs should be the top priority, even if the environment suffers to some extent.
  3 Other answer (*code if volunteered only*).

(Show Card N)
I am going to read out some statements about the environment. For each one, can you tell me whether you strongly agree, agree, disagree or strongly disagree? (*Read out and code one answer for each*):

		Strongly agree	Agree	Disagree	Strongly disagree
V105.	I would give part of my income if I were certain that the money would be used to prevent environmental pollution.	1	2	3	4
V106.	I would agree to an increase in taxes if the extra money were used to prevent environmental pollution.	1	2	3	4
V107.	The Government should reduce environmental pollution, but it should not cost me any money.	1	2	3	4

I am going to read out a list of environmental problems facing many communities. Please, tell me how serious you consider each one to be here in your own community. Is it very serious, somewhat serious, not very serious or not serious at all? (*Read out and code one answer for each problem*):

		Very serious	Somewhat serious	Not very serious	Not serious at all
V108.	Poor water quality.	1	2	3	4
V109.	Poor air quality.	1	2	3	4
V110.	Poor sewage and sanitation.	1	2	3	4

Now let's consider environmental problems in the world as a whole. Please, tell me how serious you consider each of the following to be for the world as a whole. Is it very serious, somewhat serious, not very serious or not serious at all? (*Read out and code one answer for each problem*):

		Very serious	Somewhat serious	Not very serious	Not serious at all
V111.	Global warming or the greenhouse effect.	1	2	3	4
V112.	Loss of plant or animal species or biodiversity.	1	2	3	4
V113.	Pollution of rivers, lakes and oceans.	1	2	3	4

(*Show Card P*)
V114. In political matters, people talk of "the left" and "the right." How would you place your views on this scale, generally speaking? (*Code one number*):

Left									Right
1	2	3	4	5	6	7	8	9	10

V115. Imagine two secretaries, of the same age, doing practically the same job. One finds out that the other earns considerably more than she does. The better paid secretary, however, is quicker, more efficient and more reliable at her job. In your opinion, is it fair or not fair that one secretary is paid more than the other? (*Code one answer*):

1 Fair
2 Not fair

(*Show Card Q*)
V116. Now I'd like you to tell me your views on various issues. How would you place your views on this scale? 1 means you agree completely with the statement on the left; 10 means you agree completely with the statement on the right; and if your views fall somewhere in between, you can choose any number in between. (*Code one number for each issue*):

Incomes should be   We need larger income differences
made more equal   as incentives for individual effort
1   2   3   4   5   6   7   8   9   10

V117. Private ownership of   Government ownership of
business and industry   business and industry
should be increased   should be increased
1   2   3   4   5   6   7   8   9   10

V118. The government should   People should take more
take more responsibility to ensure   responsibility to
that everyone is provided for   provide for themselves
1   2   3   4   5   6   7   8   9   10

V119. Competition is good. It   Competition is harmful. It
stimulates people to work hard   brings out the worst in people
and develop new ideas
1   2   3   4   5   6   7   8   9   10

V120. In the long run, hard work   Hard work doesn't generally
usually brings a better life   bring success —it's more a matter
of luck and connections
1   2   3   4   5   6   7   8   9   10

V121. People can only get rich   Wealth can grow so there's
at the expense of others   enough for everyone
1   2   3   4   5   6   7   8   9   10

(Show Card R)
V122. Some people believe that individuals can decide their own destiny, while others think that it is impossible to escape a predetermined fate. Please tell me which comes closest to your view on this scale on which 1 means "everything in life is determined by fate," and 10 means that "people shape their fate themselves." (*Code one number*):

Everything is   People shape their
determined by fate   fate themselves
1   2   3   4   5   6   7   8   9   10

(Show Card S)
V123. All things considered, would you say that the world is better off, or worse off, because of science and technology? Please tell me which comes closest to your view on this scale: 1 means that "the world is a lot worse off," and 10 means that "the world is a lot better off." (*Code one number*):

A lot worse off   A lot better off
1   2   3   4   5   6   7   8   9   10

V124. How about people from other countries coming here to work. Which one of the following do you think the government should do? (*Read out and code one answer*):
   1   Let anyone come who wants to?
   2   Let people come as long as there are jobs available?
   3   Place strict limits on the number of foreigners who can come here?
   4   Prohibit people coming here from other countries?

I'd like to ask you how much you trust people from various groups. Could you tell me for each whether you trust people from this group completely, somewhat, not very much or not at all? (*Read out and code one answer for each*):

		Trust completely	Trust somewhat	Do not trust very much	Do not trust at all
V125.	Your family	1	2	3	4
V126.	Your neighborhood	1	2	3	4
V127.	People you know personally	1	2	3	4
V128.	People you meet for the first time	1	2	3	4
V129.	People of another religion	1	2	3	4
V130.	People of another nationality	1	2	3	4

I am going to name a number of organizations. For each one, could you tell me how much confidence you have in them: is it a great deal of confidence, quite a lot of confidence, not very much confidence or none at all? (*Read out and code one answer for each*):

		A great deal	Quite a lot	Not very much	None at all
V131.	The [**churches**]*	1	2	3	4
V132.	The armed forces	1	2	3	4
V133.	The press	1	2	3	4
V134.	Television	1	2	3	4
V135.	Labor unions	1	2	3	4
V136.	The police	1	2	3	4
V137.	The courts	1	2	3	4
V138.	The government (in your nation's capital)	1	2	3	4
V139.	Political parties	1	2	3	4
V140.	Parliament	1	2	3	4
V141.	The Civil service	1	2	3	4
V142.	Major Companies	1	2	3	4
V143.	Environmental organizations	1	2	3	4
V144.	Women's organizations	1	2	3	4

		A great deal	Quite a lot	Not very much	None at all
V145.	Charitable or humanitarian organizations	1	2	3	4
V146.	The [**European Union**]**	1	2	3	4
V147.	The United Nations	1	2	3	4

* [*Substitute "religious leaders" in non-Christian countries*]
** [*Substitute appropriate regional organization outside Europe (e.g., in North America, NAFTA)*]

I'm going to describe various types of political systems and ask what you think about each as a way of governing this country. For each one, would you say it is a very good, fairly good, fairly bad or very bad way of governing this country? (*Read out and code one answer for each*):

		Very good	Fairly good	Fairly bad	Very bad
V148.	Having a strong leader who does not have to bother with parliament and elections	1	2	3	4
V149.	Having experts, not government, make decisions according to what they think is best for the country	1	2	3	4
V150.	Having the army rule	1	2	3	4
V151.	Having a democratic political system	1	2	3	4

(Show Card T)
Many things may be desirable, but not all of them are essential characteristics of democracy. Please tell me for each of the following things how essential you think it is as a characteristic of democracy. Use this scale where 1 means "not at all an essential characteristic of democracy" and 10 means it definitely is "an essential characteristic of democracy" (*read out and code one answer for each*):

		Not an essential characteristic of democracy								An essential characteristic of democracy	
V152.	Governments tax the rich and subsidize the poor.	1	2	3	4	5	6	7	8	9	10
V153.	Religious authorities interpret the laws.	1	2	3	4	5	6	7	8	9	10
V154.	People choose their leaders in free elections.	1	2	3	4	5	6	7	8	9	10
V155.	People receive state aid for unemployment.	1	2	3	4	5	6	7	8	9	10
V156.	The army takes over when government is incompetent.	1	2	3	4	5	6	7	8	9	10

		Not an essential characteristic of democracy							An essential characteristic of democracy		
V157.	Civil rights protect people's liberty against oppression.	1	2	3	4	5	6	7	8	9	10
V158.	The economy is prospering.	1	2	3	4	5	6	7	8	9	10
V159.	Criminals are severely punished.	1	2	3	4	5	6	7	8	9	10
V160.	People can change the laws in referendums.	1	2	3	4	5	6	7	8	9	10
V161.	Women have the same rights as men.	1	2	3	4	5	6	7	8	9	10

(Show Card U)
V162. How important is it for you to live in a country that is governed democratically? On this scale where 1 means it is "not at all important" and 10 means "absolutely important" what position would you choose? (*Code one number*):

Not at all important									Absolutely important
1	2	3	4	5	6	7	8	9	10

(Show Card V)
V163. And how democratically is this country being governed today? Again using a scale from 1 to 10, where 1 means that it is "not at all democratic" and 10 means that it is "completely democratic," what position would you choose? (*Code one number*):

Not at all democratic									Completely democratic
1	2	3	4	5	6	7	8	9	10

V164. How much respect is there for individual human rights nowadays in this country? Do you feel there is (*read out and code one answer*):

1 A great deal of respect for individual human rights
2 Fairly much respect
3 Not much respect
4 No respect at all

V165. Have you heard of the Millennium Development Goals?

1 Yes
2 No

V166. In 2000, leaders representing almost all the world's countries agreed to carry out a number of programs to improve the lives of the peoples of low-income countries. These programs are known as the Millennium Development Goals. I'm going to read out some of the problems that these programs involve. I would like you to indicate which of these problems you consider most serious. Which of the following problems do you consider the most serious one **for the world as a whole**? (*Read out and code one answer under "most serious for the world"*):

V167. And which is the second most serious problem for the world as a whole? (*Code one answer under "next most serious for the world"*):

	Most serious in the world	Second most serious in the world
People living in poverty and need.	1	1
Discrimination against girls and women.	2	2
Poor sanitation and infectious diseases.	3	3
Inadequate education.	4	4
Environmental pollution.	5	5

V168. Which of these problems do you consider the most serious one **in your own country**? (*Code one answer under "most serious for own country"*):

V169. And which is the next most serious **for your own country**? (*Code one answer under "next most serious for own country"*):

	Most serious in own country	Next most serious in own country
People living in poverty and need.	1	1
Discrimination against girls and women.	2	2
Poor sanitation and infectious diseases.	3	3
Inadequate education.	4	4
Environmental pollution.	5	5

(*NOTE: V170 to V177 are only asked in OECD-countries!*)

(Show Card W)
I'm going to read out a list of global problems, and goals that world leaders have set to reduce them. Indicate for each of these goals how high a priority your own country's leaders should give to it, using this card. (*Read out and code one answer for each goal*):

	This battery only in Split B, OECD	Top priority	High priority	Medium priority	Low priority
V170.	About 25 percent of the world's population lives in extreme poverty —that is on less than one dollar per day. The goal is to cut this percentage in half by 2015.	1	2	3	4
V171.	At present, more than 130 million children of primary school age are not in school. The goal is to ensure that by 2015, all children will be able to finish primary school.	1	2	3	4

	This battery only in Split B, OECD	Top priority	High priority	Medium priority	Low priority
V172.	About eight out of every 100 children who are born around the world, die before their fifth birthday. The goal is to reduce this proportion by two-thirds, by 2015.	1	2	3	4
V173.	About five million people become infected with HIV/AIDS each year. The goal is to stop the spread of HIV/AIDS.	1	2	3	4
V174.	About 840 million people around the world live in slums. The goal is to make a significant improvement in the housing of at least 100 million people.	1	2	3	4

V175. In 2003, this country's government allocated [**a tenth of one percent**]* of the national income to foreign aid—that is, [**$US 38.05**]** per person. Do you think this amount is too low, too high, or about right? (*Code one answer*):

    1 Too low
    2 About right
    3 Too high

* [*Restate this figure using information for your country from the 1st table at the end of this document!*]
** [*Restate this figure using information for your country from the 2nd table at the end of this document!*]
(*If respondent answered "too low," go to next question! Otherwise skip next question!*)

V176. How much more do you think this country should contribute? (*Read out and code one answer*):

    1 About one and a half times as much
    2 About twice as much
    3 About three times as much
    4 About four times as much
    5 More than four times as much

V177. Would you be willing to pay higher taxes in order to increase your country's foreign aid to poor countries? (*Code one answer!*)

    1 Yes
    2 No

V178. Thinking at your own country's problems, should your country's leaders give top priority to help reducing poverty in the world or should they give top priority to solve your own country's problems? Use this scale where 1 means "top priority to help reducing misery in the world" and 10 means "top priority to solve my own country's problems." (*Code one answer*):

Working with the Values Surveys files   107

Top priority to help								Top priority to solve my
reducing poverty in the world								own country's problems
1	2	3	4	5	6	7	8	9	10

Some people believe that certain kinds of problems could be better handled by the United Nations or regional organizations, such as the European Union, rather than by each national government separately. Others think that these problems should be left entirely to the national governments. I'm going to mention some problems. For each one, would you tell me whether you think that policies in this area should be decided by the national governments, by regional organizations, or by the United Nations? (*Read out and code one answer for each problem*):

		National governments	Regional organizations	United Nations
V179.	Peacekeeping	1	2	3
V180.	Protection of the environment	1	2	3
V181.	Aid to developing countries	1	2	3
V182.	Refugees	1	2	3
V183.	Human Rights	1	2	3

V184. Now let's turn to another topic. How often, if at all, do you think about the meaning and purpose of life? (*Read out and code one answer!*)

1 Often
2 Sometimes
3 Rarely
4 Never

V185. Do you belong to a religion or religious denomination? If yes, which one? (*Code answer due to list below. Code 0, if respondent answers to have no denomination!*)

No: Do not belong to a denomination	0
Yes: Roman Catholic	1
Protestant	2
Orthodox (Russian/Greek/etc.)	3
Jew	4
Muslim	5
Hindu	6
Buddhist	7
Other (*write in*):_____	8

(*NOTE: If your own society does not fit into this coding system, please devise an alternative, following this as closely as possible; for example, in Islamic countries, ask about Sunni, Shia, etc. Send a list of the categories used here along with your data.*)

(Show Card X)
V186. Apart from weddings and funerals, about how often do you attend religious services these days? *(Code one answer)*:

    1   More than once a week
    2   Once a week
    3   Once a month
    4   Only on special holy days
    5   Once a year
    6   Less often
    7   Never, practically never

(NOTE: In Islamic societies, ask how frequently the respondent prays!)

V187. Independently of whether you attend religious services or not, would you say you are *(read out and code one answer)*:

    1   A religious person
    2   Not a religious person
    3   An atheist

Generally speaking, do you think that the [**churches**]* in your country are giving adequate answers to *(read out and code one answer for each)*:

		Yes	No
V188.	The moral problems and needs of the individual	1	2
V189.	The problems of family life	1	2
V190.	People's spiritual needs	1	2
V191.	The social problems facing our society	1	2

[In non-Christian societies substitute "religious authorities" for "churches"!]

(Show Card Y)
V192. How important is God in your life? Please use this scale to indicate. 10 means "very important" and 1 means "not at all important." *(Code one number)*:

Not at all important   Very important
  1   2   3   4   5   6   7   8   9   10

V193. Do you take some moments of prayer, meditation or contemplation or something like that?

    1   Yes
    2   No

(Show Card Z)
How strongly do you agree or disagree with each of the following statements? *(Read out and code one answer for each statement)*:

		Strongly agree	Agree	Neither agree nor disagree	Disagree	Strongly disagree
V194.	Politicians who do not believe in God are unfit for public office.	1	2	3	4	5
V195.	Religious leaders should not influence how people vote in elections.	1	2	3	4	5
V196.	It would be better for [**Brazil**]* if more people with strong religious beliefs held public office.	1	2	3	4	5
V197.	Religious leaders should not influence government decisions.	1	2	3	4	5

* [*Substitute your own nationality for "Brazil"*]

(*Show Card AA*)
Please tell me for each of the following statements whether you think it can always be justified, never be justified, or something in between, using this card. (*Read out and code one answer for each statement*):

		Never justifiable								Always justifiable
V198.	Claiming government benefits to which you are not entitled	1	2	3	4	5	6	7	8	9	10
V199.	Avoiding a fare on public transport	1	2	3	4	5	6	7	8	9	10
V200.	Cheating on taxes if you have a chance	1	2	3	4	5	6	7	8	9	10
V201.	Someone accepting a bribe in the course of their duties	1	2	3	4	5	6	7	8	9	10
V202.	Homosexuality	1	2	3	4	5	6	7	8	9	10
V203.	Prostitution	1	2	3	4	5	6	7	8	9	10
V204.	Abortion	1	2	3	4	5	6	7	8	9	10
V205.	Divorce	1	2	3	4	5	6	7	8	9	10
V206.	Euthanasia—ending of the life of the incurable sick	1	2	3	4	5	6	7	8	9	10
V207.	Suicide	1	2	3	4	5	6	7	8	9	10
V208.	For a man to beat his wife	1	2	3	4	5	6	7	8	9	10

V209. How proud are you to be [**French**]*? (*Read out and code one answer*):
  1 Very proud
  2 Quite proud

3 Not very proud
4 Not at all proud
5 I am not [**French**]* (*do not read out! Code only if volunteered!*)

* [*Substitute your own nationality for "French"*]

(*Show Card AB*)
People have different views about themselves and how they relate to the world. Using this card, would you tell me how strongly you agree or disagree with each of the following statements about how you see yourself? (*Read out and code one answer for each statement*):

		Strongly agree	Agree	Disagree	Strongly disagree
V210.	I see myself as a world citizen.	1	2	3	4
V211.	I see myself as member of my local community.	1	2	3	4
V212.	I see myself as citizen of the [**French**]* nation.	1	2	3	4
V213.	I see myself as citizen of the [**European Union**]**	1	2	3	4
V214.	I see myself as an autonomous individual.	1	2	3	4

* [*Substitute your country's nationality for "French"*]
** [*Substitute appropriate regional organization for "European Union"*]

Are your mother or father immigrants to this country or not? Please, indicate separately for each of them (*read out and code one answer for each*):

		Immigrant	Not an immigrant
V215.	Mother	1	2
V216.	Father	1	2

In your opinion, how important should the following be as requirements for somebody seeking citizenship of your country? Specify for each requirement if you consider it as very important, rather important or not important (*read out and code one answer for each requirement*):

		Very important	Rather important	Not important
V217.	Having ancestors from my country	1	2	3
V218.	Being born on my country's soil	1	2	3
V219.	Adopting the customs of my country	1	2	3
V220	Abiding by my country's laws	1	2	3

(*Show Card AC*)

V221. Turning to the question of ethnic diversity, with which of the following views do you agree? Please use this scale to indicate your position (*code one number*):

Ethnic diversity erodes a country's unity									Ethnic diversity enriches life
1	2	3	4	5	6	7	8	9	10

V222. What language do you normally speak at home? (*Code one answer!*)
    1 English
    2 Spanish
    3 French
    4 Chinese
    5 Japanese

[*NOTE: modify the list of languages to fit your own society. Optional if only one language is spoken!*]

People use different sources to learn what is going on in their country and the world. For each of the following sources, please indicate whether you used it last week or did not use it last week to obtain information (*read out and code one answer for each*):

		Used it last week	Did not use it last week
V223.	Daily newspaper	1	2
V224.	News broadcasts on radio or TV	1	2
V225.	Printed magazines	1	2
V226.	In depth reports on radio or TV	1	2
V227.	Books	1	2
V228.	Internet, Email	1	2
V229.	Talk with friends or colleagues	1	2

V230. How often, if ever, do you use a personal computer? (*Read out and code one answer*):
    1 Never
    2 Occasionally
    3 Frequently
    4 Don't know what a computer is (*do not read out, code only if volunteered!*)

(*Show Card AD*)

V231. If there were a national election tomorrow, for which party on this list would you vote? Just call out the number on this card. If you are uncertain, which party appeals to you most? (*Code one answer*):
    01 Party 1
    02 Party 2
    03 Party 3
    04 etc.

[*NOTE: use two-digit code to cover the major parties in given society!*]

V232. And which party would be your second choice? If you are uncertain, which one appeals you second most? (*Code one answer*):

    01 Party 1
    02 Party 2
    03 Party 3
    04 etc.

V233. And is there a party that you would never vote for? (*Code one answer*):

    01 Party 1
    02 Party 2
    03 Party 3
    04 etc.

[OPTIONAL]
V233a. Generally speaking, do you think of yourself as a Christian Democrat, a Social Democrat, a supporter of some other party or don't you have any strong party loyalty?

    01 Party 1
    02 Party 2
    03 Party 3
    04 Party 4
    05 Non-partisan

[*NOTE: This question is optional because it may not work in societies having a fragmented or unstable part system. One can only name a few parties on card AA*].

V234. Did you vote in your country's recent elections to the national parliament? (*Code one answer*):

    1 Yes
    2 No

DEMOGRAPHICS

V235. (*Code respondent's sex by observation*):

    1 Male
    2 Female

V236. Can you tell me your year of birth, please? 19____ (*write in last two digits*)

V237. This means you are ____ years old (*write in age in two digits*).

V238. What is the highest educational level that you have attained? [*NOTE: if respondent indicates to be a student, code highest level s/he expects to complete*]:

    1 No formal education
    2 Incomplete primary school
    3 Complete primary school
    4 Incomplete secondary school: technical/vocational type

5 Complete secondary school: technical/vocational type
6 Incomplete secondary: university-preparatory type
7 Complete secondary: university-preparatory type
8 Some university-level education, without degree
9 University-level education, with degree

V239. At what age did you (or will you) complete your full time education, either at school or at an institution of higher education? Please exclude apprenticeships
[NOTE: if respondent indicates to be a student, code highest level s/he expects to complete]:

_____ (write in age in two digits)

V240. Do you live with your parents? (Code one answer):
1 Yes
2 No

V241. Are you employed now or not? If yes, about how many hours a week? If more than one job: only for the main job (code one answer):

Yes, has paid employment:	
Full time employee (30 hours a week or more)	1
Part time employee (less than 30 hours a week)	2
Self employed	3
No, no paid employment:	
Retired/pensioned	4
Housewife not otherwise employed	5
Student	6
Unemployed	7
Other (write in):_____	8

(NOTE: If answer is "yes" and respondent has a job, continue with next question. If no, continue with V249!)

V242. In which profession/occupation do you work? If more than one job, the main job? What is/was your job there?
_____ (write in and code due to list below but do not read out list!)
1 Employer/manager of establishment with 10 or more employees
2 Employer/manager of establishment with less than 10 employees
3 Professional worker lawyer, accountant, teacher, etc.
4 Supervisory - office worker: supervises others.
5 Non-manual - office worker: non-supervisory
6 Foreman and supervisor
7 Skilled manual worker
8 Semi-skilled manual worker

114   Working with the Values Surveys files

      9 Unskilled manual worker
    10 Farmer: has own farm
    11 Agricultural worker
    12 Member of armed forces, security personnel
    13 Never had a job

V243. Are you working for the government or for a private business or industry ?(*read out and code one answer*):
    1 Government or public organization
    2 Private business or industry
    3 Private non-profit organization (if volunteered)

V244. Are the tasks you perform at work mostly manual or non-manual? Use this scale where 1 means "mostly manual tasks" and 10 means "mostly non-manual tasks" (*code one answer*):

Mostly manual tasks   Mostly non-manual tasks
1   2   3   4   5   6   7   8   9   10

V245. Are the tasks you perform at work mostly routine tasks or mostly not routine? Use this scale where 1 means "mostly routine tasks" and 10 means "mostly not routine tasks" (*code one answer*):

Mostly routine tasks   Mostly not routine tasks
1   2   3   4   5   6   7   8   9   10

V246. How much independence do you have in performing your tasks at work? Use this scale to indicate your degree of independence where 1 means "no independence at all" and 10 means "complete independence" (*code one answer*):

No independence at all   Complete independence
1   2   3   4   5   6   7   8   9   10

V247. Do you supervise other people at work? (*Code one answer*):
    1 Yes
    2 No

V248. Are you the chief wage earner in your household? (*Code one answer*):
    1 Yes (*in this case skip next two questions and continue with V250*)
    2 No   (*in this case continue with next question*)

V249. Is the chief wage earner of your household employed now or not? (*Code one answer*):
    1 Yes
    2 No

V250. In which profession/occupation does he/she work (or did work)? If more than one job, the main job? What is/was his/her job there?
_____ (*write in and code due to list below but do not read out list!*)
1   Employer/manager of establishment with 10 or more employees
2   Employer/manager of establishment with less than 10 employees
3   Professional worker lawyer, accountant, teacher, etc.
4   Supervisory - office worker: supervises others.
5   Non-manual - office worker: non-supervisory
6   Foreman and supervisor
7   Skilled manual worker
8   Semi-skilled manual worker
9   Unskilled manual worker
10 Farmer: has own farm
11 Agricultural worker
12 Member of armed forces, security personnel
13 Never had a job

V251. During the past year, did your family (*read out and code one answer*):
1   Save money
2   Just get by
3   Spent some savings
4   Spent savings and borrowed money

V252. People sometimes describe themselves as belonging to the working class, the middle class, or the upper or lower class. Would you describe yourself as belonging to the (*read out and code one answer*):
1   Upper class
2   Upper middle class
3   Lower middle class
4   Working class
5   Lower class

(*Show Card AE*)
V253. On this card is a scale of incomes on which 1 indicates the "lowest income decile" and 10 the "highest income decile" in your country. We would like to know in what group your household is. Please, specify the appropriate number, counting all wages, salaries, pensions and other incomes that come in. (*Code one number*):

Lowest decile   Highest decile
   1   2   3   4   5   6   7   8   9   10

V254. (*Code how interested the respondent was during the interview*):
1   Respondent was very interested
2   Respondent was somewhat interested
3   Respondent was not interested

116   Working with the Values Surveys files

V255. (*Code size of town*):
- 1   Under 2,000
- 2   2,000 - 5,000
- 3   5 - 10,000
- 4   10 - 20,000
- 5   20 - 50,000
- 6   50 - 100,000
- 7   100 - 500,000
- 8   500,000 and more

V256. (*Code ethnic group by observation*):
- 1   Caucasian white
- 2   Negro Black
- 3   South Asian Indian, Pakistani, etc.
- 4   East Asian Chinese, Japanese, etc.
- 5   Arabic, Central Asian
- 6   Other (*write in*): _____

V257. (*Code region where the interview was conducted*):
- 1   New England
- 2   Middle Atlantic states
- 3   South Atlantic
- 4   East South Central
- 5   West South Central
- 6   East North Central
- 7   West North Central
- 8   Rocky Mountain states
- 9   Northwest
- 10 California

[*NOTE: use 2-digit regional code appropriate to your own society*]

V258. (*Code language in which interview was conducted*):
- 1   English
- 2   French
- 3   Spanish

[*NOTE: if relevant, use codes appropriate to your own society*]

V259. Weight variable (*Provide a 4-digit weight variable to correct your sample to reflect national distributions of key variables. If no weighting is necessary, simply code each case as "1." It is especially important to correct for education. For example, if your sample contains 10 percent more university-educated respondents as there are in the adult population, members of this group should be downweighted by 10 percent, giving them a weight of .9, coded as "90"*).

Tables

Family Important in Life
(A001) For each of the following, indicate how important it is in your life: Family
Very important (%)

Country	1981	1990	1995	2000	2006	Change
Albania			96	96		0
Algeria				95		
Andorra					87	
Argentina		91	87	90	90	−1
Armenia			86			
Australia			90		94	4
Austria		86		89		3
Azerbaijan			85			
Bangladesh			94	97		3
Belarus			77	84	78	1
Belgium		84		88		4
Bosnia and Herz.				97	98	1
Brazil		91	93		87	−4
Britain		89		90	95	6
Bulgaria		76	89	84	89	13
Burkina Faso					95	
Canada		92		94	94	2
Chile		85	90	96	90	5
China		62	77	61	78	16
Colombia			86			
Croatia			85	79		−6
Cyprus					95	
Czech		86	91	85		−1
Denmark		88		87		−1
Dominican Rep.			86			
Egypt				96	98	2
El Salvador			97			
Estonia		69	78	68		−1
Ethiopia					93	
Finland		84	81	80	87	3
France		82		88	86	4
Georgia			95		99	4
Germany (East)		85	83	74	86	1
Germany (West)		71	75	79	75	4
Ghana					94	
Greece			83			
Guatemala					98	
Hong Kong					56	
Hungary		89	90	90		1
Iceland		91		94		3
India		77	91	93	91	14
Indonesia				99	98	−1
Iran				95	94	−1
Iraq				98	96	−2
Ireland		91		92		1
Israel						
Italy		87		90	93	6
Japan			78	91	93	93	15
Jordan				96	97	1

Country	1981	1990	1995	2000	2006	Change
Kyrgyzstan				87		
Latvia		73	68	72		−1
Lithuania		65	74	67		2
Luxembourg				87		
Macedonia			98	98		0
Malaysia					96	
Mali					93	
Malta		96		96		0
Mexico	85	72	97	95		10
Moldova			79	86	83	4
Montenegro				88	92	4
Morocco				93	96	3
Netherlands	81			81	83	2
New Zealand			93		93	0
Nigeria		94	98	99		5
Northern Ireland		94		88		−6
Norway		88	88		90	2
Pakistan			82	93		11
Peru			88	83	81	−7
Philippines			96	99		3
Poland		91	90	91	94	3
Portugal		62		85		23
Puerto Rico			93	96		3
Romania		83	89	85	86	3
Russia		79	84	76	90	11
Rwanda					63	
Saudi Arabia				95		
Serbia			89	92	94	5
Singapore				94		
Slovakia		88	91	88		0
Slovenia		81	83	82	89	8
South Africa		90	94	95	96	6
South Korea		93	90	90	92	−1
Spain		83	82	86	89	6
Sweden		87	90	90	92	5
Switzerland		87	82		86	−1
Taiwan			78		92	14
Tanzania				93		
Thailand					86	
Trinidad					96	
Turkey		87	98	97	98	11
Uganda				90		
Ukraine			87	84	88	1
Uruguay			92		89	−3
USA		93	95	96	94	1
Venezuela			98	98		0
Vietnam				82	81	−1
Zambia					92	
Zimbabwe				97		

Friends important in life
(A002) For each of the following, indicate how important it is in your life: Friends
Very important (%)

Country	1981	1990	1995	2000	2006	Change
Albania			19	32		13
Algeria				36		
Andorra					49	
Argentina		51	49	50	59	8
Armenia			45			
Australia			63		59	−4
Austria		35		42		7
Azerbaijan			35			
Bangladesh			16	32		16
Belarus		37	32	27		−10
Belgium		47		47		0
Bosnia and Herz.			70	71		1
Brazil		57	58		37	−20
Britain		48		58	69	21
Bulgaria		38	41	36	42	4
Burkina Faso					56	
Canada		51		62	65	14
Chile		19	28	29	24	5
China		22	30	20	29	7
Colombia			34			
Croatia			48	38		−10
Cyprus				65		
Czech		23	39	27		4
Denmark		53		55		2
Dominican Rep.			36			
Egypt				37	42	5
El Salvador			65			
Estonia		23	27	27		4
Ethiopia				79		
Finland		43	56	53	62	19
France		41		49	59	18
Georgia			74		78	4
Germany (East)		34	40	42	55	21
Germany (West)		37	47	48	49	12
Ghana					43	
Greece				42		
Guatemala					43	
Hong Kong				33		
Hungary		27	38	33		6
Iceland		49		48		−1
India		30	38	40	43	13
Indonesia				56	57	1
Iran				30	30	0
Iraq				60	61	1
Ireland		54		61		7
Israel						
Italy		39		36	47	8
Japan		34	49	48	46	12
Jordan				48	64	16

Country	1981	1990	1995	2000	2006	Change
Kyrgyzstan				48		
Latvia		16	24	25		9
Lithuania		19	22	18		−1
Luxembourg				48		
Macedonia			50	50		0
Malaysia					43	
Mali					58	
Malta		29		32		3
Mexico		25	26	39	36	11
Moldova			21	35	23	2
Montenegro			48	43		−5
Morocco				43	52	9
Netherlands		59		59	58	−1
New Zealand			57		56	−1
Nigeria		53	53	64		11
Northern Ireland		53		64		11
Norway		68	59		65	−3
Pakistan			26	19		−7
Peru			22	25	22	0
Philippines			39	37		−2
Poland		21	26	28	36	15
Portugal		20		33		13
Puerto Rico			29	33		4
Romania		25	21	26	25	0
Russia		29	29	27	39	10
Rwanda					49	
Saudi Arabia				53		
Serbia			48	58	56	8
Singapore				38		
Slovakia		28	32	34		6
Slovenia		38	41	42	51	13
South Africa		24	31	38	36	12
South Korea		52	46	45	47	−5
Spain		45	41	43	49	4
Sweden		69	70	71	71	2
Switzerland		51	56		56	5
Taiwan			29		40	11
Tanzania				32		
Thailand					33	
Trinidad					41	
Turkey		55	70	74	62	7
Uganda				73		
Ukraine			35	39	39	4
Uruguay			57		52	−5
USA		53	69	65	66	13
Venezuela			42	53		11
Vietnam				22	22	0
Zambia					48	
Zimbabwe				35		

Leisure time important in life

(A003) For each of the following, indicate how important it is in your life: Leisure time
Very important (%)

Country	1981	1990	1995	2000	2006	Change
Albania			12	14		2
Algeria				24		
Andorra					51	
Argentina		40	26	36	41	1
Armenia			24			
Australia			45		46	1
Austria		37		38		1
Azerbaijan			30			
Bangladesh			11	23		12
Belarus		37	30	25		−12
Belgium		40		39		−1
Bosnia and Herz.			48	45		−3
Brazil		52	54		27	−25
Britain	44		48	45		1
Bulgaria		36	22	23	28	−8
Burkina Faso					21	
Canada	42			39	43	1
Chile		33	43	54	49	16
China		14	11	7	12	−2
Colombia			40			
Croatia			34	26		−8
Cyprus					52	
Czech		24	26	20		−4
Denmark		48		45		−3
Dominican Rep.			31			
Egypt				9	13	4
El Salvador			62			
Estonia		25	22	20		−5
Ethiopia					48	
Finland		47	35	40	43	−4
France		31		37	38	7
Georgia			36		40	4
Germany (East)		36	33	21	33	−3
Germany (West)		40	32	34	24	−16
Ghana					53	
Greece				43		
Guatemala					59	
Hong Kong					24	
Hungary		32	34	32		0
Iceland		36		34		−2
India		16	11	29	24	8
Indonesia				17	23	6
Iran				30	36	6
Iraq				32	33	1
Ireland		32		40		8
Israel						
Italy		34		29	31	−3
Japan		24	40	44	41	17
Jordan				17	37	20

Country	1981	1990	1995	2000	2006	Change
Kyrgyzstan				25		
Latvia		21	20	17		−4
Lithuania		17	19	15		−2
Luxembourg				39		
Macedonia			49	42		−7
Malaysia					39	
Mali					36	
Malta		47		49		2
Mexico		28	32	51	55	27
Moldova			23	25	21	−2
Montenegro			26	25		−1
Morocco				40	24	−16
Netherlands		50		52	54	4
New Zealand			47		50	3
Nigeria		68	51	52		−16
Northern Ireland	31			44		13
Norway		42	39		49	7
Pakistan			13	5		−8
Peru			29	23	33	4
Philippines			14	15		1
Poland		31	24	24	30	−1
Portugal		15		21		6
Puerto Rico			47	53		6
Romania		25	27	24	27	2
Russia		29	26	19	31	2
Rwanda					44	
Saudi Arabia				31		
Serbia			26	31	41	15
Singapore				30		
Slovakia		29	26	32		3
Slovenia		28	33	33	43	15
South Africa		28	35	37	39	11
South Korea		25	23	24	25	0
Spain		38	31	35	44	6
Sweden		55	52	54	54	−1
Switzerland		47	40		37	−10
Taiwan			26		35	9
Tanzania				12		
Thailand					26	
Trinidad					51	
Turkey		24	41	43	47	23
Uganda				43		
Ukraine			26	25	30	4
Uruguay			46		43	−3
USA		43	42	42	42	−1
Venezuela			61	66		5
Vietnam				7	7	0
Zambia					34	
Zimbabwe				28		

Politics important in life
(A004) For each of the following, indicate how important it is in your life: Politics
Very important (%)

Country	1981	1990	1995	2000	2006	Change
Albania			23	31		8
Algeria			52			
Andorra				32		
Argentina		31	31	24	33	2
Armenia			50			
Australia			50		50	0
Austria		35		41		6
Azerbaijan			37			
Bangladesh			50	51		1
Belarus		37	41	30		−7
Belgium		25		33		8
Bosnia and Herz.			49	38		−11
Brazil		42	51		55	13
Britain		41		34	41	0
Bulgaria		46	26	34	23	−23
Burkina Faso					49	
Canada		48		40	46	−2
Chile		31	20	30	21	−10
China			59	63	68	56	−3
Colombia			32			
Croatia			26	32		6
Cyprus					37	
Czech		37	26	33		−4
Denmark		43		42		−1
Dominican Rep.			39			
Egypt				50	36	−14
El Salvador			38			
Estonia		42	28	21		−21
Ethiopia				74		
Finland		26	20	19	28	2
France		33		35	48	15
Georgia			46		63	17
Germany (East)		57	47	38	39	−18
Germany (West)		42	55	38	43	1
Ghana					49	
Greece				37		
Guatemala					41	
Hong Kong					28	
Hungary		26	27	19		−7
Iceland		26		36		10
India		40	34	40	40	0
Indonesia				39	40	1
Iran				44	50	6
Iraq				55	66	11
Ireland		28		35		7
Israel						
Italy		31		34	38	7
Japan			54	65	68	66	12
Jordan				45	51	6

Country	1981	1990	1995	2000	2006	Change
Kyrgyzstan				47		
Latvia		44	27	24		−20
Lithuania		51	28	46		−5
Luxembourg				38		
Macedonia			32	37		5
Malaysia					46	
Mali					53	
Malta	31		38			7
Mexico		41	48	48	48	7
Moldova			28	37	26	−2
Montenegro			29	28		−1
Morocco				27	36	9
Netherlands		53		57	45	−8
New Zealand			44		41	−3
Nigeria		39	44	52		13
Northern Ireland	28		34			6
Norway		50	45		58	8
Pakistan			20	14		−6
Peru			38	44	29	−9
Philippines			49	56		7
Poland		39	31	31	30	−9
Portugal	20			28		8
Puerto Rico			36	40		4
Romania	21	25	25	22		1
Russia	37	28	39	35		−2
Rwanda					63	
Saudi Arabia				56		
Serbia			24	25	22	−2
Singapore				44		
Slovakia		33	29	30		−3
Slovenia		25	15	15	16	−9
South Africa		58	44	36	47	−11
South Korea		71	66	51	52	−19
Spain		22	24	22	29	7
Sweden		45	47	56	63	18
Switzerland		40	36		56	16
Taiwan			44		30	−14
Tanzania				71		
Thailand					74	
Trinidad					29	
Turkey		27	53	41	38	11
Uganda				56		
Ukraine			30	37	37	7
Uruguay			37		34	−3
USA		51	59	57	61	10
Venezuela			27	34		7
Vietnam				78	70	−8
Zambia					55	
Zimbabwe				42		

Work important in life

(A005) For each of the following, indicate how important it is in your life: Work
Very important (%)

Country	1981	1990	1995	2000	2006	Change
Albania			80	82		2
Algeria				93		
Andorra					46	
Argentina		76	70	73	70	−6
Armenia			67			
Australia			51		36	−15
Austria		62		64		2
Azerbaijan			54			
Bangladesh			83	92		9
Belarus		55	48	49		−6
Belgium		56		65		9
Bosnia and Herz.			79	72		−7
Brazil		82	84		65	−17
Britain	49			40	38	−11
Bulgaria		57	54	62	51	−6
Burkina Faso					91	
Canada	59			53	48	−11
Chile		75	66	76	63	−12
China			64	65	50	45	−19
Colombia				72		
Croatia			55	47		−8
Cyprus					58	
Czech		58	49	53		−5
Denmark	51			40		−11
Dominican Rep.			66			
Egypt				72	59	−13
El Salvador			95			
Estonia		32	61	51		19
Ethiopia				90		
Finland		54	49	51	42	−12
France		61		70	64	3
Georgia			58		78	20
Germany (East)		61	61	60	59	−2
Germany (West)		35	41	41	41	6
Ghana					94	
Greece				59		
Guatemala					95	
Hong Kong					27	
Hungary		59	51	58		−1
Iceland		56		54		−2
India		86	83	78	69	−17
Indonesia				89	86	−3
Iran				79	77	−2
Iraq				86	84	−2
Ireland		65		50		−15
Israel						
Italy		62		62	62	0
Japan		40	55	49	49	9
Jordan				64	69	5

Country	1981	1990	1995	2000	2006	Change
Kyrgyzstan				55		
Latvia		33	56	70		37
Lithuania		42	46	60		18
Luxembourg				54		
Macedonia			87	77		−10
Malaysia					71	
Mali					88	
Malta		82		76		−6
Mexico		67	62	87	85	18
Moldova			53	43	43	−10
Montenegro			55	59		4
Morocco				90	86	−4
Netherlands		50		47	31	−19
New Zealand			48		37	−11
Nigeria		94	88	89		−5
Northern Ireland	57			40		−17
Norway		73	59		53	−20
Pakistan			68	61		−7
Peru			75	69	71	−4
Philippines			83	93		10
Poland		68	64	78	62	−6
Portugal		35		58		23
Puerto Rico			75	75		0
Romania		69	59	71	55	−14
Russia		46	49	58	51	5
Rwanda					64	
Saudi Arabia				63		
Serbia			64	55	61	−3
Singapore				61		
Slovakia		64	48	62		−2
Slovenia		73	55	62	47	−26
South Africa		71	78	75	78	7
South Korea		69	58	62	62	−7
Spain		65	59	59	52	−13
Sweden		67	65	55	54	−13
Switzerland	51	49			54	3
Taiwan			45		63	18
Tanzania				96		
Thailand					57	
Trinidad					82	
Turkey		59	78	74	57	−2
Uganda				81		
Ukraine			49	63	41	−8
Uruguay			71		71	0
USA		62	53	54	46	−16
Venezuela			94	93		−1
Vietnam				57	41	−16
Zambia					78	
Zimbabwe				90		

Religion important in life
(A006) For each of the following, indicate how important it is in your life: Religion
Very important (%)

Country	1981	1990	1995	2000	2006	Change
Albania			25	28		3
Algeria				91		
Andorra					8	
Argentina		40	37	46	32	−8
Armenia			27			
Australia			23		20	−3
Austria		25		21		−4
Azerbaijan			30			
Bangladesh			82	88		6
Belarus		12	22	12		0
Belgium		17		21		4
Bosnia and Herz.			40	40		0
Brazil		57	65		52	−5
Britain		18		13	20	2
Bulgaria		12	16	16	19	7
Burkina Faso					84	
Canada		30		33	34	4
Chile		51	43	47	37	−14
China		1	4	3	7	6
Colombia			49			
Croatia			26	24		−2
Cyprus				51		
Czech		9	9	8		−1
Denmark		9		8		−1
Dominican Rep.			51			
Egypt				97	96	−1
El Salvador			87			
Estonia		4	8	5		1
Ethiopia					81	
Finland		14	13	12	18	4
France		14		11	13	−1
Georgia			49		80	31
Germany (East)		16	6	4	9	−7
Germany (West)		13	15	9	13	0
Ghana					90	
Greece				33		
Guatemala					83	
Hong Kong					5	
Hungary		23	22	19		−4
Iceland		24		19		−5
India		49	49	57	51	2
Indonesia				98	95	−3
Iran				80	78	−2
Iraq				94	96	2
Ireland		48		38		−10
Israel						
Italy		31		33	34	3
Japan			6	7	7	6	0
Jordan				96	95	−1

Country	1981	1990	1995	2000	2006	Change
Kyrgyzstan				32		
Latvia		7	13	11		4
Lithuania		16	13	12		−4
Luxembourg				15		
Macedonia			35	48		13
Malaysia					81	
Mali					90	
Malta		72		67		−5
Mexico		34	44	66	59	25
Moldova			31	35	32	1
Montenegro			24	19		−5
Morocco				94	91	−3
Netherlands		21		16	13	−8
New Zealand			20		17	−3
Nigeria			85	91	93	8
Northern Ireland		34		27		−7
Norway		15	12		11	−4
Pakistan			79	82		3
Peru			55	53	50	−5
Philippines			78	87		9
Poland		52	47	45	48	−4
Portugal		19		28		9
Puerto Rico			71	76		5
Romania		42	38	51	58	16
Russia		12	14	13	13	1
Rwanda					39	
Saudi Arabia				89		
Serbia			26	29	26	0
Singapore				59		
Slovakia		25	24	27		2
Slovenia		17	16	12	15	−2
South Africa		64	71	73	71	7
South Korea		26	20	23	21	−5
Spain		21	25	19	15	−6
Sweden		10	10	11	9	−1
Switzerland		24	16		17	−7
Taiwan			13		12	−1
Tanzania				85		
Thailand					56	
Trinidad					78	
Turkey		61	77	78	75	14
Uganda				72		
Ukraine			21	23	17	−4
Uruguay				24	23	−1
USA		53	58	59	56	3
Venezuela			61	64		3
Vietnam				10	7	−3
Zambia					78	
Zimbabwe				78		

Feeling of happiness

(A007) Taking all things together, would you say you are
Very happy (%)

Country	1981	1990	1995	2000	2006	Change
Albania			3	10		7
Algeria				16		
Andorra					28	
Argentina	17	32	29	33	32	15
Armenia			6			
Australia	35		43		36	1
Austria		29		36		7
Azerbaijan			11			
Bangladesh			18	15		−3
Belarus		6	4	5		−1
Belgium	32	39		41		9
Bosnia and Herz.			15	25		10
Brazil		21	22		34	13
Britain	38	35	33		50	12
Bulgaria		6	9	8	10	4
Burkina Faso					24	
Canada	35	29		45	46	11
Chile		33	28	36	33	0
China		28	23	12	21	−7
Colombia			23		49	26
Croatia			8	14		6
Cyprus					41	
Czech		7	9	11		4
Denmark	30	42		45		15
Dominican Rep.			32			
Egypt				18	10	−8
El Salvador			56			
Estonia		3	5	7		4
Ethiopia					30	
Finland	17	20	24	25	29	12
France	20	25		33	36	16
Georgia			12		12	0
Germany (East)		13	15	19	17	4
Germany (West)	10	15	20	18	20	10
Ghana					50	
Greece				18		
Guatemala					45	
Hong Kong					7	
Hungary	11	11	14	18		7
Iceland	42	41		47		5
India		24	30	25	29	5
Indonesia				20	25	5
Iran				23	18	−5
Iraq				13	6	−7
Ireland	39	43		42		3
Israel				27		
Italy	11	15		18	18	7
Japan	15	17	33	28	28	13
Jordan				12	29	17

Country	1981	1990	1995	2000	2006	Change
Kyrgyzstan				20		
Latvia		1	4	7		6
Lithuania		3	4	4		1
Luxembourg				34		
Macedonia			13	19		6
Malaysia					36	
Mali					39	
Malta	13	38		31		18
Mexico	34	25	27	57	58	24
Moldova			4	6	10	6
Montenegro			14	8		−6
Morocco				26	25	−1
Netherlands	33	46		46	42	9
New Zealand			33		38	5
Nigeria		39	46	67		28
Northern Ireland	38	37		45		7
Norway	28	29	30		37	9
Pakistan			28	20		−8
Peru			28	31	28	0
Philippines			40	39		−1
Poland		9	18	15	21	12
Portugal		13		17		4
Puerto Rico			43	53		10
Romania		6	5	4	7	1
Russia		5	6	6	10	5
Rwanda					12	
Saudi Arabia				44		
Serbia			14	12	10	−4
Singapore				35		
Slovakia		6	7	8		2
Slovenia		9	13	15	18	9
South Africa	27	27	41	43	47	20
South Korea		10	12	10	15	5
Spain	19	20	19	20	14	−5
Sweden	28	40	39	36	42	14
Switzerland		35	39		41	6
Taiwan			30		23	−7
Tanzania				56		
Thailand				40		
Trinidad				50		
Turkey		29	49	30	37	8
Uganda				25		
Ukraine			5	6	11	6
Uruguay			21		30	9
USA	31	39	46	39	45	14
Venezuela			54	57		3
Vietnam				49	23	−26
Zambia					18	
Zimbabwe				20		

State of health (subjective)
(A008) All in all, how would you describe your state of health these days? Would you say it is...
Very good/good (%)

Country	1981	1990	1995	2000	2006	Change
Albania			72	75		3
Algeria				44		
Andorra					84	
Argentina	51	60	61	65	79	28
Armenia			51			
Australia	75		79		76	1
Austria		62				
Azerbaijan			58			
Bangladesh			47	58		11
Belarus		27	27			0
Belgium	72	74				2
Bosnia and Herz.			62	68		6
Brazil		69	70		74	5
Britain	75	73			73	−2
Bulgaria		51	58		54	3
Burkina Faso					72	
Canada	82	80		81	80	−2
Chile		54	61	68	67	13
China		56	68	61	61	5
Colombia			76		72	−4
Croatia			51			
Cyprus					76	
Czech		49	53			4
Denmark	76	78				2
Dominican Rep.			68			
Egypt				68	67	−1
El Salvador			67			
Estonia		36	39			3
Ethiopia				65		
Finland	73	76	72		66	−7
France	63	66			72	9
Georgia			49	42		−7
Germany (East)		55	56		61	6
Germany (West)	59	57	61		73	14
Ghana					80	
Greece						
Guatemala				64		
Hong Kong				63		
Hungary	37	31	47			10
Iceland	71	74				3
India		63	57	63	69	6
Indonesia				74	76	2
Iran				76	68	−8
Iraq				77	66	−11
Ireland	80	81				1
Israel						
Italy	54	59			74	20
Japan	45	44	54	55	54	9
Jordan				84	87	3

Country	1981	1990	1995	2000	2006	Change
Kyrgyzstan				61		
Latvia		32	36			4
Lithuania		43	45			2
Luxembourg						
Macedonia			73	71		−2
Malaysia					89	
Mali					63	
Malta	57					
Mexico	32	69	56	65	64	32
Moldova			32	30	54	22
Montenegro			54	59		5
Morocco				75	75	0
Netherlands	75	72			71	−4
New Zealand			79		82	3
Nigeria		78	75	89		11
Northern Ireland	76	77				1
Norway	75	74	79		79	4
Pakistan			66	66		0
Peru			51	49	48	−3
Philippines			52	56		4
Poland		37	41		54	17
Portugal		44				
Puerto Rico			68	73		5
Romania		47	53		54	7
Russia		26	26		42	16
Rwanda					34	
Saudi Arabia				89		
Serbia			52	52	54	2
Singapore						
Slovakia			47	52		5
Slovenia			43	46	57	14
South Africa	70	74	72	81	79	9
South Korea	33		79	78	82	49
Spain	50	57	70	75	80	30
Sweden	71	80	77		78	7
Switzerland			80	83	83	3
Taiwan			48		86	38
Tanzania				64		
Thailand					76	
Trinidad					70	
Turkey		60	63	64	68	8
Uganda				73		
Ukraine			27		49	22
Uruguay				78	77	−1
USA	77	79	78	83	81	4
Venezuela				74		
Vietnam				58	60	2
Zambia					72	
Zimbabwe				64		

Child qualities: independence

(A009) Here is a list of qualities which children can be encouraged to learn at home. Which, if any, do you consider to be especially important?

Independence (%)

Country	1981	1990	1995	2000	2006	Change
Albania			32	57		25
Algeria				26		
Andorra					48	
Argentina	42	43	41	37	44	2
Armenia			32			
Australia	25		53		63	38
Austria		64		70		6
Azerbaijan			60			
Bangladesh			57	78		21
Belarus			31	30	32	1
Belgium	20	36		42		22
Bosnia and Herz.			35	52		17
Brazil		26	20		29	3
Britain	25	41	49	53	58	33
Bulgaria		62	38	42	46	−16
Burkina Faso					31	
Canada	24	44		62	58	34
Chile		31	34	52	41	10
China		84	50	74	68	−16
Colombia			27		33	6
Croatia			64			
Cyprus					44	
Czech		52	22	69		17
Denmark	57	81		81		24
Dominican Rep.			40			
Egypt				73	26	−47
El Salvador			36			
Estonia		43	54	22		−21
Ethiopia				79		
Finland		58	56	59	69	11
France	18	27		29	38	20
Georgia			51		54	3
Germany (East)		67	45	70	75	8
Germany (West)	50	74	58	70	77	27
Ghana					37	
Greece				58		
Guatemala				28		
Hong Kong				24		
Hungary	51	70	44	73		22
Iceland	39	89		76		37
India		30	37	56	67	37
Indonesia				76	82	6
Iran				53	63	10
Iraq				29	29	0
Ireland	30	43		49		19
Israel				69		
Italy	24	34		41	58	34
Japan	47	64	60	82	80	33
Jordan				21	43	22

Country	1981	1990	1995	2000	2006	Change
Kyrgyzstan				55		
Latvia		73	38	51		−22
Lithuania		81	72	78		−3
Luxembourg				49		
Macedonia			62	59		−3
Malaysia					79	
Mali					42	
Malta	8	33		30		22
Mexico	15	47	43	44	41	26
Moldova			36	56	45	9
Montenegro			52	59		7
Morocco				37	55	18
Netherlands	28	50		54	64	36
New Zealand			54		53	−1
Nigeria		16	20	26		10
Northern Ireland	17	37		51		34
Norway	53	86	89		90	37
Pakistan			22	13		−9
Peru			21	39	27	6
Philippines			51	68		17
Poland		12	32	23	42	30
Portugal		21		24		3
Puerto Rico			28	51		23
Romania		24	51	30	29	5
Russia		29	28	30	43	14
Rwanda				26		
Saudi Arabia				70		
Serbia			51	61	64	13
Singapore				72		
Slovakia		48	22	62		14
Slovenia		33	71	70	83	50
South Africa	20	20	32	58	60	40
South Korea	45	54	60	77	67	22
Spain	25	37	25	39	31	6
Sweden	18	36	61	69	78	60
Switzerland		43	43		74	31
Taiwan			66		80	14
Tanzania				42		
Thailand					48	
Trinidad					55	
Turkey		19	21	16	40	21
Uganda				32		
Ukraine			34	31	30	−4
Uruguay			52		49	−3
USA	32	52	44	62	46	14
Venezuela			23	45		22
Vietnam				56	59	3
Zambia					55	
Zimbabwe				27		

Child qualities: hard work

(A010) Here is a list of qualities which children can be encouraged to learn at home. Which, if any, do you consider to be especially important?

Hard work (%)

Country	1981	1990	1995	2000	2006	Change
Albania			57	64		7
Algeria				67		
Andorra					59	
Argentina	50	53	55	57	55	5
Armenia			84			
Australia	12		36		48	36
Austria		14		9		−5
Azerbaijan			77			
Bangladesh			8	59		51
Belarus		80	84	92		12
Belgium	32	34		43		11
Bosnia and Herz.			46	54		8
Brazil		51	47		61	10
Britain	15	28	37	38	44	29
Bulgaria		91	92	87	87	−4
Burkina Faso					80	
Canada	20	35		51	52	32
Chile		12	17	26	26	14
China			65	73	86	82	17
Colombia			18		19	1
Croatia			64			
Cyprus					53	
Czech		84	79	74		−10
Denmark	2	2		2		0
Dominican Rep.			50			
Egypt				38	55	17
El Salvador			38			
Estonia		92	87	81		−11
Ethiopia				54		
Finland		6	15	11	15	9
France	33	53		50	62	29
Georgia			82		90	8
Germany (East)		16	14	22	27	11
Germany (West)	20	14	6	23	28	8
Ghana					79	
Greece				31		
Guatemala				29		
Hong Kong				19		
Hungary	28	70	34	71		43
Iceland	24	78		44		20
India		67	72	85	81	14
Indonesia				66	59	−7
Iran				62	69	7
Iraq					63	
Ireland	24	28		37		13
Israel				24		
Italy	13	24		36	39	26
Japan	15	31	24	27	32	17
Jordan				45	42	−3

Country	1981	1990	1995	2000	2006	Change
Kyrgyzstan				87		
Latvia		91	86	85		−6
Lithuania		92	89	88		−4
Luxembourg				57		
Macedonia			24	37		13
Malaysia					49	
Mali					73	
Malta	32	60		43		11
Mexico	18	23	36	29	24	6
Moldova			87	87	79	−8
Montenegro				68	82	14
Morocco				69	51	−18
Netherlands	12	14		14	29	17
New Zealand			37		41	4
Nigeria			82	83	80	−2
Northern Ireland	19	29		41		22
Norway	4	7	11		13	9
Pakistan			54	56		2
Peru			63	59	54	−9
Philippines			58	73		15
Poland		87	16	86	21	−66
Portugal		69		67		−2
Puerto Rico			30	52		22
Romania		71	64	82	83	12
Russia		93	91	91	88	−5
Rwanda					83	
Saudi Arabia				42		
Serbia			68	75	68	0
Singapore				64		
Slovakia		83	70	75		−8
Slovenia		32	33	29	34	2
South Africa	30	27	56	70	71	41
South Korea	40	64	62	72	73	33
Spain	41	37	64	45	63	22
Sweden	4	5	7	4	10	6
Switzerland		38	43		27	−11
Taiwan			42		55	13
Tanzania				83		
Thailand					23	
Trinidad					65	
Turkey		73	62	72	79	6
Uganda				84		
Ukraine			83	89	76	−7
Uruguay			27		22	−5
USA	26	49	53	60	54	28
Venezuela			55	27		−28
Vietnam				76	89	13
Zambia					81	
Zimbabwe				84		

Child qualities: feeling of responsibility

(A011) Here is a list of qualities which children can be encouraged to learn at home. Which, if any, do you consider to be especially important?

Feeling of responsibility (%)

Country	1981	1990	1995	2000	2006	Change
Albania			31	68		37
Algeria				58		
Andorra					90	
Argentina	58	80	79	76	71	13
Armenia			69			
Australia	30		67		72	42
Austria		85		87		2
Azerbaijan			66			
Bangladesh			39	53		14
Belarus		81	62	77		−4
Belgium	37	71		80		43
Bosnia and Herz.			62	71		9
Brazil		72	65		78	6
Britain	24	46	67	56	60	36
Bulgaria		68	64	76	73	5
Burkina Faso					39	
Canada	40	75		77	73	33
Chile		88	74	85	85	−3
China		67	34	64	64	−3
Colombia			77		83	6
Croatia			67			
Cyprus				78		
Czech		61	69	66		5
Denmark	62	86		81		19
Dominican Rep.			84			
Egypt				51	77	26
El Salvador			67			
Estonia		76	77	79		3
Ethiopia				47		
Finland		84	87	86	90	6
France	40	72		73	78	38
Georgia			68		82	14
Germany (East)		84	91	79	90	6
Germany (West)	62	85	93	84	78	16
Ghana					44	
Greece				83		
Guatemala					64	
Hong Kong					26	
Hungary	45	66	85	74		29
Iceland	49	94		81		32
India		60	48	68	68	8
Indonesia				82	84	2
Iran				72	81	9
Iraq				76	83	7
Ireland	22	61		55		33
Israel				65		
Italy	48	83		82	87	39
Japan	69	84	88	91	91	22
Jordan				65	62	−3

Country	1981	1990	1995	2000	2006	Change
Kyrgyzstan				78		
Latvia		75	80	74		−1
Lithuania		72	74	78		6
Luxembourg				79		
Macedonia			74	74		0
Malaysia					79	
Mali					45	
Malta	38	56		77		39
Mexico	56	77	65	78	78	22
Moldova			66	83	70	4
Montenegro			67	68		1
Morocco				64	69	5
Netherlands	54	87		87	90	36
New Zealand			59		63	4
Nigeria		36	28	33		−3
Northern Ireland	9	38		53		44
Norway	64	90	92		90	26
Pakistan			69	50		−19
Peru			77	79	73	−4
Philippines			58	67		9
Poland		68	78	73	82	14
Portugal		72		64		−8
Puerto Rico			84	74		−10
Romania		56	83	62	69	13
Russia		70	70	76	81	11
Rwanda					54	
Saudi Arabia				57		
Serbia			65	72	67	2
Singapore				81		
Slovakia		64	69	67		3
Slovenia		71	70	76	74	3
South Africa	30	48	51	65	57	27
South Korea	54	91	88	92	90	36
Spain	63	78	70	82	70	7
Sweden	63	89	88	87	92	29
Switzerland		77	80		89	12
Taiwan			81		92	11
Tanzania				41		
Thailand					61	
Trinidad					58	
Turkey		66	67	64	75	9
Uganda				55		
Ukraine			66	75	66	0
Uruguay				83	80	−3
USA	43	72	70	72	57	14
Venezuela				74	88	14
Vietnam				70	75	5
Zambia					52	
Zimbabwe				48		

Child qualities: imagination

(A012) Here is a list of qualities which children can be encouraged to learn at home. Which, if any, do you consider to be especially important?

Imagination (%)

Country	1981	1990	1995	2000	2006	Change
Albania			11	29		18
Algeria				12		
Andorra					41	
Argentina	22	31	25	24	26	4
Armenia			16			
Australia	13		27		44	31
Austria		24		22		−2
Azerbaijan			14			
Bangladesh			14	36		22
Belarus		7	9	10		3
Belgium	9	18		26		17
Bosnia and Herz.			26	23		−3
Brazil		12	8		26	14
Britain	13	17		38	38	25
Bulgaria		16	7	19	17	1
Burkina Faso					19	
Canada	11	23		30	32	21
Chile		32	24	35	27	−5
China		27	22	35	21	−6
Colombia			19		18	−1
Croatia			17			
Cyprus					24	
Czech		5	5	7		2
Denmark	12	37		37		25
Dominican Rep.			12			
Egypt				15	10	−5
El Salvador			10			
Estonia		13	9	11		−2
Ethiopia					39	
Finland		27	24	29	38	11
France	14	23		18	25	11
Georgia			10		10	0
Germany (East)		28	27	27	35	7
Germany (West)	15	33	40	29	42	27
Ghana					17	
Greece				22		
Guatemala					12	
Hong Kong					2	
Hungary	7	9	13	11		4
Iceland	6	49		18		12
India		22	11	28	25	3
Indonesia				29	18	−11
Iran				11	18	7
Iraq					9	
Ireland	8	14		25		17
Israel				23		
Italy	9	17		12	15	6
Japan	11	24		26	35	31	20
Jordan				6	17	11

Country	1981	1990	1995	2000	2006	Change
Kyrgyzstan				38		
Latvia		11	10	7		−4
Lithuania		6	7	5		−1
Luxembourg				25		
Macedonia			12	13		1
Malaysia					22	
Mali					24	
Malta	2	11		7		5
Mexico	13	31	29	25	25	12
Moldova			13	27	21	8
Montenegro			17	12		−5
Morocco				10	26	16
Netherlands	12	23		32	26	14
New Zealand			28		35	7
Nigeria		6	6	11		5
Northern Ireland	9	13			32	23
Norway	12	31	37		55	43
Pakistan			8	7		−1
Peru			19	23	13	−6
Philippines			10	13		3
Poland		10	11	12	21	11
Portugal		18		16		−2
Puerto Rico			13	19		6
Romania		17	39	14	18	1
Russia		11	6	7	15	4
Rwanda					18	
Saudi Arabia				31		
Serbia			13	10	22	9
Singapore				13		
Slovakia		8	5	3		−5
Slovenia		10	8	12	16	6
South Africa	6	9	10	19	15	9
South Korea	6	6	8	33	43	37
Spain	26	39	22	29	20	−6
Sweden	16	40	39	41	57	41
Switzerland			30	22	44	14
Taiwan			15		17	2
Tanzania				61		
Thailand					28	
Trinidad					6	
Turkey		23	26	23	23	0
Uganda				11		
Ukraine			11	11	28	17
Uruguay			31		32	1
USA	10	26	24	30	32	22
Venezuela			13	24		11
Vietnam				20	16	−4
Zambia					20	
Zimbabwe				12		

Child qualities: tolerance and respect for other people

(A013) Here is a list of qualities which children can be encouraged to learn at home. Which, if any, do you consider to be especially important?

Tolerance and respecto for other people (%)

Country	1981	1990	1995	2000	2006	Change
Albania			81	80		−1
Algeria				54		
Andorra					88	
Argentina	44	78	73	70	70	26
Armenia			48			
Australia	67		81		91	24
Austria		66		72		6
Azerbaijan			59			
Bangladesh			69	71		2
Belarus		80	60	72		−8
Belgium	45	68		85		40
Bosnia and Herz.			63	73		10
Brazil		66	59		65	−1
Britain	62	80	86	83	85	23
Bulgaria		52	46	60	53	1
Burkina Faso					69	
Canada	53	80		82	84	31
Chile		79	62	76	79	0
China		62	43	73	61	−1
Colombia			68		84	16
Croatia			64			
Cyprus					71	
Czech		66	60	63		−3
Denmark	58	81		87		29
Dominican Rep.			68			
Egypt				65	71	6
El Salvador			59			
Estonia		70	60	71		1
Ethiopia				36		
Finland		80	82	83	86	6
France	59	78		85	87	28
Georgia			54		73	19
Germany (East)		74	86	70	77	3
Germany (West)	43	77	91	71	69	26
Ghana					71	
Greece			53			
Guatemala				59		
Hong Kong				14		
Hungary	31	62	64	67		36
Iceland	58	93		84		26
India		59	52	63	56	−3
Indonesia				63	59	−4
Iran				59	64	5
Iraq				78	85	7
Ireland	56	76		77		21
Israel				82		
Italy	43	67		75	74	31
Japan	41	60	58	71	75	34
Jordan				67	75	8

Country	1981	1990	1995	2000	2006	Change
Kyrgyzstan				65		
Latvia		70	73	69		−1
Lithuania		57	54	59		2
Luxembourg				77		
Macedonia			71	75		4
Malaysia					74	
Mali					60	
Maita	24	40		61		37
Mexico	39	64	57	72	78	39
Moldova			63	78	67	4
Montenegro				64	57	−7
Morocco				65	59	−6
Netherlands	59	89		92	86	27
New Zealand			78		82	4
Nigeria			75	64	59	−16
Northern Ireland	60	80		76		16
Norway	32	64	66		92	60
Pakistan			54	53		−1
Peru			63	73	66	3
Philippines			48	60		12
Poland		76	82	79	84	8
Portugal		68		67		−1
Puerto Rico			74	61		−13
Romania		56	72	58	59	3
Russia		70	69	68	68	−2
Rwanda					64	
Saudi Arabia				56		
Serbia			50	65	64	14
Singapore				69		
Slovakia		55	57	57		2
Slovenia		74	72	70	75	1
South Africa	51	59	68	74	77	26
South Korea	25	55	47	65	56	31
Spain	44	73	76	80	72	28
Sweden	71	91	90	92	94	23
Switzerland			77	79	91	14
Taiwan			59		80	21
Tanzania				84		
Thailand				58		
Trinidad				82		
Turkey		69	61	62	69	0
Uganda				57		
Ukraine			61	66	57	−4
Uruguay			71		82	11
USA	52	72	75	80	69	17
Venezuela			57	80		23
Vietnam				68	50	−18
Zambia					58	
Zimbabwe				77		

Child qualities: thrift, saving money and things

(A014) Here is a list of qualities which children can be encouraged to learn at home. Which, if any, do you consider to be especially important?

Thrift, saving money and things (%)

Country	1981	1990	1995	2000	2006	Change
Albania			67	55		−12
Algeria				18		
Andorra				23		
Argentina	16	15	16	15	16	0
Armenia			38			
Australia	15		18		33	18
Austria		56		49		−7
Azerbaijan			59			
Bangladesh			51	57		6
Belarus			53	53	46	−7
Belgium	36	36		44		8
Bosnia and Herz.			39	39		0
Brazil		30	39		29	−1
Britain	8	28	29	32	25	17
Bulgaria		39	43	38	42	3
Burkina Faso					48	
Canada	15	21		28	28	13
Chile		29	30	35	38	9
China		56	62	57	63	7
Colombia			25		48	23
Croatia			29			
Cyprus				40		
Czech		39	44	30		−9
Denmark	14	19		10		−4
Dominican Rep.			11			
Egypt				8	28	20
El Salvador			30			
Estonia		35	30	44		9
Ethiopia				52		
Finland		38	29	21	27	−11
France	31	36		38	43	12
Georgia			32		29	−3
Germany (East)		58	65	43	59	1
Germany (West)	29	45	41	36	42	13
Ghana					20	
Greece				30		
Guatemala				39		
Hong Kong				2		
Hungary	33	49	42	40		7
Iceland	12	69		21		9
India		24	42	62	55	31
Indonesia				52	47	−5
Iran				30	39	9
Iraq				28	32	4
Ireland	14	22		22		8
Israel				20		
Italy	18	27		35	39	21
Japan	31	40	44	48	52	21
Jordan				19	24	5

Country	1981	1990	1995	2000	2006	Change
Kyrgyzstan				43		
Latvia		46	41	45		−1
Lithuania		37	39	40		3
Luxembourg				47		
Macedonia			44	39		−5
Malaysia					51	
Mali					44	
Malta	32	41		54		22
Mexico	12	33	49	38	39	27
Moldova			42	42	53	11
Montenegro			25	38		13
Morocco				36	45	9
Netherlands	17	29		21	42	25
New Zealand			25		33	8
Nigeria		8	10	10		2
Northern Ireland	8	25		27		19
Norway	12	22	13		14	2
Pakistan			57	55		−2
Peru			19	23	11	−8
Philippines			30	45		15
Poland		44	57	39	54	10
Portugal		35		32		−3
Puerto Rico			23	24		1
Romania		37	61	31	53	16
Russia		61	55	52	52	−9
Rwanda					24	
Saudi Arabia				31		
Serbia			30	31	35	5
Singapore				38		
Slovakia		38	44	38		0
Slovenia		58	40	35	40	−18
South Africa	15	16	28	36	37	22
South Korea	34	53	66	68	73	39
Spain	11	23	19	32	19	8
Sweden	32	48	42	30	39	7
Switzerland		42	37		22	−20
Taiwan			49		67	18
Tanzania				54		
Thailand					58	
Trinidad					32	
Turkey		36	29	30	38	2
Uganda				11		
Ukraine			49	51	41	−8
Uruguay			27		23	−4
USA	10	29	29	23	25	15
Venezuela			45	39		−6
Vietnam				48	60	12
Zambia					23	
Zimbabwe				21		

132

Child qualities: determination, perseverance

(A015) Here is a list of qualities which children can be encouraged to learn at home. Which, if any, do you consider to be especially important?

Determination, perseverance (%)

Country	1981	1990	1995	2000	2006	Change
Albania			41	53		12
Algeria				17		
Andorra					37	
Argentina	17	29	28	23	25	8
Armenia			57			
Australia	18		36		51	33
Austria		39		36		−3
Azerbaijan			47			
Bangladesh			53	36		−17
Belarus		40	41	49		9
Belgium	21	39		45		24
Bosnia and Herz.			41	44		3
Brazil		25	35		31	6
Britain	18	29	35	40	38	20
Bulgaria		41	44	57	56	15
Burkina Faso					27	
Canada	22	38		47	48	26
Chile		31	34	43	46	15
China		45	36	16	25	−20
Colombia			19		20	1
Croatia			44			
Cyprus				41		
Czech		31	35	28		−3
Denmark	12	31		32		20
Dominican Rep.			27			
Egypt				9	22	13
El Salvador			14			
Estonia		51	49	50		−1
Ethiopia				30		
Finland		39	44	51	65	26
France	18	39		39	54	36
Georgia			37		27	−10
Germany (East)		54	45	50	64	10
Germany (West)	28	50	37	47	61	33
Ghana					43	
Greece				54		
Guatemala					23	
Hong Kong					6	
Hungary	17	12	62	30		13
Iceland	12	75		29		17
India			28	29	46	41	13
Indonesia				44	42	−2
Iran				28	30	2
Iraq					21	
Ireland	10	26		29		19
Israel				31		
Italy	18	29		34	44	26
Japan	25	59	61	69	67	42
Jordan				16	32	16

Country	1981	1990	1995	2000	2006	Change
Kyrgyzstan				51		
Latvia		40	48	36		−4
Lithuania		34	36	37		3
Luxembourg				39		
Macedonia			47	43		−4
Malaysia					33	
Mali					24	
Malta	4	21		16		12
Mexico	10	37	42	35	36	26
Moldova			29	34	25	−4
Montenegro				42	44	2
Morocco				16	27	11
Netherlands	16	32		35	37	21
New Zealand			39		49	10
Nigeria		21	40	23		2
Northern Ireland	10	18		33		23
Norway	12	33	35		42	30
Pakistan			31	29		−2
Peru			24	34	17	−7
Philippines			29	37		8
Poland		27		34	26	−1
Portugal		20		27		7
Puerto Rico			22	24		2
Romania		40	63	19	30	−10
Russia		40	41	39	53	13
Rwanda					59	
Saudi Arabia				40		
Serbia			44	41	49	5
Singapore				37		
Slovakia		29	31	25		−4
Slovenia		42	48	54	63	21
South Africa	18	32	30	39	33	15
South Korea	27	31	36	42	45	18
Spain	13	22	21	29	30	17
Sweden	17	33	32	29	49	32
Switzerland			45		68	23
Taiwan			34		35	1
Tanzania				57		
Thailand					46	
Trinidad					26	
Turkey		20	21	22	37	17
Uganda				36		
Ukraine			42	46	49	7
Uruguay			44		39	−5
USA	15	35	41	45	38	23
Venezuela			19	45		26
Vietnam				50	63	13
Zambia					38	
Zimbabwe				33		

133

Child qualities: religious faith

(A016) Here is a list of qualities which children can be encouraged to learn at home. Which , if any, do you consider to be especially important?

Religious faith (%)

Country	1981	1990	1995	2000	2006	Change
Albania			30	36		6
Algeria				77		
Andorra					7	
Argentina	19	28	36	43	24	5
Armenia			12			
Australia	22		21		21	−1
Austria		23		20		−3
Azerbaijan			19			
Bangladesh			78	70		−8
Belarus		6	15	12		6
Belgium	16	17		17		1
Bosnia and Herz.			25	30		5
Brazil		46	57		56	10
Britain	12	20	17	17	18	6
Bulgaria		11	16	15	18	7
Burkina Faso					68	
Canada	23	31		33	31	8
Chile		54	46	41	38	−16
China		1	3		2	1
Colombia			42		48	6
Croatia			19			
Cyprus				34		
Czech		9	9	7		−2
Denmark	7	9		8		1
Dominican Rep.			59			
Egypt				87	90	3
El Salvador			67			
Estonia		3	5	6		3
Ethiopia				41		
Finland		13	11	14	12	−1
France	10	13		8	9	−1
Georgia			31		68	37
Germany (East)		16	6	6	7	−9
Germany (West)	16	19	17	15	12	−4
Ghana					73	
Greece				39		
Guatemala					59	
Hong Kong					1	
Hungary	8	24	18	17		9
Iceland	8	50		10		2
India		29	36	47	41	12
Indonesia				93	91	−2
Iran				71	71	0
Iraq				92	90	−2
Ireland	41	57		42		1
Israel				29		
Italy	20	35		31	34	14
Japan	6	7	6	7	6	0
Jordan				85	85	0

Country	1981	1990	1995	2000	2006	Change
Kyrgyzstan				23		
Latvia		9	14	12		3
Lithuania		21	22	20		−1
Luxembourg				17		
Macedonia			22	27		5
Malaysia					60	
Mali					60	
Malta	43	55		57		14
Mexico	35	40	42	52	39	4
Moldova			28	42	42	14
Montenegro			13	22		9
Morocco				77	68	−9
Netherlands	12	14		9	10	−2
New Zealand			16		15	−1
Nigeria		74	72	68		−6
Northern Ireland	33	44		39		6
Norway	11	14	12		9	−2
Pakistan			81	86		5
Peru			52	56	45	−7
Philippines			63	60		−3
Poland		63		42	46	−17
Portugal		31		23		−8
Puerto Rico			72	69		−3
Romania		43	58	59	63	20
Russia		8	9	9	10	2
Rwanda					38	
Saudi Arabia				71		
Serbia			13	21	25	12
Singapore				47		
Slovakia		31	28	33		2
Slovenia		21	19	18	16	−5
South Africa	35	51	64	65	55	20
South Korea	14	19	17	21	21	7
Spain	21	25	22	20	11	−10
Sweden	5	6	5	5	6	1
Switzerland		24	21		13	−11
Taiwan			9		9	0
Tanzania				75		
Thailand					29	
Trinidad					67	
Turkey		44	42	45	42	−2
Uganda				67		
Ukraine			20	19	15	−5
Uruguay			18		18	0
USA	38	55	55	53	50	12
Venezuela			43	45		2
Vietnam				8	6	−2
Zambia					61	
Zimbabwe				74		

Child qualities: unselfishness

(A017) Here is a list of qualities which children can be encouraged to learn at home. Which, if any, do you consider to be especially important?

Unselfishness (%)

Country	1981	1990	1995	2000	2006	Change
Albania			12	12		0
Algeria			17			
Andorra					19	
Argentina	7	5	16	13	9	2
Armenia			31			
Australia	38		40		54	16
Austria		7		5		−2
Azerbaijan			17			
Bangladesh			16	16		0
Belarus		27	17	17		−10
Belgium	14	27		36		22
Bosnia and Herz.			26	38		12
Brazil		29	32		40	11
Britain	41	57		60	55	14
Bulgaria		22	45	15	49	27
Burkina Faso					39	
Canada	20	42		46	46	26
Chile		8	26	35	33	25
China		31	28	37	32	1
Colombia			37		53	16
Croatia			29			
Cyprus					43	
Czech			37	32	36	−1
Denmark	25	51		56		31
Dominican Rep.			12			
Egypt				22	52	30
El Salvador			28			
Estonia		25	17	16		−9
Ethiopia					36	
Finland		21	18	22	30	9
France	22	40		40	56	34
Georgia			20		17	−3
Germany (East)		8	6	11	7	−1
Germany (West)	4	8	5	6	7	3
Ghana					33	
Greece				26		
Guatemala					42	
Hong Kong					2	
Hungary	14	26	29	23		9
Iceland	21	75		35		14
India		32	23	37	34	2
Indonesia				47	33	−14
Iran				29	33	4
Iraq					9	
Ireland	23	53		49		26
Israel				49		
Italy	2	40		41	44	42
Japan	28	44	38	53	50	22
Jordan				31	56	25

Country	1981	1990	1995	2000	2006	Change
Kyrgyzstan				24		
Latvia		16	20	12		−4
Lithuania		33	28	29		−4
Luxembourg				27		
Macedonia			61	47		−14
Malaysia					30	
Mali					34	
Malta	18	39		46		28
Mexico	25	11	36	49	48	23
Moldova			9	11	32	23
Montenegro			33	40		7
Morocco				11	37	26
Netherlands	9	22		28	24	15
New Zealand			33		38	5
Nigeria		17	14	23		6
Northern Ireland	29	49		51		22
Norway	6	10	11		20	14
Pakistan			35	38		3
Peru			16	50	60	44
Philippines			31	38		7
Poland		9	14	12	18	9
Portugal		30		40		10
Puerto Rico			40	28		−12
Romania		20	23	7	23	3
Russia		24	21	21	20	−4
Rwanda					50	
Saudi Arabia				52		
Serbia			28	34	33	5
Singapore				27		
Slovakia		22	19	19		−3
Slovenia		33	29	38	38	5
South Africa	19	21	23	32	30	11
South Korea	12	11	11	15	12	0
Spain	4	8	14	12	33	29
Sweden	10	29	24	33	35	25
Switzerland		39	33		22	−17
Taiwan			21		30	9
Tanzania				46		
Thailand					31	
Trinidad					23	
Turkey		28	23	23	32	4
Uganda				30		
Ukraine			19	16	13	−6
Uruguay			55		61	6
USA	19	37	35	39	36	17
Venezuela			38	53		15
Vietnam				39	33	−6
Zambia					38	
Zimbabwe				32		

Child qualities: obedience

(A018) Here is a list of qualities which children can be encouraged to learn at home. Which, if any, do you consider to be especially important?

Obedience (%)

Country	1981	1990	1995	2000	2006	Change
Albania			58	54		–4
Algeria				56		
Andorra					39	
Argentina	19	32	32	37	42	23
Armenia			18			
Australia	41		29		37	–4
Austria		25		18		–7
Azerbaijan			25			
Bangladesh			19	19		0
Belarus			22	35	34	12
Belgium	29	36		42		13
Bosnia and Herz.			41	47		6
Brazil		41	59		56	15
Britain	36	42	51	47	46	10
Bulgaria		19	20	15	24	5
Burkina Faso					70	
Canada	21	28		31	31	10
Chile		52	46	55	52	0
China		9	29	15	15	6
Colombia			43		59	16
Croatia			21			
Cyprus				47		
Czech		21	14	17		–4
Denmark	13	20		14		1
Dominican Rep.			51			
Egypt				53	68	15
El Salvador			62			
Estonia		19	27	28		9
Ethiopia					39	
Finland		26	28	30	33	7
France	18	53		36	41	23
Georgia			23		22	–1
Germany (East)		24	14	16	18	–6
Germany (West)	14	22	11	12	14	0
Ghana					82	
Greece				11		
Guatemala				47		
Hong Kong					2	
Hungary	31	45	31	30		–1
Iceland	16	68		17		1
India		56	70	56	56	0
Indonesia				53	53	0
Iran				41	32	–9
Iraq				74	73	–1
Ireland	33	35		48		15
Israel				16		
Italy	26	32		28	26	0
Japan	6	10	6	4	5	–1
Jordan				47	64	17

Country	1981	1990	1995	2000	2006	Change
Kyrgyzstan				37		
Latvia		15	19	20		5
Lithuania		25	23	17		–8
Luxembourg				27		
Macedonia			18	11		–7
Malaysia					26	
Mali					52	
Malta	24	56		41		17
Mexico	44	45	50	59	58	14
Moldova			39	41	17	–22
Montenegro			41	47		6
Morocco				51	51	0
Netherlands	23	33		25	41	18
New Zealand			22		24	2
Nigeria		71	71	73		2
Northern Ireland	51	56		58		7
Norway	26	31	26		29	3
Pakistan			33	44		11
Peru			50	61	54	4
Philippines			44	44		0
Poland		42	49	35	49	7
Portugal		49		37		–12
Puerto Rico			52	56		4
Romania		19	14	19	17	–2
Russia		26	34	34	37	11
Rwanda					79	
Saudi Arabia				67		
Serbia			39	32	44	5
Singapore				47		
Slovakia		36	27	26		–10
Slovenia		40	28	25	31	–9
South Africa	36	39	50	55	46	10
South Korea	13	18	14	13	11	–2
Spain	29	42	44	49	37	8
Sweden	13	25	16	12	16	3
Switzerland		21	26		21	0
Taiwan			33		16	–17
Tanzania				76		
Thailand				54		
Trinidad					72	
Turkey		31	32	40	45	14
Uganda				69		
Ukraine			38	36	49	11
Uruguay			28		39	11
USA	28	38	37	32	32	4
Venezuela			50	51		1
Vietnam				56	32	–24
Zambia					68	
Zimbabwe				67		

Life satisfaction

(A019) All things considered, how satisfied are you with your life as a whole these days?

(%) Satisfied (7 thru 10)

Country	1981	1990	1995	2000	2006	Change
Albania			20	30		10
Algeria				43		
Andorra					70	
Argentina	58	68	62	68	81	23
Armenia			19			
Australia	83		78		76	−7
Austria		80		82		2
Azerbaijan			31			
Bangladesh			48	32		−16
Belarus		33	17	23		−10
Belgium	73	76		75		2
Bosnia and Herz.			43	40		−3
Brazil		67	62		74	7
Britain	75	75	76	73	79	4
Bulgaria		25	23	37	31	6
Burkina Faso					29	
Canada	81	84		81	82	1
Chile			69	57	63	65	−4
China			68	59	53	57	−11
Colombia				85		85	0
Croatia			48	58		10
Cyprus					73	
Czech		58	52	67		9
Denmark	84	85		85		1
Dominican Rep.				66		
Egypt				43	43	0
El Salvador			69			
Estonia		44	26	44		0
Ethiopia					23	
Finland	87	78	84	84	86	−1
France	58	58		67	65	7
Georgia			25		24	−1
Germany (East)		59	58	70	59	0
Germany (West)	70	71	70	78	71	1
Ghana					51	
Greece				60		
Guatemala					78	
Hong Kong					49	
Hungary	61	44	38	39		−22
Iceland	86	85		87		1
India		52	53	28	38	−14
Indonesia				61	58	−3
Iran				51	51	0
Iraq				31	19	−12
Ireland	80	80		86		6
Israel				65		
Italy	58	70		69	64	6
Japan	51	51	53	51	65	14
Jordan				36	66	30

Country	1981	1990	1995	2000	2006	Change
Kyrgyzstan				53		
Latvia		38	25	33		−5
Lithuania		43	30	34		−9
Luxembourg				80		
Macedonia			33	31		−2
Malaysia					61	
Mali					41	
Malta	77	81		86		9
Mexico	83	72	72	79	82	−1
Moldova			14	18	34	20
Montenegro			48	40		−8
Morocco				39	21	−18
Netherlands	81	84		89	86	5
New Zealand			76		80	4
Nigeria		54	57	64		10
Northern Ireland	77	83		83		6
Norway	80	77	78		87	7
Pakistan				8		
Peru			46	50	64	18
Philippines			54	54		0
Poland		54	49	47	62	8
Portugal		63		64		1
Puerto Rico			79	85		6
Romania		44	27	37	40	−4
Russia		31	21	26	49	18
Rwanda					20	
Saudi Arabia				65		
Serbia			38	39	46	8
Singapore				71		
Slovakia			53	47	46		−7
Slovenia			46	50	67	66	20
South Africa	58	60	47	51	67	9
South Korea	26	60		46	54	28
Spain	56	67	54	64	75	19
Sweden	85	84	81	79	84	−1
Switzerland			86	82	84	−2
Taiwan				49	56	7
Tanzania				21		
Thailand					69	
Trinidad					67	
Turkey		48	44	39	74	26
Uganda				37		
Ukraine			13	24	43	30
Uruguay				64	74	10
USA	77	79	77	79	79	2
Venezuela				56	70	14
Vietnam				44	61	17
Zambia					47	
Zimbabwe				19		

Freedom feeling

(A020) Some people feel they have completely free choice and control over their lives, while other people feel that what they do has no real effect on what happens to them. Indicate how much freedom of choice and control you feel you have over the way your life turns out.

(%) A great deal (7 thru 10)

Country	1981	1990	1995	2000	2006	Change
Albania			22	46		24
Algeria				56		
Andorra					76	
Argentina	61	68	63	68	77	16
Armenia			36			
Australia	68		76		79	11
Austria		71		68		−3
Azerbaijan			40			
Bangladesh				50	33	−17
Belarus			31	37		6
Belgium	48	57		58		10
Bosnia and Herz.			43	50		7
Brazil		62	66		73	11
Britain	60	64		66	70	10
Bulgaria		28	31	48	41	13
Burkina Faso					36	
Canada	70	76		77	76	6
Chile		61	61	64	65	4
China		63	59	64	66	3
Colombia			78		81	3
Croatia			55	63		8
Cyprus					71	
Czech		53	52	60		7
Denmark	63	64		72		9
Dominican Rep.			70			
Egypt				43	44	1
El Salvador			70			
Estonia		50	46	44		−6
Ethiopia					46	
Finland	80	79	82	79	77	−3
France	50	45		51	55	5
Georgia			49		50	1
Germany (East)		52	52	66	52	0
Germany (West)	64	63	70	74	64	0
Ghana					65	
Greece				65		
Guatemala					75	
Hong Kong					46	
Hungary	60	49	51	45		−15
Iceland	73	70		81		8
India		50	55	22	27	−23
Indonesia				67	68	1
Iran				55	62	7
Iraq				43	35	−8
Ireland	63	65		69		6
Israel						
Italy	39	55		51	51	12
Japan	35	29	32	39	42	7
Jordan				64	73	9

Country	1981	1990	1995	2000	2006	Change
Kyrgyzstan				61		
Latvia		48	40	41		−7
Lithuania		54	45	51		−3
Luxembourg				63		
Macedonia			49	42		−7
Malaysia					73	
Mali					44	
Malta	65	65		75		10
Mexico	74	70	73	80	86	12
Moldova			40	45	63	23
Montenegro			52	45		−7
Morocco				46	32	−14
Netherlands	46	52		65	60	14
New Zealand			79		81	2
Nigeria			57	62	67	10
Northern Ireland	50	75		75		25
Norway	56	67	70		82	26
Pakistan				11		
Peru			57	64	63	6
Philippines			57	53		−4
Poland		47		47	56	9
Portugal		51		58		7
Puerto Rico			83	83		0
Romania		49	52	58	74	25
Russia		47	33	37	63	16
Rwanda					50	
Saudi Arabia				55		
Serbia			46	44	53	7
Singapore				71		
Slovakia		54	50	50		−4
Slovenia		44	58	64	70	26
South Africa	49	65	53	58	76	27
South Korea	27	72		64	63	36
Spain	54	57	45	58	62	8
Sweden	65	74	72	74	83	18
Switzerland			66	68	75	9
Taiwan				68	70	2
Tanzania				41		
Thailand					66	
Trinidad					76	
Turkey			32	42	69	37
Uganda				52		
Ukraine			31	33	46	15
Uruguay				61	78	17
USA	72	76	73	82	81	9
Venezuela				77	82	5
Vietnam				65	61	−4
Zambia					66	
Zimbabwe				43		

Most people can be trusted

(A021) Generally speaking, would you say that most people can be trusted or that you need to be very careful in dealing with people?

Most people can be trusted (%)

Country	1981	1990	1995	2000	2006	Change
Albania			27	24		−3
Algeria				11		
Andorra					21	
Argentina	26	23	18	16	17	−9
Armenia			25			
Australia	48		40		48	0
Austria		32		33		1
Azerbaijan			21			
Bangladesh			21	24		3
Belarus			25	24	42	17
Belgium	29	34		29		0
Bosnia and Herz.				26	17	−9
Brazil		6	3		9	3
Britain	43	44	30	29	30	−13
Bulgaria			30	29	27	22	−8
Burkina Faso					15	
Canada	48	53		37	42	−6
Chile		23	21	23	12	−11
China			60	52	55	52	−8
Colombia			11		14	3
Croatia			25	21		−4
Cyprus					13	
Czech			27	29	25	−2
Denmark	53	58		67		14
Dominican Rep.				26		
Egypt				38	18	−20
El Salvador			15			
Estonia			28	22	23	−5
Ethiopia					24	
Finland	56	63	49	57	59	3
France	25	23		21	19	−6
Georgia			19		18	−1
Germany (East)		26	25	43	28	2
Germany (West)	32	38	42	32	41	9
Ghana					9	
Greece				24		
Guatemala					16	
Hong Kong					41	
Hungary	34	25	23	22		−12
Iceland	40	44		41		1
India			35	38	41	23	−12
Indonesia				52	43	−9
Iran				65	11	−54
Iraq				48	41	−7
Ireland	41	47		36		−5
Israel				23		
Italy	27	35		33	29	2
Japan	41	42	42	43	39	−2
Jordan				28	31	3

Country	1981	1990	1995	2000	2006	Change
Kyrgyzstan				17		
Latvia		19	25	17		−2
Lithuania		31	22	26		−5
Luxembourg				25		
Macedonia			8	14		6
Malaysia					9	
Mali					17	
Malta	10	24		21		11
Mexico	17	33	31	22	16	−1
Moldova			22	15	18	−4
Montenegro				32	34	2
Morocco				23	13	−10
Netherlands	45	53		60	44	−1
New Zealand			49		51	2
Nigeria		23	17	26		3
Northern Ireland	44	44		39		−5
Norway	61	65	65		74	13
Pakistan			19	31		12
Peru			5	11	6	1
Philippines			6	9		3
Poland		32	18	18	19	−13
Portugal		22		12		−10
Puerto Rico			6	23		17
Romania		16	19	10	20	4
Russia		37	24	24	27	−10
Rwanda					5	
Saudi Arabia				53		
Serbia			30	19	15	−15
Singapore				15		
Slovakia		22	27	16		−6
Slovenia		17	16	22	18	1
South Africa	26	29	16	13	43	17
South Korea	38	34	30	27	30	−8
Spain	35	34	30	36	20	−15
Sweden	57	66	60	66	68	11
Switzerland			43	37	51	8
Taiwan			38		24	−14
Tanzania				8		
Thailand					42	
Trinidad					4	
Turkey		10	5	16	5	−5
Uganda				8		
Ukraine			31	27	28	−3
Uruguay			22		28	6
USA	41	51	36	36	38	−3
Venezuela			14	16		2
Vietnam				41	52	11
Zambia					12	
Zimbabwe				11		

139

Membership in church or religious organization

(A022) Now I am going to read off a list of voluntary organizations; for each one, could you tell me whether you are an active member, an inactive member or not a member of that type of organization?

Active member in a church or religious organization (%)

Country	1981	1990	1995	2000	2006	Change
Albania			5			
Algeria						
Andorra					11	
Argentina	7		15		17	10
Armenia			1			
Australia	11		21		17	6
Austria						
Azerbaijan			1			
Bangladesh			24			
Belarus			2			
Belgium						
Bosnia and Herz.			16			
Brazil			31		52	21
Britain					18	
Bulgaria			1		2	1
Burkina Faso					24	
Canada					29	
Chile			29		23	−6
China					2	
Colombia			29		24	−5
Croatia			16			
Cyprus					6	
Czech			5			
Denmark						
Dominican Rep.			36			
Egypt					1	
El Salvador			40			
Estonia			2			
Ethiopia					30	
Finland			9		18	9
France					5	
Georgia			1		3	2
Germany (East)			8		10	2
Germany (West)			16		17	1
Ghana					72	
Greece						
Guatemala						
Hong Kong						
Hungary			9			
Iceland						
India			14		22	8
Indonesia					38	
Iran					20	
Iraq						
Ireland						
Israel						
Italy					9	
Japan	4		5		4	0
Jordan					3	

Country	1981	1990	1995	2000	2006	Change
Kyrgyzstan						
Latvia					4	
Lithuania					3	
Luxembourg						
Macedonia					4	
Malaysia					16	
Mali					39	
Malta						
Mexico				41	42	1
Moldova				13	13	0
Montenegro				3		
Morocco					1	
Netherlands					15	
New Zealand				21	18	−3
Nigeria				68		
Northern Ireland						
Norway				8	8	0
Pakistan						
Peru				24	25	1
Philippines				13		
Poland					13	
Portugal						
Puerto Rico				55		
Romania				15	5	−10
Russia				2	2	0
Rwanda					53	
Saudi Arabia						
Serbia				2	4	2
Singapore						
Slovakia				9		
Slovenia				7	12	5
South Africa				60	52	−8
South Korea	11			16	19	8
Spain				17	9	−8
Sweden				8	7	−1
Switzerland				17	20	3
Taiwan				8	7	−1
Tanzania						
Thailand					20	
Trinidad					43	
Turkey				1	1	0
Uganda						
Ukraine				2	5	3
Uruguay				14	15	1
USA				51	48	−3
Venezuela				21		
Vietnam					6	
Zambia					63	
Zimbabwe						

Membership in cultural activities

(A023) Now I am going to read off a list of voluntary organizations; for each one, could you tell me whether you are an active member, an inactive member or not a member of that type of organization?

Active member in art, music or educational organization (%)

Country	1981	1990	1995	2000	2006	Change
Albania			3			
Algeria						
Andorra					22	
Argentina	3		10		7	4
Armenia			8			
Australia	4		25		19	15
Austria						
Azerbaijan			2			
Bangladesh				18		
Belarus			2			
Belgium						
Bosnia and Herz.			5			
Brazil			11		10	–1
Britain					21	
Bulgaria			2		1	–1
Burkina Faso					5	
Canada				20		
Chile			13		13	0
China			6		6	0
Colombia			5		4	–1
Croatia			7			
Cyprus					6	
Czech			3			
Denmark						
Dominican Rep.			24			
Egypt					1	
El Salvador			10			
Estonia			5			
Ethiopia				18		
Finland			8		10	2
France					11	
Georgia			3		1	–2
Germany (East)			9		4	–5
Germany (West)			12		11	–1
Ghana				23		
Greece						
Guatemala						
Hong Kong						
Hungary			2			
Iceland						
India			12		13	1
Indonesia				17		
Iran				10		
Iraq						
Ireland						
Israel						
Italy					10	
Japan	1		6		10	9
Jordan					1	

Country	1981	1990	1995	2000	2006	Change
Kyrgyzstan						
Latvia			5			
Lithuania			3			
Luxembourg						
Macedonia			5			
Malaysia					10	
Mali					17	
Malta						
Mexico			23		14	–9
Moldova			5		8	3
Montenegro			3			
Morocco					4	
Netherlands				20		
New Zealand			25		26	1
Nigeria			19			
Northern Ireland						
Norway			15		13	–2
Pakistan						
Peru			11		12	1
Philippines			5			
Poland					5	
Portugal						
Puerto Rico			14			
Romania			4		1	–3
Russia			3		4	1
Rwanda					5	
Saudi Arabia						
Serbia			2		3	1
Singapore						
Slovakia			2			
Slovenia			4		9	5
South Africa			16		11	–5
South Korea	2		7		9	7
Spain			8		6	–2
Sweden			13		13	0
Switzerland			17		20	3
Taiwan			4		4	0
Tanzania						
Thailand					11	
Trinidad					16	
Turkey			3		2	–1
Uganda						
Ukraine			2		4	2
Uruguay			12		8	–4
USA			22		25	3
Venezuela			10			
Vietnam					6	
Zambia					21	
Zimbabwe						

Membership in labor unions

(A024) Now I am going to read off a list of voluntary organizations; for each one, could you tell me whether you are an active member, an inactive member or not a member of that type of organization?

Active member in labour union (%)

Country	1981	1990	1995	2000	2006	Change
Albania			2			
Algeria						
Andorra					3	
Argentina	1		2		1	0
Armenia			1			
Australia	1		12		9	8
Austria						
Azerbaijan			3			
Bangladesh			4			
Belarus			2			
Belgium						
Bosnia and Herz.			8			
Brazil			10		9	−1
Britain					9	
Bulgaria			5		3	−2
Burkina Faso					4	
Canada				13		
Chile			5		4	−1
China			6		5	−1
Colombia			4		1	−3
Croatia			6			
Cyprus					7	
Czech			3			
Denmark						
Dominican Rep.			7			
Egypt					0	
El Salvador			1			
Estonia			1			
Ethiopia					6	
Finland			4		12	8
France					6	
Georgia			1		1	0
Germany (East)			8		2	−6
Germany (West)			6		4	−2
Ghana					8	
Greece						
Guatemala						
Hong Kong						
Hungary			8			
Iceland						
India			7		16	9
Indonesia					2	
Iran					5	
Iraq						
Ireland						
Israel						
Italy					3	
Japan	2		3		2	0
Jordan					1	

Country	1981	1990	1995	2000	2006	Change
Kyrgyzstan						
Latvia			2			
Lithuania			1			
Luxembourg						
Macedonia			5			
Malaysia					5	
Mali					13	
Malta						
Mexico			11		8	−3
Moldova			6		7	1
Montenegro			3			
Morocco					3	
Netherlands					7	
New Zealand			6		7	1
Nigeria			10			
Northern Ireland						
Norway			16		14	−2
Pakistan						
Peru			4		4	0
Philippines			3			
Poland			2		5	3
Portugal						
Puerto Rico			6			
Romania			10		4	−6
Russia			7		3	−4
Rwanda					13	
Saudi Arabia						
Serbia			2		2	0
Singapore						
Slovakia			2			
Slovenia			5		9	4
South Africa			8		6	−2
South Korea	1		2		2	1
Spain			3		3	0
Sweden			13		10	−3
Switzerland			6		5	−1
Taiwan			9		3	−6
Tanzania						
Thailand					8	
Trinidad					5	
Turkey			3		1	−2
Uganda						
Ukraine			3		5	2
Uruguay			5		3	−2
USA			10		7	−3
Venezuela			5			
Vietnam					8	
Zambia					6	
Zimbabwe						

Membership in political party

(A025) Now I am going to read off a list of voluntary organizations; for each one, could you tell me whether you are an active member, an inactive member or not a member of that type of organization?

Active member in political party (%)

Country	1981	1990	1995	2000	2006	Change
Albania			13			
Algeria						
Andorra				3		
Argentina	5		3		2	-3
Armenia			1			
Australia	1		3		2	1
Austria						
Azerbaijan			2			
Bangladesh			11			
Belarus			0			
Belgium						
Bosnia and Herz.			6			
Brazil			7		5	-2
Britain				3		
Bulgaria			2		2	0
Burkina Faso				7		
Canada				5		
Chile			3		2	-1
China			6		6	0
Colombia			6		3	-3
Croatia			3			
Cyprus				9		
Czech			3			
Denmark						
Dominican Rep.			11			
Egypt				1		
El Salvador			2			
Estonia			1			
Ethiopia				6		
Finland			2		3	1
France				3		
Georgia			2		0	-2
Germany (East)			3		2	-1
Germany (West)			4		2	-2
Ghana				15		
Greece						
Guatemala						
Hong Kong						
Hungary			3			
Iceland						
India			9		18	9
Indonesia				5		
Iran				2		
Iraq						
Ireland						
Israel						
Italy				3		
Japan	2		2		2	0
Jordan				1		

Country	1981	1990	1995	2000	2006	Change
Kyrgyzstan						
Latvia			1			
Lithuania			1			
Luxembourg						
Macedonia			6			
Malaysia					5	
Mali					20	
Malta						
Mexico			9		10	1
Moldova			1		3	2
Montenegro			5			
Morocco					1	
Netherlands					3	
New Zealand			2		2	0
Nigeria			7			
Northern Ireland						
Norway			3		4	1
Pakistan						
Peru			3		5	2
Philippines			4			
Poland			1		1	0
Portugal						
Puerto Rico			24			
Romania			5		3	-2
Russia			1		1	0
Rwanda					13	
Saudi Arabia						
Serbia			3		3	0
Singapore						
Slovakia			2			
Slovenia			1		2	1
South Africa			12		8	-4
South Korea	1		2		1	0
Spain			2		1	-1
Sweden			5		3	-2
Switzerland			7		8	1
Taiwan			3		2	-1
Tanzania						
Thailand					7	
Trinidad					4	
Turkey			5		2	-3
Uganda						
Ukraine			1		2	1
Uruguay			6		3	-3
USA			20		24	4
Venezuela			4			
Vietnam					14	
Zambia					17	
Zimbabwe						

Membership in environmental organization

(A026) Now I am going to read off a list of voluntary organizations; for each one, could you tell me whether you are an active member, an inactive member or not a member of that type of organization?

Active member in environmental organization (%)

Country	1981	1990	1995	2000	2006	Change
Albania			1			
Algeria						
Andorra					6	
Argentina	0		3		2	2
Armenia			1			
Australia	1		7		4	3
Austria						
Azerbaijan			0			
Bangladesh			6			
Belarus			1			
Belgium						
Bosnia and Herz.			3			
Brazil			6		4	−2
Britain					6	
Bulgaria			0	0	0	
Burkina Faso					5	
Canada					6	
Chile			4		2	−2
China			2		4	2
Colombia			4		3	−1
Croatia			1			
Cyprus				1		
Czech			1			
Denmark						
Dominican Rep.			9			
Egypt				0		
El Salvador						
Estonia			0			
Ethiopia				8		
Finland			1	2		1
France					6	
Georgia			0	0	0	0
Germany (East)			1	1		0
Germany (West)			3	2		−1
Ghana				10		
Greece						
Guatemala						
Hong Kong						
Hungary			1			
Iceland						
India			5	11	6	
Indonesia				20		
Iran				2		
Iraq						
Ireland						
Israel						
Italy				1		
Japan	0		1	2	2	
Jordan				.	1	

Country	1981	1990	1995	2000	2006	Change
Kyrgyzstan						
Latvia			1			
Lithuania			0			
Luxembourg						
Macedonia			2			
Malaysia					4	
Mali					27	
Malta						
Mexico			10		6	−4
Moldova			1		2	1
Montenegro			0			
Morocco					1	
Netherlands					4	
New Zealand			5		7	2
Nigeria			15			
Northern Ireland						
Norway			1		1	0
Pakistan						
Peru			3		5	2
Philippines			7			
Poland					2	
Portugal						
Puerto Rico			6			
Romania			2		0	−2
Russia			0	0	0	
Rwanda					7	
Saudi Arabia						
Serbia			0		1	1
Singapore						
Slovakia			1			
Slovenia			1		3	2
South Africa			8		5	−3
South Korea	2		6		2	0
Spain			3		1	−2
Sweden			2		1	−1
Switzerland			5		5	0
Taiwan			1		2	1
Tanzania						
Thailand					10	
Trinidad					5	
Turkey			1		1	0
Uganda						
Ukraine			1		1	0
Uruguay			4		2	−2
USA			9		10	1
Venezuela			6			
Vietnam					8	
Zambia					7	
Zimbabwe						

Membership in professional organization

(A027) Now I am going to read off a list of voluntary organizations; for each one, could you tell me whether you are an active member, an inactive member or not a member of that type of organization?

Active member in professional association (%)

Country	1981	1990	1995	2000	2006	Change
Albania			5			
Algeria						
Andorra					10	
Argentina	2		5		3	1
Armenia			2			
Australia	2		20		16	14
Austria						
Azerbaijan			1			
Bangladesh			9			
Belarus			0			
Belgium						
Bosnia and Herz.			5			
Brazil			10		9	−1
Britain				14		
Bulgaria			1		1	0
Burkina Faso					6	
Canada				17		
Chile			7		4	−3
China			2		2	0
Colombia			5		3	−2
Croatia			6			
Cyprus					6	
Czech			4			
Denmark						
Dominican Rep.			18			
Egypt				2		
El Salvador			5			
Estonia			1			
Ethiopia				9		
Finland			2		2	0
France				6		
Georgia			1		0	−1
Germany (East)			4		3	−1
Germany (West)			5		4	−1
Ghana				8		
Greece						
Guatemala						
Hong Kong						
Hungary			6			
Iceland						
India			7		12	5
Indonesia				15		
Iran				4		
Iraq						
Ireland						
Israel						
Italy				7		
Japan	2		7		5	3
Jordan					3	

Country	1981	1990	1995	2000	2006	Change
Kyrgyzstan						
Latvia			3			
Lithuania			1			
Luxembourg						
Macedonia			4			
Malaysia					3	
Mali					16	
Malta						
Mexico			11		10	−1
Moldova			2		7	5
Montenegro			4			
Morocco					2	
Netherlands					4	
New Zealand			17		18	1
Nigeria			19			
Northern Ireland						
Norway			9		8	−1
Pakistan						
Peru			7		7	0
Philippines			4			
Poland				3		
Portugal						
Puerto Rico			18			
Romania			4		1	−3
Russia			1		2	1
Rwanda					15	
Saudi Arabia						
Serbia			3		2	−1
Singapore						
Slovakia			3			
Slovenia			5		6	1
South Africa			10		5	−5
South Korea	2		6		2	0
Spain			4		3	−1
Sweden			5		6	1
Switzerland			11		15	4
Taiwan			2		4	2
Tanzania						
Thailand					11	
Trinidad					7	
Turkey			5		1	−4
Uganda						
Ukraine			1		2	1
Uruguay			4		2	−2
USA			21		20	−1
Venezuela				8		
Vietnam					11	
Zambia					13	
Zimbabwe						

Membership in charitable/humanitarian organization

(A028) Now I am going to read off a list of voluntary organizations; for each one, could you tell me whether you are an active member, an inactive member or not a member of that type of organization?

Active member in charitable/humanitarian organization (%)

Country	1981	1990	1995	2000	2006	Change
Albania			1			
Algeria						
Andorra					13	
Argentina	5		6		6	1
Armenia			2			
Australia	8		18		17	9
Austria						
Azerbaijan			0			
Bangladesh				4		
Belarus			0			
Belgium						
Bosnia and Herz.			3			
Brazil			15		14	−1
Britain				21		
Bulgaria		1		1		0
Burkina Faso					3	
Canada				21		
Chile			8		9	1
China			3		3	0
Colombia			5		4	−1
Croatia			5			
Cyprus					5	
Czech			1			
Denmark						
Dominican Rep.			12			
Egypt				1		
El Salvador			10			
Estonia			1			
Ethiopia				12		
Finland			4		9	5
France				9		
Georgia			1		0	−1
Germany (East)			7		3	−4
Germany (West)			8		5	−3
Ghana					9	
Greece						
Guatemala						
Hong Kong						
Hungary			2			
Iceland						
India			8		11	3
Indonesia				18		
Iran				11		
Iraq						
Ireland						
Israel						
Italy					9	
Japan	2	1			2	0
Jordan					3	

Country	1981	1990	1995	2000	2006	Change
Kyrgyzstan						
Latvia			1			
Lithuania			1			
Luxembourg						
Macedonia			3			
Malaysia					5	
Mali					19	
Malta						
Mexico			9		14	5
Moldova			2		2	0
Montenegro			3			
Morocco					2	
Netherlands					7	
New Zealand			20		23	3
Nigeria			14			
Northern Ireland						
Norway			9		12	3
Pakistan						
Peru			6		10	4
Philippines			5			
Poland					3	
Portugal						
Puerto Rico			21			
Romania			2		1	−1
Russia			1		1	0
Rwanda					15	
Saudi Arabia						
Serbia			2		1	−1
Singapore						
Slovakia			1			
Slovenia			3		8	5
South Africa			11		6	−5
South Korea	3		6		2	−1
Spain			5		5	0
Sweden			7		10	3
Switzerland			7		13	6
Taiwan			7		6	−1
Tanzania						
Thailand					9	
Trinidad					13	
Turkey			2		1	−1
Uganda						
Ukraine			0		2	2
Uruguay			4		4	0
USA			26		29	3
Venezuela			7			
Vietnam					12	
Zambia					9	
Zimbabwe						

Active/Inactive membership of sport or recreation

(A029) Now I am going to read off a list of voluntary organizations; for each one, could you tell me whether you are an active member, an inactive member or not a member of that type of organization?

Active member in Sport or recreation (%)

Country	1981	1990	1995	2000	2006	Change
Albania			11			
Algeria						
Andorra					48	
Argentina			16		19	3
Armenia			100			
Australia			53		49	−4
Austria						
Azerbaijan			7			
Bangladesh			25			
Belarus			6			
Belgium						
Bosnia and Herz.			26			
Brazil			26		20	−6
Britain					41	
Bulgaria			4		3	−1
Burkina Faso					16	
Canada					43	
Chile			35		29	−6
China			16		17	1
Colombia			19		15	−4
Croatia			22			
Cyprus					23	
Czech			24			
Denmark						
Dominican Rep.			41			
Egypt					5	
El Salvador			15			
Estonia			14			
Ethiopia					51	
Finland			32		36	4
France					31	
Georgia			3		1	−2
Germany (East)			31		25	−6
Germany (West)			48		47	−1
Ghana					40	
Greece						
Guatemala						
Hong Kong						
Hungary			14			
Iceland						
India			21		64	43
Indonesia					24	
Iran					29	
Iraq						
Ireland						
Israel						
Italy					29	
Japan			22		27	5
Jordan					4	

Country	1981	1990	1995	2000	2006	Change
Kyrgyzstan						
Latvia			9			
Lithuania			7			
Luxembourg						
Macedonia			21			
Malaysia					31	
Mali					48	
Malta						
Mexico				48	32	−16
Moldova			10		14	4
Montenegro					14	
Morocco					13	
Netherlands					44	
New Zealand						
Nigeria				58	56	−2
Northern Ireland					41	
Norway				39	42	3
Pakistan						
Peru				33	18	−15
Philippines					16	
Poland					14	
Portugal						
Puerto Rico				30		
Romania			10		2	−8
Russia			6		13	7
Rwanda					27	
Saudi Arabia						
Serbia			14		18	4
Singapore						
Slovakia			21			
Slovenia			19		30	11
South Africa			39		35	−4
South Korea			50		35	−15
Spain			20		14	−6
Sweden			45		44	−1
Switzerland				48	50	2
Taiwan			13		19	6
Tanzania						
Thailand					26	
Trinidad					35	
Turkey			6		3	−3
Uganda						
Ukraine			5		10	5
Uruguay			17		13	−4
USA			43		40	−3
Venezuela			29			
Vietnam					14	
Zambia					48	
Zimbabwe						

Active/Inactive membership of any other organization

(A030) Now I am going to read off a list of voluntary organizations; for each one, could you tell me whether you are an active member, an inactive member or not a member of that type of organization?

Active member in any other organization (%)

Country	1981	1990	1995	2000	2006	Change
Albania			5			
Algeria						
Andorra					1	
Argentina			5		3	−2
Armenia			100			
Australia			22		6	−16
Austria						
Azerbaijan			0			
Bangladesh			17			
Belarus			1			
Belgium						
Bosnia and Herz.			13			
Brazil			13		100	87
Britain					1	
Bulgaria			1		100	99
Burkina Faso					52	
Canada					12	
Chile			19		2	−17
China			15		2	−13
Colombia			5		2	−3
Croatia			8			
Cyprus					9	
Czech			17			
Denmark						
Dominican Rep.			33			
Egypt						
El Salvador			5			
Estonia			2			
Ethiopia					57	
Finland			21		5	−16
France					2	
Georgia			1		0	−1
Germany (East)			14		7	−7
Germany (West)			20		7	−13
Ghana						
Greece						
Guatemala						
Hong Kong						
Hungary			9			
Iceland						
India			8		40	32
Indonesia					11	
Iran						
Iraq						
Ireland						
Israel						
Italy					12	
Japan			9		17	8
Jordan					100	

Country	1981	1990	1995	2000	2006	Change
Kyrgyzstan						
Latvia			4			
Lithuania			1			
Luxembourg						
Macedonia			13			
Malaysia					75	
Mali					88	
Malta						
Mexico			19		3	−16
Moldova					2	
Montenegro			7			
Morocco					7	
Netherlands					2	
New Zealand						
Nigeria			31		34	3
Northern Ireland			10			
Norway			31		27	−4
Pakistan						
Peru			18		3	−15
Philippines			9			
Poland					9	
Portugal						
Puerto Rico			21			
Romania			3		0	−3
Russia			1			
Rwanda						
Saudi Arabia						
Serbia			6		85	79
Singapore						
Slovakia			13			
Slovenia			13		5	−8
South Africa			16		63	47
South Korea			20		5	−15
Spain			10		6	−4
Sweden			35		40	5
Switzerland			11		100	89
Taiwan			13		100	87
Tanzania						
Thailand					11	
Trinidad					7	
Turkey			3		2	−1
Uganda						
Ukraine			1			
Uruguay			7		3	−4
USA			31		5	−26
Venezuela			15			
Vietnam					29	
Zambia						
Zimbabwe						

Environmental protection vs. economic growth

(B001) Here are two statements people sometimes make when discussing the environment and economic growth. Which of them comes closer to your own point of view?

Protecting the environment (%)

Country	1981	1990	1995	2000	2006	Change
Albania			45	48		3
Algeria				34		
Andorra					84	
Argentina			44	45	74	30
Armenia			44			
Australia			61		67	6
Austria						
Azerbaijan			50			
Bangladesh			46	55		9
Belarus			58			
Belgium						
Bosnia and Herz.			43	43		0
Brazil			49		64	15
Britain				61		
Bulgaria			43		47	4
Burkina Faso				56		
Canada				63	71	8
Chile			56	51	68	12
China			60	61	64	4
Colombia				70		
Croatia			59			
Cyprus				64		
Czech			53			
Denmark						
Dominican Rep.			72			
Egypt				51	45	−6
El Salvador			85			
Estonia			45			
Ethiopia				23		
Finland			43		66	23
France				54		
Georgia			64	57		−7
Germany (East)			34		38	4
Germany (West)			45		36	−9
Ghana				48		
Greece						
Guatemala				62		
Hong Kong				40		
Hungary			31			
Iceland						
India			29	48	52	23
Indonesia				35	35	0
Iran				45	48	3
Iraq						
Ireland						
Israel				32		
Italy					61	
Japan			46	49	53	7
Jordan				53	55	2

Country	1981	1990	1995	2000	2006	Change
Kyrgyzstan				51		
Latvia			45			
Lithuania			35			
Luxembourg						
Macedonia			51	48		−3
Malaysia					49	
Mali					49	
Malta						
Mexico			53	56	64	11
Moldova			61	57	60	−1
Montenegro			44	35		−9
Morocco				55	55	0
Netherlands				49		
New Zealand			50		65	15
Nigeria			34	46		12
Northern Ireland						
Norway			63		77	14
Pakistan			50	7		−43
Peru			45	61	66	21
Philippines			69	64		−5
Poland			49		42	−7
Portugal						
Puerto Rico			67	66		−1
Romania			53		52	−1
Russia			56		55	−1
Rwanda				59		
Saudi Arabia				40		
Serbia			46	45	56	10
Singapore			36			
Slovakia			47			
Slovenia			47		54	7
South Africa			30	35	31	1
South Korea			70	53	36	−34
Spain			55	53	64	9
Sweden			65	72	64	−1
Switzerland			43		75	32
Taiwan			64		50	−14
Tanzania				62		
Thailand					46	
Trinidad					59	
Turkey			54	69	56	2
Uganda				38		
Ukraine			57		55	−2
Uruguay			64		49	−15
USA			52	61	56	4
Venezuela			45	70		25
Vietnam				61	60	−1
Zambia					37	
Zimbabwe				36		

Environment: Income

(B002) I would give part of my income if I were certain that the money would be used to prevent environmental pollution

Strongly agree/Agree (%)

Country	1981	1990	1995	2000	2006	Change
Albania				70		
Algeria						
Andorra					63	
Argentina		62		67	56	−6
Armenia						
Australia				59		
Austria		60		49		−11
Azerbaijan						
Bangladesh				79		
Belarus				58		
Belgium		55		60		5
Bosnia and Herz.				76		
Brazil		73			53	−20
Britain		67		49		−18
Bulgaria		83		61	57	−26
Burkina Faso					80	
Canada		73		70	70	−3
Chile		84		70	57	−27
China		78		82	82	4
Colombia						
Croatia				82		
Cyprus					73	
Czech		85		77		−8
Denmark		84		79		−5
Dominican Rep.						
Egypt				49		
El Salvador						
Estonia		77		48		−29
Ethiopia				79		
Finland		67		54	57	−10
France		61		46		−15
Georgia				78		
Germany (East)		63		29	28	−35
Germany (West)		53		32	44	−9
Ghana					83	
Greece				82		
Guatemala					85	
Hong Kong					63	
Hungary		60		54		−6
Iceland		78		63		−15
India		81		67	68	−13
Indonesia				72		
Iran					85	
Iraq						
Ireland		69		55		−14
Israel						
Italy		69		65	61	−8
Japan		68		70	66	−2
Jordan					73	

Country	1981	1990	1995	2000	2006	Change
Kyrgyzstan				79		
Latvia		77		70		−7
Lithuania		75		30		−45
Luxembourg				64		
Macedonia				79		
Malaysia					62	
Mali					81	
Malta		69		60		−9
Mexico		81		79	84	3
Moldova				68	65	−3
Montenegro				60		
Morocco					45	
Netherlands		82		74		−8
New Zealand					39	
Nigeria		78				
Northern Ireland		75		44		−31
Norway		80			69	−11
Pakistan						
Peru				81	77	−4
Philippines				72		
Poland		75		61	53	−22
Portugal		83		60		−23
Puerto Rico				82		
Romania				52	38	−14
Russia		78		63		−15
Rwanda					65	
Saudi Arabia						
Serbia				80	55	−25
Singapore				63		
Slovakia		76		57		−19
Slovenia		89		82	70	−19
South Africa				53	54	1
South Korea		84		84	77	−7
Spain		68		58	49	−19
Sweden		81		79	70	−11
Switzerland					65	
Taiwan					83	
Tanzania				84		
Thailand					86	
Trinidad					75	
Turkey				77	84	7
Uganda				45		
Ukraine				63	47	−16
Uruguay					44	
USA		74		69	23	−51
Venezuela						
Vietnam				96	96	0
Zambia					49	
Zimbabwe				69		

150

Environment: Taxes
(B003) I would agree to an increase in taxes if the extra money were used to prevent environmental pollution
Strongly agree/Agree (%)

Country	1981	1990	1995	2000	2006	Change
Albania			12	19		7
Algeria						
Andorra					9	
Argentina		13	7	9	8	−5
Armenia			13			
Australia			13		13	0
Austria		13		6		−7
Azerbaijan			19			
Bangladesh			27	18		−9
Belarus		20	18	14		−6
Belgium		11		12		1
Bosnia and Herz.			23	25		2
Brazil		46	42		8	−38
Britain		10		6		−4
Bulgaria		21	19	11	12	−9
Burkina Faso					30	
Canada		14		11	11	−3
Chile		28	20	21	16	−12
China		23	21	10	15	−8
Colombia			21			
Croatia			23	14		−9
Cyprus					22	
Czech		17	15	10		−7
Denmark		27		22		−5
Dominican Rep.			37			
Egypt					8	
El Salvador			31			
Estonia		13	14	4		−9
Ethiopia				24		
Finland		14	13	8	10	−4
France		11		9		−2
Georgia			21		14	−7
Germany (East)		10	9	3	3	−7
Germany (West)		8	15	4	5	−3
Ghana					26	
Greece				19		
Guatemala					13	
Hong Kong					3	
Hungary		8	16	8		0
Iceland		11		7		−4
India		18	14	13	26	8
Indonesia					8	
Iran					16	
Iraq						
Ireland		8		6		−2
Israel						
Italy		11		7	8	−3
Japan		5	9	7	6	1
Jordan					18	

Country	1981	1990	1995	2000	2006	Change
Kyrgyzstan				13		
Latvia		20	10	8		−12
Lithuania		15	7	3		−12
Luxembourg				16		
Macedonia			20	20		0
Malaysia					10	
Mali					38	
Malta		27		5		−22
Mexico		17	18	16	15	−2
Moldova			16	6	14	−2
Montenegro			29	22		−7
Morocco					12	
Netherlands		19		10		−9
New Zealand			10		9	−1
Nigeria		32	26			−6
Northern Ireland		8		3		−5
Norway		27	24		25	−2
Pakistan						
Peru			15	9	11	−4
Philippines			12	15		3
Poland		22	13	11	9	−13
Portugal		24		5		−19
Puerto Rico			28	26		−2
Romania			19	13	8	−11
Russia		16	17	9		−7
Rwanda					16	
Saudi Arabia						
Serbia			25	26	15	−10
Singapore				4		
Slovakia		13	14	9		−4
Slovenia		13	10	8	10	−3
South Africa			14	9	11	−3
South Korea		36	23	8	5	−31
Spain		17	16	9	6	−11
Sweden		39	34	28	12	−27
Switzerland			9		11	2
Taiwan			22		7	−15
Tanzania				40		
Thailand					10	
Trinidad					10	
Turkey		25	28	13	16	−9
Uganda				11		
Ukraine			12	14	8	−4
Uruguay			16		4	−12
USA		13	12	13	4	−9
Venezuela			33			
Vietnam				23	31	8
Zambia					11	
Zimbabwe				7		

Environment: No cost

(B004) The Government should reduce environmental pollution, but it should not cost me any money

Strongly agree/Agree (%)

Country	1981	1990	1995	2000	2006	Change
Albania				63		
Algeria						
Andorra					69	
Argentina		72		86	87	15
Armenia						
Australia				63		
Austria		61		64		3
Azerbaijan						
Bangladesh				96		
Belarus				75		
Belgium		63		65		2
Bosnia and Herz.				60		
Brazil		65			82	17
Britain		58		76		18
Bulgaria		74		81	76	2
Burkina Faso					71	
Canada		52		64	65	13
Chile		58		74	84	26
China		46		36	41	−5
Colombia						
Croatia				78		
Cyprus					69	
Czech		42		54		12
Denmark		29		30		1
Dominican Rep.						
Egypt					87	
El Salvador						
Estonia		72		87		15
Ethiopia				56		
Finland		51		62	52	1
France		74		84		10
Georgia				78		
Germany (East)		48		73	78	30
Germany (West)		57		67	74	17
Ghana					52	
Greece				71		
Guatemala					80	
Hong Kong					53	
Hungary		75		86		11
Iceland		28		32		4
India		52		55	64	12
Indonesia					88	
Iran					91	
Iraq						
Ireland		60		70		10
Israel						
Italy		78		81	90	12
Japan				56	58	2
Jordan					91	

Country	1981	1990	1995	2000	2006	Change
Kyrgyzstan				61		
Latvia		71		87		16
Lithuania		69		89		20
Luxembourg				63		
Macedonia				82		
Malaysia					87	
Mali					77	
Malta		63		66		3
Mexico		40		71	67	27
Moldova				68	75	7
Montenegro				78		
Morocco					93	
Netherlands		19		23		4
New Zealand					69	
Nigeria		61				
Northern Ireland		63		71		8
Norway		44			42	−2
Pakistan						
Peru				72	73	1
Philippines				71		
Poland		48		71	77	29
Portugal		91		76		−15
Puerto Rico				66		
Romania				76	84	8
Russia		49		80		31
Rwanda					77	
Saudi Arabia						
Serbia				55	67	12
Singapore				74		
Slovakia		64		79		15
Slovenia		56		63	60	4
South Africa				78	78	0
South Korea		50		67	69	19
Spain		76		88	90	14
Sweden		36		43	30	−6
Switzerland					49	
Taiwan					40	
Tanzania				66		
Thailand					66	
Trinidad					78	
Turkey				75	73	−2
Uganda				60		
Ukraine				81	89	8
Uruguay					82	
USA		54		57	29	−25
Venezuela						
Vietnam				38	48	10
Zambia					68	
Zimbabwe				70		

Men more right to a job

(C001) Do you agree or disagree with the following statement?
When jobs are scarce, men should have more right to a job than women

Agree (%)

Country	1981	1990	1995	2000	2006	Change
Albania			49	47		−2
Algeria				67		
Andorra					5	
Argentina		24	25	26	25	1
Armenia			60			
Australia			26		13	−13
Austria		50		29		−21
Azerbaijan			64			
Bangladesh			56	68		12
Belarus		38	45	25		−13
Belgium		37		25		−12
Bosnia and Herz.			39	29		−10
Brazil		39	36		22	−17
Britain	35	25	21	16		−19
Bulgaria		46	35	37	23	−23
Burkina Faso					52	
Canada	19		16	13		−6
Chile		37	30	25	28	−9
China		41	43	45	42	1
Colombia			29			
Croatia			34	21		−13
Cyprus					34	
Czech		51	32	19		−32
Denmark		11		6		−5
Dominican Rep.			15			
Egypt				90	88	−2
El Salvador			27			
Estonia		45	33	14		−31
Ethiopia					6	
Finland		15	14	9	10	−5
France	33			22	19	−14
Georgia			65		53	−12
Germany (East)		31	22	25	17	−14
Germany (West)		31	22	28	21	−10
Ghana					54	
Greece				20		
Guatemala					19	
Hong Kong					22	
Hungary		42	44	23		−19
Iceland		6		4		−2
India		49	51	57	51	2
Indonesia				52	55	3
Iran				73	69	−4
Iraq				78	84	6
Ireland		36		16		−20
Israel						
Italy		40		27	22	−18
Japan		34	33	32	27	−7
Jordan				82	88	6

Country	1981	1990	1995	2000	2006	Change
Kyrgyzstan				49		
Latvia		34	25	20		−14
Lithuania		66	32	23		−43
Luxembourg				24		
Macedonia			49	43		−6
Malaysia					49	
Mali					62	
Malta		70		49		−21
Mexico		23	25	31	25	2
Moldova			52	45	38	−14
Montenegro			32	30		−2
Morocco				82	51	−31
Netherlands		25		12	13	−12
New Zealand			13		8	−5
Nigeria		48	57	60		12
Northern Ireland		34		17		−17
Norway		16	14		6	−10
Pakistan			76	67		−9
Peru			20	15	18	−2
Philippines			50	67		17
Poland		55	45	38	31	−24
Portugal		38		27		−11
Puerto Rico			34	21		−13
Romania		42	39	38	35	−7
Russia		40	49	36	36	−4
Rwanda					25	
Saudi Arabia				70		
Serbia			33	31	13	−20
Singapore				39		
Slovakia		55	39	24		−31
Slovenia		29	26	18	14	−15
South Africa		39	36	36	36	−3
South Korea		42	43	39	35	−7
Spain		29	27	19	18	−11
Sweden		8	8	2	2	−6
Switzerland			29		22	−7
Taiwan			57		41	−16
Tanzania				27		
Thailand					32	
Trinidad					25	
Turkey		51	59	58	53	2
Uganda				40		
Ukraine			38	30	31	−7
Uruguay			26		22	−4
USA	24	21		10	7	−17
Venezuela			33	31		−2
Vietnam				49	41	−8
Zambia					34	
Zimbabwe				41		

153

Employers should give priority to people of own nationality

(C002) Do you agree or disagree with the following statement?
When jobs are scarce, employers should give priority to people of own nationality over immigrants

Agree (%)

Country	1981	1990	1995	2000	2006	Change
Albania			98	80		−18
Algeria				87		
Andorra					31	
Argentina		60	78	73	70	10
Armenia			66			
Australia			45		40	−5
Austria		77		74		−3
Azerbaijan			86			
Bangladesh			89	92		3
Belarus		56	73	85		29
Belgium		63		51		−12
Bosnia and Herz.			25	7		−18
Brazil		82	88		82	0
Britain		53	53	59	53	0
Bulgaria		87	84	88	76	−11
Burkina Faso				72		
Canada		52		51	46	−6
Chile		83	73	82	80	−3
China		65	78	72	66	1
Colombia						
Croatia			78	88		10
Cyprus					69	
Czech		85	92	83		−2
Denmark		53		34		−19
Dominican Rep.			46			
Egypt				99	98	−1
El Salvador						
Estonia		82	47	47		−35
Ethiopia				55		
Finland		71	72	64	56	−15
France		63		54	42	−21
Georgia			83		87	4
Germany (East)		69	71	70	63	−6
Germany (West)		62	43	59	49	−13
Ghana					85	
Greece				78		
Guatemala					80	
Hong Kong					72	
Hungary		87	87	90		3
Iceland		87		70		−17
India		84	89	85	75	−9
Indonesia				88	87	−1
Iran				94	89	−5
Iraq						
Ireland		69		74		5
Israel						
Italy		71		61	64	−7
Japan		65	62	61	63	−2
Jordan				94	98	4

Country	1981	1990	1995	2000	2006	Change
Kyrgyzstan				73		
Latvia		80	41	74		−6
Lithuania		92	93	94		2
Luxembourg				44		
Macedonia			79	78		−1
Malaysia					86	
Mali					84	
Malta		92		94		2
Mexico		82	74	80	75	−7
Moldova			61	65	76	15
Montenegro			81	85		4
Morocco				94	85	−9
Netherlands		33		26	42	9
New Zealand			51		52	1
Nigeria		80	84	81		1
Northern Ireland		62		74		12
Norway		59	41		35	−24
Pakistan				57		
Peru			86	73	82	−4
Philippines			75	85		10
Poland		64	91	91	81	17
Portugal		86		65		−21
Puerto Rico			78	77		−1
Romania		75	75	74	65	−10
Russia		63	75	73	81	18
Rwanda					73	
Saudi Arabia				53		
Serbia			81	80	45	−36
Singapore				86		
Slovakia		89	86	88		−1
Slovenia		79	81	76	74	−5
South Africa		73	83	83	80	7
South Korea		72	90	84	77	5
Spain		76	72	60	58	−18
Sweden		35	26	11	11	−24
Switzerland				62	49	−13
Taiwan			91		91	0
Tanzania				71		
Thailand					61	
Trinidad					84	
Turkey		75	79	67	64	−11
Uganda				92		
Ukraine			65	70	68	3
Uruguay				83	72	−11
USA		52	60	50	53	1
Venezuela				85	81	−4
Vietnam				79	74	−5
Zambia					77	
Zimbabwe				79		

Important aspects in a job first choice

(C003) Here are some of the things many people take into account in relation to their work. Regardless of whether you're actually looking for a job, which one would you, personally, place first if you were looking for a job?

A safe job with no risk (%)

Country	1981	1990	1995	2000	2006	Change
Albania			45	38		−7
Algeria						
Andorra					19	
Argentina			35	42	36	1
Armenia			17			
Australia			24		23	−1
Austria						
Azerbaijan			14			
Bangladesh			39	35		−4
Belarus			20			
Belgium						
Bosnia and Herz.			32	43		11
Brazil			35		47	12
Britain					18	
Bulgaria			33		35	2
Burkina Faso					34	
Canada				19	20	1
Chile			28	41	32	4
China			28	34	35	7
Colombia			39			
Croatia			35			
Cyprus					43	
Czech			20			
Denmark						
Dominican Rep.			20			
Egypt				44		
El Salvador			49			
Estonia			31			
Ethiopia				29		
Finland			32		35	3
France					38	
Georgia			14		36	22
Germany (East)			48		56	8
Germany (West)			35		53	18
Ghana					45	
Greece						
Guatemala					46	
Hong Kong						
Hungary			38			
Iceland						
India			36	41	44	8
Indonesia					45	
Iran					31	
Iraq						
Ireland						
Israel				20		
Italy					38	
Japan			40	34	36	−4
Jordan					24	

Country	1981	1990	1995	2000	2006	Change
Kyrgyzstan				22		
Latvia			30			
Lithuania			27			
Luxembourg						
Macedonia			49	41		−8
Malaysia					26	
Mali					23	
Malta						
Mexico			34	40	39	5
Moldova			27	21	20	−7
Montenegro			35	29		−6
Morocco				42	18	−24
Netherlands					15	
New Zealand			21		16	−5
Nigeria			36			
Northern Ireland						
Norway			32		26	−6
Pakistan						
Peru			33	39	37	4
Philippines			49	47		−2
Poland				32		
Portugal						
Puerto Rico			44	38		−6
Romania			31		34	3
Russia			23		22	−1
Rwanda					35	
Saudi Arabia						
Serbia			35	27	44	9
Singapore				31		
Slovakia			15			
Slovenia			38		41	3
South Africa			37	40	40	3
South Korea			59	50	57	−2
Spain			41	33	42	1
Sweden			25		12	−13
Switzerland			31		20	−11
Taiwan			48		49	1
Tanzania				36		
Thailand					36	
Trinidad					29	
Turkey			35		32	−3
Uganda				46		
Ukraine			19		17	−2
Uruguay			32		44	12
USA			23	15	20	−3
Venezuela			42	42		0
Vietnam				46	56	10
Zambia					32	
Zimbabwe				38		

Important aspects in a job second choice

(C004) Here are some of the things many people take into account in relation to their work. Regardless of whether you're actually looking for a job, which one would you, personally, place first if you were looking for a job?

A good income (%)

Country	1981	1990	1995	2000	2006	Change
Albania			20	31		11
Algeria						
Andorra					37	
Argentina			24	28	28	4
Armenia			24			
Australia			30		25	−5
Austria						
Azerbaijan			22			
Bangladesh			30	31		1
Belarus			30			
Belgium						
Bosnia and Herz.			22	32		10
Brazil			30		26	−4
Britain				30		
Bulgaria			34		33	−1
Burkina Faso					30	
Canada				26	32	6
Chile			23	35	23	0
China			32	27	28	−4
Colombia			15			
Croatia			35			
Cyprus					37	
Czech			30			
Denmark						
Dominican Rep.			29			
Egypt				40		
El Salvador						
Estonia			31			
Ethiopia				22		
Finland			21		23	2
France				28		
Georgia			26		34	8
Germany (East)			27		31	4
Germany (West)			23		33	10
Ghana					37	
Greece						
Guatemala				31		
Hong Kong						
Hungary			28			
Iceland						
India			26	34	33	7
Indonesia					33	
Iran					37	
Iraq						
Ireland						
Israel				32		
Italy					31	
Japan			34	29	30	−4
Jordan					23	

Country	1981	1990	1995	2000	2006	Change
Kyrgyzstan				29		
Latvia			36			
Lithuania			27			
Luxembourg						
Macedonia			43	32		−11
Malaysia					22	
Mali					25	
Malta						
Mexico			30	31	33	3
Moldova			29	24	19	−10
Montenegro			35	21		−14
Morocco				32	23	−9
Netherlands					28	
New Zealand			34		33	−1
Nigeria			36			
Northern Ireland						
Norway			22		24	2
Pakistan						
Peru			30	28	25	−5
Philippines			31	26		−5
Poland					29	
Portugal						
Puerto Rico			30	26		−4
Romania			27		32	5
Russia			30		27	−3
Rwanda					25	
Saudi Arabia						
Serbia			37	24	38	1
Singapore				27		
Slovakia			24			
Slovenia			29		31	2
South Africa			29	32		3
South Korea			42	41	46	4
Spain			27	28	38	11
Sweden			26		24	−2
Switzerland			24		22	−2
Taiwan			34		27	−7
Tanzania				51		
Thailand					37	
Trinidad					34	
Turkey			29		38	9
Uganda				42		
Ukraine			27		23	−4
Uruguay			24		29	5
USA			33	31	34	1
Venezuela			28	22		−6
Vietnam				26	28	2
Zambia					33	
Zimbabwe				31		

Satisfaction with the financial situation of household
(C005) How satisfied are you with the financial situation of your household?
(%) Satisfied (7 thru 10)

Country	1981	1990	1995	2000	2006	Change
Albania			20	22		2
Algeria				45		
Andorra					50	
Argentina	37	36	29	37	56	19
Armenia			13			
Australia	61		54		54	−7
Austria		66				
Azerbaijan			19			
Bangladesh			42	29		−13
Belarus		27	8			−19
Belgium	69	70				1
Bosnia and Herz.			27	27		0
Brazil		37	36		43	6
Britain	62	55			58	−4
Bulgaria		17	12		16	−1
Burkina Faso					20	
Canada	70	69		63	65	−5
Chile		41	41	36	40	−1
China		46	45	39	46	0
Colombia			81			
Croatia			22			
Cyprus				49		
Czech		34	28			−6
Denmark	68	66				−2
Dominican Rep.			47			
Egypt				40	29	−11
El Salvador			50			
Estonia		31	15			−16
Ethiopia				19		
Finland	71	59	62		70	−1
France	46	42			49	3
Georgia			9		11	2
Germany (East)		43	38		38	−5
Germany (West)	62	60	57		53	−9
Ghana					38	
Greece						
Guatemala				46		
Hong Kong				43		
Hungary	51	30	22			−29
Iceland	55	53				−2
India		47	47	26	31	−16
Indonesia				52	48	−4
Iran				37	43	6
Iraq				32	20	−12
Ireland	64	59				−5
Israel						
Italy	54	66			55	1
Japan	45	41	48	46	46	1
Jordan				25	51	26

Country	1981	1990	1995	2000	2006	Change
Kyrgyzstan				39		
Latvia		21	10			−11
Lithuania			15			
Luxembourg						
Macedonia			24	21		−3
Malaysia					53	
Mali					40	
Malta	68	69				1
Mexico	72	51	68	60	69	−3
Moldova			8	14	26	18
Montenegro			23	20		−3
Morocco				28	19	−9
Netherlands	77	76			63	−14
New Zealand			54		60	6
Nigeria		38	42	54		16
Northern Ireland	62	58				−4
Norway	71	56	60		76	5
Pakistan			30	5		−25
Peru			28	31	39	11
Philippines			42	39		−3
Poland		27	21		30	3
Portugal		43				
Puerto Rico			61	70		9
Romania		29	15		29	0
Russia		27	9		27	0
Rwanda					16	
Saudi Arabia				65		
Serbia			16	15	25	9
Singapore				56		
Slovakia		27	22			−5
Slovenia		23	31		49	26
South Africa	44	43	31	33	50	6
South Korea	25	40	34	40	39	14
Spain	43	49	34	47	40	−3
Sweden	69	63	52		67	−2
Switzerland		82	69		76	−6
Taiwan			39		46	7
Tanzania				16		
Thailand					58	
Trinidad					47	
Turkey		21	25	16	43	22
Uganda				29		
Ukraine			7		23	16
Uruguay				56	45	−11
USA	58	61	57	57	57	−1
Venezuela				32	47	15
Vietnam				34	46	12
Zambia					40	
Zimbabwe					12	

157

Work: Efficiency is paid more

(C006) Imagine two secretaries, of the same age, doing practically the same job. One finds out that the other earns considerably more than she does. The better paid secretary, however, is quicker, more efficient and more reliable at her job. In your opinion, is it fair or not fair that one secretary is paid more?

Fair (%)

Country	1981	1990	1995	2000	2006	Change
Albania			93	83		−10
Algeria				82		
Andorra					81	
Argentina	74	83	72	60	54	−20
Armenia			94			
Australia			82		84	2
Austria		90		89		−1
Azerbaijan			93			
Bangladesh			94	82		−12
Belarus		92	93	85		−7
Belgium	63	73		71		8
Bosnia and Herz.			86	89		3
Brazil		79	77		67	−12
Britain	68	76		73		5
Bulgaria		86	82	90	85	−1
Burkina Faso					77	
Canada	74	83		81	78	4
Chile		62	69	67	68	6
China		97	82	93	85	−12
Colombia			82		61	−21
Croatia			88	91		3
Cyprus				90		
Czech		46	96	97		51
Denmark	59	76		82		23
Dominican Rep.			91			
Egypt				97	97	0
El Salvador			70			
Estonia		95	96	85		−10
Ethiopia					78	
Finland	51	74	56	76	80	29
France	63	78		77		14
Georgia			92		70	−22
Germany (East)		96	93	89	90	−6
Germany (West)	70	84	90	86	74	4
Ghana					83	
Greece				88		
Guatemala				81		
Hong Kong				86		
Hungary	74	90	92	85		11
Iceland	64	75		86		22
India			77	79	63	66	−11
Indonesia				87	84	−3
Iran				79	76	−3
Iraq						
Ireland	59	73		65		6
Israel						
Italy	48	79		78	73	25
Japan	68	59	80	88	85	17
Jordan				83	80	−3

Country	1981	1990	1995	2000	2006	Change
Kyrgyzstan				89		
Latvia		95	93	81		−14
Lithuania		93	89	84		−9
Luxembourg				81		
Macedonia			68	72		4
Malaysia					70	
Mali					75	
Malta	62	76		77		15
Mexico	78	85	73	78	70	−8
Moldova			87	86	80	−7
Montenegro			88	83		−5
Morocco				95	72	−23
Netherlands	62	71		75		13
New Zealand			91		91	0
Nigeria		79	81	77		−2
Northern Ireland	64	71		72		8
Norway	57	54	54		56	−1
Pakistan						
Peru			81	75	77	−4
Philippines			70	68		−2
Poland		90		88	80	−10
Portugal		70		75		5
Puerto Rico			77	77		0
Romania		88	85	89	82	−6
Russia		94	93	93		−1
Rwanda					48	
Saudi Arabia				71		
Serbia			81	88	84	3
Singapore				91		
Slovakia		39	91	91		52
Slovenia		91	88	89	86	−5
South Africa	70		58	67	58	−12
South Korea	71	73		87	79	8
Spain	70	74	67	66	72	2
Sweden	59	62	57	76	82	23
Switzerland		68	82		85	17
Taiwan				92	95	3
Tanzania				76		
Thailand					82	
Trinidad					68	
Turkey		72	79	79	82	10
Uganda				76		
Ukraine			90	92	87	−3
Uruguay			73		68	−5
USA	80	85	86	91	41	−39
Venezuela				78		
Vietnam				94	92	−2
Zambia					59	
Zimbabwe				59		

To develop talents you need to have a job

(C007) Do you agree or disagree with the following statements: To fully develop your talents, you need to have a job
Agree (%)

Country	1981	1990	1995	2000	2006	Change
Albania				80		
Algeria						
Andorra					67	
Argentina				89	92	3
Armenia						
Australia					51	
Austria						
Azerbaijan						
Bangladesh				78		
Belarus				75		
Belgium				51		
Bosnia and Herz.				84		
Brazil					71	
Britain				53		
Bulgaria				87	82	−5
Burkina Faso					92	
Canada				54	51	−3
Chile				73	77	4
China				83	83	0
Colombia						
Croatia				63		
Cyprus					74	
Czech				80		
Denmark				73		
Dominican Rep.						
Egypt					75	
El Salvador						
Estonia				80		
Ethiopia					86	
Finland				59	57	−2
France				78		
Georgia					82	
Germany (East)				90	86	−4
Germany (West)				81	70	−11
Ghana					77	
Greece				68		
Guatemala					81	
Hong Kong						
Hungary				82		
Iceland				36		
India				79	76	−3
Indonesia					82	
Iran						
Iraq						
Ireland				61		
Israel				87		
Italy				73	62	−11
Japan				64	63	−1
Jordan					90	

Country	1981	1990	1995	2000	2006	Change
Kyrgyzstan				90		
Latvia				85		
Lithuania				71		
Luxembourg				69		
Macedonia				68		
Malaysia					82	
Mali					94	
Malta				50		
Mexico				69	74	5
Moldova				80	68	−12
Montenegro				78		
Morocco				97	88	−9
Netherlands				38		
New Zealand				58		
Nigeria						
Northern Ireland						
Norway					65	
Pakistan						
Peru				61	75	14
Philippines				92		
Poland				92	88	−4
Portugal				90		
Puerto Rico				50		
Romania				79	81	2
Russia				80		
Rwanda					85	
Saudi Arabia						
Serbia				65	62	−3
Singapore				72		
Slovakia				67		
Slovenia				72	71	−1
South Africa				70	80	10
South Korea				89	89	0
Spain				69	66	−3
Sweden				50	41	−9
Switzerland					77	
Taiwan						
Tanzania				96		
Thailand					87	
Trinidad					59	
Turkey				88	87	−1
Uganda				67		
Ukraine				80	74	−6
Uruguay					74	
USA				48	20	−28
Venezuela						
Vietnam				94	92	−2
Zambia					51	
Zimbabwe				72		

Humiliating to receive money without having to work for it

(C008) Do you agree or disagree with the following statements:
Humiliating to receive money without having to work for it

Agree (%)

Country	1981	1990	1995	2000	2006	Change
Albania				76		
Algeria						
Andorra					36	
Argentina				69	74	5
Armenia						
Australia					46	
Austria						
Azerbaijan						
Bangladesh				96		
Belarus				54		
Belgium				42		
Bosnia and Herz.				59		
Brazil					57	
Britain				39		
Bulgaria				72	71	−1
Burkina Faso					57	
Canada				48	46	−2
Chile				61	54	−7
China				73	70	−3
Colombia						
Croatia				67		
Cyprus					64	
Czech				47		
Denmark				37		
Dominican Rep.						
Egypt					83	
El Salvador						
Estonia				53		
Ethiopia					82	
Finland				43	42	−1
France				44		
Georgia					59	
Germany (East)				40	45	5
Germany (West)				38	37	−1
Ghana					54	
Greece				54		
Guatemala					60	
Hong Kong					36	
Hungary				51		
Iceland				42		
India				81	78	−3
Indonesia					75	
Iran						
Iraq						
Ireland				48		
Israel				60		
Italy				67	59	−8
Japan				42	41	−1
Jordan					73	

Country	1981	1990	1995	2000	2006	Change
Kyrgyzstan				56		
Latvia				63		
Lithuania				70		
Luxembourg				55		
Macedonia				73		
Malaysia					66	
Mali					69	
Malta				64		
Mexico				56	55	−1
Moldova				57	53	−4
Montenegro				74		
Morocco				94	74	−20
Netherlands				26		
New Zealand				36		
Nigeria						
Northern Ireland						
Norway					54	
Pakistan						
Peru				65	66	1
Philippines				78		
Poland				64	60	−4
Portugal				57		
Puerto Rico				62		
Romania				65	62	−3
Russia				64		
Rwanda					67	
Saudi Arabia						
Serbia				72	56	−16
Singapore				58		
Slovakia				54		
Slovenia				53	45	−8
South Africa				53	55	2
South Korea				66	57	−9
Spain				44	48	4
Sweden				40	31	−9
Switzerland					46	
Taiwan						
Tanzania				66		
Thailand					64	
Trinidad					49	
Turkey				88	91	3
Uganda				54		
Ukraine				63	51	−12
Uruguay					65	
USA				37	20	−17
Venezuela						
Vietnam				72	86	14
Zambia					47	
Zimbabwe				64		

People who don't work turn lazy

(C009) Do you agree or disagree with the following statements: People who don't work turn lazy

Agree (%)

Country	1981	1990	1995	2000	2006	Change
Albania				80		
Algeria						
Andorra					61	
Argentina				78	80	2
Armenia						
Australia					58	
Austria						
Azerbaijan						
Bangladesh				85		
Belarus				66		
Belgium				50		
Bosnia and Herz.				63		
Brazil					74	
Britain				43		
Bulgaria				68	73	5
Burkina Faso					72	
Canada				53	54	1
Chile				67	76	9
China				86	82	−4
Colombia						
Croatia				68		
Cyprus					74	
Czech				79		
Denmark				65		
Dominican Rep.						
Egypt				89		
El Salvador						
Estonia				65		
Ethiopia					85	
Finland				55	60	5
France				54		
Georgia					78	
Germany (East)				41	54	13
Germany (West)				52	43	−9
Ghana					80	
Greece				56		
Guatemala					82	
Hong Kong						
Hungary				74		
Iceland				17		
India				85	77	−8
Indonesia					84	
Iran						
Iraq						
Ireland				57		
Israel				75		
Italy				76	73	−3
Japan				72	72	0
Jordan					90	

Country	1981	1990	1995	2000	2006	Change
Kyrgyzstan				79		
Latvia				75		
Lithuania				55		
Luxembourg				61		
Macedonia				78		
Malaysia					73	
Mali					86	
Malta				74		
Mexico				80	78	−2
Moldova				20	67	47
Montenegro				77		
Morocco				89	74	−15
Netherlands					34	
New Zealand					48	
Nigeria						
Northern Ireland						
Norway					54	
Pakistan						
Peru				80	80	0
Philippines				65		
Poland				78	76	−2
Portugal				70		
Puerto Rico				78		
Romania				80	83	3
Russia				74		
Rwanda					95	
Saudi Arabia						
Serbia				77	64	−13
Singapore				77		
Slovakia				79		
Slovenia				86	81	−5
South Africa				55	60	5
South Korea				85	86	1
Spain				63	68	5
Sweden				37	40	3
Switzerland					53	
Taiwan						
Tanzania				88		
Thailand					77	
Trinidad					79	
Turkey				90	91	1
Uganda				75		
Ukraine				66	70	4
Uruguay					74	
USA				53	25	−28
Venezuela						
Vietnam				88	88	0
Zambia					63	
Zimbabwe					69	

Work is a duty towards society

(C010) Do you agree or disagree with the following statements: Work is a duty towards society

Agree (%)

Country	1981	1990	1995	2000	2006	Change
Albania				63		
Algeria						
Andorra					49	
Argentina				79	83	4
Armenia						
Australia					57	
Austria						
Azerbaijan						
Bangladesh				97		
Belarus				63		
Belgium				62		
Bosnia and Herz.				49		
Brazil					76	
Britain				49		
Bulgaria				75	58	-17
Burkina Faso					90	
Canada				65	69	4
Chile				68	79	11
China				86	79	-7
Colombia						
Croatia				61		
Cyprus					73	
Czech				63		
Denmark				70		
Dominican Rep.						
Egypt					94	
El Salvador						
Estonia				60		
Ethiopia					88	
Finland				61	66	5
France				56		
Georgia					70	
Germany (East)				63	69	6
Germany (West)				64	63	-1
Ghana					94	
Greece				49		
Guatemala					90	
Hong Kong					77	
Hungary				70		
Iceland				58		
India				82	75	-7
Indonesia					63	
Iran						
Iraq						
Ireland				60		
Israel				70		
Italy				67	69	2
Japan				61	63	2
Jordan					98	

Country	1981	1990	1995	2000	2006	Change
Kyrgyzstan				68		
Latvia				67		
Lithuania				45		
Luxembourg				69		
Macedonia				67		
Malaysia					72	
Mali					93	
Malta				88		
Mexico				78	84	6
Moldova				52	49	-3
Montenegro				54		
Morocco				96	88	-8
Netherlands				59		
New Zealand				50		
Nigeria						
Northern Ireland						
Norway					81	
Pakistan						
Peru				84	85	1
Philippines				76		
Poland				73	67	-6
Portugal				86		
Puerto Rico				86		
Romania				79	71	-8
Russia				56		
Rwanda					96	
Saudi Arabia						
Serbia				65	50	-15
Singapore				75		
Slovakia				63		
Slovenia				76	75	-1
South Africa				77	75	-2
South Korea				61	62	1
Spain				63	71	8
Sweden				58	62	4
Switzerland					70	
Taiwan						
Tanzania					97	
Thailand					82	
Trinidad					88	
Turkey				89	89	0
Uganda				80		
Ukraine				53	53	0
Uruguay					80	
USA				58	25	-33
Venezuela						
Vietnam				95	92	-3
Zambia					74	
Zimbabwe				85		

Work should come first even if it means less spare time

(C011) Do you agree or disagree with the following statements: Work should come first even if it means less spare time

Agree (%)

Country	1981	1990	1995	2000	2006	Change
Albania				88		
Algeria						
Andorra					23	
Argentina				77	83	6
Armenia						
Australia					27	
Austria						
Azerbaijan						
Bangladesh				93		
Belarus				35		
Belgium				33		
Bosnia and Herz.				68		
Brazil					66	
Britain				26		
Bulgaria				53	69	16
Burkina Faso					72	
Canada				45	36	−9
Chile				53	59	6
China				84	67	−17
Colombia						
Croatia				54		
Cyprus					62	
Czech				56		
Denmark				49		
Dominican Rep.						
Egypt					94	
El Salvador						
Estonia				48		
Ethiopia					87	
Finland				39	37	−2
France				34		
Georgia					78	
Germany (East)				64	65	1
Germany (West)				43	59	16
Ghana					84	
Greece				38		
Guatemala					78	
Hong Kong						
Hungary				78		
Iceland				34		
India				72	73	1
Indonesia					84	
Iran						
Iraq						
Ireland				35		
Israel				67		
Italy				49	48	−1
Japan				19	21	2
Jordan					91	

Country	1981	1990	1995	2000	2006	Change
Kyrgyzstan				74		
Latvia				50		
Lithuania				55		
Luxembourg				40		
Macedonia				79		
Malaysia					69	
Mali					86	
Malta				45		
Mexico				70	63	−7
Moldova				65	50	−15
Montenegro				69		
Morocco				94	82	−12
Netherlands				23		
New Zealand				31		
Nigeria						
Northern Ireland						
Norway					50	
Pakistan						
Peru				75	76	1
Philippines				83		
Poland				62	61	−1
Portugal				46		
Puerto Rico				52		
Romania				80	76	−4
Russia				50		
Rwanda					92	
Saudi Arabia						
Serbia				66	53	−13
Singapore				54		
Slovakia				61		
Slovenia				56	51	−5
South Africa				73	75	2
South Korea				39	43	4
Spain				50	52	2
Sweden				29	36	7
Switzerland					47	
Taiwan						
Tanzania				87		
Thailand					83	
Trinidad					73	
Turkey				72	71	−1
Uganda				81		
Ukraine				47	41	−6
Uruguay					69	
USA				36	15	−21
Venezuela						
Vietnam				79	77	−2
Zambia					64	
Zimbabwe				86		

Child needs a home with father and mother

(D001) If someone says a child needs a home with both a father and a mother to grow up happily, would you tend to agree or disagree?

Tend to agree (%)

Country	1981	1990	1995	2000	2006	Change
Albania			98	99		1
Algeria				97		
Andorra					62	
Argentina	88	95	94	91	87	−1
Armenia			98			
Australia	97		71		69	−28
Austria		93		88		−5
Azerbaijan			92			
Bangladesh			98	99		1
Belarus			98	94		−4
Belgium	87	92		83		−4
Bosnia and Herz.			94	95		1
Brazil		88	87		81	−7
Britain	66	74		63		−3
Bulgaria		95	97	97	95	0
Burkina Faso					86	
Canada	66	78		71	62	−4
Chile		93	86	83	74	−19
China		98	91	95	97	−1
Colombia			86			
Croatia			86	84		−2
Cyprus					92	
Czech		96	96	87		−9
Denmark	58	73		67		9
Dominican Rep.			85			
Egypt				99	99	0
El Salvador			94			
Estonia		99	96	96		−3
Ethiopia					91	
Finland	55	86	72	59	55	0
France	86	94		87		1
Georgia			98		99	1
Germany (East)		97	89	91	90	−7
Germany (West)	91	94	85	90	86	−5
Ghana					95	
Greece				96		
Guatemala					93	
Hong Kong				90		
Hungary		99	97	96		−3
Iceland	77	78		71		−6
India		97	85	95	90	−7
Indonesia				89	81	−8
Iran				86	97	11
Iraq						
Ireland	74	83		68		−6
Israel						
Italy	92	97		92	93	1
Japan	88	95	94	90	89	1
Jordan				98	97	−1

Country	1981	1990	1995	2000	2006	Change
Kyrgyzstan				98		
Latvia		99	96	93		−6
Lithuania		94	88	81		−13
Luxembourg				84		
Macedonia			96	97		1
Malaysia					92	
Mali					89	
Malta	94	94		93		−1
Mexico	89	88	72	86	84	−5
Moldova			97	97	89	−8
Montenegro			95	97		2
Morocco				98	84	−14
Netherlands	77	79		66		−11
New Zealand			77		68	−9
Nigeria		97	94	97		0
Northern Ireland	78	81		69		−9
Norway	79	86	85		67	−12
Pakistan				98		
Peru			92	94	94	2
Philippines			95	97		2
Poland		99	97	97	95	−4
Portugal		94		72		−22
Puerto Rico			78	76		−2
Romania		97	96	95	97	0
Russia		97	97	95		−2
Rwanda					88	
Saudi Arabia				95		
Serbia			90	89	85	−5
Singapore				93		
Slovakia		97	98	95		−2
Slovenia		94	93	88	87	−7
South Africa	81	91	90	89	90	9
South Korea	91		96	97	92	1
Spain	87	93	89	87	78	−9
Sweden	71	85	82	60	47	−24
Switzerland			90		80	−10
Taiwan			98		88	−10
Tanzania				97		
Thailand					97	
Trinidad					80	
Turkey		96	97	97	96	0
Uganda				95		
Ukraine			96	97	92	−4
Uruguay			90		82	−8
USA	63	74	76	63	29	−34
Venezuela			83	89		6
Vietnam				97	98	1
Zambia					74	
Zimbabwe			98			

Marriage is an out-dated institution

(D002) Do you agree or disagree with the following statement?: "Marriage is an out-dated institution"

Agree (%)

Country	1981	1990	1995	2000	2006	Change
Albania			5	9		4
Algeria				13		
Andorra					39	
Argentina	23	9	15	20	30	7
Armenia			14			
Australia	13		19		18	5
Austria		12		19		7
Azerbaijan			18			
Bangladesh			92	5		−87
Belarus		16	19	17		1
Belgium	18	23		31		13
Bosnia and Herz.			12	10		−2
Brazil		27	30		21	−6
Britain	15	18		27		12
Bulgaria		11	19	17	28	17
Burkina Faso					11	
Canada	13	12		23	22	9
Chile		15	19	31	30	15
China		15	8	14	12	−3
Colombia			25			
Croatia			15	10		−5
Cyprus				18		
Czech		8	13	10		2
Denmark	19	18		15		−4
Dominican Rep.			11			
Egypt				4		
El Salvador			15			
Estonia		11	18	16		5
Ethiopia					10	
Finland	17	13	21	19	19	2
France	32	29		35		3
Georgia			15		4	−11
Germany (East)		14	28	20	22	8
Germany (West)	17	15	30	20	21	4
Ghana					12	
Greece				16		
Guatemala					18	
Hong Kong					22	
Hungary	17	11	15	16		−1
Iceland	13	6		8		−5
India		5	25	20	20	15
Indonesia				3	4	1
Iran				20	18	−2
Iraq						
Ireland	13	10		21		8
Israel						
Italy	23	14		17	19	−4
Japan	23	7	12	10	6	−17
Jordan				13	11	−2

Country	1981	1990	1995	2000	2006	Change
Kyrgyzstan				33		
Latvia		9	21	16		7
Lithuania		9	16	21		12
Luxembourg				34		
Macedonia			17	18		1
Malaysia					14	
Mali					21	
Malta	13	6		7		−6
Mexico	18	17	29	20	29	11
Moldova			29	31	16	−13
Montenegro				18	12	−6
Morocco				5	8	3
Netherlands	16	21		25		9
New Zealand			16		15	−1
Nigeria		13	17	15		2
Northern Ireland	14	14		24		10
Norway	13	10	13		17	4
Pakistan				1		
Peru			21	20	20	−1
Philippines			13	19		6
Poland		6	11	9	9	3
Portugal		22		25		3
Puerto Rico			11	13		2
Romania		9	14	12	14	5
Russia		15	17	21		6
Rwanda					12	
Saudi Arabia				17		
Serbia			17	18	17	0
Singapore				15		
Slovakia		7	12	12		5
Slovenia		18	25	27	23	5
South Africa	18	10	20	27	22	4
South Korea	13		15	16	13	0
Spain	25	16	17	21	33	8
Sweden	15	14	16	20	22	7
Switzerland			13	26	28	15
Taiwan				16	10	−6
Tanzania				8		
Thailand					25	
Trinidad					13	
Turkey		11	8	9	5	−6
Uganda				19		
Ukraine			17	17	23	6
Uruguay			21		25	4
USA	9	8	11	10	5	−4
Venezuela			31	25		−6
Vietnam				9	8	−1
Zambia					13	
Zimbabwe				11		

Woman as a single parent

(D003) If a woman wants to have a child as a single parent but she doesn't want to have a stable relationship with a man, do you approve or disapprove?

Approve (%)

Country	1981	1990	1995	2000	2006	Change
Albania			31	12		−19
Algeria				6		
Andorra					82	
Argentina	29	58	61	62	65	36
Armenia			37			
Australia	35		36		41	6
Austria		39		38		−1
Azerbaijan			24			
Bangladesh				4		
Belarus		47	53	61		14
Belgium	34	31		50		16
Bosnia and Herz.			40	39		−1
Brazil		51	52		46	−5
Britain	33	36		33	33	0
Bulgaria		47	39	50	39	−8
Burkina Faso					8	
Canada	36	38		46	48	12
Chile		60	65	73	75	15
China		6	7	2	6	0
Colombia			76		68	−8
Croatia			62	66		4
Cyprus					16	
Czech		27	41	39		12
Denmark	74	67		52		−22
Dominican Rep.			48			
Egypt				5	2	−3
El Salvador			28			
Estonia		32	58	29		−3
Ethiopia				39		
Finland	58	56	61	55	55	−3
France	65	39		49	63	−2
Georgia			41		23	−18
Germany (East)		34	63	31	38	4
Germany (West)	27	24	55	30	31	4
Ghana					6	
Greece				31		
Guatemala					62	
Hong Kong					12	
Hungary	27	39	40	39		12
Iceland	88	84		82		−6
India		3	7	10	14	11
Indonesia				4	3	−1
Iran				3	3	0
Iraq						
Ireland	22	23		29		7
Israel						
Italy	38	40		28	37	−1
Japan	13	15	24	23	22	9
Jordan				2	2	0

Country	1981	1990	1995	2000	2006	Change
Kyrgyzstan				30		
Latvia		26	60	55		29
Lithuania			55	70	62	7
Luxembourg				46		
Macedonia			43	53		10
Malaysia					17	
Mali					11	
Malta	18	16		15		−3
Mexico	49	43	39	50	61	12
Moldova			44	38	37	−7
Montenegro			54	37		−17
Morocco				2	2	0
Netherlands	35	40		51	57	22
New Zealand			15		20	5
Nigeria		9	6	18		9
Northern Ireland	23	24		30		7
Norway	36	27	23		34	−2
Pakistan				0		
Peru			42	49	40	−2
Philippines			12	14		2
Poland		13	20	42	33	20
Portugal		38		38		0
Puerto Rico			44	57		13
Romania		38	46	49	48	10
Russia		42	52	53	44	2
Rwanda					31	
Saudi Arabia				4		
Serbia			55	54	49	−6
Singapore				15		
Slovakia		25	36	23		−2
Slovenia		60	68	56	46	−14
South Africa	20	15	22	28	30	10
South Korea	31			22	5	−26
Spain	39	65	75	72	80	41
Sweden	41	25	26	31	49	8
Switzerland			37	40	40	3
Taiwan			11		18	7
Tanzania				15		
Thailand					26	
Trinidad					25	
Turkey		6	13	8	8	2
Uganda				18		
Ukraine			33	41	35	2
Uruguay			66		69	3
USA	34	37	40	42	51	17
Venezuela			63	65		2
Vietnam				16	15	−1
Zambia					23	
Zimbabwe				7		

Being a housewife just as fulfilling

(D004) For each of the following statements I read out, can you tell me how much you agree with each. "Being a housewife is just as fulfilling as working for pay"

Agree strongly/Agree (%)

Country	1981	1990	1995	2000	2006	Change
Albania			15	46		31
Algeria				66		
Andorra					47	
Argentina		62	61	75	64	2
Armenia			75			
Australia			69		73	4
Austria		63				
Azerbaijan			73			
Bangladesh				21	29	8
Belarus		81	62	64		−17
Belgium		68		62		−6
Bosnia and Herz.				86	75	−11
Brazil		61	61		51	−10
Britain		61		60	68	7
Bulgaria		87	75	47	62	−25
Burkina Faso					33	
Canada		71		83	81	10
Chile		73	66	69	59	−14
China		88	69	90	72	−16
Colombia			66		56	−10
Croatia			72	48		−24
Cyprus				53		
Czech		70	41	77		7
Denmark		55		54		−1
Dominican Rep.			49			
Egypt				74	91	17
El Salvador			70			
Estonia		71	66	59		−12
Ethiopia				17		
Finland		54	82	80	84	30
France		60		63	53	−7
Georgia			79		66	−13
Germany (East)		34	29	27	35	1
Germany (West)		54	47	48	52	−2
Ghana					25	
Greece				42		
Guatemala					73	
Hong Kong					91	
Hungary		76	80	59		−17
Iceland		71		64		−7
India		46	65	64	63	17
Indonesia				23	86	63
Iran				75		
Iraq				82	82	0
Ireland		72				
Israel						
Italy		53		55	54	1
Japan		83	89	89	92	9
Jordan				76	77	1

Country	1981	1990	1995	2000	2006	Change
Kyrgyzstan				73		
Latvia		66	63	40		−26
Lithuania		85	83	77		−8
Luxembourg				63		
Macedonia			42	51		9
Malaysia					59	
Mali					51	
Malta		87		87		0
Mexico		68	60	72	74	6
Moldova			65	72	46	−19
Montenegro			64	65		1
Morocco				64	58	−6
Netherlands		55		51	57	2
New Zealand			67		68	1
Nigeria		49	40	44		−5
Northern Ireland		70				
Norway		53	61		57	4
Pakistan			59	76		17
Peru			62	73	60	−2
Philippines			85	86		1
Poland		63	56	60	61	−2
Portugal		53		49		−4
Puerto Rico			72	81		9
Romania		48	47	48	35	−13
Russia		86	70	64	58	−28
Rwanda					29	
Saudi Arabia				69		
Serbia			70	69	46	−24
Singapore				71		
Slovakia		46	45	71		25
Slovenia		63	68	54	68	5
South Africa			57	64	52	−5
South Korea		67	89	88	91	24
Spain		59	60	60	53	−6
Sweden		62	66	51	48	−14
Switzerland					65	
Taiwan			86		82	−4
Tanzania				43		
Thailand					18	
Trinidad					68	
Turkey		79	76	76	77	−2
Uganda				34		
Ukraine			67	57	58	−9
Uruguay			67		75	8
USA		74	81	80	79	5
Venezuela			61	65		4
Vietnam				86	77	−9
Zambia					44	
Zimbabwe				66		

Men make better political leaders than women do

(D005) For each of the following statements I read out, can you tell me how much you agree with each. "On the whole, men make better political leaders than women do"

Strongly disagree/Disagree (%)

Country	1981	1990	1995	2000	2006	Change
Albania			47	49		2
Algeria				30		
Andorra					90	
Argentina			62	68	68	6
Armenia			17			
Australia			76		76	0
Austria						
Azerbaijan			28			
Bangladesh			44	33		−11
Belarus			30			
Belgium						
Bosnia and Herz.			44	63		19
Brazil			53		69	16
Britain				80		
Bulgaria			39		53	14
Burkina Faso					37	
Canada				81	84	3
Chile			58	60	56	−2
China			46	50	46	0
Colombia			67		71	4
Croatia			46			
Cyprus					64	
Czech			49			
Denmark						
Dominican Rep.			59			
Egypt				16	8	−8
El Salvador			63			
Estonia			31			
Ethiopia					77	
Finland			79		81	2
France				78		
Georgia			20		32	12
Germany (East)			82		81	−1
Germany (West)			87		80	−7
Ghana					22	
Greece						
Guatemala					68	
Hong Kong				63		
Hungary			48			
Iceland						
India			51	42	37	−14
Indonesia				39	39	0
Iran				34	21	−13
Iraq				10	10	0
Ireland						
Israel						
Italy					81	
Japan			40	57	56	16
Jordan				12	19	7

Country	1981	1990	1995	2000	2006	Change
Kyrgyzstan				43		
Latvia			34			
Lithuania			44			
Luxembourg						
Macedonia			54	59		5
Malaysia					32	
Mali					21	
Malta						
Mexico			56	61	72	16
Moldova			33	40	48	15
Montenegro			35	45		10
Morocco				29	42	13
Netherlands					82	
New Zealand			82		84	2
Nigeria			26	20		−6
Northern Ireland						
Norway			84		86	2
Pakistan			38	51		13
Peru			70	76	83	13
Philippines			42	37		−5
Poland			39		55	16
Portugal						
Puerto Rico			70	81		11
Romania			33		45	12
Russia			40		38	−2
Rwanda					48	
Saudi Arabia				25		
Serbia			44	53	59	15
Singapore				49		
Slovakia			32			
Slovenia			55		70	15
South Africa			48	59	49	1
South Korea			37	52	45	8
Spain			74	81	79	5
Sweden			82	81	92	10
Switzerland					85	
Taiwan			52		56	4
Tanzania				56		
Thailand				49		
Trinidad					75	
Turkey			42	41	39	−3
Uganda				31		
Ukraine			37		49	12
Uruguay			62		80	18
USA			67	78	73	6
Venezuela			59	60		1
Vietnam				44	43	−1
Zambia					50	
Zimbabwe				48		

University is more important for a boy than for a girl

(D006) For each of the following statements I read out, can you tell me how much you agree with each.
"A university education is more important for a boy than for a girl"

Agree strongly/Agree (%)

Country	1981	1990	1995	2000	2006	Change
Albania			20	15		−5
Algeria				28		
Andorra					2	
Argentina			19	15	14	−5
Armenia			42			
Australia			11		7	−4
Austria						
Azerbaijan			37			
Bangladesh			41	63		22
Belarus			41			
Belgium						
Bosnia and Herz.			24	20		−4
Brazil			24		11	−13
Britain				7		
Bulgaria			19		11	−8
Burkina Faso					35	
Canada				5	5	0
Chile			24	31	29	5
China			24	9	21	−3
Colombia			11		10	−1
Croatia			25			
Cyprus					10	
Czech			33			
Denmark						
Dominican Rep.			20			
Egypt				31	38	7
El Salvador			14			
Estonia			34			
Ethiopia					8	
Finland			14		7	−7
France					7	
Georgia			34		24	−10
Germany (East)			12		15	3
Germany (West)			10		17	7
Ghana					22	
Greece						
Guatemala					21	
Hong Kong					22	
Hungary			20			
Iceland						
India			31	42	46	15
Indonesia				17	20	3
Iran				38	56	18
Iraq				46	49	3
Ireland						
Israel						
Italy					8	
Japan			38	23	24	−14
Jordan				39	37	−2

Country	1981	1990	1995	2000	2006	Change
Kyrgyzstan				28		
Latvia			27			
Lithuania			23			
Luxembourg						
Macedonia			13	12		−1
Malaysia					46	
Mali					50	
Malta						
Mexico			32	31	25	−7
Moldova			32	23	17	−15
Montenegro			25	24		−1
Morocco				40	30	−10
Netherlands					6	
New Zealand			8		5	−3
Nigeria			36	44		8
Northern Ireland						
Norway			11		4	−7
Pakistan			40	23		−17
Peru			28	20	13	−15
Philippines			37	37		0
Poland			35		16	−19
Portugal						
Puerto Rico			13	11		−2
Romania			32		19	−13
Russia			34		29	−5
Rwanda					29	
Saudi Arabia				62		
Serbia			27	21	14	−13
Singapore				15		
Slovakia			37			
Slovenia			23		11	−12
South Africa			17	17	20	3
South Korea			37	24	25	−12
Spain			17	12	13	−4
Sweden			9	7	1	−8
Switzerland					9	
Taiwan			24		15	−9
Tanzania				16		
Thailand					28	
Trinidad					9	
Turkey			26	25	19	−7
Uganda				23		
Ukraine			36		33	−3
Uruguay			12		7	−5
USA			17	8	8	−9
Venezuela			21	15		−6
Vietnam				24	21	−3
Zambia					24	
Zimbabwe				19		

Make my parents proud

(D007) For each of the following statements I read out, can you tell me how much you agree with each.
"One of my main goals in life has been to make my parents proud"

Agree strongly/Agree (%)

Country	1981	1990	1995	2000	2006	Change
Albania			79	94		15
Algeria				92		
Andorra					68	
Argentina			77	85	80	3
Armenia			84			
Australia			69		68	−1
Austria						
Azerbaijan			86			
Bangladesh			93	96		3
Belarus			64			
Belgium						
Bosnia and Herz.			84	89		5
Brazil			88		88	0
Britain				77		
Bulgaria			77		80	3
Burkina Faso				97		
Canada				82	78	−4
Chile			71	84	87	16
China			73	61	73	0
Colombia			93			
Croatia			70			
Cyprus					86	
Czech			65			
Denmark						
Dominican Rep.			89			
Egypt				99	96	−3
El Salvador			96			
Estonia			65			
Ethiopia					94	
Finland			35		34	−1
France					74	
Georgia			85		90	5
Germany (East)			69		60	−9
Germany (West)			47		40	−7
Ghana					97	
Greece						
Guatemala					99	
Hong Kong					71	
Hungary			61			
Iceland						
India			92	89	90	−2
Indonesia				92	97	5
Iran				92	94	2
Iraq				96	96	0
Ireland						
Israel						
Italy					74	
Japan			37	73	70	33
Jordan				99	96	−3

Country	1981	1990	1995	2000	2006	Change
Kyrgyzstan				89		
Latvia			56			
Lithuania			56			
Luxembourg						
Macedonia			80	84		4
Malaysia					95	
Mali					97	
Malta						
Mexico		79	93		94	15
Moldova			78	93	85	7
Montenegro			86	74		−12
Morocco				97	92	−5
Netherlands					63	
New Zealand			58		53	−5
Nigeria			96	98		2
Northern Ireland						
Norway			54		48	−6
Pakistan				97		
Peru			93	96	93	0
Philippines			90	96		6
Poland			85		88	3
Portugal						
Puerto Rico			94	96		2
Romania			76		72	−4
Russia			64		83	19
Rwanda					97	
Saudi Arabia				96		
Serbia			76	75	73	−3
Singapore				94		
Slovakia			69			
Slovenia			65		72	7
South Africa			92	93	94	2
South Korea			60	75	76	16
Spain			80	85	84	4
Sweden			51	38	36	−15
Switzerland			49		56	7
Taiwan			64		85	21
Tanzania				88		
Thailand					98	
Trinidad					93	
Turkey			92	96	98	6
Uganda				94		
Ukraine			65		73	8
Uruguay			68		83	15
USA			77	82	76	−1
Venezuela			95	97		2
Vietnam				97	92	−5
Zambia					89	
Zimbabwe					96	

Live up to what my friends expect

(D008) For each of the following statements I read out, can you tell me how much you agree with each.
"I make a lot of effort to live up to what my friends expect"

Agree strongly/Agree (%)

Country	1981	1990	1995	2000	2006	Change
Albania			59	51		–8
Algeria				71		
Andorra					34	
Argentina			28	25	30	2
Armenia			73			
Australia			34		26	–8
Austria						
Azerbaijan			74			
Bangladesh			64	59		–5
Belarus			57			
Belgium						
Bosnia and Herz.			64	34		–30
Brazil			75		58	–17
Britain				31		
Bulgaria			74		26	–48
Burkina Faso					79	
Canada				45	29	–16
Chile			27	35	48	21
China			87	76	75	–12
Colombia			41			
Croatia			42			
Cyprus					58	
Czech			54			
Denmark						
Dominican Rep.			70			
Egypt				72	78	6
El Salvador						
Estonia			42			
Ethiopia					85	
Finland			38		38	0
France				61		
Georgia			89		91	2
Germany (East)			32		33	1
Germany (West)			20		28	8
Ghana					39	
Greece						
Guatemala					67	
Hong Kong					56	
Hungary			40			
Iceland						
India			67	55	66	–1
Indonesia				58	29	–29
Iran				53	71	18
Iraq						
Ireland						
Israel						
Italy					58	
Japan			50	65	54	4
Jordan				87	94	7

Country	1981	1990	1995	2000	2006	Change
Kyrgyzstan				75		
Latvia			51			
Lithuania			41			
Luxembourg						
Macedonia			39	35		–4
Malaysia					62	
Mali					87	
Malta						
Mexico			29	54	62	33
Moldova			54	70	19	–35
Montenegro			76	69		–7
Morocco				74	71	–3
Netherlands					12	
New Zealand			30		26	–4
Nigeria			72	77		5
Northern Ireland						
Norway			19		26	7
Pakistan			48			
Peru			67	57	57	–10
Philippines			71	56		–15
Poland			59		51	–8
Portugal						
Puerto Rico			66	52		–14
Romania			49		25	–24
Russia			52		30	–22
Rwanda					76	
Saudi Arabia				68		
Serbia			63	63	23	–40
Singapore				44		
Slovakia			66			
Slovenia			57		40	–17
South Africa			40	32	33	–7
South Korea			64	72	77	13
Spain			48	58	53	5
Sweden			38		25	–13
Switzerland			46		40	–6
Taiwan			59		64	5
Tanzania				40		
Thailand					43	
Trinidad					15	
Turkey			69		86	17
Uganda				80		
Ukraine			53		32	–21
Uruguay			28		51	23
USA			41	33	30	–11
Venezuela			49	37		–12
Vietnam				77	64	–13
Zambia					42	
Zimbabwe				50		

Be willing to fight in war for your country

(E001) Of course, we all hope that there will not be another war, but if it were to come to that, would you be willing to fight for your country?

Yes (%)

Country	1981	1990	1995	2000	2006	Change
Albania			81	72		−9
Algeria						
Andorra					41	
Argentina	59	63	67	65	58	−1
Armenia			80			
Australia	75		75		63	−12
Austria		66		55		−11
Azerbaijan			97			
Bangladesh			89	96		7
Belarus		92	88	84		−8
Belgium	34	39				5
Bosnia and Herz.			81	75		−6
Brazil		35	72		61	26
Britain	69	74			62	−7
Bulgaria		91	74		59	−32
Burkina Faso					85	
Canada	64	68		66	59	−5
Chile		83	74	60	58	−25
China		97	93	97	87	−10
Colombia						
Croatia			80	85		5
Cyprus				84		
Czech		81	54			−27
Denmark	72	89				17
Dominican Rep.			79			
Egypt				78		
El Salvador			69			
Estonia		92	75			−17
Ethiopia				77		
Finland	77	88	84	88	84	7
France	48	66		59	60	12
Georgia			72		70	−2
Germany (East)		53	50	36	33	−20
Germany (West)	47	42	49	46	35	−12
Ghana					89	
Greece						
Guatemala				70		
Hong Kong				52		
Hungary	87	77	69			−18
Iceland	74	77				3
India		92	94	82	81	−11
Indonesia					92	
Iran					81	
Iraq				37	37	0
Ireland	61	61				0
Israel				80		
Italy	36	31		60	43	7
Japan	33	20	24	25	25	−8
Jordan					93	

Country	1981	1990	1995	2000	2006	Change
Kyrgyzstan				87		
Latvia		97	68			−29
Lithuania		84	68	73		−11
Luxembourg				54		
Macedonia			83	80		−3
Malaysia					79	
Mali					88	
Malta	80	62				−18
Mexico	79	74	71	75	75	−4
Moldova			80	85	68	−12
Montenegro			90	65		−25
Morocco				94	77	−17
Netherlands	57	69			48	−9
New Zealand			65		63	−2
Nigeria		80	67			−13
Northern Ireland	59	61				2
Norway	90	91	89		88	−2
Pakistan						
Peru			90	81	77	−13
Philippines			88	87		−1
Poland		91	83		74	−17
Portugal		68				
Puerto Rico			67	76		9
Romania		92	86	84	68	−24
Russia		84	82	75	84	0
Rwanda					95	
Saudi Arabia						
Serbia			83	72	61	−22
Singapore				87		
Slovakia			75	64		−11
Slovenia			95	90	85	74	−21
South Africa	50	77	70	65	61	11
South Korea	92	87	82	75	72	−20
Spain	66	59	59	43	45	−21
Sweden	87	89	92		86	−1
Switzerland			77	70	65	−12
Taiwan				86	86	0
Tanzania				93		
Thailand				90		
Trinidad					68	
Turkey			93	96	97	4
Uganda				65		
Ukraine			84	73	67	−17
Uruguay			56		53	−3
USA	74	79	77	71	67	−7
Venezuela			86	82		−4
Vietnam				98	95	−3
Zambia					65	
Zimbabwe				55		

Less importance placed on work

(E002) I'm going to read out a list of various changes in our way of life that might take place in the near future. Please tell me for each one, if it were to happen, whether you think it would be a good thing, a bad thing, or don't you mind?

Good (%)

Country	1981	1990	1995	2000	2006	Change
Albania			6	10		4
Algeria				9		
Andorra					66	
Argentina	40	20	22	21	21	-19
Armenia			22			
Australia	29		33		37	8
Austria		23		31		8
Azerbaijan			30			
Bangladesh			2	7		5
Belarus			28	18	20	-8
Belgium	31	44		50		19
Bosnia and Herz.			17	15		-2
Brazil		18	22		27	9
Britain	24	32		54	43	19
Bulgaria		41	19	36	21	-20
Burkina Faso					10	
Canada	26	31		31	37	11
Chile		18	23	34	36	18
China		8	19	17	17	9
Colombia			12		33	21
Croatia			10	34		24
Cyprus					37	
Czech		8	7	10		2
Denmark	29	27		33		4
Dominican Rep.			10			
Egypt				2	5	3
El Salvador			18			
Estonia			14	14		0
Ethiopia					47	
Finland	17	24	19	26	33	16
France	63	35		66	51	-12
Georgia			38		20	-18
Germany (East)		15	25	30	22	7
Germany (West)	31	35	32	41	27	-4
Ghana					17	
Greece				30		
Guatemala					26	
Hong Kong					31	
Hungary	11	25	39	19		8
Iceland	32	33		43		11
India		7	10	14	18	11
Indonesia				5	7	2
Iran				16	15	-1
Iraq					33	
Ireland	22	22		36		14
Israel				34		
Italy	23	25		25	30	7
Japan	5	6	7	5	5	0
Jordan				28	25	-3

Country	1981	1990	1995	2000	2006	Change
Kyrgyzstan				15		
Latvia			14	9		-5
Lithuania		12	15	14		2
Luxembourg				48		
Macedonia			19	24		5
Malaysia					31	
Mali					20	
Malta	21	44		31		10
Mexico	24	28	18	28	43	19
Moldova			14	24	27	13
Montenegro			18	20		2
Morocco				43	8	-35
Netherlands	28	35		38	34	6
New Zealand			28		35	7
Nigeria			14	23	34	20
Northern Ireland	20	22		42		22
Norway	12	16	26		20	8
Pakistan				10		
Peru			18	13	13	-5
Philippines			24	33		9
Poland		22	21	16	28	6
Portugal		37		19		-18
Puerto Rico			23	32		9
Romania		20	19	13		-7
Russia		26	15	15	22	-4
Rwanda					3	
Saudi Arabia				31		
Serbia			12	14	20	8
Singapore				28		
Slovakia		5	8	8		3
Slovenia		12	16	20	17	5
South Africa	19	15	21	20	24	5
South Korea	11	16	17	11	12	1
Spain	39	52	37	45	41	2
Sweden	15	27	38	51	49	34
Switzerland		46	41			-5
Taiwan			12		8	-4
Tanzania				6		
Thailand					27	
Trinidad					13	
Turkey		16	16	27	24	8
Uganda				11		
Ukraine			22	21	29	7
Uruguay			15		29	14
USA	22	23	28	33	43	21
Venezuela			16	21		5
Vietnam				28	25	-3
Zambia					14	
Zimbabwe				10		

More emphasis on technology

(E003) I'm going to read out a list of various changes in our way of life that might take place in the near future. Please tell me for each one, if it were to happen, whether you think it would be a good thing, a bad thing, or don't you mind?

Good (%)

Country	1981	1990	1995	2000	2006	Change
Albania			80	61		–19
Algeria				87		
Andorra					55	
Argentina	66	78	67	67	62	–4
Armenia			83			
Australia	59		58		44	–15
Austria		42		56		14
Azerbaijan			77			
Bangladesh			92	89		–3
Belarus		84	83	82		–2
Belgium	51	56		57		6
Bosnia and Herz.			66	70		4
Brazil		79	70		72	–7
Britain	59	66	70	69	59	0
Bulgaria		81	67	84	80	–1
Burkina Faso					61	
Canada	59	64		57	63	4
Chile			73	52	57	60	–13
China		95	92	97	89	–6
Colombia			83		85	2
Croatia			63	79		16
Cyprus					63	
Czech		84	68	76		–8
Denmark	36	59		62		26
Dominican Rep.			51			
Egypt				89	77	–12
El Salvador			72			
Estonia		84	77	75		–9
Ethiopia					73	
Finland	47	68	45	55	60	13
France	67	76		58	63	–4
Georgia			82		73	–9
Germany (East)		83	61	61	61	–22
Germany (West)	57	52	51	63	47	–10
Ghana					87	
Greece				52		
Guatemala					80	
Hong Kong					38	
Hungary	84	75	70	60		–24
Iceland	74	69		85		11
India		85	55	57	50	–35
Indonesia				63	67	4
Iran				80	77	–3
Iraq					92	
Ireland	63	61		69		6
Israel				78		
Italy	61	61		65	58	–3
Japan	66	65	66	61	67	1
Jordan				94	91	–3

Country	1981	1990	1995	2000	2006	Change
Kyrgyzstan				79		
Latvia		81	71	87		6
Lithuania		88	72	79		–9
Luxembourg				64		
Macedonia			71	65		–6
Malaysia					56	
Mali					71	
Malta	73	74		88		15
Mexico	78	78	64	76	83	5
Moldova			80	76	66	–14
Montenegro			76	76		0
Morocco				92	67	–25
Netherlands	33	48		49	49	16
New Zealand			38		48	10
Nigeria			96	82	86	–10
Northern Ireland	59	60		61		2
Norway	41	47	46		58	17
Pakistan				77		
Peru			79	78	80	1
Philippines			82	67		–15
Poland		90	81	80	77	–13
Portugal		70		72		2
Puerto Rico			75	80		5
Romania			76	85	75	–1
Russia		84	89	88	78	–6
Rwanda					87	
Saudi Arabia				77		
Serbia			82	81	68	–14
Singapore				69		
Slovakia			75	65	79		4
Slovenia			87	75	79	75	–12
South Africa	60	84	69	63	67	7
South Korea	88	90	67	69	74	–14
Spain	61	63	57	60	69	8
Sweden	34	35	34	35	44	10
Switzerland			57	40		–17
Taiwan			93		79	–14
Tanzania				90		
Thailand					44	
Trinidad					73	
Turkey		90	95	90	75	–15
Uganda				72		
Ukraine			76	89	78	2
Uruguay			64		66	2
USA	66	69	52	56	61	–5
Venezuela			86	87		1
Vietnam				78	85	7
Zambia					52	
Zimbabwe				77		

174

Greater respect for authority

(E004) I'm going to read out a list of various changes in our way of life that might take place in the near future. Please tell me for each one, if it were to happen, whether you think it would be a good thing, a bad thing, or don't you mind?

Good (%)

Country	1981	1990	1995	2000	2006	Change
Albania			41	34		−7
Algeria				63		
Andorra					32	
Argentina	61	69	64	71	76	15
Armenia			63			
Australia	68		73		59	−9
Austria		47		40		−7
Azerbaijan			61			
Bangladesh			87	92		5
Belarus		71	68	72		1
Belgium	60	49		63		3
Bosnia and Herz.			39	30		−9
Brazil		81	83		78	−3
Britain	70	73	81	70	79	9
Bulgaria			78	57	69	46	−32
Burkina Faso					70	
Canada	76	64		69	71	−5
Chile			80	55	56	66	−14
China		24	41	64	61	37
Colombia			89		92	3
Croatia			23	50		27
Cyprus					67	
Czech		62	47	52		−10
Denmark	36	35		38		2
Dominican Rep.			56			
Egypt				86	75	−11
El Salvador			86			
Estonia			45	44		−1
Ethiopia					50	
Finland	25	26	27	39	43	18
France	57	59		69	86	29
Georgia			75		70	−5
Germany (East)		57	39	59	59	2
Germany (West)	39	30	24	45	45	6
Ghana					93	
Greece				17		
Guatemala					91	
Hong Kong					23	
Hungary	71	61	58	67		−4
Iceland	46	42		47		1
India			54	33	43	38	−16
Indonesia				37	17	−20
Iran				71	67	−4
Iraq					89	
Ireland	84	82		78		−6
Israel				59		
Italy	62	47		51	49	−13
Japan	6	5	7	4	3	−3
Jordan				90	93	3

Country	1981	1990	1995	2000	2006	Change
Kyrgyzstan				51		
Latvia			30	49		19
Lithuania		53	39	43		−10
Luxembourg				53		
Macedonia			44	48		4
Malaysia					52	
Mali					78	
Malta	93	95		92		−1
Mexico	67	65	62	75	86	19
Moldova			60	48	39	−21
Montenegro			62	45		−17
Morocco				88	71	−17
Netherlands	57	52		67	73	16
New Zealand			53		54	1
Nigeria		91	80	83		−8
Northern Ireland	86	82		77		−9
Norway	38	32	32		31	−7
Pakistan				62		
Peru			71	80	86	15
Philippines			76	68		−8
Poland		73	58	55	47	−26
Portugal		75		78		3
Puerto Rico			93	94		1
Romania			58	84	76	18
Russia		68	63	57	46	−22
Rwanda					91	
Saudi Arabia				73		
Serbia			52	55	60	8
Singapore				53		
Slovakia		54	42	68		14
Slovenia		66	36	43	38	−28
South Africa	67	88	80	76	79	12
South Korea	10	14	16	19	27	17
Spain	76	68	72	59	81	5
Sweden	31	22	21	22	24	−7
Switzerland		45	33			−12
Taiwan			45		27	−18
Tanzania				82		
Thailand					27	
Trinidad					90	
Turkey		64	65	66	56	−8
Uganda				72		
Ukraine			62	64	78	16
Uruguay				57	67	10
USA	85	77	77	71	68	−17
Venezuela			89	91		2
Vietnam				80	86	6
Zambia					62	
Zimbabwe				90		

More emphasis on family life

(E005) I'm going to read out a list of various changes in our way of life that might take place in the near future. Please tell me for each one, if it were to happen, whether you think it would be a good thing, a bad thing, or don't you mind?

Good (%)

Country	1981	1990	1995	2000	2006	Change
Albania			97	96		−1
Algeria				96		
Andorra					97	
Argentina	88	96	96	97	93	5
Armenia			92			
Australia	90		95		90	0
Austria		92		92		0
Azerbaijan			95			
Bangladesh			89	92		3
Belarus			95	93	91	−4
Belgium	84	85		90		6
Bosnia and Herz.			86	83		−3
Brazil		98	98		97	−1
Britain	82	89		90	93	11
Bulgaria		90	87	95	92	2
Burkina Faso					90	
Canada	90	94		95	95	5
Chile		97	86	92	91	−6
China		74	85	92	92	18
Colombia			99		99	0
Croatia			85	91		6
Cyprus					91	
Czech		94	92	93		−1
Denmark	88	94		95		7
Dominican Rep.			75			
Egypt				99	96	−3
El Salvador			95			
Estonia		86	96	89		3
Ethiopia					87	
Finland	92	96	93	95	95	3
France	88	90		92	93	5
Georgia			94		96	2
Germany (East)		92	91	85	91	−1
Germany (West)	84	87	83	90	81	−3
Ghana					90	
Greece				91		
Guatemala				97		
Hong Kong				75		
Hungary	96	94	98	92		−4
Iceland	95	96		96		1
India		75	54	75	75	0
Indonesia				83	87	4
Iran				91	92	1
Iraq						
Ireland	91	94		95		4
Israel				93		
Italy	88	92		92	93	5
Japan	80	85	89	89	87	7
Jordan				98	99	1

Country	1981	1990	1995	2000	2006	Change
Kyrgyzstan				93		
Latvia		85	87	92		7
Lithuania		96	92	96		0
Luxembourg				88		
Macedonia			76	82		6
Malaysia					78	
Mali					85	
Malta	95	90		99		4
Mexico	87	91	80	91	97	10
Moldova			92	87	92	0
Montenegro			95	95		0
Morocco				99	95	−4
Netherlands	70	67		68	78	8
New Zealand			90		92	2
Nigeria		92	87	94		2
Northern Ireland	88	92		90		2
Norway	93	95	95		87	−6
Pakistan				89		
Peru			94	95	96	2
Philippines			95	92		−3
Poland		97	94	95	95	−2
Portugal		94		92		−2
Puerto Rico			98	95		−3
Romania			93	95	92	−1
Russia		95	96	94	93	−2
Rwanda					92	
Saudi Arabia				90		
Serbia			93	95	89	−4
Singapore				93		
Slovakia		91	92	95		4
Slovenia		91	90	96	94	3
South Africa	82	95	91	85	87	5
South Korea	91	89	86	93	90	−1
Spain	84	89	91	88	92	8
Sweden	84	85	87	77	81	−3
Switzerland		91	90			−1
Taiwan			96		97	1
Tanzania				95		
Thailand					73	
Trinidad					95	
Turkey		95	96	96	90	−5
Uganda				78		
Ukraine			90	91	84	−6
Uruguay				94	89	−5
USA	95	95	94	95	90	−5
Venezuela			98	97		−1
Vietnam				88	93	5
Zambia					75	
Zimbabwe				96		

Opinion about scientific advance
(E006) In the long run, do you think the scientific advances we are making will help or harm mankind?
Will help (%)

Country	1981	1990	1995	2000	2006	Change
Albania			65	55		−10
Algeria				55		
Andorra					46	
Argentina	41	47	50	51	58	17
Armenia			74			
Australia	47		57		73	26
Austria		31		36		5
Azerbaijan			61			
Bangladesh			77	70		−7
Belarus		38	66	56		18
Belgium	28	34				6
Bosnia and Herz.			53	54		1
Brazil		64	66		67	3
Britain	50	47		40	53	3
Bulgaria		62	64		65	3
Burkina Faso				75		
Canada	46	55		50	57	11
Chile		43	36	42	50	7
China		58	80	80	77	19
Colombia			67			
Croatia			50	34		−16
Cyprus				56		
Czech		45	48			3
Denmark	33	43				10
Dominican Rep.			45			
Egypt				80	45	−35
El Salvador			49			
Estonia		52	69			17
Ethiopia				92		
Finland	45	42	51		64	19
France	39	42			45	6
Georgia			70		74	4
Germany (East)		52	50	48	58	6
Germany (West)	35	39	53	52	61	26
Ghana					91	
Greece						
Guatemala				55		
Hong Kong				44		
Hungary	65	55	53			−12
Iceland	54	54		66		12
India		51	50	59	63	12
Indonesia				50	54	4
Iran				73		
Iraq						
Ireland	41	40		41		0
Israel						
Italy	41	36		31	54	13
Japan	24	26	26	24	27	3
Jordan				68	70	2

Country	1981	1990	1995	2000	2006	Change
Kyrgyzstan				58		
Latvia		34	59			25
Lithuania		61	70	65		4
Luxembourg						
Macedonia			68	65		−3
Malaysia					68	
Mali					84	
Malta	42	58				16
Mexico	53	44	39	51	56	3
Moldova			75	56	59	−16
Montenegro			47	44		−3
Morocco				76	56	−20
Netherlands	24	37			42	18
New Zealand			27		33	6
Nigeria		79	74	87		8
Northern Ireland	40	46		38		−2
Norway	35	36	39		46	11
Pakistan				41		
Peru			48	54	42	−6
Philippines			45	68		23
Poland		70	72		67	−3
Portugal		47				
Puerto Rico			43	47		4
Romania		57	50		70	13
Russia		60	67		53	−7
Rwanda					96	
Saudi Arabia				65		
Serbia			59	45	48	−11
Singapore				40		
Slovakia		45	55			10
Slovenia		41	41	34	34	−7
South Africa	44	55	60	61	68	24
South Korea	57	40	30	49	67	10
Spain	47	46	48	66	72	25
Sweden	36	47	47	45	65	29
Switzerland			38		64	26
Taiwan			36		59	23
Tanzania				49		
Thailand					59	
Trinidad					43	
Turkey		72	80	87	83	11
Uganda				59		
Ukraine			55		44	−11
Uruguay			43		45	2
USA	57	62	63	55	80	23
Venezuela			72	63		−9
Vietnam				78	85	7
Zambia					60	
Zimbabwe				72		

Interest in politics
(E007) How interested would you say you are in politics?
Very/Somewhat interested (%)

Country	1981	1990	1995	2000	2006	Change
Albania			37	40		3
Algeria				24		
Andorra					41	
Argentina	43	30	25	18	24	–19
Armenia			52			
Australia			56		59	3
Austria		54		66		12
Azerbaijan			43			
Bangladesh			51	41		–10
Belarus			56	46		–10
Belgium		29		40		11
Bosnia and Herz.			49	39		–10
Brazil		47	31		49	2
Britain		47		36	44	–3
Bulgaria		73	43	54	43	–30
Burkina Faso					62	
Canada		58		47	49	–9
Chile			37	20	25	24	–13
China		67		71	64	–3
Colombia			29		22	–7
Croatia			42			
Cyprus				43		
Czech		82	56	71		–11
Denmark		54		60		6
Dominican Rep.			46			
Egypt				43	34	–9
El Salvador			15			
Estonia		60	49			–11
Ethiopia					67	
Finland	46	47	39	27	38	–8
France		38		36	37	–1
Georgia			50		55	5
Germany (East)		85	76	65	57	–28
Germany (West)		69	78	59	64	–5
Ghana					49	
Greece			42			
Guatemala				23		
Hong Kong				14		
Hungary	66	52	50			–16
Iceland		47		50		3
India		47	39	45	44	–3
Indonesia				37	36	–1
Iran				56	46	–10
Iraq				53	64	11
Ireland		37		46		9
Israel				70		
Italy		29		32	37	8
Japan	54	62	52	64	64	10
Jordan				48	41	–7

Country	1981	1990	1995	2000	2006	Change
Kyrgyzstan				48		
Latvia		79	52			–27
Lithuania		74	44	53		–21
Luxembourg				42		
Macedonia			34	47		13
Malaysia					34	
Mali					67	
Malta		36				
Mexico	36	38	44	36	34	–2
Moldova			35	49	37	2
Montenegro			39	45		6
Morocco				22	33	11
Netherlands		62		67	51	–11
New Zealand			60		56	–4
Nigeria		35	37	53		18
Northern Ireland		34		39		5
Norway		72	69		77	5
Pakistan				30		
Peru			33	48	22	–11
Philippines			49	50		1
Poland		49	42	43	42	–7
Portugal		28		32		4
Puerto Rico				40	42	2
Romania		18	40		32	14
Russia		53	35	39	38	–15
Rwanda					55	
Saudi Arabia				66		
Serbia			37	38	33	–4
Singapore				37		
Slovakia			63	58		–5
Slovenia		57	44	42	45	–12
South Africa	32	62	49	41	45	13
South Korea	48	73	62	50	39	–9
Spain		26	26	28	32	6
Sweden		47	51		60	13
Switzerland		66	40		67	1
Taiwan			41		29	–12
Tanzania				72		
Thailand					84	
Trinidad					36	
Turkey		48	62	42	39	–9
Uganda				52		
Ukraine			41	41	49	8
Uruguay			38		37	–1
USA		60	64	65	65	5
Venezuela			20	24		4
Vietnam				80	73	–7
Zambia					56	
Zimbabwe				32		

Political action: signing a petition

(E008) I'd like you to tell me, for each one, whether you have actually done any of these things, whether you might do it or would never, under any circumstances, do it. Signing a petition

Have done it (%)

Country	1981	1990	1995	2000	2006	Change
Albania			27	22		−5
Algeria			15			
Andorra				58		
Argentina	34	22	31	23	31	−3
Armenia			18			
Australia	70		79		80	10
Austria		48		56		8
Azerbaijan			10			
Bangladesh			25	14		−11
Belarus		27	10	9		−18
Belgium	24	47		72		48
Bosnia and Herz.			23	26		3
Brazil		50	47		55	5
Britain	63	75	58	81	68	5
Bulgaria		22	7	12	12	−10
Burkina Faso					15	
Canada	62	77		74	73	11
Chile			23	17	19	18	−5
China					6	
Colombia			19		15	−4
Croatia			43	37		−6
Cyprus				25		
Czech		48	26	58		10
Denmark	44	51		57		13
Dominican Rep.			15			
Egypt				20	6	−14
El Salvador			19			
Estonia		39	14	21		−18
Ethiopia				21		
Finland	29	41	39	51	50	21
France	45	54		68	66	21
Georgia			14		8	−6
Germany (East)		69	57	62	46	−23
Germany (West)	47	57	66	47	49	2
Ghana					4	
Greece				50		
Guatemala				13		
Hong Kong						
Hungary		18	25	16		−2
Iceland	37	47		53		16
India			25	27	29	29	4
Indonesia				5	6	1
Iran						
Iraq					10	
Ireland	29	42		61		32
Israel				39		
Italy	42	48		55	54	12
Japan	48	62	55	63	60	12
Jordan				8	4	−4

Country	1981	1990	1995	2000	2006	Change
Kyrgyzstan				8		
Latvia		65	31	19		−46
Lithuania		58	31	31		−27
Luxembourg				53		
Macedonia			15	27		12
Malaysia					6	
Mali					19	
Malta	19	32		33		14
Mexico	8	35	32	19	21	13
Moldova			10	18	11	1
Montenegro			15	24		9
Morocco				15	10	−5
Netherlands	35	51		61	46	11
New Zealand			91		87	−4
Nigeria		7	7	7		0
Northern Ireland	35	60		59		24
Norway	55	61	65		69	14
Pakistan				5		
Peru			21	22	25	4
Philippines			12	11		−1
Poland		18	20	21	24	6
Portugal		28		27		−1
Puerto Rico			28	20		−8
Romania			17	11	6	−11
Russia		30	11	12	8	−22
Rwanda					9	
Saudi Arabia						
Serbia			19	29	30	11
Singapore				9		
Slovakia		41	35	60		19
Slovenia		28	19	32	31	3
South Africa	17	34	19	27	15	−2
South Korea	20	42	40	52	34	14
Spain	24	21	22	27	23	−1
Sweden	54	72	72	87	79	25
Switzerland		63	68		80	17
Taiwan			11		12	1
Tanzania				10		
Thailand					3	
Trinidad					21	
Turkey		14	20	15	13	−1
Uganda				21		
Ukraine			13	14	8	−5
Uruguay			36		30	−6
USA	64	72	71	81	69	5
Venezuela			23	15		−8
Vietnam				6	6	0
Zambia					12	
Zimbabwe				5		

Political action: joining in boycotts

(E009) I'd like you to tell me, for each one, whether you have actually done any of these things, whether you might do it or would never, under any circumstances, do it. Joining in boycotts

Have done it (%)

Country	1981	1990	1995	2000	2006	Change
Albania			12	6		–6
Algeria				8		
Andorra					12	
Argentina	3	3	1	2	3	0
Armenia			12			
Australia	5		22		17	12
Austria		5		10		5
Azerbaijan			3			
Bangladesh			19	6		–13
Belarus		5	3	4		–1
Belgium	3	9		12		9
Bosnia and Herz.			9	6		–3
Brazil		10	6		8	–2
Britain	7	14		17	17	10
Bulgaria		3	3	4	2	–1
Burkina Faso				14		
Canada	15	23		19	22	7
Chile		4	2	5	3	–1
China					3	
Colombia			8		2	–6
Croatia			5	8		3
Cyprus				11		
Czech		10	10	9		–1
Denmark	10	11		25		15
Dominican Rep.			6			
Egypt				37	1	–36
El Salvador						
Estonia		3	2	3		0
Ethiopia				11		
Finland	8	13	12	15	16	8
France	12	12		13	14	2
Georgia			6		4	–2
Germany (East)		3	11	6	5	2
Germany (West)	8	10	18	10	12	4
Ghana					2	
Greece				5		
Guatemala					1	
Hong Kong						
Hungary		2	3	3		1
Iceland	7	21		18		11
India			17	18	13	15	–2
Indonesia				3	3	0
Iran						
Iraq					16	
Ireland	7	7		8		1
Israel				8		
Italy	6	11		10	20	14
Japan	3	4	7	8	7	4
Jordan				2	3	1

Country	1981	1990	1995	2000	2006	Change
Kyrgyzstan				3		
Latvia		4	8	4		0
Lithuania		7	5	5		–2
Luxembourg				9		
Macedonia			8	14		6
Malaysia					3	
Mali					9	
Malta	13	14		11		–2
Mexico	1	7	11	2	3	2
Moldova			1	4	5	4
Montenegro			8	16		8
Morocco				7	8	1
Netherlands	7	9		22	13	6
New Zealand			19		18	–1
Nigeria			13	10	8	–5
Northern Ireland	5	9		13		8
Norway	7	12	18		24	17
Pakistan				6		
Peru			3	8	5	2
Philippines			6	5		–1
Poland		6	6	4	5	–1
Portugal		4		6		2
Puerto Rico			7	8		1
Romania			3	2	1	–2
Russia		4	2	2	2	–2
Rwanda					4	
Saudi Arabia						
Serbia			7	19	16	9
Singapore				2		
Slovakia		4	11	4		0
Slovenia		8	6	8	6	–2
South Africa	8	15	12	14	12	4
South Korea	2	11	16	10	6	4
Spain	9	6	5	6	7	–2
Sweden	8	16	33	34	28	20
Switzerland			11		21	10
Taiwan			3		4	1
Tanzania				5		
Thailand					2	
Trinidad					8	
Turkey		6	9	6	5	–1
Uganda				13		
Ukraine			4	5	4	0
Uruguay			4		2	–2
USA	15	18	19	25	21	6
Venezuela			2	2		0
Vietnam				1	0	–1
Zambia					14	
Zimbabwe				5		

Political action: attending lawful demonstrations

(E010) I'd like you to tell me, for each one, whether you have actually done any of these things, whether you might do it or would never, under any circumstances, do it. attending lawful demonstrations

Have done it (%)

Country	1981	1990	1995	2000	2006	Change
Albania			19	25		6
Algeria				20		
Andorra					41	
Argentina	23	15	16	13	20	-3
Armenia			28			
Australia	12		18		22	10
Austria		10		16		6
Azerbaijan			20			
Bangladesh			23	7		-16
Belarus		18	20	16		-2
Belgium	14	23		40		26
Bosnia and Herz.			8	7		-1
Brazil		19	25		18	-1
Britain	10	14		13	16	6
Bulgaria		15	11	17	12	-3
Burkina Faso					22	
Canada	13	22		20	24	11
Chile		30	15	16	18	-12
China						
Colombia			11		14	3
Croatia			7	8		1
Cyprus					28	
Czech		33	11	28		-5
Denmark	19	27		29		10
Dominican Rep.			26			
Egypt				3	1	-2
El Salvador			5			
Estonia		26	21	11		-15
Ethiopia				26		
Finland	14	14	13	15	10	-4
France	27	33		39	38	11
Georgia			19		22	3
Germany (East)		53	22	47	36	-17
Germany (West)	15	21	26	22	24	9
Ghana					8	
Greece				48		
Guatemala					2	
Hong Kong						
Hungary		4	9	5		1
Iceland	14	24		21		7
India		17	13	23	19	2
Indonesia				11	14	3
Iran						
Iraq					19	
Ireland	13	17		22		9
Israel				25		
Italy	27	36		35	36	9
Japan	9	13	10	13	10	1
Jordan				3	4	1

Country	1981	1990	1995	2000	2006	Change
Kyrgyzstan				11		
Latvia		36	20	25		-11
Lithuania		34	17	14		-20
Luxembourg				30		
Macedonia			11	18		7
Malaysia					3	
Mali					24	
Malta	12	20		25		13
Mexico	8	22	11	4	16	8
Moldova			8	18	18	10
Montenegro			12	20		8
Morocco				12	18	6
Netherlands	13	25		32	19	6
New Zealand			21		21	0
Nigeria		20	18	17		-3
Northern Ireland	19	19		21		2
Norway	19	20	26		29	10
Pakistan			7			
Peru			12	17	24	12
Philippines		8	7			-1
Poland		16	10	9	11	-5
Portugal		21		17		-4
Puerto Rico			11	13		2
Romania		20	15	6		-14
Russia		33	21	24	15	-18
Rwanda					14	
Saudi Arabia						
Serbia			8	24	22	14
Singapore				2		
Slovakia		22	12	14		-8
Slovenia		10	9	10	13	3
South Africa	6	15	11	14	15	9
South Korea	7	20	14	23	11	4
Spain	25	24	21	26	36	11
Sweden	15	23	30	36	31	16
Switzerland		16	17		28	12
Taiwan			2		7	5
Tanzania				29		
Thailand					2	
Trinidad					15	
Turkey		6	9	8	6	0
Uganda				15		
Ukraine			18	18	16	-2
Uruguay			5		18	13
USA	13	16	16	21	17	4
Venezuela			10	8		-2
Vietnam				2	1	-1
Zambia					21	
Zimbabwe				5		

181

Self positioning in political scale

(E011) In political matters, people talk of "the left" and "the right."
How would you place your views on this scale, generally speaking?

(%) Left (1 thru 4)

Country	1981	1990	1995	2000	2006	Change
Albania			44	39		−5
Algeria				19		
Andorra					40	
Argentina	24	17	14	13	19	−5
Armenia			29			
Australia	19		23		21	2
Austria		17		20		3
Azerbaijan			25			
Bangladesh			17	8		−9
Belarus		60		22	15	−45
Belgium	19	24		27		8
Bosnia and Herz.			30	25		−5
Brazil		31	27		25	−6
Britain	21	25		26	24	3
Bulgaria		31	23	24	37	6
Burkina Faso					48	
Canada	13	16		20	24	11
Chile		30	25	31	30	0
China						
Colombia			10		12	2
Croatia			27	23		−4
Cyprus					33	
Czech		19	24	22		3
Denmark	20	24		26		6
Dominican Rep.			19			
Egypt					49	
El Salvador			17			
Estonia			19	11		−8
Ethiopia				13		
Finland	19	21	25	24	25	6
France	38	42		38	36	−2
Georgia			20		14	−6
Germany (East)		36	46	40	40	4
Germany (West)	28	29	35	26	38	10
Ghana					15	
Greece				34		
Guatemala					21	
Hong Kong					6	
Hungary		18	29	25		7
Iceland	26	30		28		2
India			30	21	22	41	11
Indonesia				9	9	0
Iran				39		
Iraq					44	
Ireland	14	12		13		−1
Israel				42		
Italy	48	41		32	43	−5
Japan	17	16	15	19	23	6
Jordan				17	32	15

Country	1981	1990	1995	2000	2006	Change
Kyrgyzstan				20		
Latvia			22	13		−9
Lithuania			20	25		5
Luxembourg				26		
Macedonia			33	28		−5
Malaysia						
Mali					33	
Malta	19	8		13		−6
Mexico	8	21	22	16	24	16
Moldova			33	30	21	−12
Montenegro			55	46		−9
Morocco				27	12	−15
Netherlands	33	32		37	34	1
New Zealand			23		24	1
Nigeria			22	34	33	11
Northern Ireland	15	10		20		5
Norway	22	27	24		29	7
Pakistan				4		
Peru			14	21	23	9
Philippines			11	11		0
Poland		16	23	28	16	0
Portugal		23		34		11
Puerto Rico			14	13		−1
Romania		18	29	18	19	1
Russia		33	26	31		−2
Rwanda					34	
Saudi Arabia						
Serbia			35	24	20	−15
Singapore						
Slovakia		25	29	33		8
Slovenia		23	21	25	27	4
South Africa	9	34	29	26	15	6
South Korea	21	13	34	32	29	8
Spain	42	47	41	40	50	8
Sweden	35	28	38	34	35	0
Switzerland		23	28		35	12
Taiwan			4		13	9
Tanzania				24		
Thailand					10	
Trinidad					19	
Turkey		25	25	22	25	0
Uganda				37		
Ukraine			26	27	18	−8
Uruguay			29		34	5
USA	19	16	17	17	8	−11
Venezuela			21	17		−4
Vietnam				2	1	−1
Zambia					14	
Zimbabwe				60		

182

Income: Larger income differences

(E012) Now I'd like you to tell me your views on various issues. How would you place your views on this scale?

(%) We need larger income differences as incentives for individual effort (7 thru 10)

Country	1981	1990	1995	2000	2006	Change
Albania			46	26		−20
Algeria				10		
Andorra					25	
Argentina		21	32	45	39	18
Armenia			24			
Australia			32		29	−3
Austria		41		52		11
Azerbaijan			32			
Bangladesh			22	12		−10
Belarus		15	19	39		24
Belgium		31		37		6
Bosnia and Herz.			25	21		−4
Brazil		34	38		37	3
Britain		22	37	36	34	12
Bulgaria		21	39	26	35	14
Burkina Faso					17	
Canada		21		35	31	10
Chile		30	40	59	48	18
China		9	43	29	35	26
Colombia			28		42	14
Croatia			42	49		7
Cyprus					39	
Czech		20	29	39		19
Denmark		19				
Dominican Rep.			14			
Egypt				6	22	16
El Salvador			28			
Estonia		9	34	16		7
Ethiopia					15	
Finland		23	58	52	42	19
France		40		46	42	2
Georgia			14		20	6
Germany (East)		13	51		63	50
Germany (West)		27	36		44	17
Ghana					15	
Greece						
Guatemala					21	
Hong Kong					67	
Hungary		33	61			28
Iceland		32		35		3
India		30	65	54	48	18
Indonesia				10	8	−2
Iran				29	58	29
Iraq				39		
Ireland		27		28		1
Israel				75		
Italy		32		29	24	−8
Japan		23	26	23	16	−7
Jordan				14	26	12

Country	1981	1990	1995	2000	2006	Change
Kyrgyzstan				38		
Latvia		15	21			6
Lithuania		15	42	43		28
Luxembourg				19		
Macedonia			42	38		−4
Malaysia					15	
Mali					13	
Malta		15				
Mexico		31	32	44	30	−1
Moldova			20	21	28	8
Montenegro			40	47		7
Morocco				16	36	20
Netherlands		22		20	31	9
New Zealand			34		35	1
Nigeria		16	27	29		13
Northern Ireland		16		36		20
Norway		24	36		40	16
Pakistan			15	53		38
Peru			27	14	15	−12
Philippines			26	20		−6
Poland		12	23	30	20	8
Portugal		53				
Puerto Rico			27	19		−8
Romania		26	27	67	53	27
Russia		15	23	21	31	16
Rwanda					28	
Saudi Arabia				15		
Serbia			44	35	27	−17
Singapore				13		
Slovakia		26	40			14
Slovenia		35	49	56	49	14
South Africa		39	43	40	37	−2
South Korea		45	25	25	21	−24
Spain		44	37		33	−11
Sweden		20	25		26	6
Switzerland			49		69	20
Taiwan			24		13	−11
Tanzania				48		
Thailand					7	
Trinidad					18	
Turkey			53	46	59	49	−4
Uganda				21		
Ukraine			21	19	17	−4
Uruguay				46	33	−13
USA		18	35	30	25	7
Venezuela				36	40	4
Vietnam				24	31	7
Zambia					26	
Zimbabwe				26		

183

Government ownership of business

(E013) Now I'd like you to tell me your views on various issues. How would you place your views on this scale?

(%) Government ownership of business and industry should be increased (1 thru 4)

Country	1981	1990	1995	2000	2006	Change
Albania			78	65		−13
Algeria				42		
Andorra					36	
Argentina		58	41	32	19	−39
Armenia			28			
Australia			62		38	−24
Austria		68		67		−1
Azerbaijan			35			
Bangladesh			55	35		−20
Belarus		29	25	36		7
Belgium		58				
Bosnia and Herz.			49	47		−2
Brazil		44	42		37	−7
Britain		46	37	39		−7
Bulgaria		56	40		31	−25
Burkina Faso				38		
Canada		69		60	53	−16
Chile		29	26	28	20	−9
China		17	24	21	21	4
Colombia			27		29	2
Croatia			75	55		−20
Cyprus				43		
Czech		65	38	48		−17
Denmark		61				
Dominican Rep.			26			
Egypt				24	14	−10
El Salvador			34			
Estonia		58	33	29		−29
Ethiopia				58		
Finland		64	59	57	45	−19
France		50		51		1
Georgia			36		46	10
Germany (East)		75	37	42	29	−46
Germany (West)		64	61	62	45	−19
Ghana					35	
Greece						
Guatemala				30		
Hong Kong				56		
Hungary		57	40			−17
Iceland		60		66		6
India		35	47	28	31	−4
Indonesia				25	23	−2
Iran				29	38	9
Iraq				17	14	−3
Ireland		60		54		−6
Israel						
Italy		54		56	40	−14
Japan		28	34	44	39	11
Jordan				31	43	12

Country	1981	1990	1995	2000	2006	Change
Kyrgyzstan				37		
Latvia		58	36			−22
Lithuania		52	47	48		−4
Luxembourg						
Macedonia			58	63		5
Malaysia					28	
Mali					26	
Malta		53				
Mexico		47	44	36	34	−13
Moldova			20	24	29	9
Montenegro			45	61		16
Morocco				47	32	−15
Netherlands		48		50		2
New Zealand			52		56	4
Nigeria		31	41			10
Northern Ireland		47		48		1
Norway		51	46		34	−17
Pakistan			56	28		−28
Peru			37	22	23	−14
Philippines			29	21		−8
Poland		33	31	27	20	−13
Portugal		53		39		−14
Puerto Rico			38	47		9
Romania		52	55	58	52	0
Russia		33	14	23		−10
Rwanda					32	
Saudi Arabia				31		
Serbia			41	52	35	−6
Singapore				37		
Slovakia		46	23			−23
Slovenia		59	49		42	−17
South Africa		66	51	48	40	−26
South Korea		48	45	43	31	−17
Spain		37	34	27	29	−8
Sweden		52	48		42	−10
Switzerland			69		40	−29
Taiwan			33		32	−1
Tanzania				48		
Thailand					16	
Trinidad					38	
Turkey		35	50	46	30	−5
Uganda				66		
Ukraine			32	34	19	−13
Uruguay			30		32	2
USA		74	74	68	29	−45
Venezuela			42	36		−6
Vietnam				36	40	4
Zambia					32	
Zimbabwe				57		

Government more responsibility

(E014) Now I'd like you to tell me your views on various issues. How would you place your views on this scale?

(%) The government should take more responsibility to ensure that everyone is provided for (1 thru 4)

Country	1981	1990	1995	2000	2006	Change
Albania			65	50		−15
Algeria				42		
Andorra					46	
Argentina		32	36	52	45	13
Armenia			65			
Australia		27		30		3
Austria		14		18		4
Azerbaijan			62			
Bangladesh			47	34		−13
Belarus		42	58	39		−3
Belgium		27		30		3
Bosnia and Herz.			52	48		−4
Brazil		40	38		54	14
Britain		34		20	27	−7
Bulgaria		34	48	30	60	26
Burkina Faso					50	
Canada		19		24	26	7
Chile		54	51	59	47	−7
China		33	42	32	41	8
Colombia			22		52	30
Croatia			70	34		−36
Cyprus				52		
Czech		25	56	28		3
Denmark		16		17		1
Dominican Rep.			41			
Egypt				54	70	16
El Salvador			35			
Estonia		34	63	41		7
Ethiopia				24		
Finland		19	31	25	27	8
France		18		16	28	10
Georgia			65		70	5
Germany (East)		22	60	42	57	35
Germany (West)		21	34	17	48	27
Ghana					54	
Greece				38		
Guatemala					47	
Hong Kong					85	
Hungary		47	65	45		−2
Iceland		25		24		−1
India		19	47	42	48	29
Indonesia				35	36	1
Iran				30	61	31
Iraq				69	78	9
Ireland		30		22		−8
Israel				78		
Italy		38		36	44	6
Japan			49	51	49	56	7
Jordan				52	65	13

Country	1981	1990	1995	2000	2006	Change
Kyrgyzstan				55		
Latvia		52	61	53		1
Lithuania		43	50	34		−9
Luxembourg				19		
Macedonia			65	68		3
Malaysia					34	
Mali					42	
Malta		38		33		−5
Mexico		34	43	40	40	6
Moldova			70	55	53	−17
Montenegro			65	76		11
Morocco				46	74	28
Netherlands		22		23	36	14
New Zealand			26		23	−3
Nigeria		53	57		68	15
Northern Ireland		35		25		−10
Norway		21	30		40	19
Pakistan			40	47		7
Peru			37	33	35	−2
Philippines			40	33		−7
Poland		35	40	35	43	8
Portugal		28		25		−3
Puerto Rico			31	20		−11
Romania		36	46	32	46	10
Russia		30	57	40	66	36
Rwanda					29	
Saudi Arabia				29		
Serbia			65	59	46	−19
Singapore				47		
Slovakia		43	67	48		5
Slovenia		41	52	50	50	9
South Africa		29	49	47	47	18
South Korea		25	78	76	72	47
Spain		41	49	46	50	9
Sweden		11	13	17	18	7
Switzerland			16		27	11
Taiwan			32		40	8
Tanzania				63		
Thailand					24	
Trinidad					41	
Turkey		49	45	51	48	−1
Uganda				46		
Ukraine			65	47	58	−7
Uruguay			60		41	−19
USA		13	17	20	25	12
Venezuela			38	41		3
Vietnam				19	28	9
Zambia					54	
Zimbabwe				60		

185

Competition is good

(E015) Now I'd like you to tell me your views on various issues. How would you place your views on this scale?
(%) Competition is good. It stimulates people to work hard and develop new ideas (1 thru 4)

Country	1981	1990	1995	2000	2006	Change
Albania			82	80		−2
Algeria						
Andorra					54	
Argentina		68	61	59	48	−20
Armenia			56			
Australia		76			67	−9
Austria		75		74		−1
Azerbaijan			64			
Bangladesh			92	71		−21
Belarus		68	63	65		−3
Belgium		59		48		−11
Bosnia and Herz.			75	73		−2
Brazil		69	69		57	−12
Britain		62		58	59	−3
Bulgaria		80	67	67	68	−12
Burkina Faso					68	
Canada		76		67	65	−11
Chile		60	47	47	44	−16
China		84	77	80	69	−15
Colombia					64	
Croatia			79	74		−5
Cyprus				62		
Czech		89	72	77		−12
Denmark		62		61		−1
Dominican Rep.			72			
Egypt				80		
El Salvador			66			
Estonia		81	76	52		−29
Ethiopia					68	
Finland		77	67	60	63	−14
France		61		46	41	−20
Georgia			73		70	−3
Germany (East)		78	72	66	67	−11
Germany (West)		75	72	68	62	−13
Ghana					85	
Greece				55		
Guatemala					59	
Hong Kong					93	
Hungary		68	67	63		−5
Iceland		80		84		4
India		74	79	64	72	−2
Indonesia					67	
Iran					78	
Iraq						
Ireland		68		64		−4
Israel						
Italy		59		57	50	−9
Japan		48	45	56	54	6
Jordan					81	

Country	1981	1990	1995	2000	2006	Change
Kyrgyzstan				66		
Latvia		80	74	68		−12
Lithuania		78	69	61		−17
Luxembourg				51		
Macedonia			75	77		2
Malaysia					57	
Mali					63	
Malta		65		76		11
Mexico		65	57	61	70	5
Moldova			60	61	54	−6
Montenegro			71	73		2
Morocco				84	56	−28
Netherlands		58		50	49	−9
New Zealand			72		76	4
Nigeria		81	78			−3
Northern Ireland		65		64		−1
Norway		78	70		74	−4
Pakistan			79			
Peru			69	67	70	1
Philippines			55	55		0
Poland		69	53	58	46	−23
Portugal		55		50		−5
Puerto Rico			63	73		10
Romania		81	78	79	74	−7
Russia		72	59	57	58	−14
Rwanda					62	
Saudi Arabia						
Serbia			79	70	51	−28
Singapore				72		
Slovakia		77	70	68		−9
Slovenia		72	70	73	63	−9
South Africa		77	74	70	64	−13
South Korea		81	60	58	65	−16
Spain		56	54	52	55	−1
Sweden		78	78	74	76	−2
Switzerland			74		67	−7
Taiwan			60		65	5
Tanzania				75		
Thailand					45	
Trinidad					69	
Turkey		60	70	65	55	−5
Uganda				80		
Ukraine			62	60	51	−11
Uruguay			51		50	−1
USA		76	74	70	66	−10
Venezuela			66	65		−1
Vietnam				58	53	−5
Zambia					62	
Zimbabwe				82		

Hard work

(E016) Now I'd like you to tell me your views on various issues. How would you place your views on this scale?

(%) Hard work doesn't generally bring success - it's more a matter of luck and connections (7 thru 10)

Country	1981	1990	1995	2000	2006	Change
Albania			4			
Algeria						
Andorra					40	
Argentina		31	35		36	5
Armenia			30			
Australia			18		22	4
Austria		16				
Azerbaijan			26			
Bangladesh			7			
Belarus		25	26			1
Belgium		29				
Bosnia and Herz.			18			
Brazil		60	61		31	−29
Britain		30			26	−4
Bulgaria		17	26		28	11
Burkina Faso					35	
Canada		18			18	0
Chile		29	28		32	3
China		35	17		19	−16
Colombia					34	
Croatia			24			
Cyprus					27	
Czech		16	33			17
Denmark		46				
Dominican Rep.			19			
Egypt					6	
El Salvador			34			
Estonia		25	20			−5
Ethiopia					18	
Finland		15	19		12	−3
France		21			35	14
Georgia			23		27	4
Germany (East)		11	37		29	18
Germany (West)		21	42		25	4
Ghana					10	
Greece						
Guatemala						
Hong Kong						
Hungary		28	33			5
Iceland		16				
India		11	10		20	9
Indonesia					16	
Iran					12	
Iraq						
Ireland		29				
Israel						
Italy		32			34	2
Japan		15	11		26	11
Jordan					26	

Country	1981	1990	1995	2000	2006	Change
Kyrgyzstan						
Latvia		38	30			−8
Lithuania		43	48			5
Luxembourg						
Macedonia			38			
Malaysia					23	
Mali					25	
Malta		28				
Mexico		25	31		18	−7
Moldova			26		24	−2
Montenegro			51			
Morocco					25	
Netherlands		32			28	−4
New Zealand			20		16	−4
Nigeria		19	19			0
Northern Ireland		19				
Norway		25	29		28	3
Pakistan			27			
Peru			18		28	10
Philippines			15			
Poland		37	44		44	7
Portugal		43				
Puerto Rico			26			
Romania		19	19		13	−6
Russia		22	30		42	20
Rwanda					43	
Saudi Arabia						
Serbia			34		39	5
Singapore						
Slovakia		26	32			6
Slovenia		21	21		22	1
South Africa		13	10		15	2
South Korea		14	20		19	5
Spain		35	25		15	−20
Sweden		28	26		21	−7
Switzerland			27		40	13
Taiwan			20		17	−3
Tanzania						
Thailand					36	
Trinidad					12	
Turkey		28	29		26	−2
Uganda						
Ukraine			33		31	−2
Uruguay			36		33	−3
USA		13	14		16	3
Venezuela			24			
Vietnam					9	
Zambia					21	
Zimbabwe						

Wealth accumulation

(E017) Now I'd like you to tell me your views on various issues. How would you place your views on this scale?

People can only get rich at the expense of others (1 thru 4) (%)

Country	1981	1990	1995	2000	2006	Change
Albania			32			
Algeria						
Andorra					26	
Argentina		16	23		27	11
Armenia			20			
Australia			24		23	−1
Austria		11				
Azerbaijan			18			
Bangladesh			28			
Belarus		16	20			4
Belgium		23				
Bosnia and Herz.			30			
Brazil		16	14		9	−7
Britain		24			24	0
Bulgaria		22	36		37	15
Burkina Faso				40		
Canada		15			13	−2
Chile		16	13		25	9
China		9	8		12	3
Colombia				18		
Croatia			26			
Cyprus					26	
Czech		24	43			19
Denmark		17				
Dominican Rep.			15			
Egypt					16	
El Salvador						
Estonia		19	14			−5
Ethiopia				28		
Finland		22	18		18	−4
France		21			22	1
Georgia			15		15	0
Germany (East)		10	24		28	18
Germany (West)		21	22		21	0
Ghana					41	
Greece						
Guatemala						
Hong Kong						
Hungary		19	27			8
Iceland		14				
India		27	42		37	10
Indonesia					11	
Iran					47	
Iraq						
Ireland		27				
Israel						
Italy		19			18	−1
Japan			16	14	13	−3
Jordan					40	

Country	1981	1990	1995	2000	2006	Change
Kyrgyzstan						
Latvia		26	16			−10
Lithuania		19	30			11
Luxembourg						
Macedonia			43			
Malaysia					15	
Mali					35	
Malta		11				
Mexico		28	27		15	−13
Moldova			24		19	−5
Montenegro			38			
Morocco					44	
Netherlands		11			28	17
New Zealand			24		19	−5
Nigeria		38	40			2
Northern Ireland		20				
Norway		18	18		14	−4
Pakistan			81			
Peru			20		13	−7
Philippines			15			
Poland		10	26		25	15
Portugal		29				
Puerto Rico			17			
Romania		29	30		26	−3
Russia		25	20		43	18
Rwanda				10		
Saudi Arabia						
Serbia			36		31	−5
Singapore						
Slovakia		29	46			17
Slovenia		36	37		31	−5
South Africa		16	24		22	6
South Korea		31	18		20	−11
Spain		33	27		37	4
Sweden		23	26		16	−7
Switzerland			27		17	−10
Taiwan			3		8	5
Tanzania						
Thailand					5	
Trinidad					16	
Turkey		30	24		38	8
Uganda						
Ukraine			20		24	4
Uruguay			25		20	−5
USA		21	16		16	−5
Venezuela			19			
Vietnam					22	
Zambia					25	
Zimbabwe						

Immigrant policy

**(E018) How about people from other countries coming here to work.
Which one of the following do you think the government should do?**

Place strict limits on the number of foreigners who can come here or Prohibit people coming here from other countries (%)

Country	1981	1990	1995	2000	2006	Change
Albania			27	25		−2
Algeria				36		
Andorra					24	
Argentina			41	44	41	0
Armenia			29			
Australia			43		40	−3
Austria				45		
Azerbaijan			22			
Bangladesh				44		
Belarus			30	47		17
Belgium				59		
Bosnia and Herz.			22	33		11
Brazil			38		44	6
Britain				61		
Bulgaria			43	60	32	−11
Burkina Faso					12	
Canada				47	45	−2
Chile			38	43	43	5
China			56	38	29	−27
Colombia						
Croatia			39	63		24
Cyprus				49		
Czech			62	66		4
Denmark				69		
Dominican Rep.			50			
Egypt				53	70	17
El Salvador						
Estonia			49	56		7
Ethiopia				32		
Finland			60	55	51	−9
France				61		
Georgia			31		72	41
Germany (East)			60	63	57	−3
Germany (West)			29	64	43	14
Ghana					43	
Greece				49		
Guatemala				28		
Hong Kong					47	
Hungary			74	85		11
Iceland				34		
India			65	65	55	−10
Indonesia				69	80	11
Iran				66	77	11
Iraq						
Ireland				45		
Israel						
Italy				43	43	0
Japan			50	43	55	5
Jordan				65	69	4

Country	1981	1990	1995	2000	2006	Change
Kyrgyzstan				40		
Latvia			49	66		17
Lithuania			55	59		4
Luxembourg				40		
Macedonia			67	67		0
Malaysia					90	
Mali					20	
Malta				69		
Mexico			38	40	43	5
Moldova			45	28	37	−8
Montenegro			48	59		11
Morocco				27	31	4
Netherlands				60		
New Zealand			41		53	12
Nigeria			46	31		−15
Northern Ireland				57		
Norway			53		43	−10
Pakistan				41		
Peru			53	41	27	−26
Philippines			75	68		−7
Poland			66	75	52	−14
Portugal				27		
Puerto Rico			70	56		−14
Romania			37	43	34	−3
Russia			46	44		−2
Rwanda					11	
Saudi Arabia				38		
Serbia			40	46	60	20
Singapore				74		
Slovakia			66	70		4
Slovenia			38	47	37	−1
South Africa			65	63	76	11
South Korea			46	37	38	−8
Spain			28	24	45	17
Sweden			58	30	29	−29
Switzerland			42		27	−15
Taiwan			65		68	3
Tanzania				72		
Thailand					79	
Trinidad					66	
Turkey			59	53	49	−10
Uganda				41		
Ukraine			26	46	27	1
Uruguay			31		21	−10
USA			62	43	26	−36
Venezuela			57	35		−22
Vietnam				21	23	2
Zambia					59	
Zimbabwe				36		

Having a strong leader

(E019) I'm going to describe various types of political systems and ask what you think about each as a way of governing this country. "Having a strong leader who does not have to bother with parliament and elections"

Very good/Fairly good (%)

Country	1981	1990	1995	2000	2006	Change
Albania			43	17		−26
Algeria				39		
Andorra					8	
Argentina			30	42	37	7
Armenia			53			
Australia			25		22	−3
Austria				16		
Azerbaijan			7			
Bangladesh			7	12		5
Belarus			55	40		−15
Belgium				32		
Bosnia and Herz.			48	37		−11
Brazil			61		64	3
Britain			27	26	28	1
Bulgaria			63	45	68	5
Burkina Faso				48		
Canada				24	23	−1
Chile			35	43	33	−2
China				19	36	17
Colombia			53		31	−22
Croatia			30	11		−19
Cyprus					45	
Czech			16	17		1
Denmark				14		
Dominican Rep.			28			
Egypt				8	16	8
El Salvador			59			
Estonia			38	19		−19
Ethiopia					31	
Finland			27	25	23	−4
France				35	34	−1
Georgia			66		54	−12
Germany (East)			18	23	22	4
Germany (West)			10	16	13	3
Ghana					22	
Greece				9		
Guatemala				59		
Hong Kong					32	
Hungary			19	20		1
Iceland				11		
India			68	59	64	−4
Indonesia				19	24	5
Iran				39	74	35
Iraq				20	21	1
Ireland				27		
Israel						
Italy				16	14	−2
Japan			32	28	24	−8
Jordan				41	18	−23

Country	1981	1990	1995	2000	2006	Change
Kyrgyzstan				61		
Latvia			46	58		12
Lithuania			64	54		−10
Luxembourg				45		
Macedonia			62	74		12
Malaysia					60	
Mali					61	
Malta				19		
Mexico			46	54		8
Moldova			57	62	67	10
Montenegro			25	15		−10
Morocco				17	27	10
Netherlands				27	43	16
New Zealand			20		19	−1
Nigeria			34	43		9
Northern Ireland				19		
Norway			14		16	2
Pakistan			62	34		−28
Peru			35	39	46	11
Philippines			65	62		−3
Poland				22	31	9
Portugal				37		
Puerto Rico			27	33		6
Romania			47	67	78	31
Russia			50	49	57	7
Rwanda						
Saudi Arabia						
Serbia			31	19	32	1
Singapore				22		
Slovakia			19	20		1
Slovenia			25	24	20	−5
South Africa			36	37	43	7
South Korea			32	28	48	16
Spain			30	21	33	3
Sweden			26	21	18	−8
Switzerland			29		17	−12
Taiwan			41		58	17
Tanzania				3		
Thailand					71	
Trinidad					35	
Turkey			38	70	58	20
Uganda				31		
Ukraine			54	59	65	11
Uruguay			27		39	12
USA			24	30	30	6
Venezuela				30	48	18
Vietnam				99	9	−90
Zambia					37	
Zimbabwe				27		

Having experts make decisions

(E020) I'm going to describe various types of political systems and ask what you think about each as a way of governing this country. "Having experts, not government, make decisions according to what they think is best for the country"

Very good/Fairly good (%)

Country	1981	1990	1995	2000	2006	Change
Albania			90	88		-2
Algeria				81		
Andorra					64	
Argentina			54	54	46	-8
Armenia			55			
Australia			43		45	2
Austria				61		
Azerbaijan			2			
Bangladesh			85	77		-8
Belarus			57	79		22
Belgium				58		
Bosnia and Herz.			85	71		-14
Brazil			83		78	-5
Britain			56	48	49	-7
Bulgaria			67	83	75	8
Burkina Faso					69	
Canada				46	41	-5
Chile			45	59	51	6
China				30	50	20
Colombia			71		44	-27
Croatia			82	87		5
Cyprus					59	
Czech			82	62		-20
Denmark				30		
Dominican Rep.			49			
Egypt				67	84	17
El Salvador			69			
Estonia			45	57		12
Ethiopia					64	
Finland			65	58	53	-12
France				50	51	1
Georgia			58		59	1
Germany (East)			68	66	68	0
Germany (West)			57	56	49	-8
Ghana					59	
Greece				13		
Guatemala				70		
Hong Kong				31		
Hungary			85	85		0
Iceland				42		
India			67	68	71	4
Indonesia				48	48	0
Iran				27	62	35
Iraq				78	74	-4
Ireland				37		
Israel						
Italy				51	49	-2
Japan			57	58	54	-3
Jordan				87	75	-12

Country	1981	1990	1995	2000	2006	Change
Kyrgyzstan				66		
Latvia			56	61		5
Lithuania			50	60		10
Luxembourg				48		
Macedonia			76	84		8
Malaysia					73	
Mali					69	
Malta				34		
Mexico			62	66	74	12
Moldova			59	50	70	11
Montenegro			86	89		3
Morocco				71	81	10
Netherlands				39	53	14
New Zealand			44		40	-4
Nigeria			68	73		5
Northern Ireland				37		
Norway			34		30	-4
Pakistan				19		
Peru			56	63	65	9
Philippines			63	63		0
Poland				87	84	-3
Portugal				50		
Puerto Rico			48	43		-5
Romania			49	85	76	27
Russia			59	51	58	-1
Rwanda						
Saudi Arabia						
Serbia			85	88	72	-13
Singapore				40		
Slovakia			84	86		2
Slovenia			80	81	79	-1
South Africa			52	55	59	7
South Korea			66	53	53	-13
Spain			59	44	43	-16
Sweden			39	41	36	-3
Switzerland			49		45	-4
Taiwan			60		65	5
Tanzania				30		
Thailand					63	
Trinidad					49	
Turkey			56	74	70	14
Uganda				36		
Ukraine			61	51	56	-5
Uruguay			39		48	9
USA			36	44	44	8
Venezuela			50	69		19
Vietnam				98	33	-65
Zambia					58	
Zimbabwe				68		

Having the army rule

(E021) I'm going to describe various types of political systems and ask what you think about each as a way of governing this country. "Having the army rule"

Very good/Fairly good (%)

Country	1981	1990	1995	2000	2006	Change
Albania			82	12		−70
Algeria				19		
Andorra					2	
Argentina			14	18	11	−3
Armenia			19			
Australia			7		7	0
Austria				2		
Azerbaijan			2			
Bangladesh			7	19		12
Belarus			14	20		6
Belgium				5		
Bosnia and Herz.			15	9		−6
Brazil			45		35	−10
Britain			6	7	13	7
Bulgaria			17	11	18	1
Burkina Faso					38	
Canada				6	7	1
Chile			30	24	18	−12
China				45	36	−9
Colombia			34		32	−2
Croatia			14	4		−10
Cyprus				20		
Czech			5	2		−3
Denmark				1		
Dominican Rep.			6			
Egypt					57	
El Salvador			39			
Estonia			5	3		−2
Ethiopia				25		
Finland			11	6	8	−3
France				4	12	8
Georgia			11		14	3
Germany (East)			2	2	3	1
Germany (West)			1	2	3	2
Ghana				16		
Greece			10			
Guatemala				25		
Hong Kong				4		
Hungary			5	3		−2
Iceland				1		
India			37	20	36	−1
Indonesia				96	95	−1
Iran				84	35	−49
Iraq				17	18	1
Ireland				4		
Israel						
Italy				4	6	2
Japan			3	2	2	−1
Jordan				59	75	16

Country	1981	1990	1995	2000	2006	Change
Kyrgyzstan				34		
Latvia			5	5		0
Lithuania			6	5		−1
Luxembourg				8		
Macedonia			10	26		16
Malaysia					55	
Mali					48	
Malta				4		
Mexico			26	33	41	15
Moldova			11	14	21	10
Montenegro			10	7		−3
Morocco				14	28	14
Netherlands				1	7	6
New Zealand			2		4	2
Nigeria			30	26		−4
Northern Ireland				2		
Norway			5		5	0
Pakistan			40	4		−36
Peru			18	15	31	13
Philippines			53	49		−4
Poland				18	21	3
Portugal				9		
Puerto Rico			9	11		2
Romania			25	28	20	−5
Russia			21	19	15	−6
Rwanda						
Saudi Arabia						
Serbia			10	10	21	11
Singapore				17		
Slovakia			5	7		2
Slovenia			6	5	4	−2
South Africa			23	17	31	8
South Korea			5	4	6	1
Spain			9	7	12	3
Sweden			4	7	5	1
Switzerland			5		4	−1
Taiwan			16		12	−4
Tanzania				14		
Thailand				54		
Trinidad				18		
Turkey			26	28	33	7
Uganda				34		
Ukraine			12	13	24	12
Uruguay			8		11	3
USA			7	9	15	8
Venezuela			26	23		−3
Vietnam				99	33	−66
Zambia					23	
Zimbabwe				13		

Having a democratic political system

(E022) I'm going to describe various types of political systems and ask what you think about each as a way of governing this country. "Having a democratic political system"

Very good/Fairly good (%)

Country	1981	1990	1995	2000	2006	Change
Albania			99	98		−1
Algeria				93		
Andorra					97	
Argentina			93	90	95	2
Armenia			85			
Australia			87		90	3
Austria				96		
Azerbaijan			97			
Bangladesh			98	98		0
Belarus			80	88		8
Belgium				91		
Bosnia and Herz.			95	95		0
Brazil			85		90	5
Britain				87	90	3
Bulgaria			86	87	87	1
Burkina Faso					95	
Canada				87	91	4
Chile			85	85	93	8
China				96	94	−2
Colombia			85		87	2
Croatia			98	98		0
Cyprus				96		
Czech			91	93		2
Denmark				98		
Dominican Rep.			91			
Egypt				99	98	−1
El Salvador			85			
Estonia			89	87		−2
Ethiopia					98	
Finland			77	88	90	13
France				89	90	1
Georgia			91		98	7
Germany (East)			95	92	94	−1
Germany (West)			96	95	95	−1
Ghana					96	
Greece				98		
Guatemala				87		
Hong Kong				89		
Hungary			91	87		−4
Iceland				98		
India			92	93	92	0
Indonesia				96	97	1
Iran				86	92	6
Iraq				91	88	−3
Ireland				92		
Israel						
Italy				97	95	−2
Japan			91	92	88	−3
Jordan				95	96	1

Country	1981	1990	1995	2000	2006	Change
Kyrgyzstan				82		
Latvia			87	88		1
Lithuania			88	86		−2
Luxembourg				92		
Macedonia			84	91		7
Malaysia					92	
Mali					88	
Malta				94		
Mexico		77	87	86		9
Moldova			85	75	88	3
Montenegro			95	95		0
Morocco				96	96	0
Netherlands				97	91	−6
New Zealand			91		94	3
Nigeria			93	95		2
Northern Ireland				93		
Norway			96		97	1
Pakistan			68	88		20
Peru			91	93	89	−2
Philippines			84	82		−2
Poland				84	84	0
Portugal				92		
Puerto Rico			91	92		1
Romania			91	89	95	4
Russia			58	62	80	22
Rwanda						
Saudi Arabia						
Serbia			90	94	80	−10
Singapore				89		
Slovakia			92	84		−8
Slovenia			86	89	87	1
South Africa			89	89	91	2
South Korea			85	85	79	−6
Spain			95	95	96	1
Sweden			96	97	98	2
Switzerland			93		96	3
Taiwan			93		93	0
Tanzania				93		
Thailand				93		
Trinidad				90		
Turkey			92	92	93	1
Uganda				94		
Ukraine			80	85	80	0
Uruguay			96		91	−5
USA			91	89	88	−3
Venezuela			87	93		6
Vietnam				95	93	−2
Zambia					92	
Zimbabwe				89		

193

Respect for human rights
(E023) How much respect is there for individual human rights nowadays this country?
A lot/Some respect (%)

Country	1981	1990	1995	2000	2006	Change
Albania				37		
Algeria				36		
Andorra					69	
Argentina				22	39	17
Armenia			23			
Australia				76		
Austria				75		
Azerbaijan		61				
Bangladesh				73		
Belarus			27	36		9
Belgium				62		
Bosnia and Herz.				37		
Brazil					47	
Britain				67		
Bulgaria				35	19	−16
Burkina Faso					62	
Canada				82	86	4
Chile				57	48	−9
China				88	85	−3
Colombia					50	
Croatia				57		
Cyprus					65	
Czech				65		
Denmark				88		
Dominican Rep.						
Egypt				72		
El Salvador						
Estonia			41	55		14
Ethiopia					32	
Finland				89	93	4
France				60		
Georgia			25		32	7
Germany (East)			43	66	53	10
Germany (West)			64	81	80	16
Ghana					81	
Greece				63		
Guatemala					32	
Hong Kong				86		
Hungary				59		
Iceland				86		
India				75	81	6
Indonesia				62	80	18
Iran				73	36	−37
Iraq				42	35	−7
Ireland				77		
Israel						
Italy				62	57	−5
Japan				62	53	−9
Jordan				74	78	4

Country	1981	1990	1995	2000	2006	Change
Kyrgyzstan				32		
Latvia			29	52		23
Lithuania			29	23		−6
Luxembourg				90		
Macedonia				32		
Malaysia					68	
Mali					84	
Malta				75		
Mexico				47	55	8
Moldova			20	21	15	−5
Montenegro				40		
Morocco				42	65	23
Netherlands				79		
New Zealand					82	
Nigeria				63		
Northern Ireland				70		
Norway					92	
Pakistan				54		
Peru				45	14	−31
Philippines				79		
Poland				55	65	10
Portugal				64		
Puerto Rico				56		
Romania				24	30	6
Russia				16		
Rwanda						
Saudi Arabia				72		
Serbia				49	21	−28
Singapore						
Slovakia				59		
Slovenia				41	46	5
South Africa				53	69	16
South Korea				47	70	23
Spain				63	63	0
Sweden				76	85	9
Switzerland					90	
Taiwan					68	
Tanzania				69		
Thailand					85	
Trinidad					34	
Turkey				24	38	14
Uganda				70		
Ukraine			18	23	32	14
Uruguay					83	
USA				74	29	−45
Venezuela				48		
Vietnam				95	93	−2
Zambia					52	
Zimbabwe				33		

Aims of country: first choice

(E024) People sometimes talk about what the aims of this country should be for the next ten years. On this card are listed some of the goals which different people would give top priority. Would you please say which one of these you, yourself, consider the most important? First choice

A high level of economic growth (%)

Country	1981	1990	1995	2000	2006	Change
Albania			84	88		4
Algeria				68		
Andorra					25	
Argentina		66	56	53	60	–6
Armenia			46			
Australia			44		53	9
Austria		52				
Azerbaijan			59			
Bangladesh			71	76		5
Belarus		73	78			5
Belgium		42				
Bosnia and Herz.			73	82		9
Brazil		52	46		58	6
Britain		44			38	–6
Bulgaria		76	78		80	4
Burkina Faso					66	
Canada		56		51	49	–7
Chile		66	56	66	59	–7
China		66	60	40	45	–21
Colombia						
Croatia			74			
Cyprus				62		
Czech		73	69			–4
Denmark		47				
Dominican Rep.			65			
Egypt				55	75	20
El Salvador			51			
Estonia		80	68			–12
Ethiopia				74		
Finland		34	40		21	–13
France		52			40	–12
Georgia			63		68	5
Germany (East)		72	71		59	–13
Germany (West)		49	58		62	13
Ghana					70	
Greece						
Guatemala					61	
Hong Kong					46	
Hungary		63	71			8
Iceland		52				
India		54	83	54	50	–4
Indonesia				85	82	–3
Iran				56	60	4
Iraq						
Ireland		55				
Israel				41		
Italy		43			60	17
Japan		43	40	42	48	5
Jordan				65	69	4

Country	1981	1990	1995	2000	2006	Change
Kyrgyzstan				70		
Latvia		83	77			–6
Lithuania		76	72			–4
Luxembourg						
Macedonia			85	77		–8
Malaysia					65	
Mali					63	
Malta		54				
Mexico		62	52	54	52	–10
Moldova			74	78	68	–6
Montenegro				66	78	12
Morocco				59	66	7
Netherlands		42			42	0
New Zealand			70		65	–5
Nigeria		67	79	71		4
Northern Ireland		53				
Norway		48	40		38	–10
Pakistan			51	76		25
Peru			66	63	61	–5
Philippines			46	58		12
Poland		73	52		61	–12
Portugal		69				
Puerto Rico			59	56		–3
Romania			64		77	13
Russia		72	71		75	3
Rwanda					26	
Saudi Arabia				47		
Serbia			69	80	74	5
Singapore				59		
Slovakia		67	73			6
Slovenia		64	51		54	–10
South Africa		61	65	64	62	1
South Korea		52	37	50	59	7
Spain		44	55	50	46	2
Sweden		51	69	58	68	17
Switzerland		29	44		39	10
Taiwan			41		70	29
Tanzania				82		
Thailand					68	
Trinidad					52	
Turkey		59	63	66	64	5
Uganda				66		
Ukraine			78		75	–3
Uruguay			67		75	8
USA		53	47	48	39	–14
Venezuela			55	64		9
Vietnam				64	68	4
Zambia					68	
Zimbabwe				66		

195

Aims of country: second choice

(E025) People sometimes talk about what the aims of this country should be for the next ten years. On this card are listed some of the goals which different people would give top priority. Would you please say which one of these you, yourself, consider the most important? Second choice

A high level of economic growth (%)

Country	1981	1990	1995	2000	2006	Change
Albania			11	7		-4
Algeria				21		
Andorra					26	
Argentina		22	26	28	27	5
Armenia			32			
Australia			32		24	-8
Austria		22				
Azerbaijan			21			
Bangladesh			17	10		-7
Belarus		15	16			1
Belgium		22				
Bosnia and Herz.			18	14		-4
Brazil		21	29		22	1
Britain		26			32	6
Bulgaria		12	12		10	-2
Burkina Faso				17		
Canada		25		31	31	6
Chile		18	25	22	24	6
China		16	25	29	26	10
Colombia						
Croatia			16			
Cyprus				17		
Czech		15	16			1
Denmark		22				
Dominican Rep.			25			
Egypt				25	18	-7
El Salvador						
Estonia		11	20			9
Ethiopia				9		
Finland		31	31		34	3
France		23			29	6
Georgia			24		22	-2
Germany (East)		15	15		26	11
Germany (West)		24	23		22	-2
Ghana					17	
Greece						
Guatemala				22		
Hong Kong				18		
Hungary		18	15			-3
Iceland		26				
India		18	0	20	24	6
Indonesia				12	13	1
Iran				26	21	-5
Iraq						
Ireland		26				
Israel				38		
Italy		25			22	-3
Japan		23	21	25	23	0
Jordan				22	18	-4

Country	1981	1990	1995	2000	2006	Change
Kyrgyzstan				17		
Latvia		9	15			6
Lithuania		13	18			5
Luxembourg						
Macedonia			11	15		4
Malaysia					17	
Mali					16	
Malta		18				
Mexico	20	20	23		25	5
Moldova			14	12	16	2
Montenegro				20	17	-3
Morocco				18	14	-4
Netherlands		30			30	0
New Zealand			18		22	4
Nigeria		20	14	17		-3
Northern Ireland	21					
Norway		29	34		38	9
Pakistan			24	17		-7
Peru			21	24	24	3
Philippines			24	21		-3
Poland		16	25		26	10
Portugal		20				
Puerto Rico			21	25		4
Romania			20		12	-8
Russia		18	17		17	-1
Rwanda					19	
Saudi Arabia				22		
Serbia			19	12	10	-9
Singapore				26		
Slovakia		18	14			-4
Slovenia		19	24		26	7
South Africa	20	18	19		20	0
South Korea	19	25	21		20	1
Spain	22	23	26		25	3
Sweden		26	19	28	21	-5
Switzerland		17	23		25	8
Taiwan			29		18	-11
Tanzania				9		
Thailand					17	
Trinidad					23	
Turkey		24	22	20	17	-7
Uganda				20		
Ukraine			13		15	2
Uruguay				22	19	-3
USA	26	30	30		35	9
Venezuela				22	18	-4
Vietnam				23	17	-6
Zambia					16	
Zimbabwe				17		

Priority: first choice

(E026) If you had to choose, which one of the things on this card would you say is most important? And which would be the next most important? First choice

Maintaining order in the nation (%)

Country	1981	1990	1995	2000	2006	Change
Albania			84	70		−14
Algeria			55			
Andorra					20	
Argentina	42	35	32	34	32	−10
Armenia			61			
Australia			23		33	10
Austria		41		38		−3
Azerbaijan			74			
Bangladesh			64	64		0
Belarus			44	52	56	12
Belgium	27	21		36		9
Bosnia and Herz.			82	67		−15
Brazil		30	29		39	9
Britain	32	24	29		32	0
Bulgaria		51	51	76	39	−12
Burkina Faso					36	
Canada	25	20		21	21	−4
Chile		39	33	35	37	−2
China		67	71	57	46	−21
Colombia			45		40	−5
Croatia			34	28		−6
Cyprus					44	
Czech			56	54	57	1
Denmark	38	59		59		21
Dominican Rep.			45			
Egypt				63	15	−48
El Salvador				26		
Estonia		59	51	57		−2
Ethiopia				22		
Finland	31	11	29	51	49	18
France	30	27		43	28	−2
Georgia			65		59	−6
Germany (East)		37	38	50	24	−13
Germany (West)	47	37	25	41	26	−21
Ghana					60	
Greece				40		
Guatemala					48	
Hong Kong						
Hungary	79	37	65	53		−26
Iceland	48	49		57		9
India		43	77	42	32	−11
Indonesia				77	62	−15
Iran				39	40	1
Iraq				66	56	−10
Ireland	40	24		38		−2
Israel				51		
Italy	47	27		32	21	−26
Japan	38	35	32	36	34	39	1
Jordan				62	57	−5

Country	1981	1990	1995	2000	2006	Change
Kyrgyzstan				60		
Latvia		54	57	54		0
Lithuania		29	45	23		−6
Luxembourg				45		
Macedonia			79	77		−2
Malaysia					58	
Mali					51	
Malta	45	49		33		−12
Mexico	38	28	36	31	29	−9
Moldova			66	63	49	−17
Montenegro				59	54	−5
Morocco				51	45	−6
Netherlands	38	29		41	30	−8
New Zealand			33		38	5
Nigeria		42	57	48		6
Northern Ireland	54	35		41		−13
Norway	68	64	66		57	−11
Pakistan			38	57		19
Peru			49	43	44	−5
Philippines			51	51		0
Poland		31	43	42	33	2
Portugal		35		31		−4
Puerto Rico			43	46		3
Romania		60	48	49	43	−17
Russia		59	64	57	54	−5
Rwanda					41	
Saudi Arabia				55		
Serbia			51	49	55	4
Singapore				67		
Slovakia		45	47	48		3
Slovenia		27	45	42	37	10
South Africa	52	44	54	42	36	−16
South Korea	48	43	47	43	36	−12
Spain	60	30	38	36	32	−28
Sweden	39	38	48	45	46	7
Switzerland		31	30		32	1
Taiwan			69		59	−10
Tanzania				83		
Thailand					60	
Trinidad					30	
Turkey		20	36	24	53	33
Uganda				52		
Ukraine			59	54	44	−15
Uruguay			26		33	7
USA		28	33	33	27	−1
Venezuela			39	45		6
Vietnam				56	59	3
Zambia					36	
Zimbabwe				38		

197

Priority: second choice

(E027) If you had to choose, which one of the things on this card would you say is most important? And which would be the next most important? Second choice

Maintaining order in the nation (%)

Country	1981	1990	1995	2000	2006	Change
Albania			10	18		8
Algeria				18		
Andorra					14	
Argentina	16	15	17	19	24	8
Armenia			22			
Australia			21		16	–5
Austria		22		22		0
Azerbaijan			14			
Bangladesh			21	15		–6
Belarus		28	27	25		–3
Belgium	25	23		23		–2
Bosnia and Herz.			10	15		5
Brazil		24	29		24	0
Britain	25	23	27		27	2
Bulgaria		19	30	15	35	16
Burkina Faso					26	
Canada	20	16		16	18	–2
Chile		15	23	21	24	9
China		18	22	25	30	12
Colombia			23		20	–3
Croatia			20	20		0
Cyprus					21	
Czech		22	21	22		0
Denmark	22	19		23		1
Dominican Rep.			22			
Egypt				22	35	13
El Salvador						
Estonia		21	24	24		3
Ethiopia				28		
Finland	22	17	25	26	25	3
France	22	18		19	20	–2
Georgia			19		18	–1
Germany (East)		25	25	21	23	–2
Germany (West)	20	20	19	24	19	–1
Ghana					20	
Greece				21		
Guatemala					25	
Hong Kong						
Hungary	11	29	24	26		15
Iceland	18	20		25		7
India		22	0	29	29	7
Indonesia				15	24	9
Iran				24	27	3
Iraq				13	12	–1
Ireland	24	23		21		–3
Israel				24		
Italy	24	19		20	16	–8
Japan	20	21	23	28	27	7
Jordan				19	19	0

Country	1981	1990	1995	2000	2006	Change
Kyrgyzstan				20		
Latvia		20	24	26		6
Lithuania		25	29	28		3
Luxembourg				22		
Macedonia			11	12		1
Malaysia					18	
Mali					23	
Malta	30	23		32		2
Mexico	19	21	21	24	20	1
Moldova			21	20	23	2
Montenegro				24	17	–7
Morocco				19	21	2
Netherlands	26	24		29	34	8
New Zealand			20		21	1
Nigeria			26	24	23	–3
Northern Ireland	23	21		21		–2
Norway	16	19	19		21	5
Pakistan			29	28		–1
Peru			22	24	23	1
Philippines			25	24		–1
Poland		24	26	30	29	5
Portugal		23		28		5
Puerto Rico			26	22		–4
Romania		20	27	26	26	6
Russia		24	25	28	29	5
Rwanda					21	
Saudi Arabia				18		
Serbia			23	26	22	–1
Singapore				19		
Slovakia		23	25	33		10
Slovenia		22	22	26	20	–2
South Africa	15	23	24	28	31	16
South Korea	25	26	32	33	39	14
Spain	17	17	23	22	22	5
Sweden	24	25	23	27	24	0
Switzerland		18	22		22	4
Taiwan			18		25	7
Tanzania				11		
Thailand					22	
Trinidad					22	
Turkey		25	25	24	18	–7
Uganda				20		
Ukraine			24	27	28	4
Uruguay			14		18	4
USA		20	22	23	24	4
Venezuela			19	23		4
Vietnam				29	17	–12
Zambia					24	
Zimbabwe				27		

Most important goal: first choice

**(E028) Here is another list. In your opinion, which one of these is most important?
And what would be the next most important? First choice**

A stable economy (%)

Country	1981	1990	1995	2000	2006	Change
Albania			71	69		−2
Algeria				54		
Andorra					36	
Argentina		64	52	53	50	−14
Armenia			58			
Australia			37		54	17
Austria		51				
Azerbaijan			55			
Bangladesh			72	67		−5
Belarus		70	66			−4
Belgium		32				
Bosnia and Herz.			74	80		6
Brazil		30	17		32	2
Britain		41			30	−11
Bulgaria		83	65		73	−10
Burkina Faso					41	
Canada		54		49	45	−9
Chile		56	42	58	43	−13
China		83	68	54	52	−31
Colombia			33			
Croatia			62			
Cyprus					54	
Czech		59	62			3
Denmark		50				
Dominican Rep.			44			
Egypt				47	70	23
El Salvador			24			
Estonia		60	60			0
Ethiopia				76		
Finland		40	45		42	2
France		26			25	−1
Georgia			58		74	16
Germany (East)		73	59		54	−19
Germany (West)		49	49		56	7
Ghana					62	
Greece						
Guatemala					61	
Hong Kong					48	
Hungary		67	70			3
Iceland		57				
India		44	67	36	30	−14
Indonesia				84	85	1
Iran				52	48	−4
Iraq						
Ireland		49				
Israel				39		
Italy		28			47	19
Japan		44	48	44	49	5
Jordan				52	62	10

Country	1981	1990	1995	2000	2006	Change
Kyrgyzstan				61		
Latvia		77	68			−9
Lithuania		61	62			1
Luxembourg						
Macedonia			82	76		−6
Malaysia					66	
Mali					53	
Malta		42				
Mexico		53	51	55	43	−10
Moldova			65	70	59	−6
Montenegro				64	68	4
Morocco				39	52	13
Netherlands		35			28	3
New Zealand			65		57	−8
Nigeria		61	74	65		4
Northern Ireland		51				
Norway		46	39		34	−12
Pakistan			38	69		31
Peru			62	65	53	−9
Philippines			47	65		18
Poland		71	50		55	−16
Portugal		47				
Puerto Rico			31	40		9
Romania		67	64		62	−5
Russia		65	63		66	1
Rwanda					34	
Saudi Arabia				35		
Serbia			63	69	66	3
Singapore				71		
Slovakia		59	69			10
Slovenia		81	68		57	−24
South Africa		55	54	43	44	−11
South Korea		53	47	64	74	21
Spain		35	47	40	40	5
Sweden		39	50	43	39	0
Switzerland		25	44		36	11
Taiwan			50		69	19
Tanzania				72		
Thailand					79	
Trinidad					35	
Turkey		35	45	42	56	21
Uganda				66		
Ukraine			69		71	2
Uruguay			58		57	−1
USA		50	45	45	44	−6
Venezuela			54	51		−3
Vietnam				68	77	9
Zambia					74	
Zimbabwe				63		

Most important goal: second choice

(E029) Here is another list. In your opinion, which one of these is most important?
And what would be the next most important? Second choice

A stable economy (%)

Country	1981	1990	1995	2000	2006	Change
Albania			20	20		0
Algeria				18		
Andorra					22	
Argentina		15	16	18	23	8
Armenia			18			
Australia			28		19	−9
Austria		22				
Azerbaijan			17			
Bangladesh			16	10		−6
Belarus			17	23		6
Belgium		22				
Bosnia and Herz.			14	15		1
Brazil		19	25		31	12
Britain		22			34	12
Bulgaria		10	22		13	3
Burkina Faso					21	
Canada		20		22	23	3
Chile		17	24	18	23	6
China		10	18	26	32	22
Colombia			25			
Croatia			17			
Cyprus				15		
Czech		19	22			3
Denmark		15				
Dominican Rep.			19			
Egypt				20	17	−3
El Salvador						
Estonia		20	20			0
Ethiopia				11		
Finland		31	24		27	−4
France		23		25		2
Georgia			22		14	−8
Germany (East)		15	17		19	4
Germany (West)		19	19		20	1
Ghana					19	
Greece						
Guatemala					24	
Hong Kong					24	
Hungary		18	18			0
Iceland		17				
India		15	0	20	22	7
Indonesia				8	10	2
Iran				25	23	−2
Iraq						
Ireland		24				
Israel				27		
Italy		21			21	0
Japan		27	22	23	20	−7
Jordan				20	15	−5

Country	1981	1990	1995	2000	2006	Change
Kyrgyzstan				20		
Latvia		13	19			6
Lithuania		22	23			1
Luxembourg						
Macedonia			12	12		0
Malaysia					16	
Mali					14	
Malta		21				
Mexico		18	21	21	26	8
Moldova			18	14	19	1
Montenegro				22	22	0
Morocco				18	18	0
Netherlands		22			26	4
New Zealand			18		25	7
Nigeria		22	17	19		−3
Northern Ireland		21				
Norway		22	27		25	3
Pakistan			20	12		−8
Peru			18	16	22	4
Philippines			25	19		−6
Poland		14	25		23	9
Portugal		20				
Puerto Rico			31	24		−7
Romania		16	19		19	3
Russia		20	23		24	4
Rwanda					23	
Saudi Arabia				19		
Serbia			20	17	20	0
Singapore				14		
Slovakia		17	16			−1
Slovenia		12	19		20	8
South Africa		19	28	37	34	15
South Korea		28	32	24	18	−10
Spain		19	20	23	26	7
Sweden		21	21	22	24	3
Switzerland		14	18		21	7
Taiwan			21		17	−4
Tanzania				11		
Thailand					12	
Trinidad					34	
Turkey		22	23	21	16	−6
Uganda				20		
Ukraine			17		14	−3
Uruguay			18		20	2
USA		22	29	24	30	8
Venezuela				22	26	4
Vietnam				21	14	−7
Zambia					14	
Zimbabwe				21		

Confidence: Churches

(E030) I am going to name a number of organisations. For each one, could you tell me how much confidence you have in them: is it a great deal of confidence, quite a lot of confidence, not very much confidence or none at all? The churches

A great deal/ Quite a lot (%)

Country	1981	1990	1995	2000	2006	Change
Albania			54	66		12
Algeria				89		
Andorra					20	
Argentina	46	45	50	60	56	10
Armenia			68			
Australia	56		42		38	−18
Austria		49		39		−10
Azerbaijan			72			
Bangladesh			99	99		0
Belarus		53	74	70		17
Belgium	65	49		40		−25
Bosnia and Herz.			67	55		−12
Brazil		75	74		77	2
Britain	49	43		34	46	−3
Bulgaria		30	58	35	61	31
Burkina Faso					80	
Canada	70	64		59	60	−10
Chile		76	80	78	70	−6
China		5			40	35
Colombia			82		80	−2
Croatia			57	64		7
Cyprus					63	
Czech		33	33	20		−13
Denmark	50	47		59		9
Dominican Rep.			72			
Egypt				84		
El Salvador			63			
Estonia		54	60	44		−10
Ethiopia					61	
Finland		32	56	58	64	32
France	56	50		46	47	−9
Georgia			80			
Germany (East)		44	20	25	28	−16
Germany (West)	47	40	35	43	48	1
Ghana					90	
Greece				55		
Guatemala					85	
Hong Kong						
Hungary	39	56	44	48		9
Iceland	71	68		65		−6
India			85	73	82	83	−2
Indonesia				97	94	−3
Iran				86		
Iraq				77	81	4
Ireland	78	72		54		−24
Israel						
Italy	61	63		67	75	14
Japan	16	11	13	10	9	−7
Jordan				91		

Country	1981	1990	1995	2000	2006	Change
Kyrgyzstan				67		
Latvia		64	64	67		3
Lithuania		73	69	71		−2
Luxembourg				48		
Macedonia			31	46		15
Malaysia					91	
Mali					93	
Malta	86	82		82		−4
Mexico		76	75	82	70	−6
Moldova			77	82	70	−7
Montenegro				38	48	10
Morocco				97		
Netherlands	41	32		29	30	−11
New Zealand			40		41	1
Nigeria			88	83	95	7
Northern Ireland	71	80		64		−7
Norway	50	45	54			4
Pakistan			79	88		9
Peru			71	71		0
Philippines			94	92		−2
Poland		84	67	69	73	−11
Portugal		57		80		23
Puerto Rico			86	84		−2
Romania		72	80	83	88	16
Russia		65	66	61	68	3
Rwanda					78	
Saudi Arabia				97		
Serbia			38	53	62	24
Singapore						
Slovakia		50	59	69		19
Slovenia		39	38	35	34	−5
South Africa		83	85	83		0
South Korea	63	58	42	49	49	−14
Spain	51	48	49	42		−9
Sweden	39	37	49	45	56	17
Switzerland		39				
Taiwan			62		31	−31
Tanzania				93		
Thailand						
Trinidad					50	
Turkey		66	70	70		4
Uganda				89		
Ukraine			67	66	73	6
Uruguay			56		50	−6
USA	77	68	76	75	66	−11
Venezuela				74	76	2
Vietnam				23	54	31
Zambia					87	
Zimbabwe				84		

201

Confidence: Armed Forces

(E031) I am going to name a number of organisations. For each one, could you tell me how much confidence you have in them: is it a great deal of confidence, quite a lot of confidence, not very much confidence or none at all? The armed forces

A great deal/ Quite a lot (%)

Country	1981	1990	1995	2000	2006	Change
Albania			58	57		−1
Algeria				67		
Andorra						
Argentina	19	28	23	27	32	13
Armenia			72			
Australia	67		68		84	17
Austria		28		39		11
Azerbaijan			56			
Bangladesh			57	74		17
Belarus			61	73	70	9
Belgium	44	33		37		−7
Bosnia and Herz.			91	70		−21
Brazil		67	71		70	3
Britain	82	81		83	79	−3
Bulgaria		69	81	58	72	3
Burkina Faso				70		
Canada	60	57		63	73	13
Chile		40	56	48	58	18
China		90		97	92	2
Colombia			61		61	0
Croatia			79	66		−13
Cyprus				74		
Czech		40	44	25		−15
Denmark	41	46		61		20
Dominican Rep.			30			
Egypt				57		
El Salvador			45			
Estonia		23	48	35		12
Ethiopia				41		
Finland		57	82	84	88	31
France	57	56		63	68	11
Georgia			52			
Germany (East)		14	39	46	46	32
Germany (West)	54	40	52	57	55	1
Ghana					76	
Greece				68		
Guatemala				36		
Hong Kong				57		
Hungary		52	58	46		−6
Iceland			24	40		16
India			93	84	92	83	−10
Indonesia				74	74	0
Iran						
Iraq				57	64	7
Ireland	76	61		60		−16
Israel						
Italy	58	48		52	68	10
Japan	37	24	62	67	75	38
Jordan				92		

Country	1981	1990	1995	2000	2006	Change
Kyrgyzstan				57		
Latvia		25	31	48		23
Lithuania		21	41	50		29
Luxembourg				54		
Macedonia			39	55		16
Malaysia					84	
Mali					83	
Malta	37	43		72		35
Mexico		47	59	54	64	17
Moldova			57	57	37	−20
Montenegro			61	51		−10
Morocco				70		
Netherlands	44	31		40	45	1
New Zealand			62		73	11
Nigeria			61	45	47	−14
Northern Ireland	77	78		56		−21
Norway	68	65	73			5
Pakistan			97	86		−11
Peru			42	22		−20
Philippines			69	74		5
Poland		65	80	67	67	2
Portugal		47		71		24
Puerto Rico			64	53		−11
Romania		82	82	83	82	0
Russia		69	69	67	67	−2
Rwanda						
Saudi Arabia						
Serbia			62	74	52	−10
Singapore						
Slovakia			46	68	77	31
Slovenia			45	45	42	37	−8
South Africa			60	57	55	−5
South Korea	87	80	71	64	52	−35
Spain	63	39		43	42	−21
Sweden	61	49	54	44	47	−14
Switzerland				50		
Taiwan				76	42	−34
Tanzania					91	
Thailand						
Trinidad					39	
Turkey			91	94	85		−6
Uganda					76	
Ukraine			68	69	59	−9
Uruguay				38	39	1
USA	80	48		86	82	82	2
Venezuela				60	64	4
Vietnam					96	98	2
Zambia					55	
Zimbabwe				62		

Confidence: The Press

(E032) I am going to name a number of organisations. For each one, could you tell me how much confidence you have in them: is it a great deal of confidence, quite a lot of confidence, not very much confidence or none at all? The press

A great deal/ Quite a lot (%)

Country	1981	1990	1995	2000	2006	Change
Albania			17	35		18
Algeria				48		
Andorra					37	
Argentina	46	27	33	38	36	−10
Armenia			34			
Australia	29		17		12	−17
Austria		17		32	15	
Azerbaijan				32		
Bangladesh			71	93		22
Belarus			25	41	41	16
Belgium	36	44		37		1
Bosnia and Herz.				52	30	−22
Brazil		55	61		43	−12
Britain	30	14		16	14	−16
Bulgaria			35	47	26	51	16
Burkina Faso					54	
Canada	45	46		35	33	−12
Chile			43	52	48	44	1
China		55		69	71	16
Colombia			45		44	−1
Croatia				22	18	−4
Cyprus					38	
Czech			39	43	38	−1
Denmark	30	31		33		3
Dominican Rep.			33			
Egypt				69		
El Salvador			46			
Estonia		63	55	42		−21
Ethiopia					27	
Finland		38	30	36	33	−5
France	32	38		36	39	7
Georgia			60			
Germany (East)		22	11	38	23	1
Germany (West)	33	34	24	36	36	3
Ghana					56	
Greece				31		
Guatemala				46		
Hong Kong					61	
Hungary	81	40	31	31		−50
Iceland	16	20		39		23
India			66	63	70	76	10
Indonesia				55	52	−3
Iran				36		
Iraq						
Ireland	44	36		34		−10
Israel						
Italy	30	39		35	25	−5
Japan	54	55	74	73	75	21
Jordan				59		

Country	1981	1990	1995	2000	2006	Change
Kyrgyzstan				44		
Latvia		60	50	45		−15
Lithuania		68	71	77		9
Luxembourg				46		
Macedonia			18	20		2
Malaysia					64	
Mali					57	
Malta	35	27		36		1
Mexico		49	51	42	50	1
Moldova			35	44	41	6
Montenegro			33	24		−9
Morocco					37	
Netherlands	28	36		56	32	4
New Zealand			34		27	−7
Nigeria		71	56	64		−7
Northern Ireland	32	16		18		−14
Norway	41	43	33			−8
Pakistan			54	52		−2
Peru			30	23		−7
Philippines			72	67		−5
Poland		48	46	47	38	−10
Portugal		36		66		30
Puerto Rico			50	41		−9
Romania		28	36	38	43	15
Russia		44	40	30	37	−7
Rwanda					71	
Saudi Arabia				63		
Serbia			23	29	21	−2
Singapore						
Slovakia		38	42	49		11
Slovenia		50	43	61	28	−22
South Africa		58	54	65		7
South Korea	69	66	65	66	64	−5
Spain	47	48	43	41		−6
Sweden	27	33	29	46	33	6
Switzerland			22			
Taiwan			41		17	−24
Tanzania				76		
Thailand						
Trinidad				20		
Turkey		42	49	33		−9
Uganda				67		
Ukraine			44	47	47	3
Uruguay			61		50	−11
USA	49	56	27	27	24	−25
Venezuela			59	65		6
Vietnam				84	89	5
Zambia					49	
Zimbabwe				54		

Confidence: Television

(E033) I am going to name a number of organisations. For each one, could you tell me how much confidence you have in them: is it a great deal of confidence, quite a lot of confidence, not very much confidence or none at all? Television

A great deal/ Quite a lot (%)

Country	1981	1990	1995	2000	2006	Change
Albania			24	54		30
Algeria				45		
Andorra					33	
Argentina			27	33	33	6
Armenia			45			
Australia			26		18	-8
Austria						
Azerbaijan			42			
Bangladesh			67	84		17
Belarus			48			
Belgium						
Bosnia and Herz.			59	41		-18
Brazil		38	57		42	4
Britain				32		
Bulgaria			69		67	-2
Burkina Faso				58		
Canada				38	32	-6
Chile			59	53	47	-12
China			74	75	1
Colombia			50		47	-3
Croatia			22			
Cyprus					40	
Czech		71	50			-21
Denmark						
Dominican Rep.			38			
Egypt				68		
El Salvador			49			
Estonia			68			
Ethiopia				28		
Finland			50	52		2
France				35		
Georgia			61			
Germany (East)			21	29		8
Germany (West)			23	40		17
Ghana				71		
Greece						
Guatemala				49		
Hong Kong				71		
Hungary			41			
Iceland						
India		33	57	72	75	42
Indonesia				61	62	1
Iran				49		
Iraq				56	71	15
Ireland						
Israel						
Italy					17	
Japan			27	68	68	70	43
Jordan				58		

Country	1981	1990	1995	2000	2006	Change
Kyrgyzstan				52		
Latvia				58		
Lithuania				76		
Luxembourg						
Macedonia			22	22		0
Malaysia					72	
Mali					63	
Malta						
Mexico			49	47	47	-2
Moldova			45	49	51	6
Montenegro			41	37		-4
Morocco					30	
Netherlands					37	
New Zealand			38		36	-2
Nigeria		69	59		72	3
Northern Ireland						
Norway			49			
Pakistan			63	57		-6
Peru			35	25		-10
Philippines			70	71		1
Poland			47		40	-7
Portugal						
Puerto Rico			39	27		-12
Romania			49		54	5
Russia			55	47	45	-10
Rwanda					58	
Saudi Arabia				67		
Serbia			25	29	19	-6
Singapore						
Slovakia		54	50			-4
Slovenia			53		34	-19
South Africa			67	77		10
South Korea			61	63	67	6
Spain			39	39		0
Sweden			49		55	6
Switzerland			31			
Taiwan			51		13	-38
Tanzania				79		
Thailand						
Trinidad					24	
Turkey			50	37		-13
Uganda				67		
Ukraine			48		53	5
Uruguay			57		51	-6
USA			29	25	25	-4
Venezuela			53	64		11
Vietnam				93	95	2
Zambia					55	
Zimbabwe				59		

Confidence: Labour Unions

(E034) I am going to name a number of organisations. For each one, could you tell me how much confidence you have in them: is it a great deal of confidence, quite a lot of confidence, not very much confidence or none at all? Labour unions

A great deal/ Quite a lot (%)

Country	1981	1990	1995	2000	2006	Change
Albania			16	33		17
Algeria				29		
Andorra					27	
Argentina	31	8	10	12	7	−24
Armenia			19			
Australia	24		26		28	4
Austria		35		31		−4
Azerbaijan			30			
Bangladesh			46	72		26
Belarus		25	45	28		3
Belgium	33	37		37		4
Bosnia and Herz.			59	26		−33
Brazil		48	55		45	−3
Britain	27	26		28	30	3
Bulgaria		32	34	15	22	−10
Burkina Faso				53		
Canada	33	35		36	32	−1
Chile		47	46	45	37	−10
China		42		73	71	29
Colombia			35		28	−7
Croatia			24	29		5
Cyprus				44		
Czech		26	42	22		−4
Denmark	51	46		48		−3
Dominican Rep.			19			
Egypt				68		
El Salvador			18			
Estonia		27	45	32		5
Ethiopia				26		
Finland		32	51	54	63	31
France	39	32		35	39	0
Georgia			28			
Germany (East)		29	38	36	29	0
Germany (West)	37	36	38	38	35	−2
Ghana				50		
Greece			14			
Guatemala				23		
Hong Kong				53		
Hungary	67	30	27	24		−43
Iceland	46	51		49		3
India		52	54	48	54	2
Indonesia				38	45	7
Iran				37		
Iraq						
Ireland	37	43		47		10
Israel						
Italy	27	34		29	34	7
Japan	31	26	47	43	38	7
Jordan				51		

Country	1981	1990	1995	2000	2006	Change
Kyrgyzstan				39		
Latvia		24	37	32		8
Lithuania			27	28	40	13
Luxembourg				52		
Macedonia			15	13		−2
Malaysia					64	
Mali					56	
Malta	40	35		49		9
Mexico		38	37	29	31	−7
Moldova			35	33	25	−10
Montenegro			35	20		−15
Morocco				22		
Netherlands	40	53		58	48	8
New Zealand			23		28	5
Nigeria		66	48	65		−1
Northern Ireland	23	24		38		15
Norway	56	59	66			10
Pakistan				26		
Peru			16	22		6
Philippines			55	54		−1
Poland		23	30	34	28	5
Portugal		29		47		18
Puerto Rico			41	42		1
Romania		30	32	27	30	0
Russia		47	43	30	39	−8
Rwanda				50		
Saudi Arabia						
Serbia			25	23	19	−6
Singapore						
Slovakia		29	35	43		14
Slovenia		27	25	31	28	1
South Africa		61	44	52		−9
South Korea	60	67	56	52	43	−17
Spain	33	40	32	30		−3
Sweden	49	40	44	42	52	3
Switzerland				37		
Taiwan			58		26	−32
Tanzania				70		
Thailand						
Trinidad					28	
Turkey		40		54	51	11
Uganda				58		
Ukraine			39	38	39	0
Uruguay			39		32	−7
USA	38	33	34	38	30	−8
Venezuela			27	23		−4
Vietnam				80	91	11
Zambia					32	
Zimbabwe				63		

205

Confidence: The Police

(E035) I am going to name a number of organisations. For each one, could you tell me how much confidence you have in them: is it a great deal of confidence, quite a lot of confidence, not very much confidence or none at all? The police

A great deal/ Quite a lot (%)

Country	1981	1990	1995	2000	2006	Change
Albania			73	65		−8
Algeria				67		
Andorra					62	
Argentina	25	26	23	24	21	−4
Armenia			32			
Australia	80		76		83	3
Austria		67		76		9
Azerbaijan			41			
Bangladesh			38	53		15
Belarus		21	38	40		19
Belgium	64	51		56		−8
Bosnia and Herz.			85	69		−16
Brazil		38	45		45	7
Britain	87	77		70	72	−15
Bulgaria		46	51	47	55	9
Burkina Faso				53		
Canada	85	84		79	82	−3
Chile		59	51	55	57	−2
China		68		73	78	10
Colombia			50		50	0
Croatia			61	53		−8
Cyprus				70		
Czech		37	44	33		−4
Denmark	86	89		91		5
Dominican Rep.			13			
Egypt				87		
El Salvador			49			
Estonia		19	51	34		15
Ethiopia				32		
Finland		76	86	90	92	16
France	66	67		66	71	5
Georgia			38			
Germany (East)		40	52	65	70	30
Germany (West)	71	70	71	75	78	7
Ghana					55	
Greece				28		
Guatemala				25		
Hong Kong				83		
Hungary		51	55	45		−6
Iceland	76	85		83		7
India		39	41	38	64	25
Indonesia				52	51	−1
Iran				61		
Iraq						
Ireland	86	86		83		−3
Israel						
Italy	68	67		67	78	10
Japan	69	59	79	50	67	−2
Jordan					91	

Country	1981	1990	1995	2000	2006	Change
Kyrgyzstan				23		
Latvia		20	31	40		20
Lithuania		28	21	26		−2
Luxembourg				72		
Macedonia			27	51		24
Malaysia					75	
Mali					67	
Malta	55	52		67		12
Mexico		32	33	30	34	2
Moldova			34	35	24	−10
Montenegro			55	40		−15
Morocco				52		
Netherlands	73	73		64	59	−14
New Zealand			81		76	−5
Nigeria		44	29	35		−9
Northern Ireland	84	80		63		−21
Norway	89	88	86			−3
Pakistan			16	29		13
Peru			22	16		−6
Philippines			55	61		6
Poland		32	53	55	47	15
Portugal		44		66		22
Puerto Rico			56	57		1
Romania		45	39	45	40	−5
Russia		35	30	29	33	−2
Rwanda					86	
Saudi Arabia						
Serbia			44	47	35	−9
Singapore						
Slovakia			34	40	44	10
Slovenia			51	47	50	38	−13
South Africa			64	75	56	−8
South Korea	73	53	47	50	59	−14
Spain	64	40		62	59	−5
Sweden	80	74	81	76	78	−2
Switzerland				69		
Taiwan				59	38	−21
Tanzania				67		
Thailand						
Trinidad					28	
Turkey			63	72	70	7
Uganda				55		
Ukraine			37	33	34	−3
Uruguay				53	53	0
USA	74	75	71	71	70	−4
Venezuela				30	41	11
Vietnam				93	91	−2
Zambia					45	
Zimbabwe				64		

Confidence: Justice System

(E036) I am going to name a number of organisations. For each one, could you tell me how much confidence you have in them: is it a great deal of confidence, quite a lot of confidence, not very much confidence or none at all? Justice system

A great deal/ Quite a lot (%)

Country	1981	1990	1995	2000	2006	Change
Albania			58			
Algeria						
Andorra				36		
Argentina	59	23	27		20	−39
Armenia			31			
Australia	60		35		52	−8
Austria		59		69		10
Azerbaijan			47			
Bangladesh			75			
Belarus		26	49	46		20
Belgium	58	45		34		−24
Bosnia and Herz.			69			
Brazil		44	55		49	5
Britain	67	54		49	60	−7
Bulgaria		45	39	28	37	−8
Burkina Faso					47	
Canada	65	54			66	1
Chile		45	45		29	−16
China		76			82	6
Colombia			48		37	−11
Croatia			51	35		−16
Cyprus					74	
Czech		45	29	23		−22
Denmark	80	79		78		−2
Dominican Rep.			15			
Egypt						
El Salvador			41			
Estonia		33	62	32		−1
Ethiopia				27		
Finland		66	69	66	82	16
France	56	58		46	40	−16
Georgia			46			
Germany (East)		41	33	50	55	14
Germany (West)	67	65	54	64	61	−6
Ghana					63	
Greece				44		
Guatemala						
Hong Kong						
Hungary	89	60	52	45		−44
Iceland	70	67		74		4
India			64	78	69	5
Indonesia					52	
Iran						
Iraq						
Ireland	58	47		55		−3
Israel						
Italy	43	32		32	52	9
Japan	71	62	80		82	11
Jordan						

Country	1981	1990	1995	2000	2006	Change
Kyrgyzstan						
Latvia		36	38	47		11
Lithuania			39	22	19	−20
Luxembourg				59		
Macedonia			24			
Malaysia					78	
Mali					63	
Malta	48	39		45		−3
Mexico		53	41		38	−15
Moldova			50		30	−20
Montenegro			60			
Morocco						
Netherlands	65	63		49	45	−20
New Zealand			47		47	0
Nigeria		64	48			−16
Northern Ireland	69	56		48		−21
Norway	84	75	70			−14
Pakistan			50			
Peru			17			
Philippines			66			
Poland		50	53	42	33	−17
Portugal		41		41		0
Puerto Rico			48			
Romania		48	45	40	29	−19
Russia		38	39	36	38	0
Rwanda					79	
Saudi Arabia						
Serbia			44		28	−16
Singapore						
Slovakia		41	42	36		−5
Slovenia		51	36	44	33	−18
South Africa		74	64			−10
South Korea	81	67	59		51	−30
Spain	50	47	47	42		−8
Sweden	73	56	63	61	74	1
Switzerland			66			
Taiwan			59		39	−20
Tanzania						
Thailand						
Trinidad					33	
Turkey		64	71	57		−7
Uganda						
Ukraine			44	32	33	−11
Uruguay			60		56	−4
USA	53	58	36		57	4
Venezuela			37			
Vietnam					90	
Zambia					50	
Zimbabwe						

Confidence: The Government

(E037) I am going to name a number of organisations. For each one, could you tell me how much confidence you have in them: is it a great deal of confidence, quite a lot of confidence, not very much confidence or none at all? The government

A great deal/ Quite a lot (%)

Country	1981	1990	1995	2000	2006	Change
Albania			41	58		17
Algeria				54		
Andorra					34	
Argentina			27	19	38	11
Armenia			42			
Australia				26	40	14
Austria						
Azerbaijan			92			
Bangladesh			81	87		6
Belarus			51			
Belgium						
Bosnia and Herz.				69	32	−37
Brazil			49		46	−3
Britain					34	
Bulgaria			60		34	−26
Burkina Faso					49	
Canada				42	39	−3
Chile		59	53	58	47	−12
China				97	92	−5
Colombia			36		51	15
Croatia			52			
Cyprus					58	
Czech		48	31			−17
Denmark						
Dominican Rep.			13			
Egypt				61		
El Salvador			41			
Estonia			50			
Ethiopia					26	
Finland			32		64	32
France					29	
Georgia			51			
Germany (East)			17		19	2
Germany (West)			24		29	5
Ghana					71	
Greece						
Guatemala					36	
Hong Kong					57	
Hungary			44			
Iceland						
India		43	58	56	55	12
Indonesia				52	56	4
Iran				69		
Iraq				40	61	21
Ireland						
Israel						
Italy					26	
Japan			30	27	31	1
Jordan				83		

Country	1981	1990	1995	2000	2006	Change
Kyrgyzstan				35		
Latvia			38			
Lithuania			36			
Luxembourg						
Macedonia			20	11		−9
Malaysia					75	
Mali					71	
Malta						
Mexico		24	42	37	45	21
Moldova			44	37	33	−11
Montenegro				48	34	−14
Morocco					58	
Netherlands					27	
New Zealand			16		41	25
Nigeria		26	28	48		22
Northern Ireland						
Norway			66			
Pakistan				39		
Peru			39	19		−20
Philippines			59	51		−8
Poland			39		18	−21
Portugal						
Puerto Rico			53	45		−8
Romania			22		27	5
Russia			26		45	19
Rwanda						
Saudi Arabia						
Serbia			35	31	26	−9
Singapore						
Slovakia		35	43			8
Slovenia			41		24	−17
South Africa			69	61		−8
South Korea			44	30	46	2
Spain		28	31	44		16
Sweden			42		42	0
Switzerland			52			
Taiwan			70		33	−37
Tanzania				83		
Thailand						
Trinidad					27	
Turkey		49	52	46		−3
Uganda				78		
Ukraine			44		30	−14
Uruguay			42		61	19
USA			31	38	38	7
Venezuela			27	56		29
Vietnam				98	98	0
Zambia					42	
Zimbabwe				51		

Confidence: The Political Parties

(E038) I am going to name a number of organisations. For each one, could you tell me how much confidence you have in them: is it a great deal of confidence, quite a lot of confidence, not very much confidence or none at all? Political parties

A great deal/ Quite a lot (%)

Country	1981	1990	1995	2000	2006	Change
Albania			23	29		6
Algeria				19		
Andorra					16	
Argentina			8	7	8	0
Armenia			16			
Australia				16	14	−2
Austria						
Azerbaijan			54			
Bangladesh			71	79		8
Belarus		23	16			−7
Belgium						
Bosnia and Herz.			43	16		−27
Brazil			32		21	−11
Britain				18		
Bulgaria			29		17	−12
Burkina Faso				29		
Canada				23	23	0
Chile		50	25	28	18	−32
China		80		93	86	6
Colombia			17		19	2
Croatia			22			
Cyprus				36		
Czech		48	15			−33
Denmark						
Dominican Rep.			9			
Egypt				51		
El Salvador			17			
Estonia			23			
Ethiopia				39		
Finland			13	28	15	
France				16		
Georgia			34			
Germany (East)			10	8		−2
Germany (West)			14	18		4
Ghana				41		
Greece						
Guatemala				12		
Hong Kong				28		
Hungary		20				
Iceland						
India		55	47	34	46	−9
Indonesia				33	31	−2
Iran				34		
Iraq						
Ireland						
Israel						
Italy				17		
Japan			16	18	18	2
Jordan				26		

Country	1981	1990	1995	2000	2006	Change
Kyrgyzstan				26		
Latvia			10			
Lithuania			14			
Luxembourg						
Macedonia			11	9		−2
Malaysia					58	
Mali					37	
Malta						
Mexico		30	35	25	24	−6
Moldova			18	24	21	3
Montenegro			24	26		2
Morocco				19		
Netherlands				23		
New Zealand			6		15	9
Nigeria		38	26	44		6
Northern Ireland						
Norway			33			
Pakistan			33	28		−5
Peru			6	8		2
Philippines			45	46		1
Poland			13		7	−6
Portugal						
Puerto Rico			21	20		−1
Romania			14		13	−1
Russia		46	19		22	−24
Rwanda					41	
Saudi Arabia						
Serbia			17	15	13	−4
Singapore						
Slovakia		35	23			−12
Slovenia			14		9	−5
South Africa		58	47	44		−14
South Korea			25	11	24	−1
Spain		61	19	27		−34
Sweden			28		33	5
Switzerland			27			
Taiwan			36		10	−26
Tanzania				59		
Thailand						
Trinidad					10	
Turkey			29	29		0
Uganda				41		
Ukraine			20		17	−3
Uruguay			36		36	0
USA			21	23	15	−6
Venezuela			15	20		5
Vietnam				92	94	2
Zambia					27	
Zimbabwe				29		

Confidence: Parliament

(E039) I am going to name a number of organisations. For each one, could you tell me how much confidence you have in them: is it a great deal of confidence, quite a lot of confidence, not very much confidence or none at all? Parliament

A great deal/ Quite a lot (%)

Country	1981	1990	1995	2000	2006	Change
Albania			61	45		−16
Algeria				33		
Andorra						
Argentina	73	17	16	11	14	−59
Armenia			30			
Australia	55		31		34	−21
Austria		41		41		0
Azerbaijan			74			
Bangladesh			84	89		5
Belarus		29	30	37		8
Belgium	38	43		36		−2
Bosnia and Herz.			54	22		−32
Brazil		24	34		25	1
Britain	41	46		36	36	−5
Bulgaria		49	45	27	21	−28
Burkina Faso					39	
Canada	44	38		41	37	−7
Chile			63	39	35	25	−38
China			81		95	92	11
Colombia			25		25	0
Croatia			42	23		−19
Cyprus				54		
Czech		43	20	12		−31
Denmark	37	42		49		12
Dominican Rep.			12			
Egypt				68		
El Salvador			31			
Estonia			44	27		−17
Ethiopia					24	
Finland		34	31	44	56	22
France	56	48		41	35	−21
Georgia			41			
Germany (East)		41	17	40	16	−25
Germany (West)	53	51	29	35	28	−25
Ghana					65	
Greece				24		
Guatemala					11	
Hong Kong				52		
Hungary	92	40	39	34		−58
Iceland	58	53		72		14
India		67	65	55	62	−5
Indonesia				43	37	−6
Iran				70		
Iraq						
Ireland	52	50		31		−21
Israel						
Italy	30	32		34	33	3
Japan	29	29	25	22	23	−6
Jordan				65		

Country	1981	1990	1995	2000	2006	Change
Kyrgyzstan				36		
Latvia			25	27		2
Lithuania			27	11		−16
Luxembourg				63		
Macedonia			16	7		−9
Malaysia					68	
Mali					57	
Malta	46	42		52		6
Mexico		35	45	23	25	−10
Moldova			41	35	28	−13
Montenegro				45	33	−12
Morocco				22		
Netherlands	45	54		55	30	−15
New Zealand			15		35	20
Nigeria			54	27	45	−9
Northern Ireland	47	46		40		−7
Norway	78	59	69			−9
Pakistan				76		
Peru			15	10		−5
Philippines			60	61		1
Poland		73	35	33	12	−61
Portugal		34		49		15
Puerto Rico			30	28		−2
Romania		21	19	19	17	−4
Russia		47	23	19	30	−17
Rwanda					79	
Saudi Arabia						
Serbia			32	23	21	−11
Singapore						
Slovakia		32	31	43		11
Slovenia		36	25	25	16	−20
South Africa			66	69	60	−6
South Korea	68	34	31	11	26	−42
Spain	49	36	37	48		−1
Sweden	47	47	45	51	56	9
Switzerland				44		
Taiwan				46	14	−32
Tanzania				79		
Thailand						
Trinidad					16	
Turkey		58	53	39		−19
Uganda				77		
Ukraine			38	27	20	−18
Uruguay			42		47	5
USA	53	46	30	38	21	−32
Venezuela			23	34		11
Vietnam				97	99	2
Zambia					41	
Zimbabwe				50		

Confidence: The Civil Services

(E040) I am going to name a number of organisations. For each one, could you tell me how much confidence you have in them: is it a great deal of confidence, quite a lot of confidence, not very much confidence or none at all? The Civil service

A great deal/ Quite a lot (%)

Country	1981	1990	1995	2000	2006	Change
Albania			23	40		17
Algeria				58		
Andorra					36	
Argentina	50	7	8	7	8	−42
Armenia			37			
Australia	47		38		39	−8
Austria		41		42		1
Azerbaijan			44			
Bangladesh			80	96		16
Belarus		20	51	23		3
Belgium	47	42		45		−2
Bosnia and Herz.			62	34		−28
Brazil		49	59		52	3
Britain	49	44		46	46	−3
Bulgaria		30	48	24	42	12
Burkina Faso				58		
Canada	52	50		50	56	4
Chile		49	46	40	35	−14
China		59		66	86	27
Colombia			32		32	0
Croatia			38	35		−3
Cyprus				56		
Czech		33	39	22		−11
Denmark	47	51		55		8
Dominican Rep.			10			
Egypt				63		
El Salvador						
Estonia			61	40		−21
Ethiopia				33		
Finland		33	34	41	60	27
France	53	49		46	54	1
Georgia			56			
Germany (East)		18	41	36	28	10
Germany (West)	36	39	48	39	35	−1
Ghana				62		
Greece			14			
Guatemala				15		
Hong Kong				61		
Hungary	74	50	52	50		−24
Iceland	48	46		56		8
India		74	70	49	54	−20
Indonesia				59	56	−3
Iran				44		
Iraq						
Ireland	55	59		61		6
Israel						
Italy	28	27		33	41	13
Japan	32	34	37	32	33	1
Jordan				66		

Country	1981	1990	1995	2000	2006	Change
Kyrgyzstan				45		
Latvia			44	49		5
Lithuania			41	21		−20
Luxembourg				60		
Macedonia			19	17		−2
Malaysia					70	
Mali					62	
Malta	57	39		49		−8
Mexico		28	43	22	25	−3
Moldova			54	47	14	−40
Montenegro			48	29		−19
Morocco				42		
Netherlands	45	46		37	31	−14
New Zealand			29		44	15
Nigeria			76	59	71	−5
Northern Ireland	60	57		52		−8
Norway	58	44	51			−7
Pakistan			47	50		3
Peru			11	9		−2
Philippines			68	71		3
Poland		58	35	33	18	−40
Portugal		32		54		22
Puerto Rico			57	27		−30
Romania		31	28	27	30	−1
Russia		48	49	38	53	5
Rwanda					55	
Saudi Arabia				70		
Serbia			33	29	23	−10
Singapore						
Slovakia			33	40	39	6
Slovenia			40	29	25	17	−23
South Africa			60	59	58	−2
South Korea	88	61	78	67	63	−25
Spain	40	35	42	41		1
Sweden	46	44	45	49	67	21
Switzerland				46		
Taiwan			60		40	−20
Tanzania				71		
Thailand						
Trinidad					34	
Turkey		50	68	58		8
Uganda				69		
Ukraine			43	39	49	6
Uruguay			45		24	−21
USA	57	59	52	55	41	−16
Venezuela			31	38		7
Vietnam				79	89	10
Zambia					41	
Zimbabwe				59		

Confidence: Major Companies

(E041) I am going to name a number of organisations. For each one, could you tell me how much confidence you have in them: is it a great deal of confidence, quite a lot of confidence, not very much confidence or none at all? Major companies

A great deal/ Quite a lot (%)

Country	1981	1990	1995	2000	2006	Change
Albania			24	49		25
Algeria				43		
Andorra					32	
Argentina	35	24	30	26	25	−10
Armenia			50			
Australia	79		59		30	−49
Austria		41		41		0
Azerbaijan			42			
Bangladesh			65	90		25
Belarus			37	68	59	22
Belgium	43	50				7
Bosnia and Herz.			59	39		−20
Brazil		58	68		58	0
Britain	50	48		40	37	−13
Bulgaria		34	34		33	−1
Burkina Faso					56	
Canada	57	51		56	37	−20
Chile		53	57	50	36	−17
China		36	61	55	56	20
Colombia			59		47	−12
Croatia			29	30		1
Cyprus					43	
Czech		24	38	20		−4
Denmark	35	38				3
Dominican Rep.			47			
Egypt				32		
El Salvador			40			
Estonia		15	61		46	
Ethiopia				37		
Finland		41	51	43	45	4
France	50	67		48	40	−10
Georgia			55			
Germany (East)		47	25	44	28	−19
Germany (West)	34	38	26	34	26	−8
Ghana					59	
Greece				20		
Guatemala				52		
Hong Kong				19		
Hungary		34	37			3
Iceland	33	40		42		9
India		61	66	46	51	−10
Indonesia				47	46	−1
Iran				31		
Iraq						
Ireland	50	52				2
Israel						
Italy		34	62	50	42	8
Japan	25	28	36	29	41	16
Jordan				54		

Country	1981	1990	1995	2000	2006	Change
Kyrgyzstan				41		
Latvia		11	46			35
Lithuania		16	32	17		1
Luxembourg				40		
Macedonia			27	23		−4
Malaysia					54	
Mali					62	
Malta	62	68				6
Mexico		46	50	46	46	0
Moldova			51	50	21	−30
Montenegro			46	29		−17
Morocco				42		
Netherlands	36	48		33		−3
New Zealand			46		41	−5
Nigeria		76	64	70		−6
Northern Ireland	54	47				−7
Norway	45	53	60			15
Pakistan				37		
Peru			31	26		−5
Philippines			64	58		−6
Poland		59	53		28	−31
Portugal		45		53		8
Puerto Rico			61	45		−16
Romania		35	37		40	5
Russia		46	23	21	36	−10
Rwanda					40	
Saudi Arabia				59		
Serbia			33	32	30	−3
Singapore						
Slovakia		31	31			0
Slovenia		33	40		30	−3
South Africa		76	74	74		−2
South Korea	54	35	35	30	50	−4
Spain	38	45	47	39		1
Sweden	42	53	65		51	9
Switzerland			40			
Taiwan			55		31	−24
Tanzania				66		
Thailand						
Trinidad					32	
Turkey		29	62	51		22
Uganda				70		
Ukraine			58	21	53	−5
Uruguay			45		37	−8
USA	50	51	54	54	27	−23
Venezuela			55	64		9
Vietnam				47	67	20
Zambia					42	
Zimbabwe				77		

212

Confidence: The Environmental Protection Movement

(E042) I am going to name a number of organisations. For each one, could you tell me how much confidence you have in them: is it a great deal of confidence, quite a lot of confidence, not very much confidence or none at all? Environmental Protection movement

A great deal/ Quite a lot (%)

Country	1981	1990	1995	2000	2006	Change
Albania			17	38		21
Algeria						
Andorra					62	
Argentina			72	67	62	−10
Armenia			47			
Australia			56		59	3
Austria						
Azerbaijan			14			
Bangladesh			79	83		4
Belarus			78			
Belgium						
Bosnia and Herz.			64	59		−5
Brazil			80		68	−12
Britain				70		
Bulgaria			45		43	−2
Burkina Faso					69	
Canada				68	72	4
Chile			78	65	60	−18
China			69	88	79	10
Colombia			70		54	−16
Croatia			53			
Cyprus				63		
Czech			57			
Denmark						
Dominican Rep.			64			
Egypt				77		
El Salvador			38			
Estonia			76			
Ethiopia				47		
Finland			41		56	15
France				65		
Georgia			42			
Germany (East)			64		57	−7
Germany (West)			71		60	−11
Ghana					63	
Greece						
Guatemala				60		
Hong Kong				78		
Hungary			45			
Iceland						
India			64	52	61	−3
Indonesia				55	65	10
Iran				55		
Iraq						
Ireland						
Israel						
Italy					68	
Japan			64	57	57	−7
Jordan				69		

Country	1981	1990	1995	2000	2006	Change
Kyrgyzstan				48		
Latvia			62			
Lithuania			63			
Luxembourg						
Macedonia			40	42		2
Malaysia					67	
Mali					73	
Malta						
Mexico			55	54	63	8
Moldova			52	52	38	−14
Montenegro			45	34		−11
Morocco				65		
Netherlands					56	
New Zealand			48		52	4
Nigeria			52	61		9
Northern Ireland						
Norway			63			
Pakistan			36			
Peru			52	48		−4
Philippines			74	74		0
Poland			79		59	−20
Portugal						
Puerto Rico			77	70		−7
Romania			48	51		3
Russia			79		63	−16
Rwanda				60		
Saudi Arabia				58		
Serbia			50	44	50	0
Singapore						
Slovakia			55			
Slovenia			58		41	−17
South Africa			56	61		5
South Korea			85	74	72	−13
Spain			64	61		−3
Sweden			74		74	0
Switzerland			43			
Taiwan			79		56	−23
Tanzania				61		
Thailand						
Trinidad				43		
Turkey			85	70		−15
Uganda				76		
Ukraine			66		50	−16
Uruguay			69		62	−7
USA			54	60	53	−1
Venezuela			55	68		13
Vietnam				79	90	11
Zambia					40	
Zimbabwe				69		

Confidence: The Women's Movement

(E043) I am going to name a number of organisations. For each one, could you tell me how much confidence you have in them: is it a great deal of confidence, quite a lot of confidence, not very much confidence or none at all? The women's movement

A great deal/ Quite a lot (%)

Country	1981	1990	1995	2000	2006	Change
Albania			37	38		1
Algeria				30		
Andorra					67	
Argentina			41	36	40	−1
Armenia			29			
Australia			43		61	18
Austria						
Azerbaijan			20			
Bangladesh			77	80		3
Belarus			70			
Belgium						
Bosnia and Herz.			61	53		−8
Brazil			69		66	−3
Britain					68	
Bulgaria			47		41	−6
Burkina Faso					71	
Canada				63	73	10
Chile			51	47	58	7
China			73	92	85	12
Colombia			52		44	−8
Croatia			29			
Cyprus					53	
Czech			41			
Denmark						
Dominican Rep.			52			
Egypt				74		
El Salvador						
Estonia			63			
Ethiopia				45		
Finland			29		63	34
France				49		
Georgia			41			
Germany (East)			54		57	3
Germany (West)			52		57	5
Ghana					67	
Greece						
Guatemala					51	
Hong Kong					75	
Hungary			35			
Iceland						
India			59	53	65	6
Indonesia				51	67	16
Iran				43		
Iraq						
Ireland						
Israel						
Italy					41	
Japan			44	45	40	−4
Jordan				53		

Country	1981	1990	1995	2000	2006	Change
Kyrgyzstan				51		
Latvia			49			
Lithuania			41			
Luxembourg						
Macedonia			29	45		16
Malaysia					70	
Mali					70	
Malta						
Mexico			44	39	65	21
Moldova			49	47	39	−10
Montenegro			37	29		−8
Morocco				41		
Netherlands				50		
New Zealand			38		42	4
Nigeria			53	54		1
Northern Ireland						
Norway			43			
Pakistan				29		
Peru			37	36		−1
Philippines			74	77		3
Poland			54		54	0
Portugal						
Puerto Rico			57	56		−1
Romania			42		49	7
Russia			70		60	−10
Rwanda					66	
Saudi Arabia				44		
Serbia			34	39	44	10
Singapore						
Slovakia			50			
Slovenia			44		39	−5
South Africa			57	63		6
South Korea			77	70	68	−9
Spain			44	48		4
Sweden			51		49	−2
Switzerland			39			
Taiwan			76		57	−19
Tanzania				80		
Thailand						
Trinidad					51	
Turkey			76	65		−11
Uganda				75		
Ukraine			62		50	−12
Uruguay			49		68	19
USA			53	59	51	−2
Venezuela			43	50		7
Vietnam				85	96	11
Zambia					51	
Zimbabwe				61		

Confidence: Charitable or humanitarian organizations

(E044) I am going to name a number of organisations. For each one, could you tell me how much confidence you have in them: is it a great deal of confidence, quite a lot of confidence, not very much confidence or none at all? Charitable or humanitarian organizations

A great deal/ Quite a lot (%)

Country	1981	1990	1995	2000	2006	Change
Albania						
Algeria						
Andorra					60	
Argentina					68	
Armenia						
Australia					68	
Austria						
Azerbaijan						
Bangladesh						
Belarus						
Belgium						
Bosnia and Herz.						
Brazil					67	
Britain					75	
Bulgaria					45	
Burkina Faso					77	
Canada					76	
Chile					63	
China					76	
Colombia					57	
Croatia						
Cyprus					66	
Czech						
Denmark						
Dominican Rep.						
Egypt						
El Salvador						
Estonia						
Ethiopia					56	
Finland					60	
France					66	
Georgia						
Germany (East)					62	
Germany (West)					68	
Ghana					69	
Greece						
Guatemala						
Hong Kong						
Hungary						
Iceland						
India					57	
Indonesia					74	
Iran						
Iraq						
Ireland						
Israel						
Italy					74	
Japan					32	
Jordan						

Country	1981	1990	1995	2000	2006	Change
Kyrgyzstan						
Latvia						
Lithuania						
Luxembourg						
Macedonia						
Malaysia					71	
Mali					68	
Malta						
Mexico					65	
Moldova					43	
Montenegro						
Morocco						
Netherlands					49	
New Zealand						
Nigeria						
Northern Ireland						
Norway						
Pakistan						
Peru						
Philippines						
Poland					65	
Portugal						
Puerto Rico						
Romania					54	
Russia					58	
Rwanda					60	
Saudi Arabia						
Serbia					49	
Singapore						
Slovakia						
Slovenia					40	
South Africa						
South Korea					71	
Spain						
Sweden					66	
Switzerland						
Taiwan					55	
Tanzania						
Thailand						
Trinidad					57	
Turkey						
Uganda						
Ukraine					55	
Uruguay					69	
USA					64	
Venezuela						
Vietnam					91	
Zambia					52	
Zimbabwe						

Confidence: The European Union

(E045) I am going to name a number of organisations. For each one, could you tell me how much confidence you have in them: is it a great deal of confidence, quite a lot of confidence, not very much confidence or none at all? The European Union

A great deal/ Quite a lot (%)

Country	1981	1990	1995	2000	2006	Change
Albania			86	84		–2
Algeria				16		
Andorra					46	
Argentina				41		
Armenia			59			
Australia						
Austria				37		
Azerbaijan			28			
Bangladesh						
Belarus			67	47		–20
Belgium		66		47		–19
Bosnia and Herz.			75	56		–19
Brazil						
Britain	47			26	26	–21
Bulgaria		50	72	43	63	13
Burkina Faso					62	
Canada						
Chile		32				
China		17		39	58	41
Colombia						
Croatia			33	44		11
Cyprus				47		
Czech			63	49	43	–20
Denmark		39		27		–12
Dominican Rep.						
Egypt						
El Salvador						
Estonia			65	31		–34
Ethiopia					43	
Finland		47	32	25	37	–10
France			73	48	39	–34
Georgia			60			
Germany (East)		64	25	34	27	–37
Germany (West)		48	34	38	35	–13
Ghana					64	
Greece				25		
Guatemala						
Hong Kong						
Hungary		63	65	59		–4
Iceland		36		45		9
India				53		
Indonesia						
Iran						
Iraq						
Ireland		71		59		–12
Israel						
Italy		74		69	67	–7
Japan						
Jordan						

Country	1981	1990	1995	2000	2006	Change
Kyrgyzstan				56		
Latvia			59	35		–24
Lithuania			52	31		–21
Luxembourg				58		
Macedonia			38	33		–5
Malaysia						
Mali					66	
Malta		58		56		–2
Mexico		27				
Moldova			72	75	54	–18
Montenegro			40	51		11
Morocco				24		
Netherlands		55		33	31	–24
New Zealand						
Nigeria						
Northern Ireland	49			40		–9
Norway		40	29			–11
Pakistan						
Peru						
Philippines						
Poland		59	61	43	46	–13
Portugal		57		69		12
Puerto Rico						
Romania		48	50	39	63	15
Russia			53	26		–27
Rwanda					49	
Saudi Arabia						
Serbia			24	27	31	7
Singapore						
Slovakia		45	56	55		10
Slovenia		46	42	37	36	–10
South Africa						
South Korea						
Spain		50	53	53		3
Sweden		58	25	29	37	–21
Switzerland				43		
Taiwan				64		
Tanzania						
Thailand						
Trinidad						
Turkey		37	49	40		3
Uganda						
Ukraine			64	45	48	–16
Uruguay						
USA						
Venezuela						
Vietnam						
Zambia					38	
Zimbabwe						

Confidence: NATO

(E046) I am going to name a number of organisations. For each one, could you tell me how much confidence you have in them: is it a great deal of confidence, quite a lot of confidence, not very much confidence or none at all? NATO (North Atlantic Treaty Organisa.)

A great deal/ Quite a lot (%)

Country	1981	1990	1995	2000	2006	Change
Albania				86		
Algeria				6		
Andorra						
Argentina						
Armenia						
Australia						
Austria				28		
Azerbaijan						
Bangladesh				89		
Belarus				21		
Belgium			46	44		−2
Bosnia and Herz.				50		
Brazil						
Britain			59	59		0
Bulgaria			28			
Burkina Faso						
Canada			50	57		7
Chile			29	50		21
China			22	26		4
Colombia						
Croatia				56		
Cyprus						
Czech			40	44		4
Denmark			52	59		7
Dominican Rep.						
Egypt						
El Salvador						
Estonia				37		
Ethiopia						
Finland			29			
France			60			
Georgia						
Germany (East)			19	40		21
Germany (West)			42	54		12
Ghana						
Greece				7		
Guatemala					30	
Hong Kong						
Hungary			42			
Iceland			35	47		12
India			35			
Indonesia						
Iran						
Iraq						
Ireland			59			
Israel						
Italy			54	56		2
Japan			27			
Jordan						

Country	1981	1990	1995	2000	2006	Change
Kyrgyzstan				40		
Latvia				36		
Lithuania				36		
Luxembourg				62		
Macedonia				27		
Malaysia						
Mali						
Malta				52		
Mexico			27	32		5
Moldova				66		
Montenegro				19		
Morocco				11		
Netherlands			47	52		5
New Zealand						
Nigeria			55			
Northern Ireland			53			
Norway			67			
Pakistan						
Peru						
Philippines				63		
Poland			38	57		19
Portugal			35	68		33
Puerto Rico						
Romania			47	35		−12
Russia			68	8		−60
Rwanda						
Saudi Arabia						
Serbia				6		
Singapore						
Slovakia			22	36		14
Slovenia			25	37		12
South Africa				60		
South Korea						
Spain			21	33		12
Sweden			36	41		5
Switzerland						
Taiwan						
Tanzania						
Thailand						
Trinidad						
Turkey				39		
Uganda				53		
Ukraine				32		
Uruguay						
USA			52	53		1
Venezuela				49		
Vietnam						
Zambia						
Zimbabwe				38		

Confidence: Education System

(E047) I am going to name a number of organisations. For each one, could you tell me how much confidence you have in them: is it a great deal of confidence, quite a lot of confidence, not very much confidence or none at all? The education system

A great deal/ Quite a lot (%)

Country	1981	1990	1995	2000	2006	Change
Albania						
Algeria						
Andorra						
Argentina		38			46	8
Armenia						
Australia						
Austria		65		86		21
Azerbaijan						
Bangladesh						
Belarus				84		
Belgium	79	73		80		1
Bosnia and Herz.						
Brazil		67				
Britain	62	47		66		4
Bulgaria		53		57		4
Burkina Faso						
Canada	67	73				6
Chile		73				
China		92				
Colombia						
Croatia				64		
Cyprus						
Czech		62		55		−7
Denmark	65	81		75		10
Dominican Rep.						
Egypt						
El Salvador						
Estonia		48		74		26
Ethiopia						
Finland		78		89		11
France	57	66		68		11
Georgia						
Germany (East)		42		78		36
Germany (West)	43	54		71		28
Ghana						
Greece				29		
Guatemala						
Hong Kong						
Hungary		61		64		3
Iceland	69	80		82		13
India		73				
Indonesia						
Iran						
Iraq						
Ireland	68	73		87		19
Israel						
Italy	56	48		53		−3
Japan		46				
Jordan						

Country	1981	1990	1995	2000	2006	Change
Kyrgyzstan						
Latvia		53		74		21
Lithuania		57		67		10
Luxembourg				68		
Macedonia						
Malaysia						
Mali						
Malta	68	79		84		16
Mexico		76				
Moldova						
Montenegro						
Morocco						
Netherlands	73	65		73		0
New Zealand						
Nigeria		84				
Northern Ireland	74	66		83		9
Norway	80	79				−1
Pakistan						
Peru						
Philippines						
Poland		77		81		4
Portugal		51		60		9
Puerto Rico						
Romania		79		79		0
Russia		55		71		16
Rwanda						
Saudi Arabia						
Serbia						
Singapore						
Slovakia		65		76		11
Slovenia		67		80		13
South Africa		77				
South Korea		64				
Spain	51	64		68		17
Sweden	62	70		68		6
Switzerland						
Taiwan						
Tanzania						
Thailand						
Trinidad						
Turkey				57		
Uganda						
Ukraine				72		
Uruguay						
USA	67	55				−12
Venezuela						
Vietnam						
Zambia						
Zimbabwe						

Confidence: The United Nations

(E048) I am going to name a number of organisations. For each one, could you tell me how much confidence you have in them: is it a great deal of confidence, quite a lot of confidence, not very much confidence or none at all? United Nations

A great deal/ Quite a lot (%)

Country	1981	1990	1995	2000	2006	Change
Albania			86	86		0
Algeria				15		
Andorra					41	
Argentina			39	42	22	−17
Armenia			70			
Australia			50		45	−5
Austria				42		
Azerbaijan			33			
Bangladesh			83	93		10
Belarus			71	53		−18
Belgium				45		
Bosnia and Herz.			72	50		−22
Brazil			70		49	−21
Britain			60	45		−15
Bulgaria			73	40	61	−12
Burkina Faso					65	
Canada				65	60	−5
Chile			63	58	43	−20
China			56	69	65	9
Colombia				50		
Croatia			27	47		20
Cyprus					41	
Czech			62	48		−14
Denmark				64		
Dominican Rep.			44			
Egypt				32		
El Salvador			51			
Estonia			70	43		−27
Ethiopia				39		
Finland			55	44	64	9
France				54	56	2
Georgia			61			
Germany (East)			34	47	36	2
Germany (West)			47	53	42	−5
Ghana				75		
Greece				19		
Guatemala				48		
Hong Kong						
Hungary			67	59		−8
Iceland				72		
India			55	53	64	9
Indonesia				48	52	4
Iran				36		
Iraq				16	13	−3
Ireland				62		
Israel						
Italy				68	59	−9
Japan			63	61	64	1
Jordan				36		

Country	1981	1990	1995	2000	2006	Change
Kyrgyzstan				59		
Latvia			65	48		−17
Lithuania			58	47		−11
Luxembourg				65		
Macedonia			43	37		−6
Malaysia					49	
Mali					68	
Malta				63		
Mexico			51	45	53	2
Moldova			76	74	48	−28
Montenegro				47	44	−3
Morocco				13		
Netherlands				55	39	−16
New Zealand			56		51	−5
Nigeria			72	70		−2
Northern Ireland				53		
Norway			73			
Pakistan				22		
Peru			52	44		−8
Philippines			75	76		1
Poland			68	58	49	−19
Portugal				71		
Puerto Rico			72	67		−5
Romania			53	44	65	12
Russia			61	27	46	−15
Rwanda					48	
Saudi Arabia				33		
Serbia			23	17	27	4
Singapore						
Slovakia			58	52		−6
Slovenia			39	49	33	−6
South Africa			59	67		8
South Korea			81	62	56	−25
Spain			50	49		−1
Sweden			66	74	78	12
Switzerland				43		
Taiwan			49		31	−18
Tanzania				82		
Thailand						
Trinidad					42	
Turkey			47	44		−3
Uganda				87		
Ukraine			68	55	47	−21
Uruguay			56		48	−8
USA			51	57	34	−17
Venezuela			43	52		9
Vietnam				61	85	24
Zambia					57	
Zimbabwe				70		

How much do you trust your family
(E049) Using the responses on this card, could you tell me how much you trust? Your family
Trust them completely (%)

Country	1981	1990	1995	2000	2006	Change
Albania						
Algeria						
Andorra					83	
Argentina		89			91	2
Armenia						
Australia				83		
Austria		89				
Azerbaijan						
Bangladesh						
Belarus						
Belgium		69				
Bosnia and Herz.						
Brazil		80		67		−13
Britain		92		86		−6
Bulgaria		86		91		5
Burkina Faso				84		
Canada		92		84		−8
Chile		81		83		2
China		88		88		0
Colombia				85		
Croatia						
Cyprus				88		
Czech		83				
Denmark		88				
Dominican Rep.						
Egypt				96		
El Salvador						
Estonia		79				
Ethiopia				91		
Finland		70		91		21
France		58		80		22
Georgia				92		
Germany (East)		87		82		−5
Germany (West)		81		82		1
Ghana				71		
Greece						
Guatemala						
Hong Kong						
Hungary		88				
Iceland		82				
India		92		86		−6
Indonesia				80		
Iran						
Iraq						
Ireland		93				
Israel						
Italy		75		87		12
Japan		69				
Jordan					97	

Country	1981	1990	1995	2000	2006	Change
Kyrgyzstan						
Latvia		84				
Lithuania		75				
Luxembourg						
Macedonia						
Malaysia					85	
Mali					92	
Malta		95				
Mexico		82			78	−4
Moldova					80	
Montenegro						
Morocco					89	
Netherlands		72			63	−9
New Zealand				97		
Nigeria					92	
Northern Ireland		78				
Norway		85			91	6
Pakistan						
Peru					76	
Philippines						
Poland		60			72	12
Portugal		83				
Puerto Rico						
Romania		60			77	17
Russia		43			92	49
Rwanda					73	
Saudi Arabia						
Serbia					92	
Singapore						
Slovakia		80				
Slovenia		91			82	−9
South Africa		74			85	11
South Korea		84			87	3
Spain		91			92	1
Sweden		84			94	10
Switzerland					81	
Taiwan					87	
Tanzania						
Thailand					80	
Trinidad					73	
Turkey					96	
Uganda						
Ukraine					77	
Uruguay					85	
USA		88			75	−13
Venezuela						
Vietnam					88	
Zambia					65	
Zimbabwe						

Who should decide: international peacekeeping

(E050) For each one, would you tell me whether you think that policies in this area should be decided by the national governments, by the United Nations, or by the national governments with UN co-ordination?

United Nations (%)

Country	1981	1990	1995	2000	2006	Change
Albania				77		
Algeria				94		
Andorra					66	
Argentina				65	66	1
Armenia						
Australia					69	
Austria						
Azerbaijan						
Bangladesh				80		
Belarus						
Belgium						
Bosnia and Herz.				85		
Brazil					71	
Britain						
Bulgaria					56	
Burkina Faso					39	
Canada				79	70	−9
Chile				53	48	−5
China				77	64	−13
Colombia						
Croatia						
Cyprus					48	
Czech						
Denmark						
Dominican Rep.						
Egypt				79	45	−34
El Salvador					66	
Estonia						
Ethiopia					44	
Finland					60	
France						
Georgia					16	
Germany (East)					61	
Germany (West)					53	
Ghana					67	
Greece						
Guatemala					34	
Hong Kong						
Hungary						
Iceland						
India				55	20	−35
Indonesia				66	80	14
Iran				72	44	−28
Iraq						
Ireland						
Israel						
Italy					64	
Japan				85	79	−6
Jordan				42	51	9

Country	1981	1990	1995	2000	2006	Change
Kyrgyzstan				73		
Latvia						
Lithuania						
Luxembourg						
Macedonia				44		
Malaysia					28	
Mali					42	
Malta						
Mexico				42	71	29
Moldova				69	41	−28
Montenegro					52	
Morocco				70	35	−35
Netherlands						
New Zealand						
Nigeria					85	
Northern Ireland				70		
Norway					72	
Pakistan						
Peru						
Philippines				51		
Poland					66	
Portugal						
Puerto Rico						
Romania					41	
Russia						
Rwanda					8	
Saudi Arabia				66		
Serbia				30	35	5
Singapore						
Slovakia						
Slovenia					37	
South Africa				64	34	−30
South Korea				50	47	−3
Spain				67	68	1
Sweden				74	72	−2
Switzerland					63	
Taiwan					57	
Tanzania				62		
Thailand					2	
Trinidad					55	
Turkey					41	
Uganda				79		
Ukraine					33	
Uruguay					71	
USA				74	23	−51
Venezuela						
Vietnam				55	38	−17
Zambia					49	
Zimbabwe				74		

Who should decide: protection of the environment

(E051) For each one, would you tell me whether you think that policies in this area should be decided by the national governments, by the United Nations, or by the national governments with UN co-ordination?

United Nations (%)

Country	1981	1990	1995	2000	2006	Change
Albania				9		
Algeria				44		
Andorra					22	
Argentina				31	37	6
Armenia						
Australia					21	
Austria						
Azerbaijan						
Bangladesh				28		
Belarus						
Belgium						
Bosnia and Herz.				11		
Brazil					19	
Britain						
Bulgaria				15		
Burkina Faso					22	
Canada				20	21	1
Chile				25	21	−4
China				20	27	7
Colombia						
Croatia						
Cyprus				14		
Czech						
Denmark						
Dominican Rep.						
Egypt				27	24	−3
El Salvador						
Estonia						
Ethiopia					40	
Finland					18	
France						
Georgia				9		
Germany (East)					35	
Germany (West)					29	
Ghana					7	
Greece						
Guatemala					37	
Hong Kong						
Hungary						
Iceland						
India				17	12	−5
Indonesia				4	5	1
Iran				36	23	−13
Iraq						
Ireland						
Israel						
Italy					20	
Japan				59	42	−17
Jordan				16	30	14

Country	1981	1990	1995	2000	2006	Change
Kyrgyzstan				47		
Latvia						
Lithuania						
Luxembourg						
Macedonia				21		
Malaysia					12	
Mali					13	
Malta						
Mexico				22	35	13
Moldova				27	8	−19
Montenegro					17	
Morocco				23	28	5
Netherlands						
New Zealand						
Nigeria					15	
Northern Ireland				24		
Norway					26	
Pakistan						
Peru						
Philippines				28		
Poland					18	
Portugal						
Puerto Rico						
Romania					10	
Russia						
Rwanda					7	
Saudi Arabia				43		
Serbia				9	17	8
Singapore						
Slovakia						
Slovenia					14	
South Africa				19	15	−4
South Korea				15	20	5
Spain				34	46	12
Sweden				27	25	−2
Switzerland					33	
Taiwan					15	
Tanzania				19		
Thailand					6	
Trinidad					18	
Turkey					20	
Uganda				13		
Ukraine					11	
Uruguay					33	
USA				27	9	−18
Venezuela						
Vietnam				34	26	−8
Zambia					14	
Zimbabwe					17	

Who should decide: aid to developing countries

(E052) For each one, would you tell me whether you think that policies in this area should be decided by the national governments, by the United Nations, or by the national governments with UN co-ordination?

United Nations (%)

Country	1981	1990	1995	2000	2006	Change
Albania				90		
Algeria				90		
Andorra					64	
Argentina				61	66	5
Armenia						
Australia				51		
Austria						
Azerbaijan						
Bangladesh				44		
Belarus						
Belgium						
Bosnia and Herz.				84		
Brazil				55		
Britain						
Bulgaria				46		
Burkina Faso				72		
Canada				53	53	0
Chile				52	61	9
China				49	56	7
Colombia						
Croatia						
Cyprus				39		
Czech						
Denmark						
Dominican Rep.						
Egypt				87	52	–35
El Salvador						
Estonia						
Ethiopia				75		
Finland				57		
France						
Georgia				64		
Germany (East)				56		
Germany (West)				41		
Ghana				58		
Greece						
Guatemala				58		
Hong Kong						
Hungary						
Iceland						
India				58	40	–18
Indonesia				51	57	6
Iran				79	59	–20
Iraq						
Ireland						
Israel						
Italy				59		
Japan				60	60	0
Jordan				73	62	–11

Country	1981	1990	1995	2000	2006	Change
Kyrgyzstan				73		
Latvia						
Lithuania						
Luxembourg						
Macedonia				63		
Malaysia					38	
Mali					63	
Malta						
Mexico				40	62	22
Moldova				72	41	–31
Montenegro				87		
Morocco				67	57	–10
Netherlands						
New Zealand						
Nigeria					58	
Northern Ireland				74		
Norway					55	
Pakistan						
Peru						
Philippines				61		
Poland					62	
Portugal						
Puerto Rico						
Romania					45	
Russia						
Rwanda					63	
Saudi Arabia				66		
Serbia				60	58	–2
Singapore						
Slovakia						
Slovenia					37	
South Africa				64	50	–14
South Korea				54	56	2
Spain				60	62	2
Sweden				74	53	–21
Switzerland					54	
Taiwan					46	
Tanzania				69		
Thailand					9	
Trinidad					59	
Turkey					48	
Uganda				84		
Ukraine					58	
Uruguay					58	
USA				61	19	–42
Venezuela						
Vietnam				57	68	11
Zambia					52	
Zimbabwe				73		

Who should decide: refugees

(E053) For each one, would you tell me whether you think that policies in this area should be decided by the national governments, by the United Nations, or by the national governments with UN co-ordination?

United Nations (%)

Country	1981	1990	1995	2000	2006	Change
Albania				73		
Algeria				91		
Andorra					56	
Argentina				24	64	40
Armenia						
Australia				45		
Austria						
Azerbaijan						
Bangladesh				65		
Belarus						
Belgium						
Bosnia and Herz.				37		
Brazil					50	
Britain						
Bulgaria					51	
Burkina Faso					64	
Canada				38	36	−2
Chile				55	57	2
China				46	50	4
Colombia						
Croatia						
Cyprus					36	
Czech						
Denmark						
Dominican Rep.						
Egypt				78	45	−33
El Salvador						
Estonia						
Ethiopia					70	
Finland					38	
France						
Georgia					22	
Germany (East)					52	
Germany (West)					42	
Ghana					67	
Greece						
Guatemala					43	
Hong Kong						
Hungary						
Iceland						
India				32	21	−11
Indonesia				38	44	6
Iran				71	61	−10
Iraq						
Ireland						
Israel						
Italy					41	
Japan				72	60	−12
Jordan				67	65	−2

Country	1981	1990	1995	2000	2006	Change
Kyrgyzstan				68		
Latvia						
Lithuania						
Luxembourg						
Macedonia				59		
Malaysia					39	
Mali					51	
Malta						
Mexico				34	46	12
Moldova				53	27	−26
Montenegro				81		
Morocco				66	58	−8
Netherlands						
New Zealand						
Nigeria					44	
Northern Ireland				72		
Norway					70	
Pakistan						
Peru						
Philippines				27		
Poland					38	
Portugal						
Puerto Rico						
Romania					36	
Russia						
Rwanda					73	
Saudi Arabia				69		
Serbia				56	42	−14
Singapore						
Slovakia						
Slovenia					27	
South Africa				57	49	−8
South Korea				63	60	−3
Spain				45	63	18
Sweden				55	42	−13
Switzerland					50	
Taiwan					51	
Tanzania				77		
Thailand					29	
Trinidad					51	
Turkey					38	
Uganda				70		
Ukraine					45	
Uruguay					61	
USA				52	15	−37
Venezuela						
Vietnam				50	59	9
Zambia					66	
Zimbabwe				65		

Who should decide: human rights

(E054) For each one, would you tell me whether you think that policies in this area should be decided by the national governments, by the United Nations, or by the national governments with UN co-ordination?

United Nations (%)

Country	1981	1990	1995	2000	2006	Change
Albania				35		
Algeria				75		
Andorra					63	
Argentina				35	47	12
Armenia						
Australia					59	
Austria						
Azerbaijan						
Bangladesh				54		
Belarus						
Belgium						
Bosnia and Herz.				42		
Brazil					41	
Britain						
Bulgaria				33		
Burkina Faso					54	
Canada				37	41	4
Chile				25	35	10
China				18	32	14
Colombia						
Croatia						
Cyprus				37		
Czech						
Denmark						
Dominican Rep.						
Egypt				50	38	−12
El Salvador						
Estonia						
Ethiopia					63	
Finland				58		
France						
Georgia				11		
Germany (East)				60		
Germany (West)				56		
Ghana				22		
Greece						
Guatemala				34		
Hong Kong						
Hungary						
Iceland						
India				25	23	−2
Indonesia				14	38	24
Iran				71	78	7
Iraq						
Ireland						
Israel						
Italy					55	
Japan				56	55	−1
Jordan				41	57	16

Country	1981	1990	1995	2000	2006	Change
Kyrgyzstan				25		
Latvia						
Lithuania						
Luxembourg						
Macedonia				41		
Malaysia					34	
Mali					51	
Malta						
Mexico				34	45	11
Moldova				37	25	−12
Montenegro				43		
Morocco				18	51	33
Netherlands						
New Zealand						
Nigeria					44	
Northern Ireland				26		
Norway					74	
Pakistan						
Peru						
Philippines				18		
Poland					42	
Portugal						
Puerto Rico						
Romania					36	
Russia						
Rwanda					33	
Saudi Arabia				51		
Serbia				26	37	11
Singapore						
Slovakia						
Slovenia					22	
South Africa				23	21	−2
South Korea				25	42	17
Spain				55	65	10
Sweden				76	74	−2
Switzerland					65	
Taiwan					31	
Tanzania				46		
Thailand					26	
Trinidad					42	
Turkey					43	
Uganda				33		
Ukraine					22	
Uruguay					43	
USA				38	16	−22
Venezuela						
Vietnam				24	30	6
Zambia					28	
Zimbabwe				25		

Neighbours: Drug addicts

**(E055) On this list are various groups of people.
Could you please sort out any that you would not like to have as neighbors?**

Drug addicts (%)

Country	1981	1990	1995	2000	2006	Change
Albania			83	85		2
Algeria				77		
Andorra					57	
Argentina		50	39	32	55	5
Armenia			93			
Australia			74		98	24
Austria		59		53		−6
Azerbaijan			97			
Bangladesh				90	2	−88
Belarus		82	82	87		5
Belgium		53		51		−2
Bosnia and Herz.				68	83	15
Brazil		58	56		69	11
Britain		62		72	84	22
Bulgaria		69	66	72	80	11
Burkina Faso					89	
Canada		63		64	81	18
Chile		55	58	53	78	23
China			76	71	90	94	18
Colombia			30		79	49
Croatia			70	69		−1
Cyprus					78	
Czech			79	74	73	−6
Denmark		53		60		7
Dominican Rep.			71			
Egypt				1		
El Salvador			89			
Estonia		87	87	90		3
Ethiopia					85	
Finland		68	79	75	83	15
France		44		48	75	31
Georgia			81			
Germany (East)		62	56	52	67	5
Germany (West)		60	48	60	63	3
Ghana					80	
Greece				45		
Guatemala					55	
Hong Kong					10	
Hungary		84	74			−10
Iceland			74		76	2
India		93	66	44	54	−39
Indonesia				59	71	12
Iran				1		
Iraq						
Ireland			64		66	2
Israel						
Italy		60		55	65	5
Japan		91				
Jordan				99		

Country	1981	1990	1995	2000	2006	Change
Kyrgyzstan				81		
Latvia		89	88	75		−14
Lithuania		89	90	86		−3
Luxembourg				43		
Macedonia			79	73		−6
Malaysia					87	
Mali					76	
Malta		64		71		7
Mexico		69	52	68	77	8
Moldova			86	91	88	2
Montenegro				87	86	−1
Morocco				92		
Netherlands		72		73	87	15
New Zealand		59		78		19
Nigeria			79		81	2
Northern Ireland		77	90	74		−3
Norway		55	66			11
Pakistan				59		
Peru			73	66		−7
Philippines			86	82		−4
Poland		76	78	69	77	1
Portugal		60		48		−12
Puerto Rico			66	47		−19
Romania		76	61	74	76	0
Russia		86	88	84	94	8
Rwanda					62	
Saudi Arabia				87		
Serbia			84	70	92	8
Singapore				73		
Slovakia		76	77	79		3
Slovenia		47	75	65	68	21
South Africa			75	62		−13
South Korea		4	2	93	99	95
Spain		57	53	53		−4
Sweden		65	72	60	77	12
Switzerland		32	49			17
Taiwan			89		97	8
Tanzania				81		
Thailand						
Trinidad					92	
Turkey		92	92	94		2
Uganda				87		
Ukraine			88	88	90	2
Uruguay			44		50	6
USA		79	83	74	91	12
Venezuela			75	73		−2
Vietnam				54	43	−11
Zambia					83	
Zimbabwe				64		

Neighbours: People of a different race

(E056) On this list are various groups of people.
 Could you please sort out any that you would not like to have as neighbors?

People of a different race (%)

Country	1981	1990	1995	2000	2006	Change
Albania						
Algeria						
Andorra					3	
Argentina					2	
Armenia						
Australia					5	
Austria						
Azerbaijan						
Bangladesh						
Belarus						
Belgium						
Bosnia and Herz.						
Brazil					4	
Britain					5	
Bulgaria					20	
Burkina Faso					10	
Canada					3	
Chile					9	
China					16	
Colombia					4	
Croatia						
Cyprus					17	
Czech						
Denmark						
Dominican Rep.						
Egypt						
El Salvador						
Estonia						
Ethiopia					17	
Finland	6				12	
France					23	
Georgia					25	
Germany (East)					7	
Germany (West)					9	
Ghana					22	
Greece						
Guatemala					5	
Hong Kong					73	
Hungary						
Iceland						
India					44	
Indonesia					32	
Iran					31	
Iraq						
Ireland						
Israel						
Italy					12	
Japan						
Jordan					52	

Country	1981	1990	1995	2000	2006	Change
Kyrgyzstan						
Latvia						
Lithuania						
Luxembourg						
Macedonia						
Malaysia					21	
Mali					22	
Malta						
Mexico	7				8	
Moldova					24	
Montenegro						
Morocco					23	
Netherlands					8	
New Zealand						
Nigeria					4	
Northern Ireland						
Norway					3	
Pakistan						
Peru					6	
Philippines						
Poland					12	
Portugal						
Puerto Rico						
Romania					18	
Russia					17	
Rwanda					37	
Saudi Arabia						
Serbia					19	
Singapore						
Slovakia						
Slovenia					14	
South Africa	25				8	
South Korea					37	
Spain					7	
Sweden					1	
Switzerland					6	
Taiwan					8	
Tanzania						
Thailand					27	
Trinidad					2	
Turkey					30	
Uganda						
Ukraine					12	
Uruguay					4	
USA					3	
Venezuela						
Vietnam					35	
Zambia					29	
Zimbabwe						

Neighbours: People who have AIDS

(E057) On this list are various groups of people.
   Could you please sort out any that you would not like to have as neighbors?

People who have AIDS (%)

Country	1981	1990	1995	2000	2006	Change
Albania			63	70		7
Algeria				68		
Andorra					7	
Argentina		32	15	12	7	−25
Armenia			85			
Australia			15		17	2
Austria		32		17		−15
Azerbaijan			89			
Bangladesh			82	6		−76
Belarus			73	58	58	−15
Belgium		24		13		−11
Bosnia and Herz.				56	58	2
Brazil		23	14		15	−8
Britain		23	14	25	12	−11
Bulgaria		63	43	52	51	−12
Burkina Faso					29	
Canada		21		12	12	−9
Chile		41	21	24	23	−18
China		76	62	79	76	0
Colombia			8		32	24
Croatia			43	51		8
Cyprus				50		
Czech		53	23	21		−32
Denmark		9		6		−3
Dominican Rep.			29			
Egypt				2		
El Salvador			67			
Estonia		63	44	42		−21
Ethiopia				14		
Finland		24	23	21	19	−5
France		15		9	32	17
Georgia			71			
Germany (East)		22	7	10	13	−9
Germany (West)		29	6	11	20	−9
Ghana					47	
Greece				27		
Guatemala				26		
Hong Kong				44		
Hungary		66	39			−27
Iceland		18		7		−11
India		93	60	39	44	−49
Indonesia				52	57	5
Iran				0		
Iraq						
Ireland			35		23	−12
Israel						
Italy			44		31	33	−11
Japan			77			
Jordan		.		96		

Country	1981	1990	1995	2000	2006	Change
Kyrgyzstan				64		
Latvia		65	49	29		−36
Lithuania		78	66	55		−23
Luxembourg				12		
Macedonia			63	52		−11
Malaysia					70	
Mali					42	
Malta		47		38		−9
Mexico		57	31	34	21	−36
Moldova			73	66	69	−4
Montenegro				83	76	−7
Morocco				81		
Netherlands		16		8	10	−6
New Zealand		28		31		3
Nigeria			17		20	3
Northern Ireland		79	89	68		−11
Norway		25	14			−11
Pakistan				7		
Peru			39	29		−10
Philippines			74	62		−12
Poland		57	51	44	38	−19
Portugal		44		27		−17
Puerto Rico			17	12		−5
Romania		66	43	47	39	−27
Russia		68	56	52	58	−10
Rwanda					38	
Saudi Arabia				84		
Serbia			69	51	61	−8
Singapore				35		
Slovakia		62	44	45		−17
Slovenia		42	50	33	31	−11
South Africa				44	27	−17
South Korea		4	5	89	93	89
Spain		35	23	21		−14
Sweden		18	8	7	5	−13
Switzerland			12			
Taiwan			72		73	1
Tanzania				32		
Thailand						
Trinidad					20	
Turkey		89	81	83		−6
Uganda				17		
Ukraine			59	59	52	−7
Uruguay			19		11	−8
USA		28	19	17	15	−13
Venezuela				58	44	−14
Vietnam				33	45	12
Zambia					18	
Zimbabwe				30		

Neighbours: Immigrants/foreign workers

(E058) On this list are various groups of people.
   Could you please sort out any that you would not like to have as neighbors?

Immigrants/foreign workers (%)

Country	1981	1990	1995	2000	2006	Change
Albania						
Algeria						
Andorra					2	
Argentina					3	
Armenia						
Australia					6	
Austria						
Azerbaijan						
Bangladesh						
Belarus						
Belgium						
Bosnia and Herz.						
Brazil					7	
Britain					14	
Bulgaria					18	
Burkina Faso					11	
Canada					4	
Chile					10	
China					20	
Colombia						
Croatia						
Cyprus					22	
Czech						
Denmark						
Dominican Rep.						
Egypt						
El Salvador						
Estonia						
Ethiopia					15	
Finland	0				16	
France					37	
Georgia					25	
Germany (East)					15	
Germany (West)					13	
Ghana					26	
Greece						
Guatemala					4	
Hong Kong					79	
Hungary						
Iceland						
India					35	
Indonesia					36	
Iran					59	
Iraq						
Ireland						
Israel						
Italy					15	
Japan						
Jordan					66	

Country	1981	1990	1995	2000	2006	Change
Kyrgyzstan						
Latvia						
Lithuania						
Luxembourg						
Macedonia						
Malaysia					57	
Mali					25	
Malta						
Mexico					10	
Moldova					19	
Montenegro						
Morocco					24	
Netherlands					9	
New Zealand						
Nigeria					7	
Northern Ireland						
Norway					5	
Pakistan						
Peru					6	
Philippines						
Poland					14	
Portugal						
Puerto Rico						
Romania					17	
Russia					32	
Rwanda					36	
Saudi Arabia						
Serbia					26	
Singapore						
Slovakia						
Slovenia					18	
South Africa	7				25	
South Korea					39	
Spain					7	
Sweden					2	
Switzerland					7	
Taiwan					24	
Tanzania						
Thailand					43	
Trinidad					5	
Turkey					31	
Uganda						
Ukraine					19	
Uruguay					5	
USA					12	
Venezuela						
Vietnam					37	
Zambia					28	
Zimbabwe						

Neighbours: Homosexuals

**(E059) On this list are various groups of people.
Could you please sort out any that you would not like to have as neighbors?**

Homosexuals (%)

Country	1981	1990	1995	2000	2006	Change
Albania			70	83		13
Algeria				81		
Andorra					6	
Argentina		39	27	22	16	−23
Armenia			83			
Australia			25		22	−3
Austria		43		25		−18
Azerbaijan			91			
Bangladesh			84	5		−79
Belarus		79	63	63		−16
Belgium		24		17		−7
Bosnia and Herz.			61	61		0
Brazil		30	26		22	−8
Britain		31	22	24	17	−14
Bulgaria		68	41	54	50	−18
Burkina Faso					81	
Canada		30		17	14	−16
Chile		57	41	33	35	−22
China		72	61	73	71	−1
Colombia			15		46	31
Croatia			45	53		8
Cyprus					51	
Czech		51	24	20		−31
Denmark		12		8		−4
Dominican Rep.			49			
Egypt				0		
El Salvador			78			
Estonia		73	64	46		−27
Ethiopia				82		
Finland		25	30	21	22	−3
France		24		16	29	5
Georgia			77			
Germany (East)		36	16	13	17	−19
Germany (West)		34	10	13	13	−21
Ghana					79	
Greece				27		
Guatemala					16	
Hong Kong					49	
Hungary		75	53			−22
Iceland		20		8		−12
India		91	61	29	41	−50
Indonesia				55	67	12
Iran				1		
Iraq						
Ireland		33		27		−6
Israel						
Italy		39		29	24	−15
Japan		69				
Jordan				98		

Country	1981	1990	1995	2000	2006	Change
Kyrgyzstan				66		
Latvia		78	59	46		−32
Lithuania		87	77	68		−19
Luxembourg				19		
Macedonia			66	53		−13
Malaysia					71	
Mali					66	
Malta		44		40		−4
Mexico		60	37	45	30	−30
Moldova			77	77	71	−6
Montenegro			82	74		−8
Morocco				93		
Netherlands		12		6	4	−8
New Zealand		48		35		−13
Nigeria			22		17	−5
Northern Ireland		76	90	74		−2
Norway		19	14			−5
Pakistan						
Peru			54	49		−5
Philippines			33	24		−9
Poland		70	66	55	51	−19
Portugal		50		25		−25
Puerto Rico			32	22		−10
Romania		75	56	65	61	−14
Russia		81	71	58	66	−15
Rwanda					63	
Saudi Arabia						
Serbia			74	49	72	−2
Singapore				46		
Slovakia		64	46	44		−20
Slovenia		43	61	44	35	−8
South Africa			50	46		−4
South Korea		4		82	87	83
Spain		30	20	16		−14
Sweden		18	11	6	4	−14
Switzerland			19			
Taiwan			73		55	−18
Tanzania				74		
Thailand						
Trinidad					66	
Turkey		92	90	90		−2
Uganda					76	
Ukraine			65	66	59	−6
Uruguay			32		16	−16
USA		39	29	23	25	−14
Venezuela			68	57		−11
Vietnam				39	29	−10
Zambia					73	
Zimbabwe				67		

Neighbours: People of a different religion

(E060) On this list are various groups of people.
Could you please sort out any that you would not like to have as neighbors?

People of a different religion (%)

Country	1981	1990	1995	2000	2006	Change
Albania			25			
Algeria				32		
Andorra					2	
Argentina				1		
Armenia						
Australia					3	
Austria						
Azerbaijan						
Bangladesh			13	66		53
Belarus						
Belgium						
Bosnia and Herz.			18			
Brazil			13		6	−7
Britain					2	
Bulgaria			17		15	−2
Burkina Faso					12	
Canada					2	
Chile					6	
China					16	
Colombia					8	
Croatia			14			
Cyprus				17		
Czech						
Denmark						
Dominican Rep.						
Egypt						
El Salvador			11			
Estonia			23			
Ethiopia				15		
Finland				10		
France				26		
Georgia			27			
Germany (East)			16		3	−13
Germany (West)			9		6	−3
Ghana				24		
Greece						
Guatemala						
Hong Kong						
Hungary						
Iceland						
India				40	44	4
Indonesia				38	34	−4
Iran				20		
Iraq				35	36	1
Ireland						
Israel						
Italy					11	
Japan						
Jordan				32		

Country	1981	1990	1995	2000	2006	Change
Kyrgyzstan						
Latvia			25			
Lithuania						
Luxembourg						
Macedonia						
Malaysia					22	
Mali					24	
Malta						
Mexico					14	
Moldova				16	26	10
Montenegro						
Morocco				34		
Netherlands					3	
New Zealand						
Nigeria						
Northern Ireland				29		
Norway						
Pakistan				8		
Peru						
Philippines						
Poland					11	
Portugal						
Puerto Rico						
Romania				30	15	−15
Russia					16	
Rwanda					36	
Saudi Arabia				40		
Serbia					15	
Singapore						
Slovakia						
Slovenia				23	13	−10
South Africa						
South Korea					26	
Spain						
Sweden					1	
Switzerland						
Taiwan					5	
Tanzania						
Thailand						
Trinidad					2	
Turkey				35		
Uganda						
Ukraine					13	
Uruguay					6	
USA					3	
Venezuela				17		
Vietnam					34	
Zambia					26	
Zimbabwe						

Neighbours: Heavy drinkers

**(E061) On this list are various groups of people.
Could you please sort out any that you would not like to have as neighbors?**

Heavy drinkers (%)

Country	1981	1990	1995	2000	2006	Change
Albania			83	81		−2
Algeria				69		
Andorra					54	
Argentina	38	45	44	37	36	−2
Armenia			86			
Australia	56		60		78	22
Austria		58		53		−5
Azerbaijan			85			
Bangladesh			90	4		−86
Belarus		82	74	83		1
Belgium	39	50		44		5
Bosnia and Herz.			69	77		8
Brazil		41	46		51	10
Britain	48	48	67	51	61	13
Bulgaria		73	42	76	65	−8
Burkina Faso					66	
Canada	58	54		51	60	2
Chile		52	54	51	60	8
China		58	65	74	73	15
Colombia			33		51	18
Croatia			64	63		−1
Cyprus				58		
Czech		79	67	75		−4
Denmark	29	34		36		7
Dominican Rep.			55			
Egypt				1		
El Salvador			90			
Estonia		90	86	84		−6
Ethiopia				58		
Finland		54	55	51	69	15
France	47	50		47	72	25
Georgia			70			
Germany (East)		72	48	53	73	1
Germany (West)	67	64	33	57	62	−5
Ghana					70	
Greece			37			
Guatemala				45		
Hong Kong				16		
Hungary	79	81	70			−9
Iceland	52	61		62		10
India		91	58	45	49	−42
Indonesia				58	69	11
Iran				1		
Iraq						
Ireland	33	34		36		3
Israel						
Italy	44	51		40	54	10
Japan	53	58				5
Jordan				94		

Country	1981	1990	1995	2000	2006	Change
Kyrgyzstan				71		
Latvia		85	86	75		−10
Lithuania		92	86	82		−10
Luxembourg				32		
Macedonia			70	64		−6
Malaysia					73	
Mali					65	
Malta	61	61		74		13
Mexico		56	42	56	50	−6
Moldova			78	85	81	3
Montenegro			73	63		−10
Morocco				86		
Netherlands	51	59		58	75	24
New Zealand	40	43		51		11
Nigeria			66		64	−2
Northern Ireland		72	79	65		−7
Norway	33	32	32			−1
Pakistan				1		
Peru			53	51		−2
Philippines			68	56		−12
Poland		85	79	78	72	−13
Portugal		51		38		−13
Puerto Rico			58	41		−17
Romania		79	58	77	69	−10
Russia		82	80	73	89	7
Rwanda				55		
Saudi Arabia						
Serbia			72	56	73	1
Singapore				64		
Slovakia		75	68	80		5
Slovenia		45	79	69	63	18
South Africa			61	50		−11
South Korea	56	17	16	76	76	20
Spain	38	40	40	39		1
Sweden	44	45	37	33	54	10
Switzerland		23	47			24
Taiwan			81		87	6
Tanzania				79		
Thailand						
Trinidad					63	
Turkey		87	89	87		0
Uganda				70		
Ukraine			77	79	82	5
Uruguay			59		50	−9
USA	56	59	63	56	70	14
Venezuela			55	57		2
Vietnam				44	33	−11
Zambia					65	
Zimbabwe				56		

Neighbours: Militant minority

(E062) On this list are various groups of people.
Could you please sort out any that you would not like to have as neighbors?

Militant minority (%)

Country	1981	1990	1995	2000	2006	Change
Albania						
Algeria						
Andorra					0	
Argentina						
Armenia						
Australia						
Austria						
Azerbaijan						
Bangladesh						
Belarus						
Belgium						
Bosnia and Herz.						
Brazil						
Britain						
Bulgaria						
Burkina Faso						
Canada						
Chile						
China					2	
Colombia						
Croatia						
Cyprus					24	
Czech						
Denmark						
Dominican Rep.						
Egypt						
El Salvador						
Estonia						
Ethiopia						
Finland						
France						
Georgia						
Germany (East)						
Germany (West)						
Ghana						
Greece						
Guatemala						
Hong Kong						
Hungary						
Iceland						
India					40	
Indonesia				48	39	−9
Iran						
Iraq						
Ireland						
Israel						
Italy						
Japan						
Jordan						

Country	1981	1990	1995	2000	2006	Change
Kyrgyzstan						
Latvia						
Lithuania						
Luxembourg						
Macedonia						
Malaysia					22	
Mali						
Malta						
Mexico					17	
Moldova						
Montenegro						
Morocco						
Netherlands						
New Zealand						
Nigeria						
Northern Ireland						
Norway						
Pakistan						
Peru						
Philippines						
Poland						
Portugal						
Puerto Rico						
Romania						
Russia						
Rwanda						
Saudi Arabia						
Serbia						
Singapore						
Slovakia						
Slovenia						
South Africa						
South Korea					88	
Spain						
Sweden						
Switzerland						
Taiwan						
Tanzania						
Thailand						
Trinidad					2	
Turkey						
Uganda						
Ukraine						
Uruguay						
USA					14	
Venezuela						
Vietnam					40	
Zambia						
Zimbabwe						

Neighbours: People with a criminal record

(E063) On this list are various groups of people.
Could you please sort out any that you would not like to have as neighbors?

People with a criminal record (%)

Country	1981	1990	1995	2000	2006	Change
Albania			94	97		3
Algeria				70		
Andorra						
Argentina	35	41	45	43		8
Armenia			78			
Australia	42		45			3
Austria		31		27		−4
Azerbaijan			69			
Bangladesh			87	4		−83
Belarus		72	67	72		0
Belgium	22	28		30		8
Bosnia and Herz.			80	89		9
Brazil		52	45			−7
Britain	39	41		48		9
Bulgaria		70	70	75		5
Burkina Faso						
Canada	37	42		45		8
Chile		46	50	63		17
China		41	62	71		30
Colombia			64			
Croatia			42	74		32
Cyprus						
Czech		70	71	64		−6
Denmark	17	28		31		14
Dominican Rep.			62			
Egypt				3		
El Salvador			78			
Estonia		63	74	69		6
Ethiopia						
Finland		34	42	39		5
France	11	19		21		10
Georgia			50			
Germany (East)		36	28	22		−14
Germany (West)	28	28	20	26		−2
Ghana						
Greece				67		
Guatemala					83	
Hong Kong					43	
Hungary	74	77	63			−11
Iceland	12	24		26		14
India		93	67	48		−45
Indonesia				55		
Iran				1		
Iraq				84	98	14
Ireland	44	52		56		12
Israel						
Italy	39	48		47		8
Japan	41	50				9
Jordan				96		

Country	1981	1990	1995	2000	2006	Change
Kyrgyzstan				68		
Latvia		63	70	57		−6
Lithuania		69	78	66		−3
Luxembourg				29		
Macedonia			78	76		−2
Malaysia						
Mali						
Malta	76	78		80		4
Mexico		69	57	70		1
Moldova			81	83		2
Montenegro			47	29		−18
Morocco				64		
Netherlands	17	29		32		15
New Zealand	39	46		47		8
Nigeria			57		53	−4
Northern Ireland		80	93	79		−1
Norway	35	37	44			9
Pakistan				58		
Peru			64	53		−11
Philippines			82	72		−10
Poland		75	78	68		−7
Portugal		59		44		−15
Puerto Rico			63	36		−27
Romania		67	66	69		2
Russia		63	64	58		−5
Rwanda						
Saudi Arabia				88		
Serbia			50	29		−21
Singapore				30		
Slovakia		74	78	82		8
Slovenia		38	55	40		2
South Africa			68	54		−14
South Korea	50	31	18	81		31
Spain	35	37	37	32		−3
Sweden	27	35	35	33		6
Switzerland		6	20			14
Taiwan			51			
Tanzania				89		
Thailand						
Trinidad						
Turkey		81	74	80		−1
Uganda				88		
Ukraine			72	72		0
Uruguay				70		
USA	48	50	61	54		6
Venezuela			68	77		9
Vietnam				48		
Zambia						
Zimbabwe				75		

234

Neighbours: Emotionally unstable people

(E064) On this list are various groups of people.
Could you please sort out any that you would not like to have as neighbors?

Emotionally unstable people (%)

Country	1981	1990	1995	2000	2006	Change
Albania			58	61		3
Algeria				44		
Andorra						
Argentina	26	21	28	22		-4
Armenia			75			
Australia	39		39			0
Austria		20		18		-2
Azerbaijan			75			
Bangladesh			66	28		-38
Belarus		63	53	60		-3
Belgium	15	21		22		7
Bosnia and Herz.			55	57		2
Brazil		16	18			2
Britain	30	28		39		9
Bulgaria		53	41	44		-9
Burkina Faso						
Canada	28	30		33		5
Chile		28	31	25		-3
China		46	56	64		18
Colombia			17			
Croatia			37	41		4
Cyprus						
Czech		29	22	19		-10
Denmark	9	11		14		5
Dominican Rep.			52			
Egypt				28		
El Salvador			81			
Estonia		37	59	54		17
Ethiopia						
Finland		24	33	29		5
France	9	17		22		13
Georgia			55			
Germany (East)		21	22	22		1
Germany (West)	28	31	27	22		-6
Ghana						
Greece				62		
Guatemala					23	
Hong Kong					18	
Hungary	66	23	55			-11
Iceland	23	32		31		8
India		69	45	39		-30
Indonesia				49		
Iran				1		
Iraq						
Ireland	23	30		25		2
Israel						
Italy	29	34		38		9
Japan	54	62				8
Jordan				66		

Country	1981	1990	1995	2000	2006	Change
Kyrgyzstan				50		
Latvia		54	62	35		-19
Lithuania		48	57	61		13
Luxembourg				19		
Macedonia			58	47		-11
Malaysia						
Mali						
Malta	32	34		30		-2
Mexico		38	37	34		-4
Moldova			57	68		11
Montenegro			79	77		-2
Morocco				69		
Netherlands	19	20		25		6
New Zealand	29	23		35		6
Nigeria			60		51	-9
Northern Ireland		57	60	52		-5
Norway	19	22	37			18
Pakistan				40		
Peru			32	38		6
Philippines			28	25		-3
Poland		49	55	58		9
Portugal		47		27		-20
Puerto Rico			42	33		-9
Romania		64	43	53		-11
Russia		51	56	54		3
Rwanda						
Saudi Arabia				63		
Serbia			71	57		-14
Singapore				58		
Slovakia		31	27	22		-9
Slovenia		37	49	30		-7
South Africa			37	39		2
South Korea	36	17	9	89		53
Spain	22	25	25	25		3
Sweden	12	17	24	17		5
Switzerland		4	17			13
Taiwan			73			
Tanzania				5		
Thailand						
Trinidad						
Turkey		72	76	76		4
Uganda				46		
Ukraine			59	63		4
Uruguay			33			
USA	44	43	51	52		8
Venezuela			46	46		0
Vietnam				38		
Zambia						
Zimbabwe				42		

Neighbours: Muslims

(E065) On this list are various groups of people.
Could you please sort out any that you would not like to have as neighbors?

Muslims (%)

Country	1981	1990	1995	2000	2006	Change
Albania				30		
Algeria						
Andorra						
Argentina		6		6		0
Armenia						
Australia						
Austria		15		15		0
Azerbaijan						
Bangladesh						
Belarus			24	27		3
Belgium		26		22		−4
Bosnia and Herz.				8		
Brazil						
Britain		17		14		−3
Bulgaria		41		21	20	−21
Burkina Faso						
Canada		10		7	11	1
Chile		12		7		−5
China		12				
Colombia						
Croatia				26		
Cyprus						
Czech		30		15		−15
Denmark		15		16		1
Dominican Rep.						
Egypt						
El Salvador						
Estonia			21	22		1
Ethiopia						
Finland		10	40	19		9
France		17		16		−1
Georgia						
Germany (East)		22		15	30	8
Germany (West)		20		10	23	3
Ghana						
Greece				21		
Guatemala					6	
Hong Kong						
Hungary		18				
Iceland		12		12		0
India		28	33			5
Indonesia						
Iran						
Iraq						
Ireland		13		14		1
Israel						
Italy		15		17		2
Japan		29				
Jordan						

Country	1981	1990	1995	2000	2006	Change
Kyrgyzstan				15		
Latvia		26		15		−11
Lithuania		34		33		−1
Luxembourg				14		
Macedonia				26		
Malaysia						
Mali						
Malta		12		28		16
Mexico		19		17		−2
Moldova				44		
Montenegro				20		
Morocco						
Netherlands		15		12		−3
New Zealand		15		16		1
Nigeria						
Northern Ireland		24		17		−7
Norway		21		19		−2
Pakistan						
Peru				14		
Philippines			29	26		−3
Poland		20		24		4
Portugal		18		8		−10
Puerto Rico						
Romania		34		31		−3
Russia		15		14		−1
Rwanda						
Saudi Arabia						
Serbia				14		
Singapore						
Slovakia		34		25		−9
Slovenia		38		23		−15
South Africa				24		
South Korea	26	21		57		31
Spain		12	12	13		1
Sweden		17	13	9	8	−9
Switzerland				18		
Taiwan				19		
Tanzania				13		
Thailand						
Trinidad						
Turkey		55				
Uganda				14		
Ukraine				24		
Uruguay						
USA		14	12	11		−3
Venezuela						
Vietnam				27		
Zambia						
Zimbabwe				18		

Neighbours: Jews

(E066) On this list are various groups of people.
    Could you please sort out any that you would not like to have as neighbors?
Jews (%)

Country	1981	1990	1995	2000	2006	Change
Albania				17		
Algeria						
Andorra						
Argentina		5	7	6		1
Armenia						
Australia						
Austria		11		8		-3
Azerbaijan						
Bangladesh				20		
Belarus			7	15		8
Belgium		13		13		0
Bosnia and Herz.				24		
Brazil						
Britain		7		6		-1
Bulgaria		30		18		-12
Burkina Faso						
Canada		6		4		-2
Chile		15	14	9		-6
China						
Colombia						
Croatia				18		
Cyprus						
Czech		14		4		-10
Denmark		3		2		-1
Dominican Rep.						
Egypt				17		
El Salvador						
Estonia		13		11		-2
Ethiopia						
Finland		5		9		4
France		7		6		-1
Georgia						
Germany (East)		9		8		-1
Germany (West)		7		4		-3
Ghana						
Greece				19		
Guatemala						
Hong Kong						
Hungary		10				
Iceland		7		4		-3
India		53				
Indonesia						
Iran						
Iraq				83	96	13
Ireland		6		11		5
Israel						
Italy		13		13		0
Japan		28				
Jordan						

Country	1981	1990	1995	2000	2006	Change
Kyrgyzstan				20		
Latvia		9		5		-4
Lithuania		18		23		5
Luxembourg				8		
Macedonia				20		
Malaysia						
Mali						
Malta		8		21		13
Mexico		19	31			12
Moldova				25		
Montenegro						
Morocco						
Netherlands		4		2		-2
New Zealand		6		12		6
Nigeria						
Northern Ireland		35				
Norway		9				
Pakistan						
Peru						
Philippines						
Poland		18		25		7
Portugal		19		11		-8
Puerto Rico						
Romania		28		23		-5
Russia		13	10	11		-2
Rwanda						
Saudi Arabia						
Serbia						
Singapore						
Slovakia		28		10		-18
Slovenia		38		17		-21
South Africa				24		
South Korea				41		
Spain		10		22		12
Sweden		6		2		-4
Switzerland						
Taiwan						
Tanzania						
Thailand						
Trinidad						
Turkey				62		
Uganda				22		
Ukraine				10		
Uruguay			10		5	-5
USA	5			9		4
Venezuela				26		
Vietnam						
Zambia						
Zimbabwe				19		

Postmaterialism
(E067) Materialist/Postmaterialist 4-item Index
Postmaterialist (%)

Country	1981	1990	1995	2000	2006	Change
Albania			5	8		3
Algeria				21		
Andorra					32	
Argentina		29	29	25	24	−5
Armenia			16			
Australia			29		23	−6
Austria		28				
Azerbaijan			12			
Bangladesh			22	21		−1
Belarus		23	19			−4
Belgium		29				
Bosnia and Herz.			10	14		4
Brazil		29	30		25	−4
Britain		29			33	4
Bulgaria		33	13		15	−18
Burkina Faso					22	
Canada		32		34	33	1
Chile		31	31	29	29	−2
China		10	8	7	10	0
Colombia						
Croatia			30			
Cyprus					24	
Czech		24	17			−7
Denmark		30				
Dominican Rep.			31			
Egypt				16	11	−5
El Salvador						
Estonia		25	24			−1
Ethiopia					25	
Finland		39	31		32	−7
France		31			27	−4
Georgia			12		10	−2
Germany (East)		26	26		34	8
Germany (West)		32	25		38	6
Ghana					18	
Greece						
Guatemala					20	
Hong Kong						
Hungary		17	10			−7
Iceland		36				
India		22	12	18	21	−1
Indonesia				15	18	3
Iran				28	21	−7
Iraq						
Ireland		28				
Israel				22		
Italy		25			29	4
Japan			34	30	34	27	−7
Jordan					14	13	−1

Country	1981	1990	1995	2000	2006	Change
Kyrgyzstan				19		
Latvia		24	23			−1
Lithuania		23	14			−9
Luxembourg						
Macedonia			13	10		−3
Malaysia					26	
Mali					18	
Malta		20				
Mexico		38	29	28	29	−9
Moldova			14	16	18	4
Montenegro			15	15		0
Morocco				21	20	−1
Netherlands	31				34	3
New Zealand			28		25	−3
Nigeria		25	26	22		−3
Northern Ireland		30				
Norway		30	36		34	4
Pakistan			13	9		−4
Peru			29	35	28	−1
Philippines			28	24		−4
Poland		29	18		25	−4
Portugal		28				
Puerto Rico			23	31		8
Romania			23		16	−7
Russia		20	12		11	−9
Rwanda					23	
Saudi Arabia				31		
Serbia			15	15	16	1
Singapore				24		
Slovakia		26	16			−10
Slovenia		37	33		31	−6
South Africa		27	17	16	18	−9
South Korea		22	22	22	22	0
Spain		29	31	30	25	−4
Sweden		30	27	31	31	1
Switzerland		29	33		30	1
Taiwan			13		9	−4
Tanzania				22		
Thailand					26	
Trinidad					21	
Turkey		24	25	26	20	−4
Uganda				19		
Ukraine			15		21	6
Uruguay			34		32	−2
USA		24	24	27	21	−3
Venezuela			24	22		−2
Vietnam				25	21	−4
Zambia					25	
Zimbabwe				19		

Thinking about meaning and purpose of life
(F001) How often, if at all, do you think about the meaning and purpose of life?
Often (%)

Country	1981	1990	1995	2000	2006	Change
Albania			42	53		11
Algeria				50		
Andorra					36	
Argentina	29	57	51	51	36	7
Armenia			60			
Australia	34		45		42	8
Austria		28		35		7
Azerbaijan			42			
Bangladesh			41	47		6
Belarus		35	47	36		1
Belgium	22	29				7
Bosnia and Herz.			34	42		8
Brazil		43	37		61	18
Britain	33	36		25	37	4
Bulgaria		44	33	49	33	-11
Burkina Faso					59	
Canada	37	44		52	47	10
Chile		53	50	51	37	-16
China		31	26	32	25	-6
Colombia			70		62	-8
Croatia			26	40		14
Cyprus					41	
Czech		30	26			-4
Denmark	29	29		37		8
Dominican Rep.			56			
Egypt				52	55	3
El Salvador			53			
Estonia		35	39	40		5
Ethiopia					75	
Finland	32	38	40	40	41	9
France	36	39			44	8
Georgia			73		74	1
Germany (East)		40	46	24	35	-5
Germany (West)	27	30	41	20	24	-3
Ghana					54	
Greece						
Guatemala					63	
Hong Kong					14	
Hungary	44	45	45			1
Iceland	37	36				-1
India		34	25	36	29	-5
Indonesia				58	57	-1
Iran				46	49	3
Iraq				50	47	-3
Ireland	26	34				8
Israel						
Italy	37	48		50	47	10
Japan	21	21	25	26	24	3
Jordan				59	67	8

Country	1981	1990	1995	2000	2006	Change
Kyrgyzstan				72		
Latvia		36	43			7
Lithuania		41	41	40		-1
Luxembourg				36		
Macedonia			51	50		-1
Malaysia					24	
Mali					58	
Malta	31	23				-8
Mexico	30	40	35	47	54	24
Moldova			49	57	60	11
Montenegro			39	37		-2
Morocco				74	65	-9
Netherlands	23	31			34	11
New Zealand			44		41	-3
Nigeria		59	51	56		-3
Northern Ireland	28	33				5
Norway	26	31	32		30	4
Pakistan			35			
Peru			41	54	37	-4
Philippines			43	62		19
Poland		38			33	-5
Portugal		46				
Puerto Rico			68	76		8
Romania		45	53		52	7
Russia		41	45	49	40	-1
Rwanda					87	
Saudi Arabia				26		
Serbia			43	39	33	-10
Singapore				39		
Slovakia		34	28			-6
Slovenia		37	33		31	-6
South Africa	38	58	51	54	54	16
South Korea	29	39		41	41	12
Spain	24	27	24	22	16	-8
Sweden	20	24	28	37	31	11
Switzerland		45	45		45	0
Taiwan			28		29	1
Tanzania				84		
Thailand					45	
Trinidad					81	
Turkey		38	49		49	11
Uganda				59		
Ukraine			43	52	37	-6
Uruguay			43		36	-7
USA	49	49	46	58	51	2
Venezuela			51	66		15
Vietnam				58	58	0
Zambia					43	
Zimbabwe				70		

How often do you attend religious services

(F002) Apart from weddings, funerals and christenings, about how often do you attend religious services these days?

Once a week or more (%)

Country	1981	1990	1995	2000	2006	Change
Albania			18	20		2
Algeria				47		
Andorra					6	
Argentina	31	32	25	24	20	−11
Armenia			7			
Australia	28		17		14	−14
Austria		26		23		−3
Azerbaijan			6			
Bangladesh			89	56		−33
Belarus		3	6	6		3
Belgium	30	27		19		−11
Bosnia and Herz.			37	33		−4
Brazil		34	36		49	15
Britain	13	14		14	16	3
Bulgaria		6	7	10	6	0
Burkina Faso					73	
Canada	31	27		28	25	−6
Chile		28	25	31	25	−3
China		1		2	16	15
Colombia			46		46	0
Croatia			22	31		9
Cyprus				16		
Czech		8	9	8		0
Denmark	3	3		3		0
Dominican Rep.			44			
Egypt				42	47	5
El Salvador			58			
Estonia			4	4		0
Ethiopia					77	
Finland	3	4	4	5	6	3
France	11	10		8	7	−4
Georgia			9		18	9
Germany (East)		13	5	6	4	−9
Germany (West)	18	18	14	16	13	−5
Ghana					83	
Greece				14		
Guatemala					70	
Hong Kong					8	
Hungary	23	14	11	11		−12
Iceland	2	2		3		1
India			55	42	32	44	−11
Indonesia				65	66	1
Iran				27	36	9
Iraq				33	33	0
Ireland	82	81		65		−17
Israel						
Italy	32	38		40	32	0
Japan	4	3	3	4	3	−1
Jordan				44	93	49

Country	1981	1990	1995	2000	2006	Change
Kyrgyzstan				19		
Latvia		3	5	7		4
Lithuania			16	15		−1
Luxembourg				20		
Macedonia			11	22		11
Malaysia						
Mali					69	
Malta	92	88		83		−9
Mexico	54	43	46	55	46	−8
Moldova			11	15	13	2
Montenegro			7	6		−1
Morocco				44		
Netherlands	25	20		14	12	−13
New Zealand			17		15	−2
Nigeria		84	89	92		8
Northern Ireland	52	50		46		−6
Norway	6	5	5		4	−2
Pakistan				74		
Peru			43	47	41	−2
Philippines			70	60		−10
Poland		66	56	59	57	−9
Portugal		39		37		−2
Puerto Rico			52	57		5
Romania		19	22	25	27	8
Russia		2	2	3	4	2
Rwanda					94	
Saudi Arabia				29		
Serbia			6	10	11	5
Singapore				42		
Slovakia		32	35	40		8
Slovenia		23	22	17	19	−4
South Africa	43		56	57	54	11
South Korea	31	21	15	30	31	0
Spain	40	29	25	26	16	−24
Sweden	6	4	4	4	3	−3
Switzerland		24	16		13	−11
Taiwan			7		6	−1
Tanzania				85		
Thailand				42		
Trinidad				45		
Turkey		35	42	36	34	−1
Uganda				79		
Ukraine			10	10	9	−1
Uruguay			13		27	14
USA	43	44	44	46	44	1
Venezuela			31	31		0
Vietnam				4	8	4
Zambia					72	
Zimbabwe				73		

Religious person

(F003) Independently of whether you go to church or not, would you say you are…

A religious person (%)

Country	1981	1990	1995	2000	2006	Change
Albania			45	68		23
Algeria				59		
Andorra					48	
Argentina	67	73	82	84	80	13
Armenia			75			
Australia	58		59		52	–6
Austria		81		81		0
Azerbaijan			88			
Bangladesh			84	97		13
Belarus		41		70	28	–13
Belgium	81	69		65		–16
Bosnia and Herz.			70	76		6
Brazil		88	85		88	0
Britain	55	57		41	49	–6
Bulgaria		36	53	52	63	27
Burkina Faso					92	
Canada	76	71		77	70	–6
Chile		77	75	71	63	–14
China		5		15	22	17
Colombia			85		80	–5
Croatia			71	84		13
Cyprus				61		
Czech		40	43	45		5
Denmark	69	73		77		8
Dominican Rep.			76			
Egypt				99	93	–6
El Salvador			70			
Estonia		21	36	41		20
Ethiopia				81		
Finland	51	59	57	64	60	9
France	53	51		46	47	–6
Georgia			89		97	8
Germany (East)		38	28	29	29	–9
Germany (West)	65	65	65	62	61	–4
Ghana					92	
Greece				80		
Guatemala				72		
Hong Kong				27		
Hungary	43	57	55	57		14
Iceland	66	75		74		8
India		83	80	79	78	–5
Indonesia				85	85	0
Iran				95	84	–11
Iraq				87	55	–32
Ireland	66	72		76		10
Israel						
Italy	84	84		86	88	4
Japan	28	26	24	26	24	–4
Jordan				86	91	5

Country	1981	1990	1995	2000	2006	Change
Kyrgyzstan				75		
Latvia		54	64	77		23
Lithuania		55	84	84		29
Luxembourg				62		
Macedonia			66	84		18
Malaysia					89	
Mali					98	
Malta	96	75		75		–21
Mexico	74	75	62	77	75	1
Moldova			82	91	84	2
Montenegro			49	73		24
Morocco				95	92	–3
Netherlands	69	61		61	58	–11
New Zealand			52		50	–2
Nigeria		93	94	97		4
Northern Ireland	61	72		61		0
Norway	48	48	47		41	–7
Pakistan				91		
Peru			82	88	82	0
Philippines				84	79	–5
Poland		96	94	94	94	–2
Portugal		75		88		13
Puerto Rico			86	83		–3
Romania		74	84	85	93	19
Russia		56	64	67	73	17
Rwanda					94	
Saudi Arabia				70		
Serbia			60	74	85	25
Singapore						
Slovakia		74	78	82		8
Slovenia		73	69	70	73	0
South Africa	69	85	83	85	83	14
South Korea				31	32	1
Spain	64	67	69	62	45	–19
Sweden	34	31	33	39	33	–1
Switzerland		73	59		63	–10
Taiwan			75		41	–34
Tanzania				94		
Thailand				35		
Trinidad				85		
Turkey		75	75	79	82	7
Uganda				94		
Ukraine			64	77	82	18
Uruguay			55		56	1
USA	83	84	82	83	78	–5
Venezuela			86	79		–7
Vietnam				38	39	1
Zambia				90		
Zimbabwe			89			

Churches give answers: moral problems

(F004) Generally speaking, do you think that the churches in your country are giving adequate answers to...
   The moral problems and needs of the individual

Yes (%)

Country	1981	1990	1995	2000	2006	Change
Albania				64		
Algeria				91		
Andorra					19	
Argentina		42		53	39	−3
Armenia						
Australia				36		
Austria		47		38		−9
Azerbaijan						
Bangladesh				62		
Belarus				56		
Belgium	48	42		36		−12
Bosnia and Herz.				54		
Brazil		44			62	18
Britain	37	36		32		−5
Bulgaria		49		45	37	−12
Burkina Faso					62	
Canada	63	54		52	46	−17
Chile		77		64	50	−27
China						
Colombia				66		
Croatia				56		
Cyprus				40		
Czech		67		37		−30
Denmark	22	20		20		−2
Dominican Rep.						
Egypt				92	70	−22
El Salvador						
Estonia			45			
Ethiopia				79		
Finland		25		42	48	23
France	45	38		35		−10
Georgia				87		
Germany (East)		58		35	37	−21
Germany (West)	41	40		54	49	8
Ghana				78		
Greece				43		
Guatemala				85		
Hong Kong						
Hungary		78		45		−33
Iceland	38	37		40		2
India		38		33	41	3
Indonesia				80	79	−1
Iran				79	64	−15
Iraq				76	77	1
Ireland	55	42		32		−23
Israel						
Italy	48	52		62	64	16
Japan		28		20	24	−4
Jordan				66	70	4

Country	1981	1990	1995	2000	2006	Change
Kyrgyzstan				61		
Latvia		88		58		−30
Lithuania				81		
Luxembourg				33		
Macedonia				47		
Malaysia					77	
Mali					80	
Malta	84	86		67		−17
Mexico			65	72	57	−8
Moldova				73	72	−1
Montenegro				52		
Morocco				96	92	−4
Netherlands	38	36		35		−3
New Zealand						
Nigeria			86	79		−7
Northern Ireland	55	55		47		−8
Norway	47	41			29	−18
Pakistan				62		
Peru				68	58	−10
Philippines				64		
Poland		80		66	66	−14
Portugal		60		56		−4
Puerto Rico				65		
Romania		62		81	79	17
Russia		88		72		−16
Rwanda					34	
Saudi Arabia				82		
Serbia				50	61	11
Singapore						
Slovakia		64		68		4
Slovenia		64		45	43	−21
South Africa				70	74	4
South Korea				47	48	1
Spain	46	43		41	35	−11
Sweden	23	19		26	30	7
Switzerland				49		
Taiwan				52		
Tanzania				80		
Thailand					85	
Trinidad					36	
Turkey				76	71	−5
Uganda				89		
Ukraine				81	68	−13
Uruguay					40	
USA	72	67		58	24	−48
Venezuela						
Vietnam				45	54	9
Zambia					66	
Zimbabwe				86		

Churches give answers: the problems of family life

(F005) Generally speaking, do you think that the churches in your country are giving adequate answers to...
   The problems of family life

Yes (%)

Country	1981	1990	1995	2000	2006	Change
Albania				53		
Algeria				90		
Andorra					15	
Argentina		49		58	43	–6
Armenia						
Australia				36		
Austria		34		29		–5
Azerbaijan						
Bangladesh				54		
Belarus				36		
Belgium	42	37		33		–9
Bosnia and Herz.				39		
Brazil		51		72		21
Britain	39	38		30		–9
Bulgaria		38		29	32	–6
Burkina Faso					64	
Canada	63	55		49	46	–17
Chile		83		68	54	–29
China						
Colombia				71		
Croatia			57			
Cyprus				35		
Czech		58		32		–26
Denmark	14	13		15		1
Dominican Rep.						
Egypt				87	64	–23
El Salvador						
Estonia				30		
Ethiopia				73		
Finland		27		40	51	24
France	36	28		27		–9
Georgia				78		
Germany (East)		43		27	31	–12
Germany (West)	38	34		42	38	0
Ghana				74		
Greece				31		
Guatemala				90		
Hong Kong						
Hungary		70		39		–31
Iceland	38	39		45		7
India		28		27	30	2
Indonesia				78	65	–13
Iran				73	65	–8
Iraq				71	68	–3
Ireland	51	36		29		–22
Israel						
Italy	48	45		48	52	4
Japan		22		16	17	–5
Jordan				62	67	5

Country	1981	1990	1995	2000	2006	Change
Kyrgyzstan				55		
Latvia		63		48		–15
Lithuania				79		
Luxembourg				24		
Macedonia				31		
Malaysia					71	
Mali					83	
Malta	89	90		75		–14
Mexico		64		73	64	0
Moldova				66	56	–10
Montenegro				34		
Morocco				97	94	–3
Netherlands	38	33		30		–8
New Zealand						
Nigeria			86	79		–7
Northern Ireland	56	59		47		–9
Norway	36	29			16	–20
Pakistan				49		
Peru				76	68	–8
Philippines				63		
Poland		81		64	65	–16
Portugal		58		45		–13
Puerto Rico				72		
Romania		53		78	70	17
Russia			74	56		–18
Rwanda					38	
Saudi Arabia				74		
Serbia				39	53	14
Singapore						
Slovakia		59		64		5
Slovenia		54		43	44	–10
South Africa				74	76	2
South Korea				39	39	0
Spain	40	43		37	28	–12
Sweden	18	14		18	22	4
Switzerland				42		
Taiwan				47		
Tanzania				81		
Thailand				78		
Trinidad				47		
Turkey				67	60	–7
Uganda				83		
Ukraine				64	62	–2
Uruguay				41		
USA	74	70		61	25	–49
Venezuela						
Vietnam				30	40	10
Zambia					69	
Zimbabwe				88		

243

Churches give answers: people's spiritual needs

(F006) Generally speaking, do you think that the churches in your country are giving adequate answers to...
   People's spiritual needs

Yes (%)

Country	1981	1990	1995	2000	2006	Change
Albania				79		
Algeria				98		
Andorra					41	
Argentina		59		68	50	−9
Armenia						
Australia				58		
Austria		68		60		−8
Azerbaijan						
Bangladesh				78		
Belarus				70		
Belgium	57	59		54		−3
Bosnia and Herz.				69		
Brazil		57			75	18
Britain	56	64		59		3
Bulgaria		56		56	48	−8
Burkina Faso					85	
Canada	78	75		73	75	−3
Chile		86		83	67	−19
China						
Colombia				76		
Croatia				86		
Cyprus					40	
Czech		80		68		−12
Denmark	33	48		51		18
Dominican Rep.						
Egypt				93	69	−24
El Salvador						
Estonia				72		
Ethiopia				76		
Finland		51		68	76	25
France	54	59		55		1
Georgia				97		
Germany (East)		64		39	42	−22
Germany (West)	54	67		59	52	−2
Ghana					85	
Greece				62		
Guatemala				95		
Hong Kong						
Hungary		90		66		−24
Iceland	54	58		54		0
India		59		43	48	−11
Indonesia				84	91	7
Iran				75	65	−10
Iraq				79	84	5
Ireland	71	71		65		−6
Israel						
Italy	56	69		72	83	27
Japan		41		34	37	−4
Jordan				66	67	1

Country	1981	1990	1995	2000	2006	Change
Kyrgyzstan				76		
Latvia		87		81		−6
Lithuania				84		
Luxembourg				46		
Macedonia				75		
Malaysia					66	
Mali					83	
Malta	96	91		85		−11
Mexico		80		83	78	−2
Moldova				82	85	3
Montenegro				75		
Morocco				97	91	−6
Netherlands	53	54		49		−4
New Zealand						
Nigeria		89		85		−4
Northern Ireland	71	80		75		4
Norway	64	55			48	−16
Pakistan				65		
Peru				80	75	−5
Philippines				81		
Poland		89		83	84	−5
Portugal			64	72		8
Puerto Rico				76		
Romania		78		89	89	11
Russia		92		75		−17
Rwanda					82	
Saudi Arabia				78		
Serbia				73	82	9
Singapore						
Slovakia		79		83		4
Slovenia		77		70	68	−9
South Africa				84	86	2
South Korea				59	58	−1
Spain	54	56		55	46	−8
Sweden	52	51		55	63	11
Switzerland				70		
Taiwan				70		
Tanzania				90		
Thailand				64		
Trinidad				52		
Turkey				83	73	−10
Uganda				92		
Ukraine				83	81	−2
Uruguay				61		
USA	85	83		75	32	−53
Venezuela						
Vietnam				60	76	16
Zambia					86	
Zimbabwe				90		

Churches give answers: the social problems

(F007) Generally speaking, do you think that the churches in your country are giving adequate answers to...
   The social problems facing our country today

Yes (%)

Country	1981	1990	1995	2000	2006	Change
Albania				33		
Algeria				77		
Andorra					14	
Argentina		37		49	40	3
Armenia						
Australia				31		
Austria		39		31		-8
Azerbaijan						
Bangladesh				58		
Belarus				23		
Belgium		28		27		-1
Bosnia and Herz.				30		
Brazil		41			47	6
Britain		31		27		-4
Bulgaria		22	14	18		-4
Burkina Faso				67		
Canada		43		38	39	-4
Chile		76		50	45	-31
China						
Colombia				66		
Croatia			41			
Cyprus				33		
Czech		38	17			-21
Denmark		8		11		3
Dominican Rep.						
Egypt				83	60	-23
El Salvador						
Estonia			14			
Ethiopia				74		
Finland		12	30	38		26
France		24	21			-3
Georgia				59		
Germany (East)		58	15	28		-30
Germany (West)		33	36	31		-2
Ghana				74		
Greece				31		
Guatemala				68		
Hong Kong						
Hungary		55		23		-32
Iceland		24		28		4
India		24		28	39	15
Indonesia				64	75	11
Iran				62	50	-12
Iraq				77	79	2
Ireland		33		28		-5
Israel						
Italy		41		43	50	9
Japan		7		7	8	1
Jordan				66	68	2

Country	1981	1990	1995	2000	2006	Change
Kyrgyzstan				27		
Latvia		42		26		-16
Lithuania				54		
Luxembourg				23		
Macedonia				22		
Malaysia					72	
Mali					81	
Malta		77		57		-20
Mexico		47		51	48	1
Moldova				39	23	-16
Montenegro				22		
Morocco				91	89	-2
Netherlands		31		37		6
New Zealand						
Nigeria		83		73		-10
Northern Ireland		52		35		-17
Norway		19			12	-7
Pakistan				45		
Peru				64	54	-10
Philippines				54		
Poland		52		41	46	-6
Portugal		47		37		-10
Puerto Rico				66		
Romania		32		52	45	13
Russia		60		26		-34
Rwanda					28	
Saudi Arabia				77		
Serbia				28	39	11
Singapore						
Slovakia		31		30		-1
Slovenia		49		34	29	-20
South Africa				58	57	-1
South Korea				23	28	5
Spain		33		31	24	-9
Sweden		12		17	20	8
Switzerland				40		
Taiwan				49		
Tanzania				74		
Thailand				73		
Trinidad				41		
Turkey				44	42	-2
Uganda				69		
Ukraine				32	38	6
Uruguay				30		
USA		56		46	18	-38
Venezuela						
Vietnam				18	61	43
Zambia				59		
Zimbabwe				72		

How important is God in your life

**(F008) How important is God in your life? Please use this scale to indicate-
10 means very important and 1 means not at all important.**

(%) Very important (9 thru 10)

Country	1981	1990	1995	2000	2006	Change
Albania			37	46		9
Algeria				97		
Andorra					23	
Argentina	38	56	65	66	63	25
Armenia			40			
Australia	32		27		34	2
Austria		29		35		6
Azerbaijan			68			
Bangladesh			90	94		4
Belarus		11	26	26		15
Belgium	17	19		23		6
Bosnia and Herz.			52	54		2
Brazil		87	93		92	5
Britain	21	21	23	18	26	5
Bulgaria		11	16	18	21	10
Burkina Faso					77	
Canada	44	37		49	49	5
Chile			69	67	72	68	-1
China			1		9	8
Colombia			90		93	3
Croatia			32	42		10
Cyprus				67		
Czech		13	15	12		-1
Denmark	11	8		9		-2
Dominican Rep.			87			
Egypt				91	98	7
El Salvador			94			
Estonia			14	10		-4
Ethiopia				80		
Finland	19	20	19	20	26	7
France	14	13		12	15	1
Georgia			49		78	29
Germany (East)		17	8	10	10	-7
Germany (West)	20	19	23	16	19	-1
Ghana					95	
Greece				43		
Guatemala					93	
Hong Kong					10	
Hungary	24	27	27	25		1
Iceland	24	24		23		-1
India		46	66	93	57	11
Indonesia				99	90	-9
Iran				90	88	-2
Iraq				96	96	0
Ireland	54	50		48		-6
Israel				60		
Italy	36	38		43	47	11
Japan	10	8	8	10	10	0
Jordan					99	98	-1

Country	1981	1990	1995	2000	2006	Change
Kyrgyzstan				55		
Latvia			25	21		-4
Lithuania			33	36		3
Luxembourg				20		
Macedonia			37	54		17
Malaysia					51	
Mali					79	
Malta	90	85		79		-11
Mexico	74	58	51	86	86	12
Moldova			41	47	56	15
Montenegro				27	31	4
Morocco				99	92	-7
Netherlands	18	18		15	15	-3
New Zealand			29		27	-2
Nigeria			92	92	91		-1
Northern Ireland	44	50		37		-7
Norway	22	18	16		13	-9
Pakistan				92	100		8
Peru				76	80	76	0
Philippines				92	90		-2
Poland		69		62	67	-2
Portugal		44		50		6
Puerto Rico				94	93		-1
Romania		48	58	69	80	32
Russia		13	24	23	27	14
Rwanda					88	
Saudi Arabia				96		
Serbia			21	27	36	15
Singapore				62		
Slovakia			36	40	40		4
Slovenia			17	22	18	22	5
South Africa	64	78	78	79	78	14
South Korea				22	19	-3
Spain	25	24	36	23	17	-8
Sweden	12	10	10	12	11	-1
Switzerland		35	26		31	-4
Taiwan			13		16	3
Tanzania				94		
Thailand					35	
Trinidad					94	
Turkey		77	85	84	85	8
Uganda				85		
Ukraine			30	33	40	10
Uruguay			38		48	10
USA	63	60	62	69	68	5
Venezuela				85	90		5
Vietnam				28	15	-13
Zambia					78	
Zimbabwe				92		

Moments of prayer, meditation

(F009) Do you take some moments of prayer, meditation or contemplation or something like that?
Yes (%)

Country	1981	1990	1995	2000	2006	Change
Albania				81		
Algeria						
Andorra				62		
Argentina		75		78	75	0
Armenia						
Australia				66		
Austria		72		70		−2
Azerbaijan						
Bangladesh				95		
Belarus				71		
Belgium	62	56		63		1
Bosnia and Herz.				81		
Brazil		89			90	1
Britain	49	54		50		1
Bulgaria		36		34	24	−12
Burkina Faso					94	
Canada	74	73		82	79	5
Chile			85	82	77	−8
China		20				
Colombia				94		
Croatia			74			
Cyprus					74	
Czech		33		39		6
Denmark	46	43		51		5
Dominican Rep.						
Egypt				94		
El Salvador						
Estonia				51		
Ethiopia					95	
Finland		22		73	70	48
France	42	46		40		−2
Georgia					67	
Germany (East)		52		31	38	−14
Germany (West)	63	69		60	57	−6
Ghana						
Greece				61		
Guatemala					95	
Hong Kong						
Hungary		58		60		2
Iceland	43	46		54		11
India		85		88	80	−5
Indonesia					95	
Iran				95		
Iraq						
Ireland	81	84		85		4
Israel						
Italy	71	75		79	78	7
Japan		41		40	41	0
Jordan					98	

Country	1981	1990	1995	2000	2006	Change
Kyrgyzstan				60		
Latvia		66		65		−1
Lithuania				59		
Luxembourg				57		
Macedonia				62		
Malaysia					85	
Mali					93	
Malta	91	88		92		1
Mexico		82		87	84	2
Moldova				88	86	−2
Montenegro				58		
Morocco					88	
Netherlands	61	68		70		9
New Zealand					64	
Nigeria		98				
Northern Ireland	74	76		71		−3
Norway	62	64			33	−29
Pakistan						
Peru				80	81	1
Philippines				97		
Poland		90		87	87	−3
Portugal			66		75	9
Puerto Rico				91		
Romania			86	94	96	10
Russia			37	35		−2
Rwanda					99	
Saudi Arabia						
Serbia				59	64	5
Singapore				81		
Slovakia		62		66		4
Slovenia		45		46	49	4
South Africa		87		91	87	0
South Korea				59	48	−11
Spain	71	61		55	33	−38
Sweden	34	34		45	47	13
Switzerland					77	
Taiwan					67	
Tanzania				97		
Thailand					76	
Trinidad					97	
Turkey				93	96	3
Uganda				93		
Ukraine				52	63	11
Uruguay					51	
USA	86	84		90	38	−48
Venezuela						
Vietnam				30	28	−2
Zambia					86	
Zimbabwe				92		

Justifiable: claiming government benefits

(F010) Please tell me for each of the following statements whether you think it can always be justified, never be justified, or something in between. Claiming government benefits to which you are not entitled

Never justifiable (%)

Country	1981	1990	1995	2000	2006	Change
Albania			5	58		53
Algeria				51		
Andorra					54	
Argentina	69	77	69	64	61	-8
Armenia			44			
Australia	74		74		73	-1
Austria		69		59		-10
Azerbaijan			62			
Bangladesh			80	92		12
Belarus		55	49	35		-20
Belgium	66	52		54		-12
Bosnia and Herz.			60	78		18
Brazil		65	55		51	-14
Britain	73	69		66	65	-8
Bulgaria		68	74	70	58	-10
Burkina Faso					55	
Canada	61	70		71	68	7
Chile		43	49	46	34	-9
China		75	58	62	41	-34
Colombia			72		76	4
Croatia			39	76		37
Cyprus				59		
Czech		50	45	65		15
Denmark	90	81		83		-7
Dominican Rep.			70			
Egypt				73	71	-2
El Salvador			74			
Estonia		61	64	36		-25
Ethiopia					66	
Finland	65	13	63	49	56	-9
France	39	38		41	41	2
Georgia			47		71	24
Germany (East)		74	66	62	70	-4
Germany (West)	61	56	57	65	55	-6
Ghana					51	
Greece				24		
Guatemala					37	
Hong Kong					49	
Hungary	82	61	55	76		-6
Iceland	73	72		68		-5
India		76	74	75	60	-16
Indonesia				42	67	25
Iran				67	37	-30
Iraq						
Ireland	72	68		70		-2
Israel						
Italy	83	66		65	75	-8
Japan	68	67		64	64	-4
Jordan				81	76	-5

Country	1981	1990	1995	2000	2006	Change
Kyrgyzstan				56		
Latvia		73	41	62		-11
Lithuania		61	54	55		-6
Luxembourg				46		
Macedonia			47	47		0
Malaysia					18	
Mali					54	
Malta	88	92		85		-3
Mexico	51	22	49	45	37	-14
Moldova			49	28	38	-11
Montenegro			50	42		-8
Morocco				85	79	-6
Netherlands	82	74		78	81	-1
New Zealand			70		71	1
Nigeria		67	68	62		-5
Northern Ireland	77	77		68		-9
Norway	80	79	71		56	-24
Pakistan				77		
Peru			48	44		-4
Philippines			32	28		-4
Poland		63	55	54	53	-10
Portugal		54		59		5
Puerto Rico			76	71		-5
Romania		71	63	70	68	-3
Russia		65	62	59	54	-11
Rwanda					36	
Saudi Arabia				55		
Serbia			56	61	28	-28
Singapore				50		
Slovakia		43	34	37		-6
Slovenia		49	41	49	2	-47
South Africa	57	74	64	57	56	-1
South Korea	63	77			49	-14
Spain	60	61	67	56	58	-2
Sweden	81	74	58	55	62	-19
Switzerland		73	62		77	4
Taiwan			54		48	-6
Tanzania				87		
Thailand					15	
Trinidad					58	
Turkey		83		90	77	-6
Uganda				69		
Ukraine			43	49	40	-3
Uruguay			78		61	-17
USA	76	68	76	64	77	1
Venezuela			69	54		-15
Vietnam				73	58	-15
Zambia					41	
Zimbabwe				78		

Justifiable: avoiding a fare on public transport

(F011) Please tell me for each of the following statements whether you think it can always be justified, never be justified, or something in between. Avoiding a fare on public transport

Never justifiable (%)

Country	1981	1990	1995	2000	2006	Change
Albania			41	47		6
Algeria				64		
Andorra					53	
Argentina	63	71	61	67	69	6
Armenia			37			
Australia	59		63		56	−3
Austria		65		55		−10
Azerbaijan			49			
Bangladesh				94	96	2
Belarus		47	31	21		−26
Belgium	61	57		60		−1
Bosnia and Herz.			58	75		17
Brazil		61	56		35	−26
Britain	60	58		48	54	−6
Bulgaria			63	60	55	−8
Burkina Faso					57	
Canada	61	62		64	59	−2
Chile			55	58	46	33	−22
China			79	76	83	64	−15
Colombia			49			
Croatia			22	48		26
Cyprus				55		
Czech		63	39	42		−21
Denmark	80	74		71		−9
Dominican Rep.			71			
Egypt				74	74	0
El Salvador						
Estonia		59	49			−10
Ethiopia				63		
Finland	68	53	59	47	54	−14
France	54	54		55	50	−4
Georgia			47		70	23
Germany (East)		73	51	67	71	−2
Germany (West)	55	52	39	53	45	−10
Ghana					48	
Greece				36		
Guatemala					34	
Hong Kong					61	
Hungary	77	53	36			−41
Iceland	61	53				−8
India			84	78	80	58	−26
Indonesia				87	79	−8
Iran				84	55	−29
Iraq						
Ireland	55	57				2
Israel						
Italy	76	64		61	64	−12
Japan	77	78	80	77	77	0
Jordan				89	86	−3

Country	1981	1990	1995	2000	2006	Change
Kyrgyzstan				55		
Latvia		58	25			−33
Lithuania		56	43	40		−16
Luxembourg				50		
Macedonia				64	69	5
Malaysia					23	
Mali					56	
Malta	93	92				−1
Mexico	48	30	47	48	37	−11
Moldova			43	22	38	−5
Montenegro			49	42		−7
Morocco				81	67	−14
Netherlands	54	59		44	66	12
New Zealand			64		61	−3
Nigeria			60	60	56	−4
Northern Ireland	68	72				4
Norway	80	75	70		50	−30
Pakistan				87		
Peru			46	54		8
Philippines			35	34		−1
Poland		72	68		52	−20
Portugal		52				
Puerto Rico			75	81		6
Romania		63	67		68	5
Russia		52	35	33	37	−15
Rwanda					51	
Saudi Arabia				57		
Serbia			54	59	30	−24
Singapore				58		
Slovakia		46	29			−17
Slovenia		61	54		3	−58
South Africa	54		64	57	50	−4
South Korea	63	67	49	41	39	−24
Spain	55	60	68	58	52	−3
Sweden	76	67	47		45	−31
Switzerland		78	61		67	−11
Taiwan			60		58	−2
Tanzania				90		
Thailand					18	
Trinidad					49	
Turkey		74			68	−6
Uganda				62		
Ukraine			28	34	30	2
Uruguay				71	56	−15
USA	68	61	68	50	55	−13
Venezuela			72	56		−16
Vietnam				89	75	−14
Zambia					37	
Zimbabwe				83		

Justifiable: cheating on taxes

(F012) Please tell me for each of the following statements whether you think it can always be justified, never be justified, or something in between. Cheating on taxes if you have a chance

Never justifiable (%)

Country	1981	1990	1995	2000	2006	Change
Albania			44	58		14
Algeria				76		
Andorra					61	
Argentina	64	81	71	77	85	21
Armenia			41			
Australia	48		62		63	15
Austria		62		60		-2
Azerbaijan			48			
Bangladesh				96	98	2
Belarus		44	41	26		-18
Belgium	44	34		39		-5
Bosnia and Herz.			63	80		17
Brazil		61	47		39	-22
Britain	53	53		56	58	5
Bulgaria		57	65	68	54	-3
Burkina Faso				55		
Canada	65	59		69	70	5
Chile		76	65	69	65	-11
China		81	79	77	63	-18
Colombia			72		80	8
Croatia			32	56		24
Cyprus					68	
Czech		69	41	60		-9
Denmark	65	57		66		1
Dominican Rep.			70			
Egypt				80	77	-3
El Salvador			81			
Estonia		65	42	39		-26
Ethiopia					75	
Finland	59	40	55	50	56	-3
France	45	46		49	48	3
Georgia			53		74	21
Germany (East)		67	54	58	70	3
Germany (West)	49	40	40	57	47	-2
Ghana					100	
Greece				37		
Guatemala					54	
Hong Kong					61	
Hungary		56	60	67		11
Iceland	54	56		58		4
India		82	77	80	63	-19
Indonesia				79	79	0
Iran				89	65	-24
Iraq						
Ireland	44	49		59		15
Israel						
Italy	73	55		57	61	-12
Japan	81	82	82	84	83	2
Jordan				85	85	0

Country	1981	1990	1995	2000	2006	Change
Kyrgyzstan				58		
Latvia		64	31	60		-4
Lithuania		57	46	38		-19
Luxembourg				41		
Macedonia			61	68		7
Malaysia					27	
Mali					55	
Malta	84	84		80		-4
Mexico	48	37	51	69	60	12
Moldova			39	26	35	-4
Montenegro			48	46		-2
Morocco				95	79	-16
Netherlands	40	44		47	62	22
New Zealand			60		60	0
Nigeria		63	68	58		-5
Northern Ireland	52	68		61		9
Norway	41	43	48		50	9
Pakistan				91		
Peru			63	64		1
Philippines			38	41		3
Poland		50	55	61	55	5
Portugal		39		54		15
Puerto Rico			74	78		4
Romania		68	64	57	66	-2
Russia		53	47	47	51	-2
Rwanda					48	
Saudi Arabia						
Serbia			56	64	32	-24
Singapore				68		
Slovakia		59	35	60		1
Slovenia		68	54	60	2	-66
South Africa	50	62	68	61	54	4
South Korea	76	90	72	75	73	-3
Spain	49	56	69	57	65	16
Sweden	70	56	49	50	53	-17
Switzerland			63	54	62	-1
Taiwan			64		64	0
Tanzania				85		
Thailand					29	
Trinidad					67	
Turkey		90		92	81	-9
Uganda				55		
Ukraine			41	41	37	-4
Uruguay				80	69	-11
USA	66	68	74	63	73	7
Venezuela			71	70		-1
Vietnam				88	77	-11
Zambia					34	
Zimbabwe				83		

Justifiable: someone accepting a bribe

(F013) Please tell me for each of the following statements whether you think it can always be justified, never be justified, or something in between. Someone accepting a bribe in the course of their duties

Never justifiable (%)

Country	1981	1990	1995	2000	2006	Change
Albania			46	53		7
Algeria				89		
Andorra					84	
Argentina	81	95	88	92	91	10
Armenia			63			
Australia	75		86		81	6
Austria		72		73		1
Azerbaijan			53			
Bangladesh			98	99		1
Belarus		72	67	39		−33
Belgium	62	59		69		7
Bosnia and Herz.			74	88		14
Brazil		88	46		72	−16
Britain	76	76		68	72	−4
Bulgaria		80	67	79	67	−13
Burkina Faso					56	
Canada	76	76		82	79	3
Chile		84	74	70	72	−12
China		86	90	83	73	−13
Colombia			81		79	−2
Croatia			60	76		16
Cyprus					74	
Czech		57	56	53		−4
Denmark	92	91		93		1
Dominican Rep.			76			
Egypt				94	88	−6
El Salvador			89			
Estonia		68	82	67		−1
Ethiopia					75	
Finland	78	74	83	79	73	−5
France	54	63		68	63	9
Georgia			73		85	12
Germany (East)		64	74	61	76	12
Germany (West)	61	62	74	66	65	4
Ghana					59	
Greece				64		
Guatemala					60	
Hong Kong					67	
Hungary	71	64	34	54		−17
Iceland	82	84		87		5
India		85	79	85	64	−21
Indonesia				82	87	5
Iran				93	73	−20
Iraq				85	94	9
Ireland	80	85		83		3
Israel				86		
Italy	67	76		79	86	19
Japan	67	70	77	83	77	10
Jordan				97	96	−1

Country	1981	1990	1995	2000	2006	Change
Kyrgyzstan				73		
Latvia		75	62	74		−1
Lithuania		59	69	66		7
Luxembourg				70		
Macedonia			82	87		5
Malaysia					36	
Mali					54	
Malta	98	96		94		−4
Mexico	70	52	57	73	65	−5
Moldova			64	49	61	−3
Montenegro			78	84		6
Morocco				97	82	−15
Netherlands	66	68		74	80	14
New Zealand			82		83	1
Nigeria		65	71	63		−2
Northern Ireland	89	85		79		−10
Norway	84	80	85		77	−7
Pakistan				92		
Peru			75	73		−2
Philippines			35	39		4
Poland		80	85	78	84	4
Portugal		73		74		1
Puerto Rico			88	90		2
Romania		67	73	80	82	15
Russia		85	81	72	74	−11
Rwanda					49	
Saudi Arabia				77		
Serbia			84	86	39	−45
Singapore				78		
Slovakia		53	46	40		−13
Slovenia		79	74	74	1	−78
South Africa	63	79	75	68	58	−5
South Korea	61	84	80	80	75	14
Spain	77	79	83	72	74	−3
Sweden	74	74	69	67	62	−12
Switzerland		82	78		79	−3
Taiwan			75		79	4
Tanzania				92		
Thailand					28	
Trinidad					80	
Turkey		91		94	84	−7
Uganda				69		
Ukraine			71	65	54	−17
Uruguay				91	75	−16
USA	79	80	89	80	83	4
Venezuela			67	75		8
Vietnam				94	84	−10
Zambia					40	
Zimbabwe				91		

Justifiable: homosexuality

(F014) Please tell me for each of the following statements whether you think it can always be justified, never be justified, or something in between. Homosexuality

Never justifiable (%)

Country	1981	1990	1995	2000	2006	Change
Albania			68	81		13
Algeria				93		
Andorra					6	
Argentina	69	60	34	40	30	–39
Armenia			71			
Australia	41		31		22	–19
Austria		49		27		–22
Azerbaijan			89			
Bangladesh				99		
Belarus		80	68	57		–23
Belgium	51	42		28		–23
Bosnia and Herz.			66	72		6
Brazil		69	56		31	–38
Britain	43	42	21	25	21	–22
Bulgaria		80	51	58	33	–47
Burkina Faso				79		
Canada	51	37		26	20	–31
Chile		77	44	37	25	–52
China		92	88	92	78	–14
Colombia			61		46	–15
Croatia			40	63		23
Cyprus					43	
Czech		39	10	26		–13
Denmark	34	36		21		–13
Dominican Rep.			53			
Egypt				100		
El Salvador			81			
Estonia		76	66	56		–20
Ethiopia				76		
Finland	47	32	37	27	21	–26
France	47	39		24	15	–32
Georgia			82		91	9
Germany (East)		44	27	25	15	–29
Germany (West)	42	32	15	19	8	–34
Ghana					73	
Greece				24		
Guatemala				46		
Hong Kong				39		
Hungary	86	73	46	89		3
Iceland	46	24		12		–34
India		93	77	71	64	–29
Indonesia				95	89	–6
Iran				94	82	–12
Iraq						
Ireland	58	51		38		–20
Israel				38		
Italy	63	42		30	51	–12
Japan	52	60	42	30	24	–28
Jordan				98	99	1

Country	1981	1990	1995	2000	2006	Change
Kyrgyzstan				81		
Latvia		82	55	77		–5
Lithuania		88	75	78		–10
Luxembourg				21		
Macedonia			81	76		–5
Malaysia					43	
Mali					63	
Malta		83		61		–22
Mexico	72	55	52	50	34	–38
Moldova			74	64	62	–12
Montenegro				68	86	18
Morocco						
Netherlands	21	12		7	16	–5
New Zealand			30		22	–8
Nigeria		72	80	78		6
Northern Ireland	65	65		44		–21
Norway	50	45	27		6	–44
Pakistan				96		
Peru			44	57		13
Philippines			29	29		0
Poland		78	60	61	53	–25
Portugal		69		41		–28
Puerto Rico			60	51		–9
Romania		86	67	80	73	–13
Russia		88	80	72	65	–23
Rwanda					76	
Saudi Arabia				85		
Serbia			65	75	36	–29
Singapore				62		
Slovakia		50	18	24		–26
Slovenia		60	50	42	23	–37
South Africa	62	71	61	50	47	–15
South Korea	63	90	67	53	45	–18
Spain	56	42	24	17	10	–46
Sweden	39	37	12	9	4	–35
Switzerland		41	19		13	–28
Taiwan			65		40	–25
Tanzania				94		
Thailand				23		
Trinidad					72	
Turkey		84		85	74	–10
Uganda				89		
Ukraine			71	71	55	–16
Uruguay			45		18	–27
USA	65	54	45	31	33	–32
Venezuela			71	62		–9
Vietnam				82	71	–11
Zambia					59	
Zimbabwe				96		

Justifiable: prostitution

(F015) Please tell me for each of the following statements whether you think it can always be justified, never be justified, or something in between. Prostitution

Never justifiable (%)

Country	1981	1990	1995	2000	2006	Change
Albania			59	80		21
Algeria				93		
Andorra					18	
Argentina	68	73	44	51	43	−25
Armenia			65			
Australia	35		29		24	−11
Austria		47		38		−9
Azerbaijan			84			
Bangladesh				95		
Belarus		70	60	48		−22
Belgium	50	46				−4
Bosnia and Herz.			63	77		14
Brazil		73	68		48	−25
Britain	46	44	20	41	31	−15
Bulgaria		70	61		46	−24
Burkina Faso					66	
Canada	50	42		46	40	−10
Chile			77	51	48	36	−41
China			92	91	93	84	−8
Colombia				64		72	8
Croatia				37	79		42
Cyprus					58	
Czech		51	34	46		−5
Denmark	41	42				1
Dominican Rep.			54			
Egypt				93		
El Salvador			85			
Estonia		61	54			−7
Ethiopia					68	
Finland	48	29	40	41	40	−8
France	45	46			42	−3
Georgia			74		91	17
Germany (East)		52	30	43	36	−16
Germany (West)	39	32	17	34	14	−25
Ghana					69	
Greece				41		
Guatemala					49	
Hong Kong					43	
Hungary	85	69	51			−34
Iceland	60	53		50		−10
India		83	74	74	63	−20
Indonesia				94	88	−6
Iran				95	83	−12
Iraq						
Ireland	69	61		60		−9
Israel				48		
Italy	69	57		57	58	−11
Japan	65	71	63	64	67	2
Jordan				98	99	1

Country	1981	1990	1995	2000	2006	Change
Kyrgyzstan				74		
Latvia		64	45			−19
Lithuania		78	66	65		−13
Luxembourg				47		
Macedonia			76	82		6
Malaysia					45	
Mali					56	
Malta	95	94				−1
Mexico	67	48	53	58	42	−25
Moldova			70	61	62	−8
Montenegro				61	80	19
Morocco						
Netherlands	27	19			21	−6
New Zealand			29		25	−4
Nigeria			66	75	77	11
Northern Ireland	76	65		69		−7
Norway	72	65	43		21	−51
Pakistan				96		
Peru			55	66		11
Philippines				44	43	−1
Poland		78	64		58	−20
Portugal		70				
Puerto Rico			71			
Romania		78	58	74	69	−9
Russia		77	69	63	64	−13
Rwanda					68	
Saudi Arabia				87		
Serbia			64	75	37	−27
Singapore				63		
Slovakia		57	34			−23
Slovenia		60	51	50	7	−53
South Africa	63	72	71	62	56	−7
South Korea	65	78	61	59	50	−15
Spain	58	48	29	31	23	−35
Sweden	54	65	31		41	−13
Switzerland		42	23		19	−23
Taiwan			66		49	−17
Tanzania				93		
Thailand					29	
Trinidad					70	
Turkey		82			73	−9
Uganda				74		
Ukraine			66	69	55	−11
Uruguay			44		21	−23
USA	64	60	58	49	49	−15
Venezuela			68	66		−2
Vietnam				92	79	−13
Zambia					45	
Zimbabwe				93		

Justifiable: abortion

(F016) Please tell me for each of the following statements whether you think it can always be justified, never be justified, or something in between. Abortion

Never justifiable (%)

Country	1981	1990	1995	2000	2006	Change
Albania			5	26		21
Algeria				79		
Andorra					9	
Argentina	49	45	48	65	55	6
Armenia			23			
Australia	30		24		17	−13
Austria		32		24		−8
Azerbaijan			30			
Bangladesh				90		
Belarus		25	19	18		−7
Belgium	36	24		29		−7
Bosnia and Herz.			28	37		9
Brazil		64	75		63	−1
Britain	30	20	15	26	20	−10
Bulgaria		25	22	19	17	−8
Burkina Faso					64	
Canada	38	20		31	26	−12
Chile		75	68	67	57	−18
China		15	31	56	68	53
Colombia			74		74	0
Croatia			21	37		16
Cyprus				38		
Czech		11	9	13		2
Denmark	21			13		−8
Dominican Rep.			59			
Egypt				56		
El Salvador			91			
Estonia		14	15	21		7
Ethiopia					63	
Finland	19	10	19	10	14	−5
France	21	18		15	15	−6
Georgia			29		54	25
Germany (East)		20	17	15	18	−2
Germany (West)	28	18	20	31	17	−11
Ghana					65	
Greece				18		
Guatemala					65	
Hong Kong				37		
Hungary	32	24	18	32		0
Iceland	22	11		12		−10
India		38	54	65	59	21
Indonesia				88	84	−4
Iran				77	61	−16
Iraq				77	85	8
Ireland	78	52		55		−23
Israel				27		
Italy	30	22		32	39	9
Japan	31	28	23	15	15	−16
Jordan				84	92	8

Country	1981	1990	1995	2000	2006	Change
Kyrgyzstan				58		
Latvia		23	12	37		14
Lithuania		30	34	29		−1
Luxembourg				19		
Macedonia			33	40		7
Malaysia					43	
Mali					55	
Malta	96	85		90		−6
Mexico	64	39	56	67	55	−9
Moldova			36	41	46	10
Montenegro			26	32		6
Morocco				83	76	−7
Netherlands	29	13		15	20	−9
New Zealand			19		16	−3
Nigeria		52	71	74		22
Northern Ireland	41	40		46		5
Norway	19	14	15		5	−14
Pakistan				60		
Peru			64	74		10
Philippines			58	54		−4
Poland		44	43	45	50	6
Portugal		31		35		4
Puerto Rico			78	74		−4
Romania		23	27	40	48	25
Russia		19	18	17	33	14
Rwanda					67	
Saudi Arabia				62		
Serbia			16	20	24	8
Singapore				49		
Slovakia		20	24	25		5
Slovenia		14	25	19	22	8
South Africa	50	54	64	59	55	5
South Korea	31	38	37	37	30	−1
Spain	49	28	33	28	17	−32
Sweden	16	13	5	5	3	−13
Switzerland		52	21		15	−37
Taiwan				46	34	−12
Tanzania				90		
Thailand					37	
Trinidad					64	
Turkey			37	64	63	26
Uganda				72		
Ukraine			29	32	30	1
Uruguay			47		34	−13
USA	43	34	36	30	32	−11
Venezuela			69	71		2
Vietnam				61	55	−6
Zambia					47	
Zimbabwe				92		

254

Justifiable: divorce

(F017) Please tell me for each of the following statements whether you think it can always be justified, never be justified, or something in between. Divorce

Never justifiable (%)

Country	1981	1990	1995	2000	2006	Change
Albania			4	18		14
Algeria				26		
Andorra					3	
Argentina	30	24	17	25	17	−13
Armenia			18			
Australia	16		10		6	−10
Austria		17		12		−5
Azerbaijan			27			
Bangladesh			74	82		8
Belarus		20	14	9		−11
Belgium	28	18		13		−15
Bosnia and Herz.			13	14		1
Brazil		32	30		19	−13
Britain	14	13	4	12	7	−7
Bulgaria		29	21	17	12	−17
Burkina Faso					46	
Canada	19	13		11	9	−10
Chile		46	34	27	17	−29
China		15	14	57	57	42
Colombia			34		37	3
Croatia			8	25		17
Cyprus					17	
Czech		10	4	7		−3
Denmark	11	13		7		−4
Dominican Rep.			27			
Egypt				16	29	13
El Salvador			57			
Estonia		11	8	11		0
Ethiopia					56	
Finland	9	5	7	3	5	−4
France	13	11		8	9	−4
Georgia			21		32	11
Germany (East)		13	11	11	6	−7
Germany (West)	13	8	7	14	5	−8
Ghana					52	
Greece				7		
Guatemala					28	
Hong Kong					22	
Hungary	20	23	9	24		4
Iceland	7	4		4		−3
India		51	47	51	47	−4
Indonesia				54	46	−8
Iran				55	45	−10
Iraq				65	74	9
Ireland	45	30		27		−18
Israel				12		
Italy	21	17		18	19	−2
Japan	21	17	12	6	5	−16
Jordan				43	68	25

Country	1981	1990	1995	2000	2006	Change
Kyrgyzstan				45		
Latvia		16	5	25		9
Lithuania		24	23	19		−5
Luxembourg				11		
Macedonia			33	36		3
Malaysia					31	
Mali					41	
Malta	82	74		60		−22
Mexico	48	26	37	37	26	−22
Moldova			33	29	28	−5
Montenegro			12	9		−3
Morocco				41	31	−10
Netherlands	19	8		5	11	−8
New Zealand			6		5	−1
Nigeria		42	58	54		12
Northern Ireland	29	27		23		−6
Norway	16	14	6		2	−14
Pakistan				66		
Peru			29	42		13
Philippines			40	42		2
Poland		31	26	26	23	−8
Portugal		21		16		−5
Puerto Rico			39	35		−4
Romania		23	23	33	35	12
Russia		16	13	11	17	1
Rwanda					43	
Saudi Arabia				27		
Serbia			11	13	21	10
Singapore				35		
Slovakia		15	9	14		−1
Slovenia		15	19	14	30	15
South Africa	34	39	40	31	31	−3
South Korea	33	38	27	21	18	−15
Spain	28	18	16	12	7	−21
Sweden	10	7	2	2	1	−9
Switzerland		23	9		5	−18
Taiwan			33		22	−11
Tanzania				53		
Thailand				22		
Trinidad				41		
Turkey		24		42	44	20
Uganda				57		
Ukraine			17	24	19	2
Uruguay			22		10	−12
USA	22	18	12	7	9	−13
Venezuela			36	30		−6
Vietnam				50	54	4
Zambia					28	
Zimbabwe				74		

Justifiable: euthanasia

(F018) Please tell me for each of the following statements whether you think it can always be justified, never be justified, or something in between. Euthanasia (terminating the life of the incurably sick)

Never justifiable (%)

Country	1981	1990	1995	2000	2006	Change
Albania			46	47		1
Algeria				85		
Andorra					8	
Argentina	79	57	45	48	44	−35
Armenia			39			
Australia	24		15		14	−10
Austria		39		31		−8
Azerbaijan			47			
Bangladesh			92	97		5
Belarus		34	18	19		−15
Belgium	41	21		14		−27
Bosnia and Herz.			43	44		1
Brazil		65	61		49	−16
Britain	27	23		21	13	−14
Bulgaria		47	43	42	19	−28
Burkina Faso					63	
Canada	34	23		21	21	−13
Chile		63	53	45	38	−25
China		15	21	53	55	40
Colombia			45		57	12
Croatia			23	39		16
Cyprus					48	
Czech		34	13	18		−16
Denmark	18	21		12		−6
Dominican Rep.			53			
Egypt				78	91	13
El Salvador			83			
Estonia		36	18	22		−14
Ethiopia				71		
Finland	25	12	16	15	14	−11
France	26	22		13	10	−16
Georgia			57		68	11
Germany (East)		39		30	22	−17
Germany (West)	27	30		29	22	−5
Ghana					50	
Greece				30		
Guatemala				47		
Hong Kong				20		
Hungary	64	39	14	42		−22
Iceland	30	20		18		−12
India		52	56	63	49	−3
Indonesia				84	74	−10
Iran				76	55	−21
Iraq						
Ireland	69	56		52		−17
Israel						
Italy	56	42		40	37	−19
Japan	25	18	13	10	8	−17
Jordan				91	94	3

Country	1981	1990	1995	2000	2006	Change
Kyrgyzstan				55		
Latvia		41	13	30		−11
Lithuania		42	27	23		−19
Luxembourg				20		
Macedonia			62	56		−6
Malaysia					38	
Mali					54	
Malta	90	81		70		−20
Mexico	50	34	49	56	41	−9
Moldova			58	50	36	−22
Montenegro			31	35		4
Morocco				92	71	−21
Netherlands	19	12		8	14	−5
New Zealand			12		13	1
Nigeria			50	64	64	14
Northern Ireland	44	41		42		−2
Norway	55	30	18		15	−40
Pakistan				100		
Peru			49			
Philippines			51	48		−3
Poland		68	46	52	47	−21
Portugal		54		41		−13
Puerto Rico			65	69		4
Romania		49	44	56	56	7
Russia		49	30	24	26	−23
Rwanda					68	
Saudi Arabia				80		
Serbia			27	35	24	−3
Singapore				47		
Slovakia		42	21	25		−17
Slovenia		45	31	27	16	−29
South Africa	35	44	50	41	43	8
South Korea	30		30	24	21	−9
Spain	53	36	29	24	19	−34
Sweden	29	19	6	10	6	−23
Switzerland		26	15		12	−14
Taiwan			27		13	−14
Tanzania				89		
Thailand					19	
Trinidad					57	
Turkey		63		65	57	−6
Uganda				80		
Ukraine			34	31	29	−5
Uruguay			39		29	−10
USA	43	32	30	24	25	−18
Venezuela			67	55		−12
Vietnam				51	49	−2
Zambia					40	
Zimbabwe				89		

256

Justifiable: suicide

(F019) Please tell me for each of the following statements whether you think it can always be justified, never be justified, or something in between. Suicide

Never justifiable (%)

Country	1981	1990	1995	2000	2006	Change
Albania			62	68		6
Algeria				94		
Andorra					40	
Argentina	82	82	70	77	74	−8
Armenia			60			
Australia	48		47		43	−5
Austria		48		48		0
Azerbaijan			73			
Bangladesh			98	99		1
Belarus		60	67	50		−10
Belgium	65	51		44		−21
Bosnia and Herz.			76	81		5
Brazil		89	87		75	−14
Britain	48	41	40	32		−16
Bulgaria		66	68	71	56	−10
Burkina Faso					70	
Canada	65	52		53	51	−14
Chile		81	74	71	62	−19
China		54	52	83	69	15
Colombia			82		87	5
Croatia			37	81		44
Cyprus				65		
Czech		49	25	48		−1
Denmark	51	56		51		0
Dominican Rep.			76			
Egypt				95	95	0
El Salvador			94			
Estonia		56	66	61		5
Ethiopia				78		
Finland	55	31	49	39	36	−19
France	38	33		27	35	−3
Georgia			78		92	14
Germany (East)		55	32	55	35	−20
Germany (West)	47	40	25	53	36	−11
Ghana					68	
Greece			54			
Guatemala					66	
Hong Kong					59	
Hungary	72	65	55	81		9
Iceland	56	57		63		7
India		81	70	72	57	−24
Indonesia				97	91	−6
Iran				95	76	−19
Iraq						
Ireland	75	63		70		−5
Israel						
Italy	76	67		62	70	−6
Japan	50	56	58	48	48	−2
Jordan				97	97	0

Country	1981	1990	1995	2000	2006	Change
Kyrgyzstan				84		
Latvia		60	42	75		15
Lithuania		69	65	75		6
Luxembourg				40		
Macedonia			84	83		−1
Malaysia					44	
Mali					57	
Malta	97	92		94		−3
Mexico	73	48	74	81	64	−9
Moldova			79	67	69	−10
Montenegro			47	53		6
Morocco				98	88	−10
Netherlands	46	31		27	38	−8
New Zealand			48		47	−1
Nigeria		73	80	76		3
Northern Ireland	68	58		69		1
Norway	66	57	52		33	−33
Pakistan				97		
Peru			72	75		3
Philippines			61	56		−5
Poland		71	63	65	60	−11
Portugal		72		60		−12
Puerto Rico			87	90		3
Romania		76	75	87	83	7
Russia		66	68	68	67	1
Rwanda					70	
Saudi Arabia				88		
Serbia			55	73	39	−16
Singapore				73		
Slovakia		54	33	37		−17
Slovenia		55	47	47	8	−47
South Africa	60	71	70	67	58	−2
South Korea	44	64	52	51	45	1
Spain	65	65	60	52	51	−14
Sweden	52	44	26	28	26	−26
Switzerland		54	38		29	−25
Taiwan				63	58	−5
Tanzania				96		
Thailand					37	
Trinidad					76	
Turkey		80		90	79	−1
Uganda				91		
Ukraine			69	74	64	−5
Uruguay			70		53	−17
USA	71	61	60	57	54	−17
Venezuela				83	80	−3
Vietnam				85	75	−10
Zambia					53	
Zimbabwe				92		

Politicians who don't believe in God are unfit for public office

(F020) How much do you agree or disagree with each of the following statement:
Politicians who do not believe in God are unfit for public office

Agree strongly/Agree (%)

Country	1981	1990	1995	2000	2006	Change
Albania				44		
Algeria				78		
Andorra					3	
Argentina				36	33	−3
Armenia						
Australia				13		
Austria				14		
Azerbaijan						
Bangladesh				71		
Belarus				26		
Belgium				7		
Bosnia and Herz.				14		
Brazil					49	
Britain				11		
Bulgaria				24	28	4
Burkina Faso					49	
Canada				19	18	−1
Chile				34	30	−4
China						
Colombia						
Croatia				28		
Cyprus					39	
Czech				6		
Denmark				4		
Dominican Rep.						
Egypt				88		
El Salvador						
Estonia				14		
Ethiopia					49	
Finland				14	9	−5
France				9		
Georgia					83	
Germany (East)				8	7	−1
Germany (West)				17	15	−2
Ghana					73	
Greece				37		
Guatemala					59	
Hong Kong						
Hungary				14		
Iceland				9		
India				42	49	7
Indonesia				89	88	−1
Iran					75	
Iraq				87	87	0
Ireland				15		
Israel						
Italy				15	13	−2
Japan				8	7	−1
Jordan				81	69	−12

Country	1981	1990	1995	2000	2006	Change
Kyrgyzstan				36		
Latvia				22		
Lithuania				24		
Luxembourg				13		
Macedonia				35		
Malaysia					64	
Mali					59	
Malta				41		
Mexico				41	26	−15
Moldova				45	43	−2
Montenegro				21		
Morocco				87	53	−34
Netherlands				2		
New Zealand				14		
Nigeria					9	
Northern Ireland				82		
Norway					4	
Pakistan				95		
Peru					39	
Philippines				71		
Poland				17	18	1
Portugal				15		
Puerto Rico				65		
Romania				52	49	−3
Russia				21		
Rwanda					44	
Saudi Arabia						
Serbia				27	41	14
Singapore						
Slovakia				22		
Slovenia				11	11	0
South Africa				51	48	−3
South Korea				10	15	5
Spain				11	11	0
Sweden				4	4	0
Switzerland						
Taiwan					10	
Tanzania				66		
Thailand					64	
Trinidad					68	
Turkey				61	55	−6
Uganda				63		
Ukraine				33	45	12
Uruguay					13	
USA				38	14	−24
Venezuela				52		
Vietnam				19	18	−1
Zambia					55	
Zimbabwe				54		

Religious leaders should not influence how people vote

(F021) How much do you agree or disagree with each of the following statement:
Religious leaders should not influence how people vote in elections

Agree strongly/Agree (%)

Country	1981	1990	1995	2000	2006	Change
Albania				77		
Algeria				38		
Andorra					87	
Argentina				75	66	−9
Armenia						
Australia					75	
Austria				85		
Azerbaijan						
Bangladesh				74		
Belarus				82		
Belgium				79		
Bosnia and Herz.				75		
Brazil					67	
Britain				70		
Bulgaria				83	83	0
Burkina Faso					70	
Canada				77	78	1
Chile				69	61	−8
China						
Colombia						
Croatia				84		
Cyprus					76	
Czech				81		
Denmark				85		
Dominican Rep.						
Egypt				57		
El Salvador						
Estonia				84		
Ethiopia					56	
Finland				68	70	2
France				86		
Georgia					62	
Germany (East)				72	77	5
Germany (West)				75	68	−7
Ghana					72	
Greece				78		
Guatemala					64	
Hong Kong						
Hungary				77		
Iceland				81		
India				68	67	−1
Indonesia				87	78	−9
Iran					60	
Iraq				51	52	1
Ireland				78		
Israel						
Italy				79	71	−8
Japan				74	75	1
Jordan				75	72	−3

Country	1981	1990	1995	2000	2006	Change
Kyrgyzstan				68		
Latvia				84		
Lithuania				81		
Luxembourg				82		
Macedonia				80		
Malaysia					54	
Mali					68	
Malta				90		
Mexico				64	57	−7
Moldova				68	63	−5
Montenegro				83		
Morocco				75	39	−36
Netherlands				66		
New Zealand				76		
Nigeria					78	
Northern Ireland				73		
Norway					86	
Pakistan				74		
Peru					69	
Philippines				75		
Poland				86	83	−3
Portugal				80		
Puerto Rico				70		
Romania				78	73	−5
Russia				82		
Rwanda					59	
Saudi Arabia						
Serbia				85	55	−30
Singapore						
Slovakia				74		
Slovenia				78	74	−4
South Africa				65	64	−1
South Korea				69	55	−14
Spain				67	74	7
Sweden				68	81	13
Switzerland						
Taiwan					88	
Tanzania				70		
Thailand					64	
Trinidad					70	
Turkey				79	72	−7
Uganda				63		
Ukraine				83	64	−19
Uruguay					62	
USA				64	27	−37
Venezuela				56		
Vietnam				69	61	−8
Zambia					50	
Zimbabwe				63		

Better if more people with strong religious beliefs in public office

(F022) How much do you agree or disagree with each of the following statement:
It would be better for [this country] if more people with strong religious beliefs held public office

Agree strongly/Agree (%)

Country	1981	1990	1995	2000	2006	Change
Albania				42		
Algeria				40		
Andorra					5	
Argentina				35	29	–6
Armenia						
Australia					15	
Austria				25		
Azerbaijan						
Bangladesh				24		
Belarus				35		
Belgium				16		
Bosnia and Herz.				23		
Brazil					48	
Britain				18		
Bulgaria				28	26	–2
Burkina Faso					60	
Canada				25	22	–3
Chile				41	40	–1
China						
Colombia						
Croatia				48		
Cyprus					21	
Czech				9		
Denmark				6		
Dominican Rep.						
Egypt				87		
El Salvador						
Estonia				26		
Ethiopia					47	
Finland				18	12	–6
France				13		
Georgia					85	
Germany (East)				15	17	2
Germany (West)				29	24	–5
Ghana					81	
Greece				32		
Guatemala					71	
Hong Kong						
Hungary				25		
Iceland				14		
India				31	38	7
Indonesia					83	
Iran					68	
Iraq				64	52	–12
Ireland				23		
Israel						
Italy				22	18	–4
Japan				5	5	0
Jordan				60	64	4

Country	1981	1990	1995	2000	2006	Change
Kyrgyzstan				44		
Latvia				44		
Lithuania				41		
Luxembourg				22		
Macedonia				23		
Malaysia					58	
Mali					74	
Malta				64		
Mexico				47	37	–10
Moldova				66	46	–20
Montenegro				34		
Morocco				57	61	4
Netherlands				12		
New Zealand				21		
Nigeria					16	
Northern Ireland				87		
Norway					6	
Pakistan				17		
Peru					61	
Philippines				75		
Poland				30	30	0
Portugal				25		
Puerto Rico				48		
Romania				65	61	–4
Russia				47		
Rwanda					62	
Saudi Arabia						
Serbia				43	37	–6
Singapore						
Slovakia				37		
Slovenia				12	10	–2
South Africa				62	57	–5
South Korea				24	18	–6
Spain				14	13	–1
Sweden				9	5	–4
Switzerland						
Taiwan					24	
Tanzania					61	
Thailand					57	
Trinidad					64	
Turkey				56	48	–8
Uganda					63	
Ukraine				56	42	–14
Uruguay					19	
USA				49	18	–31
Venezuela				56		
Vietnam				30	25	–5
Zambia					60	
Zimbabwe				66		

Religious leaders should not influence government

(F023) How much do you agree or disagree with each of the following statement:
Religious leaders should not influence government

Agree strongly/Agree (%)

Country	1981	1990	1995	2000	2006	Change
Albania				76		
Algeria				40		
Andorra				85		
Argentina				65	60	−5
Armenia						
Australia				64		
Austria				79		
Azerbaijan						
Bangladesh				71		
Belarus				73		
Belgium				73		
Bosnia and Herz.				71		
Brazil					54	
Britain				65		
Bulgaria				79	77	−2
Burkina Faso					69	
Canada				67	71	4
Chile				68	60	−8
China						
Colombia						
Croatia				79		
Cyprus					75	
Czech				74		
Denmark				85		
Dominican Rep.						
Egypt						
El Salvador						
Estonia				75		
Ethiopia					71	
Finland				58	65	7
France				82		
Georgia					51	
Germany (East)				73	70	−3
Germany (West)				71	65	−6
Ghana					57	
Greece				59		
Guatemala					59	
Hong Kong						
Hungary				70		
Iceland				70		
India				71	65	−6
Indonesia				91	57	−34
Iran				44		
Iraq						
Ireland				72		
Israel						
Italy				68	70	2
Japan				72	70	−2
Jordan					64	

Country	1981	1990	1995	2000	2006	Change
Kyrgyzstan				67		
Latvia				73		
Lithuania				76		
Luxembourg				77		
Macedonia				74		
Malaysia					46	
Mali					70	
Malta				78		
Mexico				65	55	−10
Moldova				58	56	−2
Montenegro				77		
Morocco				65	38	−27
Netherlands				60		
New Zealand				66		
Nigeria					69	
Northern Ireland						
Norway					79	
Pakistan						
Peru					63	
Philippines				76		
Poland				81	78	−3
Portugal				79		
Puerto Rico				59		
Romania				78	76	−2
Russia				68		
Rwanda					67	
Saudi Arabia						
Serbia				82	53	−29
Singapore						
Slovakia				71		
Slovenia				73	70	−3
South Africa				52	56	4
South Korea				57	48	−9
Spain				69	72	3
Sweden				52	75	23
Switzerland						
Taiwan					84	
Tanzania					69	
Thailand					60	
Trinidad					54	
Turkey				72	69	−3
Uganda				55		
Ukraine				72	58	−14
Uruguay					60	
USA				51	22	−29
Venezuela				57		
Vietnam				67	64	−3
Zambia					44	
Zimbabwe				52		

How proud of nationality

(G001) How proud are you to be [Nationality]?

Very proud (%)

Country	1981	1990	1995	2000	2006	Change
Albania			57	73		16
Algeria				74		
Andorra					40	
Argentina	49	55	58	67	62	13
Armenia			44			
Australia	70		73		68	−2
Austria		53		54		1
Azerbaijan			64			
Bangladesh				78	73	−5
Belarus		34		32	27	−7
Belgium	29	31		24		−5
Bosnia and Herz.			59	48		−11
Brazil		64	64		39	−25
Britain	52	53		49	55	3
Bulgaria		39	51	36	44	5
Burkina Faso					83	
Canada	62	60		67	71	9
Chile		53	56	72	59	6
China		43	40	26	21	−22
Colombia			85		90	5
Croatia			45	39		−6
Cyprus					55	
Czech		28	35	27		−1
Denmark	30	42		48		18
Dominican Rep.			76			
Egypt				82	73	−9
El Salvador			86			
Estonia		30	21	24		−6
Ethiopia				69		
Finland	38	38	48	55	55	17
France	31	35		40	29	−2
Georgia			65		76	11
Germany (East)		29	16	29	22	−7
Germany (West)	21	20	14	15	22	1
Ghana					93	
Greece				55		
Guatemala					88	
Hong Kong					11	
Hungary	67	47	49	51		−16
Iceland	58	54		66		8
India		75	73	71	73	−2
Indonesia				48	46	−2
Iran				92	63	−29
Iraq				77	83	6
Ireland	68	77		74		6
Israel				54		
Italy	40	40		39	42	2
Japan	30	29	26	23	22	−8
Jordan				69	70	1

Country	1981	1990	1995	2000	2006	Change
Kyrgyzstan				43		
Latvia		49	22	40		−9
Lithuania		41	19	21		−20
Luxembourg				48		
Macedonia			69	60		−9
Malaysia					69	
Mali					90	
Malta	75	79		75		0
Mexico	64	56	70	80	83	19
Moldova			36	23	19	−17
Montenegro			46	33		−13
Morocco				88	58	−30
Netherlands	18	23		20	26	8
New Zealand			65		71	6
Nigeria		68	62	72		4
Northern Ireland	49	54		29		−20
Norway	43	45	52		53	10
Pakistan			85	81		−4
Peru			80	77		−3
Philippines			74	85		11
Poland		67	70	71	63	−4
Portugal		42		78		36
Puerto Rico			86	95		9
Romania		48	45	47	38	−10
Russia		26	30	32	45	19
Rwanda					78	
Saudi Arabia				75		
Serbia			41	42	49	8
Singapore				52		
Slovakia		30	44	25		−5
Slovenia		59	61	56	57	−2
South Africa	48	64	81	66	77	29
South Korea	49	45		17	18	−31
Spain	51	45	65	53	60	9
Sweden	30	41	46	41	43	13
Switzerland		38	28		37	−1
Taiwan			15		14	−1
Tanzania				82		
Thailand					85	
Trinidad					91	
Turkey		67	78	64	81	14
Uganda				66		
Ukraine			25	24	30	5
Uruguay			74		76	2
USA	76	75	79	72	69	−7
Venezuela			94	92		−2
Vietnam				78	81	3
Zambia					63	
Zimbabwe				77		

Printed by
Impresora Publimex, S.A.
Calz. San Lorenzo 279-32
Col. Estrella Iztapalapa,
México, D.F.